A BIBLE STUDY GUIDE

LUKE

A BIBLE STUDY GUIDE

LUKE

Written By

DR. SAMUEL LEE

UBF**PRESS**

BACK TO THE BIBLE

 The **UNIVERSITY BIBLE FELLOWSHIP** is an international student organization dedicated to the task of campus evangelism. Our main work is to help college students and teenagers study the Bible and live according to its teachings.

UBF is a member of the **NAE**–National Association of Evangelicals, **Cross Global Link**, **ECFA**–Evangelical Council For Financial Accountability, **EMS**–Evangelical Missiological Society, **GIMNET**–Global Inter-Missions Network, and the **KEF**–Korea Evangelical Fellowship.

Website: http://ubf.org

All scripture quotations, unless otherwise indicated, are taken from the HOLY BIBLE, NEW INTERNATIONAL VERSION®. NIV®. Copyright © 1973, 1978, 1984 by International Bible Society. Used by permission of Zondervan. All rights reserved.

Printed in the United States of America

Library of Congress Control Number: 2011929953

ISBN 9780981982694

6558 N. Artesian Ave. Chicago, IL 60645

http://ubfpress.org

Email: ubfpress@gmail.com

UBFPRESS
BACK TO THE BIBLE

DR. SAMUEL LEE

Writing Daily Bread, the UBF devotional book, 1968

Dr. Samuel Lee's Profile

- October 9, 1931: Born in Osaka, Japan as the second son of Young Jun Lee and Eun Soon Chang
- Graduated from Shinheung High School in Jeonju, South Korea
- 1957: Worked as an evangelist for Chungwoong Church in Imsil, South Korea
- 1959: Graduated from the Chongshin Presbyterian Seminary in Seoul, South Korea
- March 26, 1959: Married Grace A. Lee, eldest daughter of Elder Chun, had three children together: Grace, Samuel, and Sarah
- 1959: Worked as co-training pastor for Dukjin Church in Jeonju
- 1959: Worked as co-training pastor for the American Southern Presbyterian Church
- 1960: Graduated with BA degree in Philosophy at Chonbuk University
- September 1, 1961: Started the UBF (University Bible Fellowship) campus movement, co-working with Sarah Barry, a missionary from the American Southern Presbyterian Church, USA, on the 2nd floor of the building located at 176-1 Daein-dong, Kwangju in South Korea
- 1966: Pioneered campus ministry at Seoul National University on the 2nd floor of the Yellow Building located at 25 Hyojae-dong Street, Jongro in South Korea
- 1967: Attended the IFES International Conference in Amsterdam
- 1968-1977: Published 32 books of the UBF devotional, Daily Bread
- 1969: Sent out the first three lay missionaries to West Germany (Suh Ingyung, Lee Hwaja, Sul Dongran)
- August 3-7, 1971: Summer Bible Conference at Soongshil University in Seoul (1,000 students attended and began to pray for the Niagara Falls Summer Bible Conference with 200 attendees within 10 years)
- September 16-22, 1974: 1st International Summer Bible Conference in Switzerland with 169 attendees
- July 1975: 1st Niagara Falls Summer Bible Conference and 2nd International Summer Bible Conference in Frankfurt with 220 attendees,

including 40 natives

- June 14, 1977: Moved to the USA as General Director of UBF world mission
- June 19, 1978: 1st World Mission Report in Seoul
- July, 1981: Niagara Falls Summer Bible Conference with 420 attendees, including 220 American students
- July 1985: 1st MSU International Summer Bible Conference
- 1985: Began to pray for the pioneering of Russia at the Seoul World Mission Report
- August 28, 1990: Three missionaries sent to pioneer Moscow State University
- 1991: Received honorary PhD in literature from Chonbuk University
- September 12, 1994: World Mission Report to celebrate the sending of 1,000 lay missionaries at the 100th Anniversary Memorial Hall of Korea Christianity
- 1995: Began to pray for North America to be a kingdom of priests and a holy nation
- May 24, 1998: 14th World Mission Report at Seoul Fencing Gymnasium with 10,000 attendees
- July 26-29, 2001: ISU International Summer Bible Conference with 2,350 attendees
- January 8, 2002 : Call to heaven (Homecoming ceremony with 1,000 guests worldwide. In all, Dr. Samuel Lee pioneered 100 chapters in Korea and sent out 1,500 self-supporting lay missionaries to 85 countries)

TABLE OF CONTENTS

FOREWORD

Dr. Samuel Lee wanted to plant in our hearts the truth of the gospel which has power to save anyone who believes.

These Luke's Gospel lectures are a precious treasure. They represent the culmination of years of study and prayer. I worked with Dr. Lee for 40 years in the University Bible Fellowship, and I came to respect him as a deep and prayerful, and at the same time, scholarly, Bible student and teacher. In Korea he wrote Daily Bread notes on the whole Bible and developed outstanding Bible study materials on Genesis, Romans, Isaiah, Mark's Gospel, and many other books of the Bible. These writings nourished the souls of Korean students and led many into deeper faith. To come to America in his mid-40s and begin writing and delivering lectures in English was a Herculean task. Without the help of the Holy Spirit and the prayers and support of many co-workers, especially the encouragement of his wife, Grace A. Lee, he could not have done it. Of all the study materials he produced in the USA, Luke's Gospel may be the most heart-moving. It is with gratitude to God that the UBF publication committee can publish these lectures.

—SARAH BARRY, UBF General Director Emeritus,
Presbyterian Missionary, Ret.

ENDORSEMENTS I

Dr. Samuel Lee was my personal shepherd for nearly 40 years. I heard his messages from the beginning of the UBF ministry and they helped me grow as a shepherd. His messages were so deep that through them I could receive the love and grace of Jesus personally. As I recall, Dr. Samuel Lee faced all kinds of hardships while serving God's work in UBF as our leader, but in the midst of adversities, he studied the Bible deeply and wrote many wonderful Bible lectures. They include his studies on the books of Luke, Matthew, Mark, John, Exodus, Joshua, Daniel, Acts, Romans, Ephesians, Philippians, 1 Peter, 2 Peter, Hebrews, and many more. He especially loved Luke's Gospel because it presents the gospel as the continuation of God's history. He put his best effort into his 1985 version. UBF Press plans to publish about 20 books of Dr. Samuel Lee's lectures in a series, and we are very happy to publish his 1985 version of Luke's Gospel as the first one. May God bless our personal Bible study and message preparation through this book.

—DR. JOHN JUN, General Director Emeritus

ENDORSEMENTS II

University Bible Fellowship was born in 1961 through the Bible teaching and co-working of the late Dr. Samuel Lee, a Presbyterian youth pastor, and Ms. Sarah Barry, a Presbyterian missionary, for Korean students. Both believed in the Bible as the word of God and taught it from the author's point of view. The student movement grew nationwide, embraced world campus mission, and sent out missionaries from the early 1970s. Behind this work of the Holy Spirit were Dr. Lee's inspiring expository Bible sermons, which came out of his deep and prayerful Bible study.

When he came to America in 1977, Dr. Samuel Lee realized that American young people really needed to know the grace and mercy of Jesus, and also, a sense of God's history. So during the 1980s, he repeatedly preached from the Gospel of Luke. Through his Sunday sermons, many American young people received Christ's grace and mercy personally and gained a sense of the redemptive work and history of God.

We are delighted to publish this study of Luke's Gospel that Dr. Lee developed in 1985, which is so outstanding in spiritual depth. May God use them as a source of blessing for his people all around the world.

—ABRAHAM KIM, PhD, UBF General Director

ENDORSEMENTS III

The following Luke's Gospel sermons were delivered by Dr. Samuel Lee at the Chicago UBF Sunday worship services in the mid 1980s with the prayer topic that young Americans might learn a sense of God's history. At that time, America was known as a Christian nation. Many people thought America did not need missionaries from other nations to preach the gospel here. But in truth, there were many, even among church attendees, who did not live with gospel faith. As Dr. Lee engaged American college students with a pastor's heart, he perceived their deep spiritual need. He was convinced that young Americans needed most the gospel of Jesus Christ, rooted in historical truth, as recorded by Luke. So he devoted himself wholeheartedly to share Luke's Gospel sermons and delivered them with passion, often with tears. In response, many young Americans came to believe the gospel message and accepted Jesus Christ personally as Lord and Savior. I worked closely with Dr. Lee to prepare these sermons, and it greatly influenced me toward a Christ-centered lifestyle and ministry. Times have changed, and the problems young people face today may be different in some ways, but the gospel is timeless, and it speaks to every culture and every generation. In publishing these studies, it is our prayer that the power of God's word, which worked so mightily through Dr. Lee, may bring Christ's blessing to the hearts of all who read it.

—RON WARD, Senior Pastor, Chicago UBF Church; North America UBF Coordinator, 2002-11

A Light to the Gentiles

"... a light for revelation to the Gentiles and for glory to your people Israel." (Luke 2:32)

THE GOSPEL ACCORDING TO St. Luke is so universal in content and inclusiveness. It is impossible to write an introduction to the gospel according to St. Luke because there is a danger that the introduction will be longer than the text. So it is summarized with a brief preface.

I.   First, Luke, the author.

Luke is known as a Gentile and a historian because of his universal point of view. But when we study the Bible broadly, we don't find any hint that Luke was a Gentile. Still, people call him a Gentile. Maybe it is because his gospel is universal: he included Gentiles just as much as Jews in regards to salvation through Jesus Christ our Lord. His narrative, "a light for the Gentiles," was his key to understanding the vast Bible and the principle of his gospel ministry. He really included the Gentile people as equals to the Jewish people even though Jewish people regarded the Gentile people as "not chosen" and "not privileged" to be called the children of God. But Luke did not have the prejudice of traditional Jews against the Gentiles. This may be the reason he was recognized by the Jewish people as a Gentile.

In his gospel, he is known as a medical doctor. In ancient times, especially in Jesus' time, medical doctors were eminently honored and well treated. Among the Jews, famous medical doctors became

19

responsible persons for the healthcare of kings of many nations. Humanly speaking, for Luke to remain as a medical doctor was very reasonable. But since converting to Christianity, his priorities were changed to Jesus first and to the proclamation of the gospel of Jesus to the whole world.

Luke was also an eminent theologian because he saw everything from a universal point of view. There was no hint of a localistic point of view.

The most beautiful part of Luke's life was his personal service to St. Paul from the time of Paul's second world mission journey to Paul's prison life in Rome. Luke dedicated himself to Paul as a private medical doctor.

II. Second, Luke gives a special position to women.

In short, the gospel according to Luke is universal; it applies to all mankind. In Palestine, the place of women was not regarded. For example, when Jesus was carrying out the Messianic ministry around the Galilean district, many people, around 5,000 men, gathered (Lk 9:14). They did not include women and children in the count because at that time, the human dignity and equality of women were not appreciated. Children were also not numbered because the bigoted Jewish people were all money lovers. So children who had no labor power or could not earn money were unimportant.

But Luke gave women a special place. Luke's gospel starts with the story of the birth of Jesus. Chapters 1-2 are all stories of women. The story of Mary the mother of Jesus was astounding, especially to our brothers and sisters in the former Soviet Union. Still, many traditional churches do not distinguish between Mary the mother of Jesus and the Savior Jesus. At the time of Jesus' birth, Mary was a country damsel. She was betrothed to Joseph, a descendant of David. One day the angel of the Lord appeared to her and said, "Greetings, you who are highly favored! The Lord is with you" (1:28 ff.). Mary was indeed afraid. But the angel told her that she would be the mother of Jesus before marrying Joseph the carpenter. She asked, "How can it be, since I am a virgin?" Luke 1:35 says, "The Holy Spirit will come upon you, and the power of the Most High will overshadow you.

So the holy one to be born will be called the Son of God." Then she learned that it is from the Lord and said in 1:38, "I am the Lord's servant. May it be to me as you have said." Then the angel left her.

How could a teenage girl accept this unutterably great mission from the angel as the favor of God? It is because the angel told the prophecy concerning the Savior Jesus in verses 31-33. It says, "You will be with child and give birth to a son, and you are to give him the name Jesus. He will be great and will be called the Son of the Most High. The Lord God will give him the throne of his father David, and he will reign over the house of Jacob forever; his kingdom will never end." Even though she asked, "How can it be?" She accepted the angel's prophetic tiding. Here we learn that Luke gave a special place to a woman who had no human rights or equality with men at that time.

In Luke 1-2, Elizabeth and Anna appear. Humanly speaking, they were useless. They were no more than senior citizens who deserved food stamps. But Luke saw them with spiritual eyes and recognized them as the lamp of God. In the sight of God, they were praying women. Right before Jesus' coming, the world was in the darkest dark time. But their prayer was a shining lamp to the dark world, and Luke gave them great honor and a special position.

Luke dealt with godly women, but also had great sympathy for those women who were in need of God's mercy. Without mercy, these women would have perished. In chapter 7, there is a story about a very sorrowful widow in a town called Nain. She married, but her husband died young. She did not remarry for the sake of her only son. One day, her only son died without any notice. She could not even cry because her mind went blank and his sudden death was completely unbelievable. But since her son died, she had to proceed with the funeral procession. We have never heard such a sorrowful story. She was not walking straight, but just tottering after the bier. When Jesus saw her, his heart went out to her, and he said, "Don't cry." The Savior of the world gave the dead boy a new life and wiped away his mother's sorrow.

There are endless stories in Luke's gospel which give a special place to women. Among many events, one is very impressive. Luke

8:2-3 say, "... and also some women who had been cured of evil spirits and diseases: Mary (called Magdalene) from whom seven demons had come out; Joanna the wife of Cuza, the manager of Herod's household; Susanna; and many others. These women were helping to support [Jesus and the Twelve] out of their own means." Even though Jesus is the Son of God, while carrying out the earthly Messianic ministry, he needed necessary funds. In addition, his jobless, young, and energetic twelve disciples consumed a three months' portion of groceries in one month. Where did the financial resources come from? That's a good question. Nobody mentions these financial resources. But Luke, who had a special place for women, recorded that some women who had been cured of evil spirits and diseases were helping to support them out of their own means. These women had been worldly. As a result, they suffered and were corrupted in the world and finally they became women of sorrows. But because of Jesus' healing touch, they became completely new creations. In actuality, they did not have regular jobs. They could make only minimum wage because they were women, even if they worked harder. But they supported Jesus and his disciples from the beginning to the end. What a surprising story! Here we learn that the hearts of women are most beautiful and most powerful. But in Jesus' time, people looked down on women. How ignorant they were. How they needed the light of life of Jesus.

How was world mission possible? Of course, it was Paul's faith in God Almighty. It was also the grace of God in his soul. Paul confessed his sinfulness. His sinful status was like a person untimely born (1Co 15:8). He was like a paralyzed man in the sight of God because of his sins and selfish ambition. But God forgave his sins when he was on the way to Damascus to annihilate the early Christians (Ac 9:1 ff.). On the way, he met the Risen Jesus. He fell down from his horse. It was the time of conversion. Despite his unforgivable sins, Jesus forgave all his sins and wanted to make him a servant of God for the Gentiles. Acts 9:15 says, "But the Lord said to Ananias, 'Go! This man is my chosen instrument to carry my name before the Gentiles and their kings and before the people of Israel.'" The grace of Jesus is indeed marvelous. The grace of Jesus is universal.

In the course of world evangelization, Paul went to Philippi. It was a Roman colony. On the Sabbath day, Paul expounded on the gospel of salvation (Ac 16:13). There was a pimp who made use of a girl who knew how to perform magic arts. This pathetic girl was converted. Then the pimp stirred up people and put Paul and Silas in prison. But they sang and praised God in the prison (16:16-25). Through this event, God gave them a life-committed convert whose name was Lydia. When Paul was looking for a place of prayer in the morning, Lydia grabbed the shoulders of Paul and Silas and said, "If you consider me a believer in the Lord, come and stay at my house" (Ac 16:15). And she persuaded both. In this moment, Lydia seemed to have been more persuasive than St. Paul, who is known as the most persuasive in the world throughout history. In this way, Luke gave a special place to women. Especially, Luke gave an honorary position to Lydia. Lydia was good at business. She was a dealer in purple cloth. Since then, she began to support the expenses of Paul's world mission journey. Praise God that he made man and woman in his image and gave them the same honor, privilege, and mission.

III. Third, the outstanding universality of Luke's gospel.

If we study Luke's gospel, we learn that, as a whole, Luke's gospel is the best literature and the most historical and evangelical. The outstanding universality of Luke's gospel is beyond comparison with other gospels. For example, Luke 15 is known as the best story. Once an English novelist was convinced that he could write a better parable than Luke 15. So the English government gave him five years of time and he tried to write a better parable of the prodigal son. The government was supposed to reward him with one million pounds. When the day came to hand in his parable, he pleaded with the government officials to give him three years more to write the parable, and after three years, another two years. Finally, he surrendered himself to Luke 15. In the gospel messages, Luke 15 is the most difficult to deliver as a message, because it is already outstanding over all literature. We cannot subtract or add a word. That's what Oscar Wilde did. Luke 15 includes the philosophy of all humanity, the theology of God's mercy and grace of salvation. We cannot tell the whole story of Luke 15 right now, but this chapter reveals the beautiful and everlasting relationship between the Father God and his children. This chapter reveals that men are happy when they realize the love of God.

Only in Luke's gospel is there the Parable of the Good Samaritan (10:25-37). Luke was known as a Gentile, even though we don't know if he was a converted diaspora Jew or a secret orthodox Jew. Whatever the reason, he is worthy to be called a Gentile, or "light for the Gentiles," after the nickname of Jesus, because he loved all human beings with the love of God. The Parable of the Good Samaritan is a very familiar story to our ears. The characters are an orthodox Jew, a religious Levite, and a vigorous merchant. They saw a man badly wounded by gangsters. But the orthodox Jew turned around and ran away with an excuse that he must keep his worship service time. The religious Levite knew he should take care of the wounded man, but in order not to miss singing in the vocal team, he ran away with full speed. But the Samaritan, a Gentile, ruined his business and gave all his money and saved this man's life. This story is not at all dogmatic. But it reveals the universal love of God. Who could have been the most happy?

Luke the historian and evangelist wrote about ten lepers (17:11-19). Since they contracted leprosy, their bodies were decaying. And they lost most of their fingers. Their eyeballs were barely supported by the sockets. What is more, they were smelly. What is worse, they were hopeless because of the leprosy spreading in their bodies. They heard the good news of Jesus Christ and secretly ran away from their lepers' shelter. As soon as they saw Jesus, they asked for his healing mercy. Luke 17:12-13 says "They stood at a distance and called out in a loud voice, 'Jesus, Master, have pity on us!'" He told them to show themselves to the priests and get a certificate of recovery. A very unusual thing happened. When they were healed, the nine Jewish lepers went to their mommies or went around claiming that they were healed by their own effort. Jesus was very sorry that they did not come back to thank him for the healing. Only one man came and thanked Jesus for his healing. He was a Samaritan, a Gentile. Jesus was very sorry that God's chosen people had all forgotten God's grace. They were saved from their leprosy, but they did not have a thankful mind. Jesus was very sorry because they were supposed to be shepherds and Bible teachers and a blessing to the Gentile people, but they were really unthankful. Their root was totally corrupted because they did not thank God. Unthankfulness is the root of sin. Jesus was very sorry because there were so many people who should study the Bible with his chosen people, but his people were worse than the lepers. On the other hand, a Gentile leper remembered his past agony in being a leper and came to Jesus and bowed down with his face to the ground and thanked him with many tears. Here we learn that Luke did not concentrate on the chosen people, but on God who is universal and whose grace extends to a Gentile leper. Thank God that his saving grace extends to all mankind.

Luke understood Luke 2:32, "... a light for revelation to the Gentiles and for glory to your people Israel." It is amazing that Luke accepted the universal love of God for the helpless.

IV. Fourth, the kingdom of God.

When we study Luke's gospel, there are many events. Therefore, sometimes we are confused about what the main focus of this gospel is. But the main focus of this gospel is the kingdom of God. Luke mentioned "the kingdom of God" 39 times in his gospel. When we compare Luke's gospel with Matthew's gospel, it is quite different. Matthew emphasized the kingdom of God or Jesus as the Messiah King through many kinds of illustrations and parables and stories. But Luke's gospel's teaching of the kingdom of God is far superior to Matthew's gospel in planting the kingdom of God in the hearts of vulgar people who are suffering under Satan's rule. Luke tried to plant faith in the kingdom of God in many ways. Luke 1:33 says, "... his kingdom will never end." Luke 6:20 says, "... for yours is the kingdom of God." Luke 8:10 says, "... the kingdom of God has been given to you." Luke 9:11 says, "... and spoke to them about the kingdom of God." Luke 10:9 says, "... the kingdom of God is near you." Luke 10:11 says again, "Yet be sure of this: The kingdom of God is near." Luke also talked about the happiness of the kingdom of God in Luke 13:29 when he referred to it as "the feast in the kingdom of God." Jesus told them in 17:21 that "the kingdom of God is within you." It means that those who truly believe can taste the kingdom of God on earth.

Why did he talk so much about the kingdom of God? Luke the historian knew what the world was like. The world is under the rule of Satan in which innocent people suffer endlessly. People who suffer most are those who achieve something through their bone-crushing efforts. The kingdom of God teaches us that man is flesh and spirit. John 6:63 says, "The Spirit gives life; the flesh counts for nothing. The words I have spoken to you are spirit and they are life." Peter said, "For, 'All men are like grass, and all their glory is like the flowers of the field; the grass withers and the flowers fall, but the word of the Lord stands forever'" (1Pe 1:24-25a). It is true. Luke 9:25 says, "What good is it for a man to gain the whole world, and yet lose or forfeit his very self?" Since modern men do not read the Bible, they lost the knowledge of who God really is and what man really is. They only think about money and future security. There is no future security except the funeral home.

But the evangelist accepted Jesus' words of promise; he believed in eternal life. John 3:16 says, "For God so loved the world that he gave his one and only Son, that whoever believes in him shall not perish but have eternal life." This is God's ultimate promise. In order to give us eternal life, our Lord Jesus Christ was crucified on the cross. God raised dead Jesus on the third day and made him King of kings and Lord of lords. And God made him the Judge. 2 Corinthians 5:10 says, "For we must all appear before the judgment seat of Christ, that each one may receive what is due him for the things done while in the body, whether good or bad."

V. Fifth, Luke's view of Jesus' discipleship training.

Luke's view of Jesus' discipleship training is far superior to those of other gospels. Luke 24 explains concisely.

First, Luke saw that Jesus' discipleship training is based on the word of God. Luke did not quote Old Testament references as frequently as Matthew did. But he mastered God's purpose of world salvation, and his proclamation of the gospel was entirely based on it. For this, Luke emphasized the gospel of Jesus: that Jesus is the Son of God and the only salvation from sin. In Jesus only, man has eternal life and receives the kingdom of God. However, Luke's gospel is a little different in color, even though basic accounts are the same. According to Luke's account, Jesus emphasized to his disciples that he should suffer and be handed over to the Gentiles and should die on the cross and rise again on the third day. Whenever Luke emphasized this, he related that Jesus' suffering and death was to fulfill the will of God and the will of God was that he would become the Lamb of God for the sin of the world. The disciples, who had been clumps of desires, were not willing to understand the way of the cross.

What did this do to them? We cannot go into all the details of how Jesus tried to plant a few words of gospel faith. Literally, Jesus failed until he was crucified on the cross on the hill of Golgotha. But there is no failure in Jesus.

Second, Jesus' discipleship training helped them open their spiritual eyes. The Risen Christ appeared in shining form to the women who came to the tomb to anoint his dead body. Right after the women heard his voice, their sorrows were gone. Heavenly sunlight smeared into their hearts. The Risen Christ also appeared to two persons who were running for their lives after the crucifixion of Jesus. They despaired. They were tragic. But the Risen Jesus had a living hope for them and taught them the Bible all over again on the way to Emmaus (24:27). At sunset, they all went into a house. Jesus began to teach them the Bible. Finally, they recognized it was the Risen Christ. Then the Risen Christ disappeared from their sight. When they met the Risen Christ, their dead hearts came back to life. They asked each other, "Were not our hearts burning within us while he talked with us?" (24:32). In this part, we learn that Jesus raised disciples by teaching the Bible until their spiritual eyes were opened. May God raise us as Bible teachers like Jesus. May God open our spiritual eyes to see the Risen Jesus. May God help us study the Bible truth, believe it in our hearts, and see from God's point of view with universal eyes so that we can really understand God who is like the Father in the Parable of the Prodigal Son in chapter 15. May God give us universal love so that we can embrace all kinds of sheep without any prejudice like Luke, a servant of God.

Lesson 1

The Birth of John the Baptist Foretold

Luke 1:5-25
Key Verse: 1:13

I. THE LIVES OF FAITH OF ZECHARIAH AND ELIZABETH (5-7)

1. What do you know about Herod and his times?
2. Who were Zechariah and Elizabeth? In what respects might they be called upright in the sight of God? What was the problem in their family? How do you think this problem affected them?

II. ZECHARIAH'S LIFE OF PRAYER (8-13)

3. What special opportunity came to Zechariah? What did it mean to burn incense at the altar while the people prayed outside? What should be his prayer topic at a time like this?
4. As he stood at the altar to offer prayer and burn incense, what happened? What was his reaction? Why?
5. What had evidently been his personal, secret, lifelong prayer topic? Why might a personal prayer topic be somewhat inappropriate for this occasion?
6. What was the angel's good news? Why do you think the angel even told him the name of his son?

III. GREAT BEFORE THE LORD (14-17)

7. How would John be a blessing to his family and neighbors?
8. In what respects would John be great? What would be special about his lifestyle? What would be his mission? What does this tell us about the people of those times?

IV. GOD TRAINS ZECHARIAH (18-25)

9. How did Zechariah respond to the angel's message concerning his son? What does this show about his sense of history? Why did he find it so hard to believe the angel's message of good news?
10. How did the angel rebuke him? What special training did he receive? What was the point of the training? What do you learn here about God who trains his servants?
11. How did Elizabeth reveal that her barrenness had been a great problem for her? What was her testimony after she became pregnant?

The Birth of John the Baptist Foretold

Luke 1:5-25
Key Verse: 1:13

> *But the angel said to him: "Do not be afraid, Zechariah; your prayer has been heard. Your wife Elizabeth will bear you a son, and you are to give him the name John."*

WHEN THE TIME WAS ripe for the fulfillment of the prophecy of John the Baptist to be born as the forerunner of the Messiah, the angel announced his birth. This story focuses on the foretelling of the birth of John the Baptist. However, there are two senior citizens in this story, John's parents, who prepared the spiritual environment for his birth. This passage teaches us the kind of people God uses in his work and history; it teaches us the character of God's history. We also learn here the integrity of John as the forerunner of the Messiah. May God give new vision and insight to those who are living in the mainstream of God's history.

I.   The lives of faith of Zechariah and Elizabeth (5-7)

Verse 5 begins with the words, "In the time of Herod king of Judea ..." The reign of Herod king of Judea from 40 BC to 4 BC was a time of tragedy. Herod called himself "Great"—but he was not. He was a puppet of the Roman Empire, just a small figure of a human being.

In history, there have been tyrants who have made the hearts of men shudder, such as Nero, Emperor of Rome; Adolph Hitler, the Nazi dictator of Germany; and Joseph Stalin, the Soviet Premier. Despite their inhumanity, at least they did not kill their children. But Herod, in his megalomania, strangled his own two sons. In many novels, even monsters are mindful of innocent little children. But this Herod, when he heard that the king of the Jews was born, ordered all the boys in Bethlehem and its vicinity who were two years old and under to be killed (Mt 2:16). "In the time of Herod" thus points to a dark, ominous, and calamitous period in the history of the Jewish nation. The time of Herod was a microcosm of the dark world of those times.

The word of God through the prophets had been life and light to the people of Israel down through the generations. But for about four hundred years after the last appearance of the Old Testament prophets, no further revelation had been given to the chosen people of God. They were like prisoners in a dungeon where there was no light or sound, only darkness. The world looked as if Satan wielded his power and the lamps of God had been extinguished. Still, God was steadily fulfilling prophecies and promises according to his own time schedule. There were also the devout who were waiting for the emergence of the Messiah. God was preparing the birth of John the Baptist through two senior citizens.

These two senior citizens were Zechariah and Elizabeth. What kind of persons were they? Look at verse 6. "Both of them were upright in the sight of God, observing all the Lord's commandments and regulations blamelessly." Who can dare say, "I am upright in the sight of God?" But the historian Luke says that Zechariah and Elizabeth were upright in the sight of God. Surely they must have appeared great, a man and woman of standing. But they were not. They were ordinary laymen. But they were upright in the sight of God. There are two reasons for this.

First, they were upright in the sight of God because they lived according to the word of God. There are two kinds of people. One kind is those who look nice in the sight of men. Among them were the religious leaders who appeared to be holy, but in the gospels, they were hypocrites who had the form of religion but denied its power. They were the source of hideous corruption and a symbol of Satan. Though they might have been the object of envy and praise in men's eyes, they were evil in the sight of God.

The other kind is Zechariah and Elizabeth. They looked like poor senior citizens who might have depended on social security benefits and lived in a nursing home. Still, they were very important persons (VIPs) in the sight of God. Why? It was because they lived according to the word of God. Though the world was dark under Herod's dominion, they were not swayed by the worldly consensus. They meditated on the law of God day and night. Zechariah and Elizabeth had reasons to complain to each other. But they did not. They woke up early and shared a daily devotional and prayed together and ate breakfast together.

Not only that, they obeyed the word of God wholeheartedly. They may have bought candy and given them to the neighborhood children and played with them. And they visited many needy people with gifts from their poor social security checks. They were poor, but they were rich because they abided in the word of life. They were old, but they looked like evergreens. They were like trees planted by streams of water which yield their fruit in season.

Compared with the great military power of the Roman Empire, the Bible studies of these two old persons seemed like that of reading newspapers and passing the time. But it was more meaningful and powerful than the might of Rome. Their personal struggles to live by the word of God made them come alive spiritually. Compared with all the other people of the world who were like dead fish floating downstream, they were like living fish swimming against the trends of the world. They were a living people among a confused and corrupted people. When God saw them, they were upright in his sight.

Second, they were upright in the sight of God because they overcame the fatalistic elements of their life. As each person has a fatalistic element in his life, so did these old people. What was their problem? Look at verse 7: "But they had no children, because Elizabeth was barren; and they were both well along in years." As we know well, children are a source of joy and comfort to all parents. I know one person who only had two daughters. He really wanted to have a son, but he would not try because he was afraid of having another daughter. When I helped him to live by faith, he tried and God granted him a son. He experienced great joy through his son. Then he tried again for another son, but this time, God gave him another daughter.

Since Zechariah and Elizabeth had no child, they were always lonely and alone. They would make melancholy smiles whenever they saw children in the streets. They were sad whenever people around them derided their childlessness. At that time, childlessness was traditionally regarded tragically. But they did not fall into fatalism. They were not bitter, nor did they doubt God's love. By faith they overcame the fatalistic problem of childlessness, and they maintained their married life until they were both well along in years. In this way, they pleased God, and God was very pleased by them.

II. Zechariah's life of prayer (8-13)

Read verses 8 and 9. Zechariah was chosen by lot to go into the temple to burn incense. Many a priest would never have the privilege of burning incense in the temple. But Zechariah was chosen. It was a great day in his life. Insomuch as he was thrilled with the privilege, he was also obliged to pray for his people, calling out their names one by one.

Read verses 11 and 12. When Zechariah was alone burning incense in the temple, the angel of the Lord appeared. When Zechariah saw him, he was startled and gripped with fear. Why? The Hebrew people thought that they would die if they saw God with their own eyes. This may be one reason why he was gripped with fear. But most likely, the moment of God's intervention struck him with an awesome fear, for God was bringing the dawn of a new day into the life and history of humanity through the advent of John the Baptist.

Look at verse 13. "But the angel said to him: 'Do not be afraid, Zechariah; your prayer has been heard. Your wife Elizabeth will bear you a son, and you are to give him the name John.'" This verse suggests another reason why he was gripped with fear. While he prayed for the people and for his nation as his priestly duty, Zechariah also prayed earnestly for himself, "O Lord, give me a son." When he heard that his prayer was answered and a son would be given him, he realized that he had prayed for a son when he should have prayed for others. Moreover, he was afraid, realizing that God had intervened in his life. This story indicates that man is basically selfish. However, Zechariah's spirit of prayer is admirable. We learn the greatness of his prayer life.

First, his prayer was persistent. He had never given up his prayer for a son. Maybe he began to pray for a son after two years of married life. Humanly, he could pray earnestly for one or two years, then give up. But he continued to pray even when his wife became like a grandma, with gray hair and wrinkles and heavy bags under her eyes. Zechariah, though he lived in a dark and faithless generation, had absolute trust in God. He never doubted God's omnipresence and omnipotence. He believed that God was sovereign over life and death, blessing and curse. How wonderful it is to believe like Zechariah and pray persistently.

Second, he had one prayer topic throughout his lifetime. By nature, human beings are forgetful. If people were not forgetful, they would die because of all the unhappy memories of the past. How difficult it is not to forget! But Zechariah kept one prayer topic throughout his lifetime. God saw this man of prayer and answered his prayer. Though he was too old, God used him as the father of John the Baptist.

It is amazing that God is with praying people. Those were times when human thinking made a lot of noise. Zechariah burning incense in the temple and the crowd of people praying outside looked like a group of sorrowful weeping widows to the people of the world. But in God's sight, these praying people were the main characters in his history, and God was present with them. God blessed that gathering as the prayer vessel for the advent of John. We learn that God is in the midst of a fellowship that prays earnestly.

III. Great before the Lord (14-17)

Verses 14-17 are the angel's prophecy concerning John, the son of Zechariah. The main point of this prophecy was that John would be great before the Lord. In verses 14-17, we can see several factors that would make John great in the sight of God.

First, he is great before God because he is a gracious gift of God. Look at verses 13 and 14 again. John's birth would bring great joy to his mother and father and to all the neighbors. Why? It may be because they would have little Zech who would be a joy to his parents and their neighbors. But this was not the reason. The angel said to

Zechariah, "You are to give him the name John," not little Zech. The name "John," according to Hebrew etymology, means, "the Lord is merciful" or "gracious gift of God." This name, therefore, refers to the grace of God that was going to descend on the family of Zechariah as well as on the devout people who were waiting for the Messiah. This joy was to see the mercy and gracious gift of God to all people through the birth of John.

Second, he is great before God because he lived a pure life. Read verse 15b. "He is never to take wine or other fermented drink, and he will be filled with the Holy Spirit even from birth." When God saw the world, it was filled with the stains of sin. Men drove themselves into break dancing to find relief from their unclean spirits. Women wore heavy makeup to cover their nasty smells. So God sent John to live a pure life against the corruption of the world. When we think about John, there are many elements of greatness in him: his full devotion to ministry, his burning conviction, his intensity of moral courage, and his humbleness and self-abnegation. However, his pure life was a most important element of his greatness before God.

John lived a pure life before God, withstanding the corruption and pleasure-seeking ways of the world. In order to live a pure life, he did not take any fermented drink or expensive food. But he ate only cold food, such as locusts and wild honey. He slept in the crevices of rocks, a very uncomfortable bed. When he lived a pure life before God, people said, "He is demon-possessed." One man tried to live a pure life before God. He did not have a girlfriend. Then even his parents wondered if he was homosexual. Likewise, it was most difficult for John to live a pure life before God. But his pure life was the power source of his inner life. When he lived such a poor and pure life, God filled him with the Holy Spirit.

Third, John is great before God because he lived up to God's calling. Read verses 16 and 17. He was sent to prepare the way for the coming Messiah. His mission was to preach the baptism of repentance to all kinds of people. Nobody wants to hurt others. Nobody wants to be hurt by others. Everybody wants to be accepted and recognized by others. So it is not easy for anybody to say to others, "Repent." These days there is a danger of being sued if one says "repent" to others because it sounds like a violation of personal rights in a democratic country. I heard that many ministers in the United States pay malpractice insurance to cover the danger of being sued.

Nobody can say "repent" to someone else unless he himself lives a life of faith. Therefore, this was the hardest task to do. But John acknowledged God's specific calling to him. It was to prepare the way of the Lord through the baptism of repentance. He did not take good care of himself. He cared for God's calling at the cost of his own life. He also cared for the dying souls of his time. He rebuked their corruption and perversion. He rebuked many irresponsible fathers to repent and come back to their children. He rebuked disobedient children to repent and live in the wisdom of the righteous God. He walked a thorny way in order to live up to God's calling. His life of mission ended with imprisonment and death by beheading. But he was not a victim of the vicious cycles of the world. He was great in the sight of God.

Fourth, John is great because he was a man of spirit. What was his source of power as a man of God? John was like a reincarnation of the prophet Elijah (17). He came in an epoch similar to that in which Elijah had lived. No one had dared to challenge King Ahab and Queen Jezebel's wickedness. But Elijah, with power and spirit, challenged them to repent. As we studied, King Herod was a most cruel man. But with the same power and spirit as that of Elijah, John challenged him to repent of his cruelty and immorality. Flesh is nothing; spirit is everything.

These days, most people look nice and pretend to be happy, but they are miserable. Their spirits are so deranged that many men look like women, and women look like wild horses. They say that the size of highways is the measure of a nation's power. But the real power of a nation depends on the spiritual condition of its people.

IV. God trains Zechariah (18-25)

The angel's message to Zechariah was God's promise that he would give him a son. This promise is similar to God's promise to Abraham in Genesis 17:16. Abraham believed it, but Zechariah could not believe it. So Zechariah said to the angel, "How can I be sure of this? I am an old man and my wife is well along in years" (18). He was a man of prayer. He had faith in God, but no faith to believe in God's sovereign rule in history. In brief, he had no sense of history. So the angel Gabriel rebuked him: "I am Gabriel. I stand in the presence of God ... And now you will be silent and not able to speak until the day this happens, because you did not believe my words" (19-20).

In spite of much training through childlessness, he needed more training in order to learn a sense of God's history. This time he received dumb training. When Zechariah came out to the people, he tried to speak with sign language. Suddenly, he became a pantomime artist. The multitude waiting outside did not know what had happened inside the temple. We are living in times when there is no awareness of history. So those of us doing God's work sometimes get confused. But we must believe that God rules the history of the world steadily and quietly through men and women of prayer.

Read verses 24 and 25. "After this his wife Elizabeth became pregnant and for five months remained in seclusion" (24). Through five months in seclusion, she came to a conclusion: "The Lord has done this for me" (25). She confessed that the Lord had intervened in her life and taken away her disgrace as a barren woman.

From God's point of view, in that dark world, Zechariah and Elizabeth were the remnants of God's history. From God's point of view, they kept the lamp of God burning. They were the main characters in God's history. They were historical persons; they were not people who remained only for awhile, wiggling around like groundbeetles and then forgotten. They were the ones God could use for the advent of John the Baptist.

Lesson 2

The Birth of Jesus Foretold

Luke 1:26-38
Key Verse: 1:32

I.   YOU WHO ARE HIGHLY FAVORED (26-30)

1.   Think about the environment in which Mary lived. What was her human situation? To what does the sixth month refer? (36)

2.   What was the angel's greeting, and why was Mary so greatly troubled and fearful?

3.   What does it mean to be "highly favored," to "find favor with God"? What was the particular mission God wanted to give Mary? Why might this be hard for her to bear humanly?

II.   HIS KINGDOM WILL NEVER END (31-33)

4.   What would be the name of Mary's son, and what does the angel's message tell us about his uniqueness and his character? What would be his mission and his privilege?

5.   What do you know about David's kingdom? (1Ch 17:10b-12; Ac 13:36) About the kingdom of the Messiah? (Isa 11:1-9; Da 7:14,18,27)

III.   I AM THE LORD'S SERVANT (34-38)

6.   What was Mary's first response? Why was it hard for her to accept the angel's words?

7.   How did the angel answer her question? How could it be possible for a virgin to bear a son? What evidence of God's power encouraged her to believe?

8.   What was Mary's decision of faith? What was the basis for her decision? What can you learn from her about obedience? Think about the great cost and the great privilege that would result from her decision.

The Birth of Jesus Foretold

Luke 1:26-38
Key Verse: 1:32

> *"He will be great and will be called the Son of the Most High.*
> *The Lord God will give him the throne of his father David ..."*

ODAY'S PASSAGE IS ABOUT the angel's Christmas message to Mary, a country girl. The core of the message is about the birth of Jesus foretold. This prophecy is parallel with the birth of John the Baptist foretold, emphasizing the spiritual environment which made the birth of Jesus possible. In this passage, the concept of God's favor upon mankind, especially upon woman, is appealing, and a full view of Jesus and his kingdom is well delineated. May God give us a sense of his work in history.

I.   You who are highly favored! (26-30)

Read verses 26 and 27. These verses show us the village in which Mary lived, and it also poetically shows us her human situation. Over 2,000 years ago, there was a small village in Galilee called Nazareth. It was probably a small, clean country village. Perhaps in the daytime, one could hear the sweet song of the oriole crying among the trees, and at night, from across the hills, one could hear the lonely hoot of the owl. Young boys collected sticks and grass from the wooded hill for firewood. Pretty girls went out to the fields to pick mulberry leaves. How happy they must have been when they met by chance! They might have wished that they could meet each other again. And the boys might have talked a lot about the girls they knew. The girls must have said something too.

Mary was a country girl and lived in such a village. And she was engaged to be married to a young man named Joseph, a descendant of David. Perhaps she was preparing for her marriage, embroidering pillow cases, trying on the new clothes she would wear after her marriage and taking them off—and then trying them on again. Perhaps she had beautiful and happy dreams of the home she would have with Joseph. She rode every night in a beautiful chariot of dreams. She was only waiting for quiet Joseph and the sweet home they would have together. Probably she wanted her sweet dream to last forever. She didn't want anything to change it.

But one day an unusual event happened. Gabriel, the angel of the Lord, came to her and said, "Greetings, you who are highly favored! The Lord is with you." What was her response to this greeting? Verse 29 says that Mary was greatly troubled at his words and wondered what kind of greeting this might be. We can understand why she was so troubled at the greeting.

Mary was abundantly satisfied with Joseph's human favor. Therefore, she didn't think she needed any favor from anybody, even from an angel. She was also troubled at the angel's words, thinking that no one should bother her beautiful dream of her upcoming marriage. At that moment, for this engaged girl, the angel's greeting sounded as if she was losing everything.

What did the angel do? He knew that Mary was afraid. But with no deviation in his challenge to her, he said, "Do not be afraid, Mary, you have found favor with God." This emphatic verse has the meaning that God's favor to Mary was absolute and irresistible and irrevocable.

It seems good to know the meaning of the word "favor" in order to better understand the angel's message. Generally, favor means to get something from someone else free of charge, such as love and kindness or a small gift or token. Many secular Christians think that to be favored by God means to receive some human blessing. But the biblical concept of the word "favor" is quite contrary to our secular concept. The Greek word "favor" (karis) has the same root and meaning as the word "grace," and the derivative words are "beauty" and "thanks." This implies that we can be thankful, beautiful, and full of grace when we receive the favor of God. Because of the nuance of the word, it seems better to say "God's grace" instead of "God's favor."

What then did it mean for Mary to be favored by God? Look at verse 31. "You will be with child and give birth to a son, and you are to give him the name Jesus." God's grace to Mary was to be used as an instrument for his work and history of redemption. More specifically, God's grace meant that Mary was to become the mother of Jesus. By the same token, God's grace is God's mission. God's grace is the bestowing of his mission on his chosen ones.

However, it was very costly for Mary to accept God's grace personally. In order to accept God's grace, she had to give up her dreams. Mary was a simple, unsophisticated country girl. Her dream must have been to have a sweet home with Joseph, being loved by him. Her beautiful dreams were about to be realized. But before her marriage, she had to conceive and bear the baby Jesus. Humanly speaking, it was impossible for her to accept such costly grace. In spite of that, this passage tells us that she gave up her dream of marriage and accepted God's grace to be the mother of Jesus. What a great sacrifice she made when she gave up her dream of marriage. Apostle Peter gave up his family, business, and everything, but he could not give up his dream of being the top man in an earthly Messianic kingdom. We know how difficult it is to give up one's dream. What a great sacrifice Mary made when she gave up her dream of marriage!

As we know, she was a pure country girl who lived in a rigid, traditional Jewish society. Her purity must have been the attraction of her beauty, which was a sweet fragrance in her community. No sooner had God's grace come upon her than she became the object of scorn and discouragement to others. This must have been unbearable shame and punishment. In spite of this, she sacrificed herself and bore in her body all the shame and punishment.

God's grace was even more costly to her than this. The grace of God to her as the mother of Jesus was too painful. As the mother of Jesus, Mary was misunderstood and ill-treated by the people as Jesus was misunderstood and ill-treated. Later, Simeon prophesied about Mary when he held the baby Jesus in his arms: "And a sword will pierce your own soul too" (Lk 2:35). In truth, the agony that followed her sacrifice was like a knife piercing her soul. She had to stand beneath the cross and feel the pain of a mother's broken heart (Jn

19:25). When Jesus was nailed to the cross, she felt the nails being driven into her own heart. She bore such a painful grace and was known as the mother of Jesus.

II. His kingdom will never end (31-33)

In verses 31-33, the angel continues to speak his message to Mary. In his message, the angel introduces who Jesus is and what his kingdom will be like, for Mary needed this knowledge of Jesus' future to accept God's grace. So also do we.

First, Jesus is great. Look at verse 32. "He will be great and will be called the Son of the Most High." General Montgomery, at the end of his book, mentioned the world's greatest leaders—Mohammed, Buddha, and Jesus—from the point of view of world history. He included Jesus as one of the greatest men because of his persuasiveness. Others say many things about the greatness of Jesus as a philanthropist, poet, pedagogue, as a man who deeply understood humanity, etc. Indeed, there is no one in the entire world as great as Jesus. But the real greatness of Jesus does not rest on his human qualities and achievements, but on the fact that he is the Son of the Most High God. Though Jesus is the Son of the Most High God, he gave up all the power and glory of the heavenly kingdom and came to this world in human form to save the world. He is great in his renunciation of all his glory and honor and privileges as the Son of the Most High. He is great because as a shepherd, he never gave up on any person, but had the faith, hope, and love of God toward every kind of person. He is great because he obeyed the will of God unto death—even death on a cross.

Second, Jesus is the King. Look at verse 32b. "The Lord God will give him the throne of his father David." This verse tells us that Jesus is a king like David. Who was David? David was a king who served the will of God in his time by shepherding his people Israel (Ac 13:36). The people of Israel—even a blind beggar—longed and waited for a king like David to come again. David was the shadow of the Messiah who was to come. Jesus came out of the root of David (Isa 11:10). Jesus was born of a kingly line. Kings of the world live for a brief time and die. But Jesus is truly an eternal king because he conquered death through his resurrection and became the eternal King of the

LESSON 2 | THE BIRTH OF JESUS FORETOLD

kingdom of God.

Third, his kingdom is forever. Look at verse 33. "And he will reign over the house of Jacob forever; his kingdom will never end." The kingdoms of the world are temporal. The British Empire was once a glorious kingdom with many colonies. Perhaps there has been no other nation with such a glorious history, tradition, and culture. But this kingdom is gone. Only the kingdom of Jesus is forever.

There is a lot said about nations and kingdoms in the Bible. Among them is the eternal kingdom over which Christ will rule. This kingdom is the climax of the redemptive history about which the Bible is written, and it is the eternal kingdom for which all Christians long and wait. The prophet Daniel wrote in his prophecy concerning the apocalyptic thought of this eternal kingdom (Da 7:14,18, 27). The kings and kingdoms of the world are represented by the Babylonian Empire with its kings, Nebuchadnezzer, Belshazzar, and Darius; and again with the kingdoms of the Medes and Persians with their kings, Xerxes and Cyrus. These kingdoms are like a large statue made of iron and clay, gold and bronze. When God's time comes, they and their power will be destroyed. There is nothing eternal in this world. This truth has been the agony of the kings of nations who have wanted to keep their kingdoms forever. The kingdoms of the world have all crumbled like iron eaten by rust. Only the kingdom of Jesus is forever. The purpose of Jesus' coming to this world was to bring us back to his eternal kingdom and make us his heirs.

III. I am the Lord's servant (34-38)

What was Mary's response? Look at verse 34. "'How will this be,' Mary asked the angel, 'since I am a virgin?'" She wondered how a virgin could bear a child, and how this terrible thing would happen in her personal life. Her wonder was understandable. The angel taught her how it would be in verse 35a. "The Holy Spirit will come upon you, and the power of the Most High will overshadow you." This verse teaches us that the virgin birth of Jesus was the work of the Holy Spirit and the work of the mighty hand of God. It also teaches us Jesus' Godhood and manhood. Jesus was conceived by the Holy Spirit, so he is the Son of God. He was born of the Virgin Mary, so he is a son of man who can sympathize with our human weaknesses. Jesus' birth by the Virgin Mary is a miracle. God did this through his Holy Spirit and by his almighty hand. Her life was not in the grip of any man or in the goddesses of fate; it was in the almighty hand of God, held in his absolute providence.

Read verses 36-37. "Even Elizabeth your relative is going to have a child in her old age, and she who was said to be barren is in her six month. For nothing is impossible with God." In these verses we realize that the mighty hand of God was with her, and God had a specific purpose and mission for her. We also realize that nothing is impossible with God. What did she do before God Almighty? Did she wander on the crossroads of her life? No! She committed her life to God. She surrendered herself to the will of God. At the crucial moment of God's history, she surrendered herself to the will of God, saying in verse 38, "I am the Lord's servant. May it be to me as you have said." In this verse, we learn a very important lesson from Mary. When she said, "I am the Lord's servant. May it be to me as you have said," she did not speak out of her emotions, or in blind resignation to fate, but on the basis of God's promise. She had simple and absolute faith in the promise of God.

When God wanted to send his Son Jesus to the world in accordance with his promise, he had to choose a woman to be the mother of Jesus. Of all women, God chose Mary, a woman pledged to be married. Why? Was it because she was a pure country girl? Was it because she looked so beautiful, like the picture of the Mona Lisa? God chose her simply because she was obedient. She obeyed what she could not obey. Her obedience prepared the spiritual environment that made possible the birth of Jesus.

On the other hand, when we look at wayward and rebellious women, we lose the joy of life and the world seems to be coming to an end. But we cannot be negative about women. We must pray with broken hearts that God would raise up 561 Mary's for this generation to serve the work of God in America. Her beauty, which came from obedience, has been a blessing to all men of the world. Many men of the world have been abundantly comforted, even by looking at her picture, or by thinking of her sweetness and her womanliness.

Contrary to this, when we look at ugly women whose desires are on the sub-human level, everything in the world looks ugly and desolate. But this passage teaches us that we can pray for them until they become beautiful and obedient like Mary the mother of Jesus. Then this land will be filled with beauty and grace, which will be inspiration and encouragement for all men of this land.

In this passage, we learn how precious is one woman of obedience. It is amazing that God used one woman of obedience, Mary, in his history so preciously. May God raise many Marys in this land!

Lesson 3

The Song of Mary

Luke 1:39-56
Key Verses: 1:46b-47

I.   MARY VISITS ELIZABETH (39-45)

1.   What happened to Mary in verses 26-38? What was her human situation after her decision of faith in verse 38?

2.   Why did she decide to visit Elizabeth instead of going to Joseph for sympathy? (36,37,39,40) What did she have to overcome in order to go to Elizabeth? What did her going to Elizabeth show about her faith?

3.   What happened in Elizabeth's life to prepare her for Mary's coming? What happened when she met Mary?

4.   If Elizabeth had thought about Mary from a human point of view, what might she have said? What did she say about Mary and the baby she would bear? How might these things have encouraged Mary?

II.   MY SOUL PRAISES THE LORD (46-56)

5.   What kind of emotions did Elizabeth's greeting awaken in Mary? (46-47) Why? What was her attitude toward God and his work in her life?

6.   What word of God dwelt in Mary's heart that enabled her to sing a song of praise? (32,45)

7.   What can we learn about Mary's relationship with God from verses 37,38,45,47,48a,49? What is the source of her joy?

8.   What does it mean to be blessed by God? How is this different from the worldly concept of blessing or happiness? What enabled her to become a blessed woman? (38)

9.   What did Mary know about God's character and his ways of working? (49,50,51-53) What do these verses teach about the Messiah?

10.   What did Mary know about God's faithfulness? What do these verses reveal about Mary's sense of history? How can we have the joy reflected in Mary's song? (cf. Rom 8:6, Col 3:16, 1Th 5:16-18)

The Song of Mary

Luke 1:39-56
Key Verses: 1:46b-47

> *"My soul glorifies the Lord and my spirit rejoices in God my Savior ..."*

T HESE DAYS, MANY PEOPLE in almost all of the fields of liberal arts, even in theology, express their despair. The direct expression of their despair may be that their eyes are filled with apprehension or that they habitually sigh. Should a Christian do the same thing? No!

Paul says in Colossians 3:16, "Let the word of Christ dwell in you richly as you teach and admonish one another with all wisdom, and as you sing psalms, hymns and spiritual songs with gratitude in your hearts to God." This verse teaches us that we Christians must let the word of God dwell in our hearts, and that we must sing all kinds of songs of praise to God. There is an implication in this verse that we Christians are all born as singers, poets, and psalmists.

There are two classic songs in verses 39-80 that we want to study. One is the song of a lovely young girl and the other, the song of an old man. It's just like a duet in an opera. The beautiful soprano of a young girl is heard, followed by the rich baritone of a white-haired old man. In this passage, we learn that our souls rejoice and can sing songs of praise when God is with us and his word dwells in us. Today we want to study Mary's song.

I. Mary visits Elizabeth (39-45)

Once Mary was a woman of beautiful dreams—marriage, a sweet home, five sons and two daughters—and so on. Mary was getting ready to be an ordinary housewife, living together with Joseph.

She must have whispered many times in her dreams, "Joe, dinner is ready!"

Then, what a surprise! One day, out of nowhere, her human dreams were shattered into pieces and her circumstances changed completely because God intervened in her life and said, "Greetings, you who are highly favored! The Lord is with you (28)." God's favor was the immeasurable grace of his mission for her to be the mother of Jesus before marriage and bear the pains and sorrows of being his mother. In this time of drastic change, she simply decided to obey the will of God and said, "I am the Lord's servant. May it be to me as you have said (38)." Still, she had to experience the painful moment of sorting out her broken dreams and, for a time, struggling to forget Joseph. She must have been more sorry about Joseph than about herself. Perhaps she thought again and again that she should first talk to Joseph and tell him plainly what had happened to her. At the same time, she must have tried to settle on some direction in which she could meet the new destiny which was to come. What did she do?

Read verses 39 and 40. Mary decided first to visit Elizabeth. This decision was based on the angel's message. How wonderful it is that Mary was not swayed by human thinking, but allowed herself to be quietly led by the angel's message! Mary hurried to a town in the hills of Judah to visit Elizabeth. It was an act of faith. This shows that Mary believed she lived under the providence of God, not fate. As Joseph lived in the same town and was her fiancée, Mary easily could have visited him. But Mary did not go to Joseph. She was a woman. But she was a pious woman. On the other hand, it was not easy for Mary to visit Elizabeth. She lived in a mountain village a long distance from Nazareth. Mary had to travel through dangerous mountains passes, possibly where there were many dangers such as wild animals and mountain bandits. She was also tired and weak because of morning sickness. Also, Mary was a virgin. Elizabeth was an old woman. They had an age gap. Elizabeth was too old to understand a young woman's problems.

It was a moment when Mary was too full of her own problems: breaking up with Joseph, conceiving a baby by the Holy Spirit, the disappointment of family and friends and their misunderstanding and criticism. It was a time when she could have forgotten all the good things, especially the word of God which she had learned, and could have been bullied and frozen by fearful problems. Nonetheless, Mary overcame her feelings and the adverse conditions. It is amazing that she remembered the word of God in that situation. How was it possible? Probably her heart was so pure that the words of God through the angel's tidings were photocopied on it. Obviously, she did not live according to feelings, but lived by the word of God. Still, we wonder how she could go to Elizabeth according to the angel's words instead of going to Joseph.

Read verse 50. This verse explains how it was possible for her. She had the fear of God. She accepted with great respect the angel's message, "The Holy Spirit will come upon you, and the power of the Most High will overshadow you. … For nothing is impossible with God (35-37)." When she tried to obey his word, God did not ignore her. God helped her to remember his word. This was the best help that God could give, for the word of God is living (Heb 4:12). With God's help, Mary waded through the sea of her feelings and walked one step after another until she finally knocked at the door of Elizabeth's home. She went there to see the work of God in Elizabeth as the angel said. She went to pray with Elizabeth.

Read verse 42. When Mary entered Zechariah's home, Elizabeth saw her with God's eyes and welcomed her saying, "Blessed are you among women, and blessed is the child you will bear!" In verse 43, she exclaims with a louder voice, "But why am I so favored, that the mother of my Lord should come to me?" A white-haired grandmother bowed her head before an unwed girl and called her, "the mother of my Lord." But Elizabeth was a spiritual woman who had spiritual eyes. She did not see Mary as an unwed mother, but the mother of Jesus, the mother of her Lord. Surely God can use this kind of woman as an important person in his work and history of redemption, especially in linking the Old and New Testament times.

After seeing what had happened in the life of Elizabeth, Mary was convinced that God's hand was in their midst. At the same time, she realized that she was a most blessed woman. She could not contain herself. She began to sing a song of praise.

II. My soul praises the Lord (46-56)

Her song in verses 46-55 may be divided into the following four strophes: first, her expression of sincere emotion (46-48a); second, the great fact for which she is called "blessed" (48b-50); third, the consequences of God's rule in history (51-53); and fourth, God's fulfillment of his promise to Israel (54,55). Her personal part extends from verses 46-50, and it contains heartfelt expressions of the glad emotions awakened by Elizabeth's salutation, which came to Mary as the confirmation of the angel's annunciation. When Gabriel first said to her, "You will be with child," she was afraid. But now she was convinced that God intervened in her life to use her as the most blessed woman.

What was it that enabled Mary to sing the praises of God? It was the Spirit of God. In John chapter 15, the vine and branch relationship is a good allegory to help in understanding Mary, whose heart was fused with the Spirit of God. Mary was the branch and God was the vine. Just as new power and life circulates into the vine when it is attached to the branch, so when Mary was touched by God, the Spirit of God mightily empowered her to sing this song of praise. We learn in the Bible that whenever one wants to serve God's will, God fills that man with his Holy Spirit. For example, Isaiah despaired while living in a dark and distressed situation. By chance, he entered the temple of God and saw the Holy God. His vision was renewed and he became the embodiment of God's hope for Israel. He delivered God's message of hope even to exiles.

When she was touched by God's Spirit, suddenly all of Mary's human thinking disappeared and the light of the great God shone upon her. It was the work of God in her heart. The same thing happened to Elizabeth. She was a barren old woman. She was too old to bear a child. But when Mary visited her, her baby leaped in her old womb according to the prophecy concerning John's birth. Nothing is impossible with God.

Mary said in verses 46-47, "How my soul praises the Lord. How my spirit rejoices in God my Savior!" (NLT). Her opening words are a burst of rapturous praise in which her full heart runs over. In this verse, there is a twofold act: she magnifies God and she rejoices. Her fountains of joy were her soul and spirit. They were not her feelings or thinking. When she was touched by the Spirit of God, her soul and spirit rejoiced. Her joy ran through her heart. The heart is the doorway into a man's soul and spirit. Her soul (or spirit) praised God when she had God in her soul. Through this we learn that those whose spirits are corrupted or those who have no God have no joy in their lives at all. Her joy overflowed in magnifying the name of God. She magnified God when she realized that God was working in history, and more specifically, in her life.

Mary also greatly rejoiced from her deep inner spirit when she perceived the fuller knowledge of God's work in her personal life. Her joy overflowed like a flowing fountain. Her spirit bounded as in a dance. How is it possible for her, when her destiny of being the mother of Jesus would be so full of misunderstanding and her future seemed to be so thorny? In short, it was God's work in her soul.

Verse 48 reads, "…for he has been mindful of the humble state of his servant. From now on all generations will call me blessed." Here, a personal testimony from her soul comes pouring out. She is nothing but a village damsel, poor and obscure. She is no more than a humble ordinary woman. So she wonders why God's eyes should have fallen on her and why he favored her. She exclaims with great joy, deeply realizing God's special favor, "From now on all generations will call me blessed." Mary had the assurance of being the blessed one. Of course Mary knew very well that her blessedness was quite different from that of worldly people. The worldly concept of "blessed" is to have a slightly better husband or a slightly better house or a slightly better future security. But to be blessed by God is to have a higher calling and a higher mission from God. Being blessed by God particularly means to sacrifice more for God and for his glory. It means to experience more pains and sufferings for his name's sake. In history, there may have been no one who suffered more than Mary, the mother of Jesus. It is very important to have the assurance of being a blessed one as a servant of God. Why was she raised up to be the most blessed one? It was because she committed her life to God and decided to obey the will of God. To obey or not to obey was optional, for she had freedom of choice. But when she decided to obey God, sacrificing her small joys, then God gave her overflowing joy—joy which made her exclaim aloud with conviction that she was the most blessed one.

God helped her to have assurance that she was the most blessed. God also gave her blessed assurance that all the people of the world down through the generations would think that she was the most blessed one. "I am the most blessed one!" What a wonderful assurance it is! But this kind of assurance comes only from God. God gives such a wonderful assurance of being blessed to those who want to stand in the forefront of God's history. Her conviction which came from the work of the Holy Spirit was true. Now no one, not even the people of the communist bloc, call her a woman of sorrow. Instead, all the people of the world see her as the most blessed woman as she is.

Read verses 49-50. In this part of the song, the personal element disappears and only thoughts about God's character remain. There are three clauses which express his twofold divinity, his power and his eternal mercy. The words expressed are mostly quotations from the Old Testament, especially from Hannah's song. Probably Mary could write her own poetry. But her application and understanding of the meaning excels that of the original writers. As a result, this poem has become Mary's own song, "The Magnificat." In these verses, she praises the Mighty God.

Who is this Mighty One? Read verses 51b-53. He is the one who rules over world history. He scatters those who are proud in their innermost thoughts. He is the one who brings down rulers from their thrones, but lifts up the humble. Though God is mighty, he is also merciful. He fills the hungry with good things. The main idea of verses 51-53 is the anticipation of the Messiah who would rule over history and who would shepherd his people with love and peace.

In the last part of the song, Mary was overwhelmed by the faithfulness of God who kept his ancient promises and helped Israel faithfully by sending his Messiah. It is amazing that a country girl is so mindful of the suffering people of Israel when she had God in her heart. Look at verses 54-56. "He has helped his servant Israel, remembering to be merciful to Abraham and his descendants forever, even as he said to our fathers." Mary was painfully thankful for the faithfulness of God. Why should God have to take care of such unfaithful people?

Mary's song reminds us of Romans 8:6, "The mind of sinful man is death, but the mind controlled by the Spirit is life and peace." In this rebellious and self-seeking generation, it is easy for us to think only of our own problems. But we must know that the mind of sinful man is death. To the contrary, it is extremely difficult to accept the word of God which clearly reveals the will of God for each person. But when we accept his words, God, by his Spirit, helps us to sing songs of praise and to rejoice no matter what the situation may be.

Lesson 4

The Song of Zechariah

Luke 1:57-80
Key Verse: 1:69

I. THE LORD'S HAND (57-66)

1. How did the neighbors and family respond to the news of a baby's birth in Zechariah's family? Why was everyone so amazed?

2. Why did everyone assume that the baby would be named "Zechariah Jr."? How was his name finally decided? What was the significance of the baby's name?

3. What happened to Zechariah after he named the baby "John"? What effect did this event have on the people of the countryside? What does this event teach about Zechariah's faith? About God's way of working?

II. A HORN OF SALVATION (67-75)

4. Read verses 67-75. Why did Zechariah praise and thank God according to verse 68? What does it mean that "he has come"?

5. Who is the "horn of salvation"? Why is he called a "horn of salvation"?

6. According to the promise of God, what does the horn of salvation do for us? What does it mean to be delivered from the hand of our enemies? (74-75) Who is our real enemy?

7. What are the two purposes of God in saving us from sin? (74-75)

III. THE RISING SUN (76-80)

8. Read verses 76-79. To whom are these verses addressed? What do they teach us about John?

9. What more can we learn here about the nature of our salvation? (76-77)

10. Read verses 78-79 again. To what does the rising sun refer? How does the rising sun which comes to us from heaven change our lives?

The Song of Zechariah

Luke 1:57-80
Key Verse: 1:69

> *"He has raised up a horn of salvation for us in the house of his servant David."*

ODAY'S PASSAGE IS ABOUT Zechariah's song. This old man sang a rhyming song of praise to God and sang joyfully with a rich baritone voice. This old man Zechariah had a spirit like that of a young man. How could he write a rhyming song and sing a song of praise instead of deeply sighing with an old man's fatalism? The answer is simple. He could sing when he had Jesus in his heart.

As the angel announced, John was born, and he was now eight days old. It was the day of his son's circumcision, a historic day in his family, so he should have sung about God's mercy and blessing on his family in giving him a son. But to our surprise, his song was mainly about Jesus the Messiah who saves people. His prophetical song teaches us two things about how Jesus saves us.

I.   The Lord's hand (57-66)

Look at verse 57. As the angel had said, Elizabeth became pregnant and gave birth to a son. In the past, her neighbors and relatives must have been very sorry that Zechariah and Elizabeth had no child. As a priestly family, this was the cause of grief for all his neighbors and of shame in their family, and furthermore, this was the crux of their faith. But one day, her neighbors and relatives heard that Elizabeth had given birth to a son. They realized that his birth was God's mercy on a family with no heir and they shared their joy.

According to Jewish custom, on the eighth day, they came to circumcise the baby. Circumcision was a ceremony which was held to purify one's life before God by cutting off a part of the foreskin in order that his life may be dedicated and consecrated to God. During circumcision, the baby is given a name before God. Their relatives unanimously wanted to name the baby after his father Zechariah. But his mother remembered what the angel had said and spoke up saying, "No! He is to be called John" (60). They wondered about this and said, "There is no one among your relatives who has that name" (61). Then, they turned to Zechariah to ask his opinion. They made signs to him, for he was still dumb. Zechariah asked for a writing tablet, and to everyone's astonishment, he wrote, "His name is John" (63). At the historic moment of his son's future destiny, he remembered what the angel of God had said. Zechariah was a typical Jew who honored Jewish traditions and heritage. He was also a human being with human desires, especially the desire for a son. Indeed, he wanted to name his son for himself because he had lived so long without an heir. But in order to obey God's will, he rose above traditions and overcame his human desires. He named his son John as the angel had said. The day he circumcised his son John, he also circumcised his own heart by dedicating his only son of his old age to God.

Look at verse 64. As soon as he named his son John, as the angel had said, his tongue was loosed and he began to speak, praising God. The neighbors were filled with awe and throughout the hill country of Judea people were talking about all these things and wondering "Why?" It was because Zechariah suddenly became a dumb man and a white-haired grandmother gave birth to a son. Also, Zechariah and Elizabeth named their son John, ignoring the Jewish heritage and tradition. They wondered especially about the child because he seemed to be an extraordinary child from birth. So they asked, "What then is this child going to be?" (66). They wondered out loud what was going to happen in this child's future. The writer Luke comments on this: "For the Lord's hand was with him" (66). God was working mightily in history through this family and through this child. Sometimes we also wonder what is going to happen, but we must have spiritual vision to see the hand of God that is with us.

II. A horn of salvation (67-75)

Look at verses 67-68. "His father Zechariah was filled with the Holy Spirit and prophesied: 'Praise be to the Lord, the God of Israel, because he has come and has redeemed his people.'" For the last four hundred years, the people of Israel had not had any word of life through the prophets. In addition, for the most part, Israel had groaned under the invasion and oppression of a foreign country; presently, they were under the yoke of the Roman Empire. They had no hope. But there was hope for them—the hope of the coming Messiah. The hope of the coming Messiah was everything to them. Now the promised Messiah was to be born, the one for whom Zechariah and devout men had wearily looked for. Zechariah was captured by surprise and rapture when he thought about the divine promises concerning the Messiah being fulfilled at last.

Look at verse 68. "Praise be to the Lord, the God of Israel, because he has come and has redeemed his people." The verb "has come" literally means "has visited." In this verse, Zechariah praises God in two ways.

First, Zechariah praises God because God has visited his people. His people were the most privileged people. God made them his own people and gave them all the best privileges that he could give. But they disobeyed his word. They rebelled against him. They provoked the wrath of God by complying with the enemy of God, Satan. God should have punished them, pouring out his wrath on them. God should have abandoned them. But God did not abandon them. In spite of their rebellion, God visited them first. This is the hardest thing for any man to do. Even King David, known as a man after God's own heart, did not visit his son Absalom when he sinned against him. But God visited his people. In order to visit his people, the Almighty God lowered himself and came to this world as a tiny baby in a manger. He is Jesus. God is faithful. God is humble.

Second, Zechariah praises God because God has visited his people to redeem them. Read verse 69 again. "He has raised up a horn of salvation for us in the house of his servant David." He visited his people to redeem them from their enemies. Here, "horn" is an emblem taken from animal horns. It implies glory and power (Ps

148:14; Dan 7:21; Hos 5:8; Ex 27:2; Rev 5:6). At the same time, "horn" is a symbol of threat and terror to oppressed people.

The people of Israel had suffered under the yoke of Egypt for four hundred years. They had tasted unbearable bitterness in a world without God's mercy. They had experienced the cursed life of mankind, working day and night under the constant whipping of Egyptian slave masters, only to eat three meals a day. After their liberation from the yoke of Egypt, they lived in the Promised Land flowing with milk and honey. But they were under constant fear and threats of enemies. They could not enjoy peace even while living in material abundance. Fear of their enemies was a dominant part of their lives in Canaan.

We can see in the book of Judges how their life in Canaan was one continuous battle with their enemies. During this time, many heroes—Gideon, Jephthah, Samson, and Barak—appeared and led them to temporary victories. However, before even taking a breath or getting a good night's sleep, they were again surrounded by their enemies and driven into fear of calamities and death.

Israel, which had only God as their king, was forced by incessant warfare with hostile enemies to raise up a man to be their king and lead them in battle. God gave them David as their shepherd and king. He destroyed all their enemies who had paralyzed them with fear. He also unified his people and brought the surrounding countries under his control to establish the kingdom of David. While King David ruled his people, they enjoyed peace. But that peace only lasted during the time of David's reign.

Read verse 69. This verse is the promise of God that he would raise up a horn of salvation to redeem his people from their enemies. In the Old Testament time, the enemies of Israel were neighboring countries. They are symbols of Satan because they planted fear in the hearts of Israel. After the coming of Jesus, the enemies of Israel, as well as the enemies of mankind, are not neighboring countries, but Satan. Because of Satan, man had to suffer in fear endlessly. Man fears the horn of Satan because it impales man, leading to a critical condition or to death. If anyone is impaled by the horn of Satan, he suffers throughout his lifetime. He is like a dead man.

I once saw a movie titled, "Matador." The matador was a coura-geous young man named Pedro. When he went into the bull ring to fight the ferocious bulls, he had great confidence in his own courage and skill, and he won several times. Then one day he did not want to fight. But he was pushed by the people, so he entered the ring. When the angry bull saw him, he fiercely pawed the ground with his hoof, then rushed out of the pen toward him. Because of fear, he lost his spirit. His mind went blank and he couldn't move. He was severely injured when he was impaled by the horns of the bull. This story is a good illustration of the fearsomeness of Satan. According to Revela-tion 17:7, Satan has seven heads and ten horns. The power of Satan is beyond comparison to that of bulls. The power of Satan is the power of sin.

But we must know that Satan does not appear so fiercely like an angry bull. Satan did not come to Eve with the formidable appear-ance of a devil with ten horns and sharp incisors. Rather, he came to Eve in the figure of a serpent, so colorful and silky. Satan usually appears like a close friend.

Satan is so deceptive. Eve, the first woman, was confident that she could talk with Satan and help him and partly enjoy him and then send him away. On the other hand, Satan the serpent, taking advantage of the woman's aesthetic sense, induced her to take the forbidden fruit. When the woman listened to Satan's clever words, she was overpowered by the power of sin. As a result, she disobeyed the word of God and took the forbidden fruit of the tree. She ate and gave the leftovers to her husband, Adam. Eve did not see the horn of Satan underneath his make-up. She was impaled by the horn of Satan. Adam was also impaled by the horn of Satan. They both became prey of Satan and were driven into Satan's dungeon together with their descendants as well.

One young man lived without purpose and the meaning of life. He found the purpose and meaning of his life through Bible study. One day, he was convinced that he should talk with his father and lead him to Christ. But Satan impaled him through the loophole of his overconfidence. He was impaled by the horn of Satan's doubt. He began to doubt the life of discipline and the life of mission. He received instead a mission from Satan to liberate those who are willing to receive discipleship training and live a life of mission. He became a slave of Satan, and now he works for Satan to plant doubt in the hearts of young and immature Christians. He knows that he is wrong. He is in great fear, so he cannot tell others his address or telephone number. But he cannot get out of this fear because he is under the power of Satan.

When we read Romans 1:29-31, we can see many kinds of ugly people: the wicked, the evil, murderers, inventors of evil-doing, the senseless, heartless, and the ruthless. Originally, they were all good people, created in the image of God, but they became like that after being wounded by the horn of Satan.

But praise be to God, the God of Israel, because he has come to redeem his people according to his promises. He has raised up a horn of salvation for us in the house of his servant David. He has crushed the horn of Satan. He saves us from the hand of Satan.

Read verses 74 and 75. "To rescue us from the hand of our enemies, and to enable us to serve him without fear in holiness and righteousness before him all our days." These verses explain God's two purposes in saving people. First, God saved them from the fear of the horn of Satan. Second, God saved them so that they can serve him without fear, in holiness and righteousness all their lives.

Exodus explains this well. The Israelite's misery in their life of slavery was unbearable. Their hard work was only for three meals a day and no more. Their fear of slave drivers was endless. God, in his great mercy, redeemed them and brought them to the land that flows with milk and honey, to serve him without fear in holiness and righteousness. This was the best happiness God could give. God saved us from the fear of Satan. God saved us from the hand of Satan so that we can live a life of mission by serving him without fear in holiness and righteousness. According to Apostle Peter, God also saved us to participate in the divine nature (2Pe 1:3-4). Whoever he may be, each person has a deep desire to follow the way of truth. Each person wants to live a holy life before God. Each person wants to do absolutely meaningful work before God. But because of the power of sin and the fear of Satan, many a man does what he really does not want to do. Praise God that he has raised up a horn of salvation for us to save us from the power of Satan and fear. Praise God that he has raised up a horn of salvation so that in him we can solve our chronic fear problem.

III. The rising sun (76-80)

Read verses 76-77. "And you, my child, will be called a prophet of the Most High; for you will go on before the Lord to prepare the way for him, to give his people the knowledge of salvation through the forgiveness of their sins…" Zechariah finally makes a brief mention of his son John. He was happy that his son would be used as a fore-runner of the Messiah. Of course, he knew that his son's life would be a life of suffering. Still, he was happy that his son would be used by God. We love our children. If we love them, we must dedicate them to God and pray that they may be used by God.

Read verses 78-79. "…because of the tender mercy of our God, by which the rising sun will come to us from heaven to shine on those living in darkness and in the shadow of death…" God, in his tender mercy, sent his one and only Son as the rising sun to shine on those living in darkness. Here, the rising sun is another name for Jesus. Darkness refers to the sinful world of mankind. And "those who are sitting in darkness" refers to the situation of mankind. In darkness, men are driven into fear. In darkness, all men, as incorrigible sinners, are tempted to sin freely. As a result, darkness deprives men of their sense of direction. Who are those who live in darkness? They are those who do not know Jesus.

Those who are in the darkness have no hope, but Jesus, the rising sun, can deliver them from darkness. Jesus drives out all the elements of darkness in one's heart, such as doubt, fear, hatred, rebellion, and the shadow of death. Jesus also illumes them with the knowledge of God. His light pours into our souls until the darkness of our sins passes away and until the new joy of life comes. Fanny Crosby was a young blind woman. Her soul was once also dark because of her blindness. She lived under the power of death. But Christ visited her and shone his light on her. She became a hymn writer and wrote many joyful hymns of praise.

Verse 79b reads, "…to guide our feet into the path of peace." Jesus came to guide our feet into the path of peace. We see many people these days who enjoy a pleasure-seeking lifestyle. For this, they even break up their families. But in truth, they do not want to spend too much money for momentary pleasures. They really don't want to take drugs, but they do. Why? They want peace, real peace. But there is no peace for them. Jesus, the rising sun, alone can give peace by pouring heavenly sunshine into our hearts. When we accept Jesus as our personal Savior, he drives out all the elements of darkness and anoints us with his Holy Spirit until we have peace that passes all understanding. Jesus is the rising sun who gives us peace and joy. God is sorry when we sit in the shadow of darkness like condemned criminals. God sent Jesus, the rising sun, to deliver us from the shadow of darkness to bring us into the path of peace. In Jesus, we have peace with God.

Lesson 5

Good News of Great Joy

Luke 2:1-20
Key Verse: 2:10

I.   THE TIMES WHEN JESUS WAS BORN (1-7)

1.   Who was Caesar Augustus and how does this passage reveal his power and influence?

2.   What was the probable purpose of his decree? How did it affect the Roman world? (What was the extent of the Roman Empire at that time? What else do you know about the Roman Empire?)

3.   How did this decree affect Joseph and Mary? What does this journey reveal about this family's lack of power? What does this suggest about those times?

4.   Describe the circumstances of Jesus' birth. What does this reveal about the atmosphere of society at that time?

5.   Even though God is not mentioned in verses 1-7, how is his sovereignty over history revealed?

6.   Compare and contrast the baby in the manger with Caesar Augustus. What can you learn here about God's history and human history?

II.   A SAVIOR HAS BEEN BORN TO YOU (8-12)

7.   Who were the first ones to learn about Jesus' birth? What were they doing? What was their first reaction to the angel? What does this event show about the shepherds?

8.   Look at the angel's message. Why is Jesus' birth good news of great joy? What does "to all the people" mean?

9.   What was the sign God gave the shepherds? What is significant about this sign? How can one see God's history in such an ordinary scene?

III.   GLORY TO GOD, PEACE ON EARTH (13-14)

10.   What did the choir of angels add to the meaning of Jesus' birth? Think about why Jesus' birth is glory to God. Think about why Jesus' birth in the manger gives peace to men.

Good News of Great Joy

Luke 2:1-20
Key Verse: 2:10

> *"But the angel said to them, 'Do not be afraid. I bring you good news of great joy that will be for all the people.'"*

ODAY'S PASSAGE IS THE angel's message to the shepherds living out in the field: "Do not be afraid. I bring you good news of great joy that will be for all the people." Luke, the historian, says the birth of Jesus is good news of great joy that will be for all the people. Let's think about how the birth of Jesus is good news of great joy that will be for all the people.

I. The times when Jesus was born (1-7)

In verses 1-7, Luke explains how the historical background served to fulfill prophecy concerning the birth of Jesus, and under what circumstances Jesus was born. Read verse 1. "In those days Caesar Augustus issued a decree that a census should be taken of the entire Roman world." In those days, the Emperor of Rome ruled the entire known world. He ruled the world from Rome with military power. This despotic empire extended its hand of invasion as far as England to the west, Asia Minor to the east, and to North Africa beyond the Mediterranean Sea. The Roman Emperor ruled the world with the philosophy of Pax Romana, which proclaimed economic protection and political stability for the colonial countries. But in reality, it was nothing but a political slogan. Those who lived in the Roman world had to live under constant threats and oppression with no way out.

These conditions existed not only in the time of Caesar Augustus, but they also exist at any time where men rule men. The extent may vary, but in the godless world, the vicious cycle of rule continues. They say that democracy is the ideal form of government, for in it people can enjoy inalienable human rights and freedom. But these days we see that in the name of democracy, capitalists exert their money power over the poor relentlessly. Communists claim that communism through its classless societies is the political ideology which makes the world a utopia. But the constant bloodshed due to class struggles proves that this is not true.

At this time, the Emperor issued a decree that a census should be taken in an attempt to levy a head tax. His order was absolutely despotic. No one was exempt. Upon hearing the order, all people trembled in fear, quit what they were doing, and hurried off to their own town to register. Everybody was expected to obey the decree unconditionally with no choice. Therefore, even a woman full-term in pregnancy had to travel on a long journey to register. Verses 4 and 5 read, "So Joseph also went up from the town of Nazareth in Galilee to Judea, to Bethlehem the town of David, because he belonged to the house and line of David. He went there to register with Mary, who was pledged to be married to him and was expecting a child." At the time of Jesus' birth, there was no mercy under the rule of Rome.

Read verses 6 and 7. "While they were there, the time came for the baby to be born, and she gave birth to her firstborn, a son. She wrapped him in cloths and placed him in a manger, because there was no room for them in the inn." A woman was ready to deliver a baby, so they looked for a room at the inn. But no one offered her a room for her to deliver a baby. So Joseph and Mary went into an animal stable to deliver a baby. The animals in the stable did not reject their coming because they could not speak. A woman was crying with labor pains, but those who heard her crying pretended not to hear. They all turned deaf ears to her. The world was too hard to survive in. The world made mankind too selfish to maintain humanity. Under the rule of the Roman Emperor, all the people were tired and weary, fearful and selfish. They were living in the darkness and in the shadow of death. This is the typical situation of mankind when man is ruled by another man without God.

II. A Savior has been born to you (8-12)

Read verses 8-10. Most narratives in the Bible are written using understatement. The Bible never exaggerates or uses unnecessary words. But verse 10 says "good news of great joy," that is, good news plus great joy. Why is the birth of Jesus good news of great joy? Where on earth is good news of great joy when the world is overflowing with bad news? The people of the world must find some joy by going on a weekend trip or by shopping with the money they earned from hard work. Some people adopt hedonism as the best lifestyle, saying, "Let's eat and drink for tomorrow we die." Nobody can say, "I have real joy." But verse 10 says, "I bring you good news of great joy that will be for all the people." Why is the birth of Jesus good news of great joy for all the people?

First, Jesus' birth is good news of great joy for all people because Jesus came as the Savior of the world. Read verse 11. "Today in the town of David a Savior has been born to you; he is Christ the Lord." From what then does Jesus save us?

In the first place, he saves us from our sorrows and fatalism. Those who do not know God's providence in their lives are all sorrowful and fatalistic. If we read John 5:1-5, we see near the Sheep Gate a pool where a great number of disabled people used to lie: the blind, the lame, and the paralyzed. This is a picture of man's condition when he lives in fatalism without knowing God. During the times when one young man's feelings and emotions were developing, his family moved more than 30 times. This planted great sorrow in his heart. Because of this sorrow, he escaped to a fantasy world and did not face reality. Another boy was very sorrowful because he lost a wrestling match with a boy who was much smaller than himself. He used to cry saying, "If I had eaten lunch, I would not have lost." Whenever he saw his parents who were so poor that they could not give him enough food to eat, he became even more sorrowful.

But Jesus came to the world as the Savior of the world. From a human point of view, Jesus was born in the most sorrowful circumstances. He was born in the land of Roman colonization. He was born like an illegitimate child. He was born in a stable and laid in a manger. He shared the fate and bore the sorrows of all sorrowful people. Isaiah wrote of Jesus who was to come: "Surely he took up our infirmities and carried our sorrows, yet we considered him stricken by God, smitten by him, and afflicted. But he was pierced for our transgressions ..." (Isa 53:4-5a).

In the second place, Jesus saves us from our sins. These days, many people take sin lightly. But sin is the most serious matter in human history. Sin takes away the absoluteness of God. As a result, man becomes relative. When man becomes relative, he loses the absolute meaning and purpose of life; he feels that everything is an accident or mischief. What is worse, this relative idea divides man's heart into many pieces until he finally becomes crazy. It's not worth it to struggle just to live. In the end, he comes to the conclusion that man is nothing and that suicide is optional.

Sin makes man fearful. Cain did not want to recognize God's sovereignty over his life. He wanted to be his own master. Was he happy when he lived without God? No. One day he was so upset about his brother Abel that he took him out to a field and beat him to death. After that, he left God's presence and lived as a restless wanderer. When he lived without God, strangely, instead of having freedom, he became so fearful that he experienced day after day the endless punishment that comes from fear. Jesus came to save us from fear.

Sin makes man very sick spiritually. When a man is sick spiritually, he can doubt the love of God and the love of his parents as well for no obvious reason. When a man is sick with sin, he becomes as dirty as a man with leprosy. When a man is sick spiritually, he becomes as heartless as a selfish tax collector or as powerless as a man with physical paralysis. Sin disfigures the image of God in a man until he looks like a devil. Sin makes a man a slave of sinful desires. Sin makes a man a slave of Satan. Most people are unhappy, not because their human situations are too poor, but because they are under the power of sin.

No one can laugh or make a smile when he is enslaved by the power of sin or Satan. About 50 years ago, when I was a student in Seoul, I went to the prisons each week to preach to the prisoners. Because the prisoners looked so sad, I tried to tell them funny and

STUDY OF LUKE'S GOSPEL

happy stories. There were about 600 prisoners in my audience, but no one laughed. One Christmas, visitors came and brought all kinds of food to the prisoners. A comedian came and put on a comic show for them. But still, no one laughed. Then one day as I was preaching, one young man started grinning. So after the sermon I asked him, "What made you smile?" He answered, "My father was able to post my bail, so tomorrow I'm getting out."

But God so loved the world that he gave his one and only Son, that whoever believes in him should not perish but have eternal life (Jn 3:16). In order to save us from our sins, he gave up heavenly glory and power and came to this world as a tiny baby in a manger. In order to save us from our sins he became the Lamb of God. When John, his forerunner, saw him coming, he cried out, "Look, the Lamb of God, who takes away the sin of the world!" (Jn 1:29). Finally, he shed his blood on the cross for our sins. On the cross he bore our sins and curse and saved us from our sins. He is our Savior. Today in the town of David a Savior has been born to you. It is good news of great joy for each of us.

Second, Jesus' birth is good news of great joy for all people because he is Christ the Lord. Christ the Lord means the King of kings, or the Messiah. How did he become our King?

Jesus became our King when he died and rose again from the dead and destroyed the horn of Satan. In the past, Satan scattered his bait here and there, and anyone he caught taking his bait, he impaled in a vital spot, making him crippled and a slave of fear. The victim then suffered throughout his lifetime, trembling and groaning. But God raised up Jesus the horn of salvation, and he crushed the horn of Satan, delivering us from Satan's dungeon.

When Jesus died for our sins to obey God's will for world salvation, God did not abandon him in the pangs of death. He raised him on the third day and made him Christ the Lord. "God exalted him to the highest place and gave him the name that is above every name, that at the name of Jesus every knee should bow, in heaven and on earth and under the earth, and every tongue confess that Jesus Christ is Lord, to the glory of God the Father" (Php 2:9-11). Therefore, he is the King of kings and he is also the King anointed by God. This is what Christ means.

Jesus is the King of peace and love. Everyone seems to be independent and nice, but without exception, everyone wants to be loved and to enjoy peace. But a man is too limited to love others limitlessly. But Jesus can and does. Where there is Christ's rule, there is no fear or doubt. There is only love and peace. Isaiah portrayed the happiness of all creation on earth when the King of peace and love rules. The wolf and the lamb say to each other, "Good morning"; the calf and the lion go on vacation together (Is 65:25). Where Christ rules, there is no more separation and no more tears.

This does not stop just as a utopian dream of Christianity. It is real and true for everyone who accepts Jesus as his personal Savior and King. One man became a punk rocker after his father ran away with another woman. He tried so hard to overcome his despair that once he even cut his hair in a mohawk. He was so helpless that he decided as a teenager to commit suicide at the age of 25. Thank God who interrupted this foolish plan and instead led him to accept Jesus as his personal Savior through Bible study.

Third, Jesus' birth is good news of great joy that will be for all the people because his kingdom is forever. Each person wants to establish a kingdom for himself and to enjoy it forever. But mortal man soon despairs when he reaches his human limitations. This was Nicodemus' spiritual agony.

In the book of Daniel, King Nebuchadnezzar saw a dazzling statue awesome in appearance. It was made of pure gold, silver, bronze, iron, and clay. Then the iron, clay, bronze, silver, and gold were broken to pieces at the same time and became like chaff on a threshing floor in the summertime. The wind then swept it away without a trace (Da 2:31-35b). This is the fate of all the world's kingdoms. Historically, kingdoms rise and wane. The kingdom of David was an ideal one, but it also did not last long enough.

The theme of the Bible concerns paradise lost and paradise restored. Because the first Adam sinned, man lost paradise. Because the second Adam obeyed, paradise was fully restored. His ultimate purpose in coming to the world was to bring us back to his kingdom. And the kingdom of Jesus is forever because Jesus destroyed the power of death and all the elements of death when God raised him from the dead. Jesus' kingdom is forever because the Lord God renewed heaven and earth through the resurrection of Jesus.

The angel said to Mary, "The Lord God will give him the throne of his father David, and he will reign over the house of Jacob forever; his kingdom will never end" (1:32b-33). God gave him authority, glory, and sovereign power; all peoples and nations of every language should worship him because his dominion is everlasting and his kingdom is forever.

Fourth, Jesus is the ruler of history. Where was he born? As prophesied in Micah 5:2, he was born in Bethlehem, the town of David, even though that's not where Mary had been living. In what circumstances was he born? Read verse 12. "This will be a sign to you: You will find a baby wrapped in cloths and lying in a manger." His birthplace did not look like the birthplace of a king. At his birth, he had no place to lay his head. So his mother did what she could; she wrapped him in cloths and laid him in the manger of a stable. Jesus is still the ruler of history.

This story began with the action of a Roman Emperor imposing a census, the result of which Mary and Joseph found themselves in Bethlehem. The census served an important function in the development of the narrative, but at the same time, it served to transfer the birthplace of Jesus from Nazareth in Galilee to Bethlehem in Judea. Through this we learn that the fiat of an earthly ruler can be utilized in the will of God to bring his more important purposes to fruition.

In this passage, Luke also contrasts Caesar's throne with the birthplace of Jesus. Luke contrasts Caesar and the baby in the manger. The power of Caesar seemed to be almighty, but his power rested on the law and military force, so it could not last. The baby wrapped in rags was tiny and helpless. But he was God's life. This was the sign of the Savior of the world and the King of all kings. And God's love abides in him. And God's will is upon him. And God's life and light are in him.

Luke contrasts Caesar Augustus and the baby in the manger to teach us about God's history. The history going on in Caesar's palace seems to be really impressive, and God's history seems small and weak like the manger. But the nations of the world are like a mist which disappears in the morning sun, and God's kingdom is forever. It is easy to look at God's history as though it was insignificant like the manger. Like Luke, we must train our eyes to see God's history. This passage puts the Roman Empire as the backdrop of Jesus' birth, and the baby in the manger as the focal point of history. Luke emphasizes here that Jesus in a manger is the ruler of history.

III. Glory to God, peace on earth (13-14)

Look at verses 13 and 14. Suddenly a great host of angels joined in a heavenly chorus. They praised God. Their hymn of praise is recorded in verse 14, "Glory to God in the highest, and on earth peace to men on whom his favor rests." These verses are a great host of angel's heavenly chorus. We learn here what the birth of Jesus means to the whole universe.

First, the birth of Jesus is glory to God in the highest. One meaning of "glory" is "to reveal." God should reveal his wrath because of men's sins. Men were doomed to die in their sins and deserved eternal punishment. But God, instead of revealing his wrath, revealed his redemptive love by sending his one and only Son, Jesus Christ, to this world. God also revealed his faithfulness by patiently keeping his promises to send the Savior of the world, and he fulfilled those promises by sending his one and only Son to this world, withholding his righteous judgment upon his rebellious people. The birth of Jesus is God's redemptive love. The birth of Jesus is glory to God in the highest. The world was filled with God's glory, honor, love, and faithfulness at the time of Jesus' birth.

Second, the birth of Jesus is peace to men on earth. Before the coming of Jesus, men were in the state of being God's enemies. Nobody can be at peace when he is in this state. When Paul was an enemy of God, the risen Jesus appeared to him and said, "Saul, Saul, why do you persecute me? It is hard for you to kick against the goads" (Ac 26:14). To be an enemy of God is nothing but to torture one's own soul. To be an enemy of God means being a slave of Satan. A slave of Satan must live in darkness and in the shadow of death. A slave of Satan must do whatever his master tells him to do. Satan never commands his slave to do good, but to do evil all the time. One who does evil feels condemnation in his soul.

People who are sick with sin are not happy. First of all, they feel powerless, nothingness, frustration, and distress all the time. They have no peace in their hearts. They cannot sleep well. Jesus came into the world to heal people sick with sin.

Jesus came into this world to make peace between God and men. Jesus came to this world to destroy all the enemies of mankind, that is, the power of sin and death. Jesus came to this world to restore everything in heaven and on earth that has been cursed because of the presence of sin and death. Jesus came to bring men and women back to his kingdom. Men can have peace when they are healed. Men can have peace when they have a clear destination in life. Men can have peace when they are reconciled with God through faith in the blood of Jesus.

The birth of Jesus is glory to God in the highest and peace to men on whom his favor rests.

Lesson 6

Jesus Presented in the Temple

Luke 2:21-40
Key Verse: 2:30

I. JESUS' CIRCUMCISION (21-24)

1. Why did Jesus' parents have him circumcised? What does circumcision signify? What is the significance of their naming the baby Jesus?

2. Why did Mary and Joseph bring the baby to the temple? What did they offer to consecrate him to God? What was significant about their offering? (Ex 13:2; Lev 12:8)

3. What do their actions show about their relationship with God and his word? Why was it necessary to do these things for Jesus? What can all parents learn from Mary and Joseph?

II. SIMEON'S FAITH (25-35)

4. Who was Simeon? How does Luke describe his spiritual life? What promise had God made to him? How did he happen to be in the temple when Mary and Joseph came in with the baby?

5. What did he do and say when he saw the child? Why did he say, "…you now dismiss your servant in peace"?

6. What was his great vision concerning this baby's future? What was the basis of his faith and vision? (Isa 49:6)

7. How did the baby's parents respond? What did Simeon say to them? What do you think it means that the child would cause the rising and falling of many in Israel? That a sword would pierce Mary's soul too? How were these prophecies fulfilled?

III. ANNA'S PRAYER (36-40)

8. Who was Anna? What can we know about her human life and human hopes?

9. What can we know about her spiritual life? What was her prayer topic? What can we learn from her?

10. What was her response to the baby Jesus? What did she believe about him? How could this hopeless old woman have such great hope and be so full of joy and thanksgiving?

Jesus Presented in the Temple

Luke 2:21-40
Key Verse: 2:30

"For my eyes have seen your salvation ..."

TODAY'S PASSAGE IS ABOUT how Jesus was presented in the temple. From this event, we learn how to present our precious children to God. At the time of the presenting of baby Jesus, two old people, Simeon and Anna, appear. These two old people had lived lives of faith in that dark time and came to see the salvation of Jesus with their own eyes. We learn from them the wisdom of God to live a victorious life in a dark world.

I.   Jesus' circumcision (21-24)

Look at verse 21. It was the eighth day since the Savior of the world had come into the world, as had been promised. He was a very special person; therefore, his circumcision and his presentation in the temple should have been very special. Being unique, extraordinary, and unprecedented, his presentation should have been more spectacular than the opening ceremony of any Olympic Games or of any wedding ceremony for the prince of a kingdom. But to our surprise, it was very ordinary.

His parents, according to Jewish custom, circumcised him on the eighth day. Circumcision was the sign of the covenant which God had made with Abraham; it was the sign of being God's covenant people. Those who wanted to be the covenant people of God were expected to be circumcised. Circumcision also meant consecration to God. For example, when Abram was complacent with his illegitimate child Ishmael, God appeared to him and said, "Walk before me and be blameless" (Ge 17:1b).

Men are inclined to live according to their sinful desires, but God wants us to live according to his holy desires. Each man craves to enjoy the life of an ordinary man with petty desires. But God wants men to be his chosen people, the people with his promises and covenant. Abraham needed to consecrate himself to be a covenant member of God's family. At that time, God commanded him to be circumcised so that he might get rid of the dirtiness in himself and stand before God consecrated. We must also have circumcision of the heart if we want to be covenant members in God's family (Ro 2:29); this is a biblical constant.

After circumcision, his parents named him Jesus, the name the angel had given him before he had been conceived. It was not easy for Joseph and Mary to name him "Jesus" because Jewish custom demanded that they name him "Joseph Jr." after his father. Also, the name Jesus means one who saves people from their sins (Mt 1:21). It was understood by the people of Israel to mean the name of the Messiah who was to come. So the name Jesus was too great a name for any human being to give a son. There was a great possibility of being misunderstood by the people if they named him Jesus. Humanly speaking, it was impossible for them to name him Jesus. Anyway, they overcame their human situation and obeyed God's command to name him Jesus.

Read verse 22. After the time of purification was over, Joseph and Mary took him to Jerusalem to publically present him to the Lord. This refers to the provisions detailed in Leviticus 12. A woman is regarded as ceremonially unclean for 40 days after the birth of a male child (or 72 days after a female child) and prohibited from entering the sanctuary. Naturally, the child is also prohibited as his place is with his mother. So together, they had to mark the end of the purification period with a purification ceremony in order to be made clean before the Holy God. Bodily cleanliness was highly regarded and assiduously practiced in early Palestine. It is also said that priests bathed twice each day and twice each night. Those who copied the scrolls bathed every time they read the word "God" in the Scriptures. Before God, it is a serious matter to have a pure body and a pure heart.

After the purification ceremony was over, a woman had to bring a lamb as a burnt offering and a pigeon as a sin offering. But if she could not afford a lamb, she could bring a pair of pigeons instead. This was called the offering of the poor, and this is what Mary brought. Here we see that Jesus was born into a poor family. This reminds us of what Apostle Paul said in 2 Corinthians 8:9, "For you know the grace of our Lord Jesus Christ, that though he was rich, yet for your sakes he became poor, so that you through his poverty might become rich."

There are many people who have much money, but do not know how to spend money effectively. Though they are rich, because they are stingy, they are poor. The more they have, the more unsatisfied they are. They suffer endlessly to make more money to fill their unsatisfied hearts. They are slaves of money. On the other hand, those who have Jesus in their hearts are indeed rich. Some of our missionaries are poor, but when Bible students have no place to go, they invite them into their small homes to live together with them. Some students who have experienced this have become healthy and rich spiritually. Those who have Jesus have thankful hearts. Why? I don't know. But they are all thankful because they know God's love, the grace of Jesus. They have compassion toward others and are eager to share what they have with the poor. They have spiritual eyes to see the richness and eternity of the kingdom of God. They want nothing and are indeed rich.

Behind these public and holy ceremonies is a confession of faith by the parents that their children are not their own, but are the children of God. In the past, parents circumcised their children, dedicated their children to God, and taught them the Law of God. But these days, few parents have this kind of conviction. They enjoy their children and thereby spoil them. Some parents spend a lot of money to give their children the best education available, but do not take the pains necessary to teach their children the word of God. Some parents are overanxious about their children and end up planting anxiety in their children's hearts. So we must present our children to God to be his own possession and covenant members of God's family.

Jesus was not only born into a poor family to make us rich, but he also became like our brother. When the time had fully come, God sent his one and only Son in the likeness of sinful flesh, born of a woman (Gal 4:4). In all things he had to become like his brothers (Heb 2:17). He was born under the law and had to undergo circumcision and purification. This was a great humiliation to Jesus who is holy. But he took upon himself the impurity of his people so as to save them from their guilt and sin.

II. Simeon's faith (25-35)

As the darkest time is right before the dawn, so the world was in deep darkness right before the coming of Jesus, the rising sun, into the world. Still, there was a man named Simeon who kept the lamp of God burning. What kind of person was he?

First, Simeon was righteous and devout before God. In that dark time, people of the world did not know what to do or what was going on. They were like people groping around in the darkness. They were anxious and fearful. They struggled hard to survive in an unpredictable situation and despaired when they found their struggle was endless with no meaning.

But Simeon was different. Luke introduces him as a man who was "righteous" and "devout." He never stood out from the people. To most people, he was an ordinary old man. But he was a very special person before God. Why was he so? Simply because he lived before God. He had God in his heart. He had the hope of God in his heart. Because of God in his life, he never despaired. In this way, he had a relationship with God and his faith was credited as righteousness before God. He was nothing but an old man. But in truth, he was the whole church of God. He reminds me of a grandfather named Young Bae Kim. I knew him when I was a young boy. At that time, most people in my town, both young and old, were distressed and sorrowful under Japanese oppression. But this grandfather was quiet and joyful all the time. He would come to the children's playground and gather many children together. Then he would tell Bible stories to the children in such an interesting way that many children loved to listen and were moved to tears. During the weekdays, he taught his three sons the Bible, English, and music until they were raised up to be international figures. Everyone thought that he was just a crazy man, but he was a sincere Christian layman. At the time of Korean liberation in 1945, most Koreans were excited and hoped for material and political prosperity, but this old grandfather never changed his lifestyle. He still lived before God quietly.

Simeon was also devout. He was an old man, but he was diligent. He did not just sit back and watch his years roll by, but was eager to find ways to serve God. He gave his heart to serve God diligently. He was eager to study the Law of God and meditate on it. As Noah wholeheartedly built the ark, working day and night, so also Simeon diligently studied the Law of God in all earnestness and was eager to obey the law of God day and night.

Second, Simeon was one of God's waiting people. Verse 25b reads, "He was waiting for the consolation of Israel." The tragic national situation of Israel in those times was simply appalling. They suffered under Roman rule. All they hoped for was to be liberated from the oppression of Rome. They were bitter and full of despair. When they were bitter, Satan came and tormented them violently. People in those times were embedded in unbelief and were plagued by their own doubts and frustration. They had no hope because there was no hope.

But Simeon had hope. He was waiting for the emergence of the Messiah. Simeon believed God's promise. He was in the same situation as his fellow citizens, but did not doubt God's love. Rather, he believed God's love as revealed in his promises that he would send the Messiah to comfort his suffering people. He was one of the waiting people who waited for the emergence of the Messiah. Because of the hope of God, he never despaired even in the midst of despair. He was a man of prayer who talked to God and also listened to what God said to him. Instead of despairing, he prayed that the Messiah would come and comfort and redeem his suffering people. He had one clear prayer topic that the Messiah would come and redeem his people. Humanly, it was an impossible prayer topic because the world was too dark and there seemed to be no hope at all. But by faith, Simeon kept this prayer topic to the end of his lifetime.

What happened to this old man when he believed and prayed? Verse 25b says "the Holy Spirit was upon him." When Simeon lived a life of faith and had a lifelong prayer topic, the Holy Spirit came upon him and gave him God's revelation that he would not die before he had seen the Lord's Christ. Here we learn that God is with those who pray and works in them with his Holy Spirit.

We learn in verses 27 and 28 that Simeon had a vision from God. He waited for a long time with great patience. Finally, his long-awaited vision was realized. He saw God's salvation in the baby Jesus lying there in his arms. In this we learn that his prayer had been answered and fulfilled. For a millennium, many prophets and devout people had hoped to see the emergence of the Messiah, but they all died without seeing him. Simeon believed and prayed that the Messiah would come and comfort his people. God gave him the privilege of seeing the Messiah with his own eyes. He could enjoy the blessing also of having his prayers answered.

In verses 29-32, we read Simeon's song of praise. We learn from his song three things about Jesus.

First, Jesus is salvation. Verse 29 reads, "Sovereign Lord, as you have promised, you now dismiss your servant in peace." In this verse, Simeon sees himself as a faithful shepherd with his Master's instructions to keep watch over his flock through the long weary night. As dawn breaks, he is released from his duty.

Why was Simeon so peaceful at his departure to an unknown world? Verses 30 and 31 tell us the answer: "For my eyes have seen your salvation, which you have prepared in the sight of all people." The baby Jesus was brought in by a peasant woman. But Simeon had eyes to see in the baby Jesus salvation for himself and for all his suffering people as well. He saw salvation from God in this child. So his dying was like going back home. We must have this kind of faith, faith that Jesus is salvation for all mankind.

Second, Jesus is light for the Gentiles and glory to the people of Israel. This idea is derived from the prophecy of Isaiah (Isa 49:6). God chose Israel to be a light for the Gentiles. In order to accomplish this mission, God did not give them material blessings; rather, he gave them the spiritual blessing to be a priestly nation—a nation of Bible teachers. They did not realize God's deep love for them. The people of Israel were very bitter before God because their national situation was like that of a shrimp caught among whales. They envied the

Gentile's material prosperity and military power and in the process, became sorrowful and fatalistic. They had no spiritual insight when they saw the world this way. As a result, they failed to see God's blessing and failed also to be a light for the Gentiles. But Jesus, a real Jew, came into the world as a light for the Gentiles to shine on those living in darkness and in the shadow of death. Here we must straighten out our concept of Gentiles. Who are the Gentiles? They are those who do not know Jesus personally. No matter who they may be, they are in the shadow of darkness. We must see all people who do not know Jesus as Gentiles and have pity on them.

In verse 32b, Simeon says that the baby Jesus is "glory to the people of Israel." From the time of the patriarchs, the Israelites were a nomad people who wandered from one grazing place to another with their flocks. God did not let them settle down in one place, but made them live as pilgrims on earth. He did this so that they might depend only on him. Because God loved them, he put them in adverse situations so that they might experience a world without his mercy and at the same time, through much suffering, experience the deep love and grace of God. Finally, from this people, God brought forth Jesus the Messiah. His birth from among the Israelites is surely glory to his people Israel.

Third, Jesus is the cause of the falling and rising of mankind. Verse 34 reads, "This child is destined to cause the falling and rising of many in Israel." The destiny of all men depends on how they see Jesus. To those who believe in him, Jesus is the rock of salvation. To those who do not believe, Jesus is the rock that makes them stumble. Jesus is also a sign that will be spoken against. In essence, men like the darkness more than the light because in the light they are exposed. So wherever Jesus appears, most people reject him and antagonize one another (Mt 10:34-35).

Verse 35b reads, "And a sword will pierce your own soul too." Simeon foresaw the baby Jesus' suffering and rejection by the people and prophesied about his mother's suffering also. The whole life of Jesus would be the cause of his mother's pain, especially his death on the cross, which would be like a sword piercing her very soul (Jn 19:25).

III. Anna's prayer (36-40)

In those times, a woman's place in every stratum of society was unimportant compared with that of men. But Luke did not hesitate to speak about one old woman named Anna who was present in the temple during Jesus' presentation. Anna was a prophetess, a daughter of the tribe of Asher. She had married when she was young and full of the dream of a sweet home in her heart. She had lived with her husband seven years after her marriage, and then as a widow until she was eighty-four. When she lost her husband, she did not become a victim of her sorrowful destiny. Who could help her in the loss of her husband at such a young age? But instead of despairing, she made a decision of faith to live in the house of God among God's people, serving them as a mother of prayer.

Verse 38 says that she prayed for the redemption of Israel. She prayed for her people who were suffering under the heel of Rome and also suffering from their sins. She prayed for the Messiah to come and save them from their suffering. At the moment she saw the baby Jesus, she saw the Messiah. Like Simeon, God's grace fell upon her at that moment and she could not but praise God with her mouth. She thanked God and spoke up about the child to everyone present in the temple, as well as to all who were looking forward to the redemption of Jerusalem.

We learn from Simeon and Anna that when they looked at God in dark times, they not only overcame themselves, but also became prayer servants of their time. They were used as lamps of God, burning in those dark times.

Lesson 7

The Boy Jesus at the Temple

Luke 2:41-52
Key Verse: 2:49

I.   WHEN HE WAS TWELVE YEARS OLD (41-50)

1. What does verse 41 reveal about the family of Joseph?

2. Why did Jesus' parents take him up to Jerusalem at the age of 12? What do you know about the Feast of the Passover? about 12-year-old boys?

3. When did Jesus' parents realize that he was missing? What did they do? Where did they look? When and where did they find him?

4. What was Jesus doing? How did the people in the temple respond to Jesus? Describe the scene in the temple court. What does this event reveal about Jesus, his inner desires, his attitude as a student, etc.?

5. Why were his parents astonished to see him? How and why did his parents rebuke him?

6. What was his answer? Why did he say "had to be"? Think about the meaning of Jesus' answer.

7. What was Jesus' view of his two fathers? What can we learn from Jesus' example?

II.   HE WAS OBEDIENT TO THEM (51-52)

8. How did Jesus keep spiritual order in his home? How long was he subject to his human parents? Why was obedience to his parents necessary even though Jesus was God's Son and he knew who he was? What can you learn from Jesus? (Heb 5:8-9)

9. How does Luke describe how Jesus grew up in Nazareth? What do you think this means? If he was perfect, why did he have to grow? What was it about his attitude that enabled him to grow? What can you learn here?

10. Why do you think Luke included this event in his Gospel?

The Boy Jesus at the Temple

Luke 2:41-52
Key Verse: 2:49

*"'Why were you searching for me?' he asked. 'Didn't you know
I had to be in my Father's house?'"*

TODAY'S PASSAGE IS A story about the boy Jesus at the temple
during the time of the Feast of the Passover. Luke the historian
opened his eyes wide and carefully observed the facts regarding Jesus' early years. Apart from this incident, which Luke alone
relates, we know nothing of Jesus' boyhood. He went with his parents
to Jerusalem to celebrate the Feast of the Passover. This event is not
so complicated, in spite of what many commentators say. But this
story is a natural one. It simply portrays a teenage boy Jesus. In this
passage, we learn what was in Jesus' subconscious mind and what
was his heart's desire.

I. "Didn't you know I had to be …" (41-50)

Read verses 41-48. Jesus' parents went to Jerusalem annually for
the Feast of the Passover. The Feast of the Passover continued for
seven days. During this special occasion, the people of Israel remembered God's great grace of deliverance from the hand of Pharaoh
after a long 430 years of slavery in Egypt. Historically, Jews who were
scattered all over the world were willing to make a pilgrimage to
Jerusalem for the Passover.

Every year his parents went to Jerusalem for the Feast of the
Passover (41). When Jesus was twelve years old, his parents took him
with them to the Passover Feast for the first time, for according to
Jewish custom, from the age of twelve, boys were considered men. It
was now legal for these young men to participate in the festivals and

ceremonies of the Law of Moses and to get married.

After the festival was over, Joseph and Mary left. When returning from the festival, it was the custom for the women to go on ahead with the younger children and the men to follow with the bigger boys. Therefore, Mary may have thought that Jesus was with Joseph, and Joseph may have thought that he was with Mary. At the end of a day's journey, they began to look for him among their relatives and friends, but to their consternation, they found that Jesus was not in their company—he was lost.

At that time, a journey was more tiring because of the poor means of transportation available to them. Common people traveled on foot, and only rich people could afford donkey carts. Because it was night when they found that the boy Jesus was missing, they had to wait until early the next morning to go back to Jerusalem. It was a full day's journey, so it was already night again when they arrived back in the city. They had to endure another anxious night, and then they began to look all over Jerusalem for the boy Jesus.

The following day—the third day since they had seen him—they discovered Jesus in the temple. They couldn't believe their eyes. Mary and Joseph wanted to dash to him and hug him. But Jesus, looking at them, waved his hand quietly and again concentrated on the discussion he was having. His mother said to him, "Son, why have you treated us like this? Your father and I have been anxiously searching for you" (48). How did he answer? "Why were you searching for me? Didn't you know I had to be in my Father's house?" (49). It seems that they didn't understand each other. But we can learn several things from Jesus.

First, the boy Jesus had great desire for the truth. The age of twelve falls in the puberty period. For the most part, ordinary teenagers eat a lot, sometimes enormous amounts because they are growing. Probably, most of the boys and girls who went to Jerusalem enjoyed eating something new and delicious, munching and crunching. They looked as if they had come to Jerusalem only to enjoy delicious food.

The teenager period is the time of blossoming. Teenagers look so fresh and pretty. One day I saw a girl who was crying at the airport in West Germany. So I ran to her and asked, "What can I do for you?"

She responded, "No, nothing. I am just crying. I saw myself in the mirror... so pretty. I was moved." Teenagers are very curious about many things, especially about the opposite sex. Probably many boys from various country districts were busy glancing out of the corner of their eyes at beautiful Jerusalem girls. Perhaps the studious kind of teenager who went to the Jerusalem temple was fascinated by the elegant temple buildings, ornamented with marble stones and gold. They were all normal, growing boys. The teenage years are a time of dreams and romanticism. Teenagers sing love songs endlessly. They also write secret diaries. Sometimes they write poems, read them, and cry many tears. Sometimes they burn with ambition. It is said that Napoleon Bonaparte, when he was a teenager, tried to catch the rainbow while riding on horseback.

The mood of the Feast had calmed down and everybody was busy trying to go back home. The boy Jesus, however, was in no hurry to return home with his parents and remained in the temple. What did he do there? Read verse 46. For three days, he stayed in the temple, sitting among the teachers, listening to them, and asking questions. It is surprising that he had so many questions to ask that after three days he was still asking many questions to the teachers of the law. It is also surprising that he could answer their questions.

Those who are truth seekers have many questions about the fundamental problems of mankind, such as origin, ontology, epistemology, purpose, and meaning. On the other hand, those who have no learning mind have no questions to ask. They are too proud to ask any questions to anybody, so they don't learn much. They also cannot answer others' questions because they did not learn much. Learning by asking questions is not humiliating. A learning mind does not abase anybody.

See Jesus! He had a great learning mind. He asked questions and answered questions. Because of his learning mind, his wisdom, sagacity, and lucid intelligence were so bright that even the teachers of the law marveled at him. Especially, his earnest search for the truth was remarkable. Jesus was a truth-seeking teenager.

What kind of questions could Jesus have asked? It is obvious that he would have asked, "Who created the world?" Probably they tried to answer him theologically, referring to many scrolls, and then became speechless. Then Jesus must have answered from the book of Genesis, "In the beginning God created the heavens and the earth." What further questions could Jesus have asked? In all likelihood, he must have asked, "Who is the Lord of the temple?" or "What is the original meaning of the Passover Feast?" His questions made them speechless, for they revealed their hypocrisy and corruption.

Teenagers who live under the structure of utilitarianism and pragmatism learn how to live according to the situation. They learn how to get instant profit and how to enjoy life in this hard world. Gradually, they lose interest in the great quest of man's meaning and purpose. In the course of living in a world where many people suppress the truth of God, teenagers see many horrible things they should not see. In their curiosity, they imitate these things. When they are growing up, both in body and spirit, they have little chance to create a close relationship with God. In the most perceptive years as a teenager, to grow without God is most dangerous and hazardous.

We can underestimate children, judging them by their outward appearance. But they have the image of God in them and they are the ones who are asking these fundamental questions of life the most because they want to know why they have to live and why they have to do so much homework.

Second, Jesus' two fathers. Mary, his mother, asked him, "Why have you treated us like this?" (48) Of course, Joseph and Mary remembered what the angel of the Lord said to them (Lk 1:31-33 and Mt 1:21). But up until now, Jesus had worked hard as a carpenter's apprentice. He had been a treasure to their family. He had been so faithful and obedient. But for the first time he did something without permission. So Mary asked, "Why have you treated us like this?" Jesus answered in verse 49, "Why were you searching for me? Didn't you know I had to be in my Father's house?" Here, Jesus is not denying that Joseph was his father, but only he affirms that God is his heavenly Father. At the age of twelve, Jesus had assurance that God is his heavenly Father. From his teenage days, he was aware that he had two fathers.

It is really great for children to grow up with an earthly father's protection and love, and at the same time, grow in the knowledge of God. Those who grew from childhood in the awareness of God are mainly stable, courageous, and historically great men and women of God. We are greatly inspired whenever we think of Abraham Lincoln's honesty, courage, and love of the truth. On the other hand, those who grew up without God in their hearts are clever, unstable, and unfaithful. Those who grew up without God mostly have their human father's image in their hearts, or in rare cases, their mother's image. How wonderful it is to have God in our hearts! How wonderful the boy Jesus was when he said, "Didn't you know I had to be in my Father's house?"

According to statistics, 70% of youngsters come to know God and most of them decide to believe God in their subconscious mind. Matthew 5:8 says, "Blessed are the pure in heart, for they will see God." Teenagers can see God because they are still pure in heart. We must not judge teenagers by their outward appearance; rather, we must respect them as young human beings.

Third, Jesus' heart's desire. Mary asked him, "Why have you treated us like this?" His response was, "Didn't you know I had to be in my Father's house?" In this case, the meaning according to the nuance in Greek is "Didn't you know that I had to be interested in my Father's business?" Jesus, in the corner of his heart, had desire to do his Father's business.

"Must" was in his heart. At that time, he worked for his father as a carpenter's apprentice. But in reality, his work in the carpenter's shop itself was for the glory of God because he had God in his heart. Necessity was in Jesus' heart. This concept of necessity is frequently found in the Gospel of Luke. Here, "must" is an inseparable quality in establishing his inherent relationship with God. When he was at home working under his carpenter father Joseph, Jesus was mindful of his parents and was obedient to them. He was also kind to his neighbors. However, he was sure that he must be in the house of God and must do God's business. When the boy Jesus lived in the consciousness of God, his consciousness formed a subconsciousness in his inner man. We know that the subconscious rules each man's heart's desire.

Because God created man for his glory, everyone has a heart's desire to live for the glory of God. One missionary said, "I will pioneer Moscow State University. I must learn how to speak Russian." After that, he concentrated on pioneering the UIC ministry and almost forgot about praying for Russia. Then one day his daughter said, "I think I must pioneer the U.S.S.R. I think I must learn to speak Russian." She is a teenager, but because she has God in her heart, she wants to do something that pleases God instead of only enjoying her privileges as the youngest.

When Dr. Albert Schweitzer was just eight years old, he dropped to his knees in his room and prayed, "Lord, bless me to study well so that I may serve you the rest of my life after my studies." He mainly studied the humanities, theology, and music. So in order to serve God more effectively, he began medical studies at the age of 30. God blessed him in this and he became a medical missionary. When he died, even the Soviet newspapers recognized him as a light in the 19th Century.

Through this, we learn that we must work hard with a sense of necessity for our earthly father as an obedient and hard-working apprentice, and at the same time, we must be sure to do God's work. When God made man, he made us to have a family for our happiness. He also allows us to work hard as small carpenters and such. But this is not all God created us for. God wants us to work for him, our Chief Carpenter. Sometimes we don't know what we are doing, but we work hard in spiritual carpentry according to the Chief Carpenter's blueprint. When we work hard for the Chief Carpenter, later we see that he has done a great work by himself through us.

II. He was obedient to them (51-52)

Let's see what Jesus did after this event. Luke the historian connects Jesus in the temple with Jesus who works hard and obediently in his father's carpentry shop after the Feast. "Then he went down to Nazareth with them and was obedient to them" (51). Joseph was a carpenter with a large family. They say that a carpenter's work in those days included the erection of houses, the making of all kinds of furniture and household equipment, and agricultural implements.

The work of carpentering must have been demanding, but Jesus was obedient continually.

Verse 52 reads, "And Jesus grew in wisdom and stature, and in favor with God and with men." This is a brief description of a beautiful teenage boy Jesus. May all teenagers of this country grow like the boy Jesus.

Lesson 8

John the Baptist Prepares the Way

Luke 3:1-38
Key Verse: 3:2b

I. THE TIMES WHEN JOHN BEGAN HIS MINISTRY (1-3)

1. Look at the names of the political and religious leaders. What do you know about each of them? What does this tell us about the times of John? What does the divided priesthood suggest about the state of religious life?

2. Where and how did John begin his ministry? What did John come to do when the word of God came to him? How does the word of God come to us?

II. ALL MANKIND WILL SEE GOD'S SALVATION (4-6)

3. How did John's life and ministry fulfill the prophecy of Isaiah?

4. What was the good news that John proclaimed? What is significant about the words, "all mankind will see God's salvation?"

III. PEOPLE'S RESPONSE TO THE MESSAGE OF REPENTANCE AND JUDGMENT (7-14)

5. Why did John rebuke the crowds? Why did he use such strong language? What keeps people from producing fruit in keeping with repentance?

6. What does the phrase, "out of these stones God can raise up children for Abraham," mean?

7. Why is it so important to repent? What are the consequences of not repenting?

8. How did the people respond to John's words? What can we learn from their attitude?

9. What direction did John give each group of people who asked? How can we apply this advice to ourselves and to the people of our times?

IV. ONE WHO BAPTIZES WITH THE HOLY SPIRIT (15-20)

10. Who did the people begin to think that John might be? How did John introduce Jesus and his ministry? What does this mean?

V. THE BAPTISM AND GENEALOGY OF JESUS (21-38)

11. How was John's baptism different from that of other people?

What was the meaning of Jesus' baptism? Why was God pleased with his Son?

12. Notice the difference in this genealogy and that recorded in Matthew. (Some scholars say that this is Mary's genealogy, while Matthew's is Joseph's.) Why do you think Luke traces Jesus' lineage back to Adam and to God?

John the Baptist Prepares the Way

Luke 3:1-38
Key Verse: 3:2b

> "... the word of God came to John son of Zechariah in the desert."

LUKE THE HISTORIAN DISPLAYS before our eyes in today's passage the beginning of the ministry of John the Baptist. In this passage, we can study what the world situation was when John began his public ministry and how he prepared the way for the Messiah.

I. The times when John began his ministry (1-3)

Read verse 1. At that time, Tiberius, the successor to Augustus Caesar, was the Emperor of Rome. He ruled the world by military power, demanding that nations either submit or be annihilated. What was worse, Judea was under the control of a Roman governor, Pontius Pilate. People call a mean and cunning person a "sneaky guy." Maybe Pilate is a good picture of a sneaky person. He washed his hands to escape the guilt of condemning Jesus to death. But history condemns him as the one who sentenced the Son of God to death. Under constant threats and fear, the Israelites trembled day and night. Judea was filled with the fear of death, bad rumors, and unpredictable disaster. They were under the rule of the power of darkness.

The internal misery of Judea was more than one could say. When Herod the Great died in 4 B.C. after reigning about 40 years, his kingdom was divided into three parts, each to be ruled over by one of his three sons, the three tetrarchs: Herod, Philip, and Lysanias. Herod II took his own brother Philip's wife, Herodias (Mk 6:18), and incited his anger. The division of the kingdom was the cause of a power struggle among the brothers, which victimized the lives of innocent people in all their respective territories. In recent decades, the bipolar struggle between democracy and communism has brought forth such tragedy among brethren of many polarized countries such as Korea and Vietnam. During the war, about three million Korean brethren killed each other. In the 1960's, Vietnamese brothers of the North and South engaged in an internecine war and perpetrated innumerable deaths among their own people. Because of the horror of war, many U.S. soldiers who served in the Vietnam War became psychiatric patients. When we watch the movie, "The Deer Hunter," about the Vietnam War, we can tell just how tragic that internecine war was.

What did the religious leaders do in that dark time? There was supposed to be only one high priest, but Luke says that there were two high priests, Annas and Caiaphas. This plainly tells us of the disorder in the high priestly office. The high priest should have been the prayer servant and conscience of the times, but he was the symbol of evil. He collaborated with politicians to destroy Jesus and made the people of the time despair and tremble in fear even more.

It was a most terrible time in world history, and it was a time when no one dared to do any good work because of fear. But it is amazing to know that in that time, God began the gospel work through John the Baptist.

Read verse 2. "The word of God came to John son of Zechariah in the desert." According to the prophecy of Isaiah, John the Baptist came as the forerunner of the Messiah, and before his ministry began, he lived in the desert. John was the son of Zechariah and Elizabeth, the one and only son of old parents. Humanly speaking, he was like a little fish caught in the rushing torrent of a stream. He could do nothing by himself. Then how could he begin the work of God in that impossible time?

First, when the word of God came to him, John could begin his work. Read verse 2. "The word of God came to John son of Zechariah in the desert." When John was in the desert, preparing himself to do the work as the forerunner of the Messiah by living a pure life, the word of God came to him. Then he was empowered to break his silence and began to cry out to the thronging people to repent of their sins.

Jeremiah was another example of a man like this. He was an ordinary man from a country priest's family. But when the word of God came to him, he was filled with the Spirit of God, and without fear, he began to deliver the message of God's judgment continually. Those who did not like to listen to his message of judgment put him in prison. Still, they could not shut his mouth. When one word came to Martin Luther, "The righteous will live by faith," (Rom 1:17), not only could he solve his inner spiritual problem, but he could also challenge the corruption and worldly power of Roman Catholicism of the times. When one word came to St. Augustine, "Let us behave decently, as in the daytime…" (Rom 13:13), he was empowered to change his intellectual hedonism, which had been incurable.

"The word of God came to John." This does not mean that John caught one word in his heart, but that the word of God from above came upon him while he was preparing his mind and heart in the desert. So we must also pray for the word of God to come to us when we wait. The word of God changes men's hearts. The word of God changed world history, for the word of God is living and active (Heb 4:12). To John, the word of God was the source of power.

Second, when the word of God came to him, John was filled with the Spirit of God. Elijah was a most outstanding prophet, mainly because of his spirit of power. In the Bible, the spirit of John the Baptist parallels that of Elijah's.

When the word of God came to John, he was empowered by the Holy Spirit. Through this, we learn the deep meaning of John 1:1-2, "In the beginning was the Word, and the Word was with God, and the Word was God. He was with God in the beginning." The Word is God himself. When the word of God came to John, he became powerful and he was not fearful at all. He was not afraid of Herod the Tetrarch, the cruelest of men, and he rebuked him to repent of taking his younger brother's wife. When the word of God came to him, he could have the spirit of Elijah, and he became as powerful as a locomotive. He went into all the country around the Jordan. His message of repentance reverberated throughout the whole country.

He stood squarely as the national leader and shepherd, and as the forerunner of Jesus Christ.

Why are most young people so fearful, too fearful to do anything? It's because they have no word of God in them. For example, when King Saul rejected the word of God, the Spirit of God left him, and he was filled with evil spirits. When he was filled with evil spirits, he was ruled by fear and hatred. All must come to Bible study and accept even one word so that the Spirit of God may fill their hearts and the evil spirit—the spirit of fear—may disappear from their hearts.

Third, when the word of God came to him, John preached the message of repentance and judgment. These days it seems to be impossible. What is worse, many people think that their human rights are invaded if someone says to them, "Repent." But John preached the baptism of repentance and the impending judgment of God. John was a true servant of God because he preached the message of repentance and judgment. Without the love of God and love for another's soul, nobody can deliver the message of repentance. God is living. God judges the living and the dead (2 Co 5:10).

II. All mankind will see God's salvation (4-6)

Read verse 4-6. "A voice of one calling in the desert, 'Prepare the way for the Lord, make straight paths for him. Every valley shall be filled in, every mountain and hill made low. The crooked roads shall become straight, the rough ways smooth." These verses quote the prophecy concerning the coming of John the Baptist as the forerunner of the Messiah (Isa 40:3-5), and are a poem concerning the announcement of a king's arrival. In short, it is the announcement of the Messiah's coming. It is also a clear warning to his people to prepare their minds and hearts to welcome the Messiah by repenting of their crooked minds and evil ways. Then all mankind will see God's salvation (6).

The gist of the poem is that "all mankind will see God's salvation." People do many things to save themselves. Each person has his own way of surviving and saving himself. I realized that everybody else is smarter than me in saving themselves. But nothing can save them from their sins, and nothing can save them from the shadow of death and from the impending judgment of God. Through Jesus alone, all mankind can see God's salvation. At this moment, we must open our hearts and accept the truth that through Jesus alone, all mankind will see God's salvation.

III. People's response to the message of repentance and judgment (7-14)

What did John do for the people coming to him? Read verses 7 and 8. "John said to the crowds coming out to be baptized by him, 'You brood of vipers! Who warned you to flee from the coming wrath? Produce fruit in keeping with repentance. And do not begin to say to yourselves, "We have Abraham as our father." For I tell you that out of these stones God can raise up children for Abraham.'" In Matthew 3:7, we see that these words refer to the Pharisees and Sadducees. It sounds very harsh when John says to them, "You brood of vipers." It means that the religious leaders were most disgusting because of their hypocrisy and spiritual pride. They thought that since they were children of Abraham, they were special and did not have to do anything for salvation. But John said that they must produce fruit in keeping with repentance (8). John told them that their empty spiritual pride was useless because God could raise up children for Abraham out of stones on the ground. If they did not repent, they would not escape the impending judgment of God (9). They were serious sinners and John's message was serious. But we don't see any specific repentance from them.

How did the ordinary people respond? They are the last persons listed in this passage, but they sincerely wanted to repent. They looked nice and happy, but in truth, they were suffering endlessly from their burdens of sin and from the hand of Satan. They really wanted to see God's salvation. Read verses 10 and 11. The crowd asked, "What should we do then?" Even the tax collectors came and asked, "What should we do?" Cruel soldiers also came and asked the same question (12-14). We must also have contrite hearts like those who came to John to confess their sins because God does not accept a bull, but rather a broken heart for the forgiveness of sins (Ps 51:16-17). We must also cry out moment by moment, "What should we do?"

John's exhortations were very plain and practical. He urged them to repent of the basic things which pulled them down in the gravity of sin. It is not surprising that they responded to the message of repentance and judgment because man is created in the image of God, and as beings who yearn for the holiness of God, most people have desire to repent of their sins and become children of God. Many people in the past boldly became monks and practiced aestheticism in order to satisfy their holy desires. These days, many go to theological seminaries hoping to somehow change their sinful natures. Men despair most, not because they have nothing to eat, but because they find themselves too sinful to repent before God.

IV. One who baptizes with the Holy Spirit (15-20)

Read verse 15. People who were spiritually thirsty and hungry came to John and were baptized. When they saw John's spiritual authority over people, they began to wonder if John might possibly be the Messiah.

Immediately, John took people's attention away from himself to focus on Jesus. He began to introduce Jesus. Read verse 16. "John answered them all, 'I baptize you with water. But one more powerful than I will come, the thongs of whose sandals I am not worthy to untie.'" John introduces Jesus as one who is so high and powerful that he doesn't even deserve to untie the thongs of his sandal. In conclusion, he says in verse 16b that Jesus baptizes with the Holy Spirit. John only baptized people with water in the Jordan River as a symbol of the cleansing of their sins. But John knew that water could not wash their sins away. Their sins were washed away only when Jesus baptized them with the Holy Spirit. Jesus is the unique one who saves us from the condition of being slaves to fear (Rom 8:15). Jesus is the unique person who solves our sin problem by giving us the baptism of the Holy Spirit.

Verse 18 says, "And with many other words, John exhorted the people and preached the good news to them." Here, Luke the historian says the message of repentance and judgment is good news to them. It's unbelievable. But it is true because the message of repentance and judgment can help people to come to Jesus for the grace of the forgiveness of sins.

V. The baptism and genealogy of Jesus (21-38)

Read verse 21. When all the people were being baptized by John, Jesus was also baptized. Why was Jesus baptized? It was not for the forgiveness of sins, but for the taking over of John's ministry as had been prophesied. Verse 22 is nothing but a vivid scene of the inauguration of the Messiah, who came through the way John had prepared. Jesus was anointed by the Holy Spirit as the Messiah so as to save us from the grip of evil spirits.

The genealogy of Jesus written by Matthew focuses on the key turning points in the history of the Israelites. It goes from Abraham to David to Jeconiah at the time of the captivity, down through Joseph. He wrote for Jewish readers.

Luke begins with Jesus, the Son of God, and traces his genealogy back through Heli, apparently the father of Mary, all the way back to Adam, the first man created by God. Luke emphasizes Jesus' relationship to the whole human race, Jew and Gentile alike. Luke's genealogy demonstrates Paul's view in Romans that Jesus is the "last Adam" (1Co 15:45). Paul also said in 1 Corinthians 15:22, "For as in Adam all die, so in Christ all will be made alive."

Lesson 9

The Temptation of Jesus

Luke 4:1-13
Key Verse: 4:4

I. MAN DOES NOT LIVE ON BREAD ALONE (1-4)

1. After Jesus was baptized and filled with the Holy Spirit, where did he go and what did he do? Why do you think the Spirit led him into the desert? What is a desert like?
2. How long was Jesus there? What was his physical condition?
3. What was the first temptation? In what respect is this temptation representative of all temptations on the material and animal level? In what respect was the devil's temptation a reasonable and logical suggestion? Why might Jesus have been especially vulnerable?
4. How did Jesus answer the devil? What does his answer mean? Why was it the best answer?

II. WORSHIP THE LORD YOUR GOD (5-8)

5. In the second temptation, what did the devil promise Jesus? To what does this temptation appeal? What was the devil's condition? Was the devil telling the truth about his power and authority?
6. What was Jesus' answer? How was it an appropriate answer? What does it mean to worship God? (Dt 6:5)

III. DO NOT PUT THE LORD YOUR GOD TO THE TEST (9-13)

7. Describe the third temptation. What was the point? How did the devil use Scripture to confuse Jesus?
8. How did Jesus answer? What was the source of this and of all his answers? What can we learn from him? What can we learn here about the nature of temptation and about how to defeat the devil?
9. Did Jesus ever face temptation again? How does the devil continue to tempt us?

The Temptation of Jesus

Luke 4:1-13
Key Verse: 4:4

"It is written: 'Man does not live on bread alone.'"

I N THIS PASSAGE THERE are three kinds of temptations on different levels: the material temptation; the temptation for power and splendor; and the temptation to test God out of spiritual pride. Living in this pragmatic society, the devil's temptation can be taken lightly. But each of the devil's temptations can cause a fateful result to each individual if he is a human being. Once yielding to the devil's temptation, one has to live as a slave of the devil in fear and anguish throughout his lifetime. What is worse, he has to live as an enemy of God with no peace. We have to learn how Jesus won the victory over the devil's temptation so that we can also win the victory over the devil and live a victorious life.

I. Man does not live on bread alone (1-4)

Read verses 1 and 2. "Jesus, full of the Holy Spirit, returned from the Jordan and was led by the Spirit in the desert, where for forty days he was tempted by the devil. He ate nothing during those days, and at the end of them he was hungry." We wonder why he was led by the Spirit in the desert when he was about to begin his ministry. Verse 2b, "He ate nothing during those days ..." suggests that he wanted to fast and pray to prepare for the work God had given him. When he was full of the Holy Spirit, the devil did not dare to tempt Jesus. But when Jesus was too hungry and weak to do anything after forty days, he was tempted in the desert where there was no one to help him. The desert was not a vacation spot or a place of picturesque beauty. It was a heap of dust and limestone rocks which were blistering and peeling.

It glowed with heat like a big furnace and precipices rose 1200 feet high and swooped down to the Dead Sea. The place where he was tempted was itself gruesome and chilling.

At this moment, we have to think about why Jesus had to undergo the devil's temptation at the outset of his ministry. Ever since Adam yielded to the devil's temptation, man was enslaved by the devil. Since then, the devil has defeated all mankind through temptations. The devil is like a soldier on high ground, strafing enemies who were scattered in disorder around the foot of a mountain. Man is helpless before the devil's temptation. Therefore, Jesus had to receive the devil's temptations and defeat him so that he could open the way for us to a victorious life.

How did the devil tempt Jesus? Read verse 3. "If you are the Son of God, tell this stone to become bread." The devil recognized Jesus' clear consciousness of being the Son of God. Thereby, he went to tempt him, saying, "Hey! Are you really the Son of God? If so, you have the ability to make stone into bread. Why is it necessary for you to sit down and starve to death even before trying? It is not necessary. Why don't you use any available means to save yourself, be they fair or foul?"

This is the temptation of the bread problem. By tempting people with the bread problem, the devil has enslaved most people of all nations down through the generations and ruled over them. But in reality, the bread problem is a material problem, and the material problem is a life security problem.

Time past and present, the devil's temptation to man to get bread by any available means has been most persuasive. These days also, the devil says to insecure people, "You've gotta eat," and "What is more important than life security? What are you going to do when you get married and have several kids?" Then most people both young and old become too anxious to do anything. One existential philosopher once said, "The 20th century is the age of anxiety." Why are people so anxious? It is mainly due to the bread problem—not because they have no bread to eat, but because they are just sick with the bread problem. The bread problem has occupied modern man's heart as if it were everything. Schools have adopted a job-oriented educational system. Most young men do not study for the pure purpose of being educated; instead, for the most part, they study to get skills and a better job to solve the bread problem for the future. As a result, most of them become like machines with skills and licenses.

In order to solve this problem, both men and women must exert every effort. Those who want to get a proper job have to study nearly 20 years and take many tests. They tremble in fear with this problem from their young age. If they fail in making an effort toward this goal, intentionally or unintentionally, they despair.

This kind of job-oriented educational system demands a man to be pragmatic. Finally, he becomes animal-like like Esau, who sold his birthright to his brother for a bowl of stew when he was famished, saying, "Look, I am about to die. What good is the birthright to me?" (Ge 25:29-32). Because of this, he became a most despised person in the Bible (Heb 12:16). If the devil had succeeded in defeating Jesus in this temptation of the bread problem, he could have continued to keep all mankind as his prisoners, chained on the superficial level as slaves of bread. But he failed.

How did Jesus answer? Read verse 4. "It is written: 'Man does not live on bread alone.'" What does it mean when Jesus said man does not live on bread alone?

First, "Man does not live on bread alone" means that man is both body and soul. Here, he is saying that there is more to a man than his physical body. Of course, Jesus knew that man is flesh, made out of the dust of the ground. Therefore, he did not deny man's need for physical bread. He also did not deny man's need to satisfy his physical desires. But Jesus did not agree that bread is everything. He refused the devil's idea that man should use any available means to get bread and that man should sweat and toil only for the bread problem. Man is flesh, but he is also a soul, created in the image of God. Therefore, a man, whoever he may be, is great, greater than anything else in the universe. And he is noble, more noble than any of the creatures of the world, for he is a soul and he has God's life in himself and he was cre-ated for a great purpose of God. This great human being needs more than physical bread. This great human being cannot be animal-like or a cursed man by working only for three meals a day. He not only must work for bread to satisfy his physical desires, but he must also do the work of God to satisfy his soul. He must live for the glory of God as originally created, not for his stomach.

Second, "Man does not live on bread alone" means that man must live by the word of truth. To the phrase, "Man does not live on bread alone," Matthew 4:4 and Deuteronomy 8:3 add, "but on every word that comes from the mouth of God." Worldly wisdom tells of innumerable skills on how to survive or save oneself in the world. But these days, materialism ranks number one. In fact, the power of money works in this society. Because of this, many people think that if they have money, they can do anything they want to do. They want to buy happiness with money. They want to violate their children's human rights and religious freedom with money by sending them to deprogramming centers. This kind of materialism is an irrevocable mistake of materialists. The tragedy is that materialism violently denies man's spiritual life. Materialism suppresses the truth of God.

How then can we survive in a materialistic society where no one can survive without money? That's a hard question to answer. However, we can find the answer in the Bible. Matthew 6:33 says, "But seek first his kingdom and his righteousness and all these things will be given to you as well." This is God's truth and promise. But these days in the material society, there are not many who believe this promise of God. There is a strong impression that many people believe God's promise and truth while they are in churches or while they are preaching. Nobody wants to suffer to live by the word of truth. In consequence, they have to live without the truth of God. In the state where the absolutes of God are absent, they have to live without any absolute meaning or purpose of life. All the efforts they exert remain barren except for three meals a day. That's all. In the end, they are all shackled by the chains of the devil and live a cursed life.

But see the history of America! American forefathers became rich and happy when they first sought God's kingdom and righteousness. In October 1978, one couple went to pioneer OSU in Columbus. At that time, the woman missionary had had two consecutive miscarriages and hadn't worked for several months. But when she went to Columbus, she made a decision of faith that she would not look for a job before finding one Bible student. What happened when she made this decision of faith? God granted her two Bible students. In addition, God gave her a nice job as a physician. This one word from Matthew 6:33 made many peoples of many nations rich and happy when they believed it.

Most importantly, we must see Jesus and what he did when he faced the devil's material temptation. When the devil tempted him, he was at the point of death after fasting for forty days. But he did not yield to the devil's temptation. He could have become worried since he had a large family with a labor class income. But he did not worry about his future security, or his family; instead, he trusted God's word of promise and obeyed God's word at the cost of his life. In this way, Jesus defeated the devil's material temptation.

II. Worship the Lord your God (5-8)

This time, Satan tempted Jesus on the human level, that is, the political level. Read verses 5 and 6. The devil led Jesus up to a high mountain and showed him in an instant all the kingdoms of the world. He wanted to make a deal, "I will give you all their authority and splendor, for it has been given to me, and I can give it to anyone I want to. So if you worship me, it will all be yours."

In the Bible, the devil is called, "the prince of this world" (Jn 12:31; 14:30; 16:11). In one sense, what the devil says is true. But in actuality, he is a liar. He cannot give away all the authority and splendor of the kingdoms of this world just as the President of the U.S.S.R. cannot, even though his power is supreme. He is a liar and wanted to test Jesus so as to arouse Jesus' political ambition to rule the world with authority and splendor. It was a great temptation to Jesus, for he should rule the world as the King of kings. Humanly speaking, he might have needed the political power and authority of the kingdoms of the world, as well as the applauding recognition of the peoples of all the kingdoms of the world.

The devil proposed a political compromise: "If you worship me, I will give all the authority and splendor of the world to you." At the same time, it was a threat and pressure on Jesus, suggesting that unless he compromised with him, he could do nothing. The problem

LESSON 9 | THE TEMPTATION OF JESUS

today is that the principle of democracy seems to be, "Compromise in order to get some benefit or recognition." Living in this land, what can we do if we do not compromise?

The devil knows very well that all men have a sense of honor. Especially, all young men are ambitious to be popular and to be top leaders. The temptation of popularity and recognition is so strong that it can cause any ambitious person to fall down. The devil always tempts us saying, "I know you want to be very popular; I know you want recognition. I know you want to rule all the kingdoms of the world in splendor and glory." Then the devil wants us to compromise with him. In response, almost all young men want to compromise repeatedly. These days, we see many teens doing drugs in order to be accepted and recognized by their friends. Many kinds of stars and talented people sacrifice their purity to be picked up as the main character of a play or a soloist for a concert. They finally became Satan worshipers.

What was Jesus' answer to this? Verse 8 says, "It is written: 'Worship the Lord your God and serve him only.'" What does it mean to worship? It doesn't mean to bow one's head to the ground two hundred times as the believers of Buddha do. Deuteronomy 6:5 explains what worship is: "Love the Lord your God with all your heart and with all your soul and with all your strength."

Man must love God wholeheartedly. Man must be loved by God. Man must live before the eyes of God. Man must seek recognition and praise from God. Man must serve God wholeheartedly and serve his children faithfully instead of hoping to rule them with power and authority like Nero or Hitler. Most importantly, man must seek God's approval, recognition, and praise instead of seeking popularity or recognition from men, for men are all terrible sinners.

III. Do not put the Lord your God to the test (9-13)

At this point, the devil tempted Jesus to test God by using Scripture. This temptation is of the third dimension, and it is a temptation within the spiritual life.

Read verses 9 and 10. The devil quoted Psalm 91:11-12. He tempted Jesus to prove himself to be the Son of God by throwing himself down from the top of the temple and landing on the ground unhurt. The devil's real intention in tempting Jesus to perform an arms show was to persuade Jesus that he could find a more efficient and easy way to fulfill his Messianic ministry than that of denying himself and taking up his own cross to obey the will of God for world salvation. In brief, the devil tempted Jesus to take an easy way and give up the way of the cross. His intention was to stop Jesus from taking up his cross of salvation.

There are many clever men who listen to the devil's counseling and who only try to discover an easy way. As a result, they become the inventors of evil. The easy way has only produced hedonists and dispirited people. The easy way sounds good, but it is a way to utter corruption and despair and fear. These days many people who are taking the broad and easy way are not happy; they are miserable because of their corruption and despair.

There is no easy way in God's world. God made man to work hard for the glory of God and for their happiness. God made man to be responsible for his own children, as well as God's children. God's way is the way of the cross. This is the way that God chose for the salvation of the world. In order to save the world, God chose one person, Abraham, and took care of him for twenty-five years until he became a real man of faith. God sent Jesus to take up his cross of raising twelve disciples and finally, to suffer pain and anguish and die on the cross to save his children from their sins.

Jesus knew that he came to this world to die on the cross, but the devil tempted him, saying, "No, no. Don't take up your cross!" To this subtle devil, Jesus answered, "Do not put the Lord your God to the test." Jesus did not doubt the way of the cross, the way which God chose for world salvation, for it is the truth of God's creation. We must love the way of the cross. We must love Jesus who took up his cross of mission.

The purpose of God's promise in Psalm 91:11-12 is that he will protect those who absolutely depend on him in doing his work, even when it requires courageous faith and dangerous risks. This promise is not at all to be used to test God. We can find the same promise of protection in Mark 16:18, "They will pick up snakes with their hands;

and when they drink deadly poison, it will not hurt them at all." This was God's promise of protection for his servants who had to risk their lives for the sake of world evangelism. I heard of one fanatic who insisted on testing God's promise; so he picked up a rattle snake. Of course, God did not respond to his foolishness. We cannot test God. We can only trust God.

But Jesus defeated Satan's temptations through obedience to the word of God. Each time he was tempted, Jesus quoted a word from the book of Deuteronomy. Jesus used the word of God as his unique weapon. Jesus trusted the word of God as the absolute truth. We only thank God for his Son Jesus who overcame the temptation of the devil and opened the way for us to win the victory over the devil's temptations.

Lesson 10

Jesus Rejected at Nazareth

Luke 4:14-30
Key Verse: 4:18a

I. WHEN JESUS TAUGHT IN THEIR SYNAGOGUE (14-19)

1. How and where did Jesus begin his ministry? What does it mean that he returned in the power of the Spirit?

2. What was the general response of the people of the Galilean countryside to Jesus? What was his relationship to the town and the synagogue of Nazareth? How did he announce his Messianic ministry?

3. How did Isaiah describe the ministry of the Messiah? How did Jesus fulfill this Scripture?

4. Think about what it means to preach good news to the poor, to proclaim freedom to the prisoners and recovery of sight for the blind, to release the oppressed, and to proclaim the year of the Lord's favor.

II. TODAY THIS SCRIPTURE IS FULFILLED (20-30)

5. How did the people of Nazareth respond to Jesus' words? What does it mean that they thought of him as Joseph's son? How did Jesus understand their seeming compliments?

6. How and why did Jesus rebuke them? What does this mean? (23-24)

7. How and why did God use and bless a Gentile widow in the days of the prophet Elijah? Why this woman, rather than an Israelite widow? (1Ki 17:7-16)

8. Who was Naaman? Why was he cleansed by Elisha? (2Ki 5:1-14)

9. What was Jesus' point in telling these stories about the prophets in the Old Testament?

10. Why did the people become angry enough to want to throw Jesus down a cliff? Why did they not succeed? What can you learn about human nature from the people of Nazareth who should know God and his work best?

Jesus Rejected at Nazareth

Luke 4:14-30
Key Verse: 4:18a

> *"The Spirit of the Lord is on me, because he has anointed me
> to preach good news to the poor."*

I N CHAPTERS 4-9 OF his gospel, Luke describes Jesus' Galilean ministry. The event described in today's passage took place in Nazareth, the hometown of Jesus. Although this was not likely the first event in Jesus' ministry, Luke chose to start here. In this passage, Jesus wanted his hometown people to believe that he is the Son of God, so he gave them a general picture of the work of the Messiah (18-19) by quoting from the book of Isaiah (Isa 61:1-2; 58:6). But his hometown people, though they enjoyed his word, rejected him. At the outset of his gospel ministry, Jesus was rejected. Through this, we learn that rejection seems to be one of the characteristics of the gospel ministry. Let's learn what Jesus did when he was rejected and what the general picture of the Messianic work is.

I. When Jesus taught in their synagogues (14-19)

Verse 14 begins with the words, "Jesus returned to Galilee in the power of the Spirit ..." At the moment he was anointed with the Holy Spirit after his baptism, heaven opened and the Holy Spirit descended on him in bodily form like a dove. Jesus can uniquely be the Messiah of the world, for he was the only one who was anointed by God with the Holy Spirit. The fact that he returned to Galilee in the power of the Spirit contrasts him with the people of the world who remain in a deranged condition under the spirit of fear (Rom 8:15).

A man's spirit makes him different. As long as his spirit is in his body, he is a man. But if his spirit leaves him, he is nothing but an animal. If his spirit leaves him, his body dissolves into the dust. The spirit is everything, but the flesh is nothing (Jn 6:63). A man's appearance does not make him bold and valiant. The power of the Holy Spirit in a man is what makes him courageous and adventurous. King Saul was a bashful man, even though he was a head taller than all the others. So when the prophet arrived to anoint him king, he hid himself among the baggage (1Sa 10:22-23). But when the Spirit of God came to him in power, he burned with anger. He took a pair of oxen and cut them into pieces in order to demonstrate his power and authority to lead the people into battle with the Philistines (1Sa 11:6-7).

Peoples of all nations honor Abraham Lincoln because of his fighting spirit. They say that during the Civil War, he prayed regularly for three hours, kneeling down in order to uphold the truth of God, until he won the war over the enemy. People of this nation like John F. Kennedy. They like him because of his frontier spirit.

When Jesus returned to Galilee in the power of the Spirit, he was like a general making a triumphal entry into a royal court. And news about him spread through the whole countryside. The power of the Spirit was soaring all the more higher in him because he was the first man, since Adam failed, to defeat the devil's temptations. Since Adam yielded to the devil's temptations, throughout the generations, all peoples of all nations have yielded to the temptations of the devil and forfeited the gift of God's Spirit. Some fell at one wink of the devil, some with one whisper, and some by the devil's constant jabbing. Historically, people have been completely defeated by the devil. All of them lived as losers in life and died in fatalism and defeatism. But uniquely, at the very place where Adam failed, Jesus withstood the devil's temptations and won the victory over the devil. His victory was the first victory over the devil's temptations and was an eternal victory for all mankind.

It is customary for victorious generals to invite people to feast with them. But what did Jesus do? Read verses 15 and 16. On a Sabbath day, he went to Nazareth, where he had been brought up. There, Jesus did not give a material feast, but a heavenly spiritual feast. He taught the Bible. He wanted to share the good news with his home-town people.

Most people cursorily think that Jesus was brought up in the backwoods. They imagine Nazareth as a remote country town. But actually, it was a big town with 20,000 inhabitants. It was situated on the lower slopes of Galilee near the plain of Jezreel. From the hill-tops of Nazareth, there were three great stretches of roads: the road from the south with pilgrims to Jerusalem on it; the great way of the sea, leading from Egypt to Damascus; and Roman military roads crisscrossing these, running north, south, east, and west. These were ancient trade routes, and consequently, in Christ's day, the region was prosperous. Jesus' life and ministry were, from the beginning, world-wide in scale and oriented toward world conquest and evangelization.

Read verses 18 and 19. "The Spirit of the Lord is on me, because he has anointed me to preach good news to the poor. He has sent me to proclaim freedom for the prisoners and recovery of sight for the blind, to proclaim the year of the Lord's favor." These verses from Isaiah were a prediction of the liberation of the people of Israel from slavery in Babylon, and at the same time, they are a summary of Messianic work. These verses are loosely quotation from Isaiah 61:1-2 and 58:6. This quotation tells us about the historical background of the people of Israel. At the time of Isaiah, the people of Israel were in Babylonian captivity. They had no hope, and on them was placed the tremendous burden of hard labor day and night. They were oppressed and broken. But God gave them through Isaiah the hope that they would be liberated. The story of their captivity is an allegorical description of those who are under the bondage of sin. In what respect, then, is Jesus good news to all people? First, Jesus is good news to the poor. Here, "the poor" refers to the spiritually poor. Luke 12:16-23 is a parable of a rich fool. A certain man whose ground produced a good crop became very rich. Then he said to himself, "You have plenty of good things laid up for many years. Take life easy; eat, drink and be merry." But God said to him, "You fool! This very night your life will be demanded from you. Then who will get what you have prepared for yourself?" This man was selfish. He was not mindful of others. He knew that he was of flesh. But he did not know that he was a soul. There are many men like this fool. They are very rich, but they are nothing but like animals and are very poor toward God.

One day, the father of a female doctor approached me during a wedding reception and said, "You know, believing in God is good, but you must also know how to make money." He was very angry at me, thinking that I had made his daughter a fool through Bible study. It was a very joyful occasion, but he was not joyful because of his money problem. Throughout his lifetime, he had worked at a bank and made some money. Two years after that wedding, he retired from the bank at the age of 55. Then, he got a stroke due to his anxiety. He spent all the money he had saved to cure his paralysis. Soon, he died.

Jesus came to this world to save us from the misery of such spiritual poverty. No one is rich without Jesus, even though he may have much money. Jesus came to free us from the misery of poverty. Jesus came to the world to make us rich.

Second, Jesus came to proclaim freedom for the prisoners. Here, "prisoners" does not refer to those in a "government hotel." Prisoners are those shackled by the power of sin. There are many kinds of prisoners: prisoners of passion, prisoners of fear, prisoners of hatred, and prisoners of guilt.

There was a promising young man who was willing to give his life for God's work. So we prayed for him earnestly day and night. But he became a prisoner of lust. He tried hard to get out of the prison of lust with his willpower, but he couldn't; he only looked like a dead man. He finally gave up everything. For the last six years, I have tried to help one of our missionaries in writing Bible messages and in speech. But I found that he did not learn anything. He was a prisoner of pride. There are also many prisoners of fear. They are under the intimidation of the devil with his seven heads and ten horns. The greatest number of prisoners are those who are prisoners of guilt. They are alive, but in reality, they are dying because of the burden of their sins. Though men want unrestricted freedom, they are not free because of their bondage to sin.

Only Jesus, full of the Holy Spirit, can give real freedom to all these prisoners. Jesus is the promised Messiah who came and crushed the devil's head. God delivered the people of Israel through Moses from the hand of King Pharaoh. Likewise, Jesus who defeated the temptations of the devil and who crushed his head through his death and resurrection can deliver us from the hand of the devil. What then should we do if we want to be delivered by him? We must accept Jesus' words. Once Jesus said to the Jews who had believed him, "If you hold to my teachings, you are really my disciples. Then you will know the truth, and the truth will set you free" (Jn 8:31-32). We are not sure if they accepted his word, but Jesus can help anyone who does accept it.

Third, Jesus came for the recovery of sight for the blind. Here, "the blind" are spiritually blind men. Since spectacles and contact lenses have been invented, most people can enjoy 20/20 vision. But there are those who are spiritually blind. Happiness is a stranger to those whose eyes are spiritually blind. Ahab was the king of Northern Israel. As a king, he had everything. But he looked at his neighbor Naboth's vineyard and wanted to get it for himself. When Naboth refused his request, saying, "It is my inheritance from my fathers," Ahab went home, sullen and angry. He did not eat before the eyes of his wife. His wife manipulated the city council and put Naboth to death by stoning, then gave the vineyard to Ahab (1Ki 21:1-16).

God chose the people of Israel and gave them the best blessing, to be shepherds for all peoples of all nations. But they were not happy about God's spiritual blessing at all. They only saw rich people and powerful nations around them and became fatalistic.

In the past, there had never been a story of a man who dared to give sight to a blind man. But the prophecy of Isaiah mentions that the Messiah would give sight to the blind. Jesus came to the world as the Messiah and Jesus gave sight to the blind.

Jesus can also restore spiritually blind men so that they can see many good things in Jesus and the beauty, richness, infinity, and majesty of the spiritual world. Paul, when he was Saul, persecuted the church of God by arresting and killing Christians. He was a spiritually blind man. But Jesus gave him spiritual sight. Later, Paul became a most influential man in Christian history.

Fourth, Jesus came to release the oppressed. The people of Israel were oppressed in their slavery to the Babylonian Empire. They could not claim human rights or religious freedom. They could not claim a national identity or weekend holidays. They were constantly under the whips of slave masters and under the quota of hard labor. Likewise, many people are oppressed by the burden of daily life and by the heavy burden of sin. They are weary and tired. This is an exact picture of a man who is oppressed by the power of sin. But our Lord Jesus came down from heaven to release them from their oppression. Jesus said in Matthew 11:28, "Come to me, all you who are weary and burdened."

In verse 19, "the year of the Lord's favor" was the prediction of the liberation of the Israelites from Babylonian captivity. Likewise, Jesus is the good news of the liberation of mankind from the oppression of the devil.

II. Today this Scripture is fulfilled (20-30)

Read verses 20-22. After proclaiming the good news of salvation, he rolled up the scroll. After giving the scroll back to the attendant, Jesus sat down among his hometown people like a friend. Even after the message had ended, their eyes were fastened on him because they were amazed by his message.

Jesus was happy to see their interest in the word of God and began by saying, "Today this scripture is fulfilled in your hearing." This meant that the promise of God that the Savior of the world would come was fulfilled. Jesus was happy to see that the good news of great joy was delivered. Jesus was happy that they heard it with their own ears. Now, in order to have real freedom and salvation, they had to accept what they heard and hold it in their hearts. They also had to sincerely repent of their sins and be forgiven. Jesus was serious about their bondage to sin.

When Jesus read their minds, to his amazement, instead of listening to his words, they were only sizing him up in order to satisfy their own wishes. So Jesus said to them, "Surely you will quote this proverb to me: 'Physician, heal yourself!'" (23a). What they really wanted to say was, "Perform miracles here in our hometown as we have heard that you did in Capernaum" (23b). They wanted Jesus to perform miracles for them so that they could enjoy power and splendor without doing anything. When Jesus pointed out their inner motive, all at once they became furious. They were filled with human thinking and said, "Isn't he just the poor son of a carpenter?"

Jesus was rejected by his hometown people. From the outset of his gospel ministry, no one accepted his good news. Jesus must have been in pain since his love toward his hometown people was betrayed. But he solved this problem with the word, "No prophet is accepted in his hometown" (24). But Jesus did not give up on them. In spite of themselves, in order to let them accept the word of God and obey, he told them stories of two persons in the Old Testament who obeyed the word of God when they could not obey.

Read verses 25 and 26. There were so many widows in Israel, but none of them were willing to listen to and obey the word of God to feed Elijah the prophet at the time of his seclusion. God was sorry. So God sent Elijah to a very poor Gentile widow. Elijah asked her, "Bring me, please, a piece of bread." She replied, "I don't have any bread—only a handful of flour in a jar and a little oil in a jug. I am gathering a few sticks to make a meal for myself and my son, that we may eat it—and die." To this woman, Elijah's imposition was too great to obey. But anyway, she obeyed him. In fact, she obeyed the word of God (1Ki 17:1-16). Because of this Gentile woman, Elijah the great prophet was succored, and the history of God continued.

Read verse 27. Because of the hot Mediterranean weather, there were many in Israel with leprosy. But in the time of Elisha the prophet, none of them were cleansed—only Naaman the Syrian. He was the commander-in-chief of the armies of Syria. He came to Elisha. But the prophet with the bald head did not even look at him; he said, "Go, wash yourself seven times in the Jordan, and your flesh will be restored and you will be cleansed" (2Ki 5:1-14). Naaman, the commander-in-chief to the king of Syria, was infuriated and humiliated before his entourage. His pride was greatly hurt by the prophet Elisha. Naaman went away angry. But on the way, he curbed his pride, repented of his disobedience to the prophet, and went to the Jordan River to be cleansed.

How did Jesus' hometown people respond to him after he shared these stories? All the people were furious and drove him out of the town. They took him to the brow of the hill on which the town was built in order to throw him down the cliff. They wanted to kill Jesus.

At the outset of his earthly ministry, he was rejected and despised. In light of the reaction of his hometown people, Jesus could not see any hope for the people of Israel to be a priestly nation. But Jesus did not mind the people's rejections so much or become negative. Rather, he saw God's sign of world evangelization through two Gentiles, a poor widow and a man with leprosy, both of whom accepted the word of God and obeyed. Let's see God's signs of mighty work instead of becoming negative when rejected.

Lesson 11

Jesus Laid His Hand on Each One

Luke 4:31-44
Key Verse: 4:40

I. JESUS' TEACHING OF THE WORD WAS HINDERED BY DEMONS (31-37)

1. What did Jesus do on the Sabbath in Capernaum? (31) What was he teaching and why? (2Ti 3:15; Jn 8:14,32) How did the people respond to the word of God? (32; Jn 4:14) What does it mean that his message had authority?

2. What happened that hindered his Bible teaching? What can we learn here about demons? What did Jesus do about the man who hindered his Bible teaching? (Lk 15:4-6)

3. How did the people respond to the authority of God's word? (36-37; Mk 1:27) What are some differences in being under the rule of God's word and under the rule of demons?

II. JESUS HEALS MANY, ONE BY ONE (38-44)

4. How and why did Jesus help Simon's mother-in-law? What did she do after being healed? What can we learn from her? How did Jesus serve the crowd? (40-41) Can you remember several stories in which Jesus helped individuals, one by one?

5. How did Jesus find time to pray? Why was prayer so important to Jesus? (Mk 1:35) Why did it not seem important to others? What does this tell us about Jesus' purpose in coming?

Jesus Laid His Hand on Each One

Luke 4:31-44
Key Verse: 4:40

> *"When the sun was setting, the people brought to Jesus all who had various kinds of sickness, and laying his hands on each one, he healed them."*

I N THIS PASSAGE, WE learn how much Jesus wanted to teach the word of God, since the word of God gives eternal life and hope in the kingdom of God. But it was not easy for Jesus to teach the word of God to the people because they wanted something else other than the word of God. At the initial stage of his messianic ministry, teaching the word of God was not easy because people demanded healing. But we learn how Jesus wanted to teach the word of God to the people as his first priority. In this short passage, we learn that Jesus cares for many people one by one.

I. Jesus' teaching of the word was hindered by the demon (31-37)

Read verse 31. "Then he went down to Capernaum, a town in Galilee, and on the Sabbath began to teach the people." This verse tells us that on the Sabbath, Jesus taught the word of God to the people. The main point of Jesus' messianic ministry was to teach the word of God to the people, because the word of God makes people wise to obtain salvation from their sins and escape from eternal condemnation (2Ti 3:15). Jesus wanted to teach the word of God so that they might come to know God. Jesus wanted to teach the word of God so that they might come to know the truth. Jesus wanted to teach them his word so that they might come to know that he is the Son of God who gives them eternal life.

How did people respond when Jesus taught the word of God in Capernaum, a town in Galilee? These thirsty souls living in the hard world experienced drinking the living water (Jn 4:14). When they heard his word, they did not know what kind of joy this was. They were overwhelmed by mysterious joy. All of them stood up and shouted, "Jesus, Jesus," in amazement at his word. Read verse 32. "They were amazed at his teaching, because his message had authority." When Jesus spoke his message with absolute faith, many believed the word. This scene reminds us of John 6:35 which says, "Then Jesus declared, 'I am the bread of life. He who comes to me will never go hungry, and he who believes in me will never be thirsty.'"

People who received the word were being revived like beautiful flowers. They didn't know why they were happy. But they knew one thing, that the message of Jesus had authority. Here, "authority" is not like the authority of a policeman who stops a car to give a man a ticket. Here, "authority" refers to the power of God which can move sinners' hearts. His message had authority because it revealed God's mercy and his great purpose for all men (4:18-19). At the moment they heard the message of Jesus, they felt free, as free as an eagle flying in the sky over a huge mountain peak. The message of Jesus gave them true freedom and a new life.

Where there was the work of God, there was also the work of a demon. In the synagogue, there was a man who was possessed by a demon, an evil spirit (33). A demon is also called an evil spirit because an evil spirit is Satan's agent. In the past, people thought the world was polluted by demons or evil spirits so that there were no more places people could dwell. The origin of Hellenism began in Greece. The Greeks developed their idea based on a humanistic point of view. They were a theists. Therefore, they did not recognize the existence of spirits of any kind. But Greece was a nation of idol worshipers. When Paul went there, he found many nameless idols and many dirty mythological stories (Ac 17:23).

Japan resembles Greece in many ways. They say that there are 800,000 family idols in Japan. They have money. But they are under the torment of the demon. Modern people think that there is no such thing as a demon or an evil spirit or Satan. Modern people ignore demons because they want to think about every thing from a scientific point of view. But in fact, they are afraid, thinking about spiritual reality. But as we see in this passage, the demon's presence is clearly identifiable and the demon bothered Jesus' ministry of teaching the word of God. To our surprise, there are many people who identify themselves as demon worshipers. However, there are few who identify themselves as Christians.

The demon was very unhappy when people were reviving their spirits and were about to sing a song of praise to God after hearing the word of God. This part reveals the characteristics of the demon. The demon knows God very well. He knew that Jesus is the Holy One of God. The demon also knew that Jesus made him helpless by taking over all his prisoners. So the demon turned out to be a general without soldiers. Lastly, the demon knew that Jesus was in control of everything. Moreover, the demon felt that he would be destroyed by Jesus. So the demon cried out. Read verse 34. "Ha! What do you want with us, Jesus of Nazareth? Have you come to destroy us? I know who you are—the Holy One of God!'" The demon felt Jesus, the Holy One of God, could destroy him.

What did Jesus do with the demons who hindered his delivering the word of life? Look at verse 35a. "'Be quiet!' Jesus said sternly. 'Come out of him!'" The demon could not but obey the Messiah's command. But the demon was cross—tempered. When the demon came out, he threw the man down before them all and came out without injuring him (35b). Whenever we want to teach the word of God, the demon's mischief follows, as a tree is followed by its shadow.

When we think about this event, we see that Jesus was sorry that his teaching the word of God was hindered. But Jesus was happy that he cast out the demon from a man. Jesus thought that one person under the torment of the demon was more important than his ministry of teaching the word of God. This part reminds us of Luke 15:4-6: "Suppose one of you has a hundred sheep and loses one of them. Does he not leave the ninety-nine in the open country and go after the lost sheep until he finds it? And when he finds it, he joyfully puts it on his shoulders and goes home. Then he calls his friends and neighbors together and says, 'Rejoice with me; I have found my lost sheep.'" Jesus cares more for one lost sheep than for 99 sheep already in the pen.

Luke again talks about the people and how they responded to the authority of the word of God. Read verses 36-37. "All the people were amazed and said to each other, 'What is this teaching? With authority and power he gives orders to evil spirits and they come out!' And the news about him spread throughout the surrounding area." People said Jesus' word had authority to cast out demons. Here we learn how they had been tormented by demons. Because of demons, they lost all the joy of life. When we carefully observe people, they suffer much mainly due to demon possession. Those who have no love relationship with God are under the demon's rule. Those who are under the demon's rule suffer from endless conflict and struggle with others over trivial matters. But those who have a love relationship with God can have beautiful love relationships with others. Those who do not have a love relationship with God cannot have a love relationship with others.

According to Mark's Gospel, people said, "What is this? A new teaching—and with authority!" (Mk 1:27b). In reality, Jesus' teaching was the old, old story. But people accepted Jesus' word as a new teaching. As we know well, people like something new all the time. In order to experience something new, many people do many strange things. One man said, "I divorced my wife in order to experience a new wife." But there is nothing new in the world (Ecc 1:9-10). Only when we come to Jesus can we experience new life, new joy, and a new vision.

II. Jesus heals Simon's mother-in-law (38-39)

Jesus left the synagogue and went to the home of Simon (38a). Obviously, Jesus heard the voice of his disciples' growling stomachs. Then Jesus felt it was urgent that he should feed his disciples. There was only one possible place to go—Simon's mother-in-law's house. But it was not easy for Jesus to go to Simon's mother-in-law's house because she was a widow and poor. And she was too sick to ask for help. Probably Simon's mother-in-law had contracted malaria.

Maybe she was sorry that her son-in-law Simon, a veteran fisherman, suddenly gave up his fishing job and began to follow Jesus of Nazareth to catch men. Simon's mother-in-law thought he should catch fish instead of catching men. When Jesus arrived at Simon's mother-in-law's house, the old grandma was in a high fever, sweating and groaning. Nobody knew her sorrow and agony of life. There is a saying which goes, "Only a widow understands a widow's heart." This saying tells us that nobody cared for Simon's mother-in-law and nobody understood Simon's mother-in-law. The situation was desperate. Jesus was not swayed by the situation. Jesus bent over her and rebuked the fever, and it left her (39a). She accepted Jesus as the one who was more than a man.

Jesus was not only compassionate with his hungry disciples, but also very compassionate with a widow suffering from a high fever. This scene reminds us of James 1:27a: "Religion that God our Father accepts as pure and faultless is this: to look after orphans and widows in their distress." In the old Jewish society, widows had no chance to remarry. They were regarded as the most sorrowful. Jesus comforted Peter's mother-in-law and made her happy to the degree that she voluntarily served Jesus and his disciples. Jesus is the God of comfort. In this part, we learn that Jesus cared for one sorrowful widow until she was willing to serve Jesus and his hungry disciples.

III. Jesus heals many, one by one (40-41)

Read verse 40. "When the sun was setting, the people brought to Jesus all who had various kinds of sickness, and laying his hands on each one, he healed them." This part explains that Jesus cares for people one by one, even though crowding people are innumerable. As we know, the heat of the Middle Eastern countries is unbearable. Therefore, most people enjoy a siesta and then begin to work right before the sunset. But Jesus worked all day long during the heat of the day. It was time for Jesus to call it a day. But unexpectedly, as if they had had appointments, the people brought all kinds of sick people to him. Among them were many demon-possessed people, shouting, "You are the Son of God!" (41). Many sick people are too pitiful even to look at. To take care of one or two people even by appointment is not easy. So how troubling it is when we have to help many people all at once.

One pastor visited his Bible student on Sunday to pick him up for worship service. But this Bible student was upset because he came without an appointment, so he called the police. But let's look at what Jesus did. Jesus was very tired. Nevertheless, Jesus was filled with compassion and healed them one by one until no one was left. There are many people in the world. But Jesus does not see them as too many people. Jesus sees each of us as the most precious one, and he cares for each of us one by one.

There are many examples of how Jesus helped the needy personally. There was a woman who was subject to bleeding. She spent all the money she had on doctors. But her sickness was only getting worse. She came to Jesus to touch the back part of his clothes. And she was healed. Jesus was on the way to Jairus' house where Jairus' daughter was about die at any moment. So at this moment, Jesus could not take care of anybody else. But Jesus took care of one smelly woman anyway, being detained from going to the house of Jairus (Lk 8:43-48). Once, Jesus was passing by Nain, and his disciples and a large crowd went along with him. As he approached the town gate, a dead person was carried out. He was the only son of his mother. When Jesus saw her, his heart went out to her and he said, "Don't cry." Then Jesus touched the coffin. The dead man broke the cover of the coffin and began to talk. Jesus gave him back to his mother. Jesus served a widow whose heart was dead (Lk 7:11-15).

We think that there are too many people, so that it is impossible to take care of people one by one. But caring for people one by one is a biblical constant. We must take care of young American students one by one until we can raise 10,000 Bible teachers. At that time, Jesus' core disciples numbered twelve. But they had no shepherd heart. So they were only dozing and yawning and waiting for Jesus to finish healing the sick. But Jesus never finished. We are just like the disciples of Jesus. But we must learn the shepherd heart of Jesus who took care of people one by one.

IV. Jesus prays early in the morning (42-44)

Read verse 42. "At daybreak Jesus went out to a solitary place. The people were looking for him and when they came to where he was, they tried to keep him from leaving them." Jesus worked hard the previous day. The next morning Jesus got up early and went to a solitary place. Luke does not say why Jesus went to a solitary place. But Mark 1:35 says, "Very early in the morning, while it was still dark, Jesus got up, left the house and went off to a solitary place, where he prayed." Jesus had no time to pray because of people's endless demands. But Jesus had time to pray. He woke up early in the morning and went to a solitary place and prayed to God. Through prayer, Jesus listened to God. Through prayer, Jesus renewed the power of God. Through prayer, Jesus renewed his pledge and his faithfulness to God. Most of all, through prayer, Jesus renewed his love relationship with God. Prayer is a measure of faith. When we pray, we must believe that our prayer has been answered (Mk 11:23).

While Jesus was praying, several people came to Jesus to persuade Jesus to stay in the town. Maybe they wanted to build a huge hospital so that Jesus could heal the sick without going around here and there. They did not know the purpose of Jesus' coming to this world. So Jesus said in verse 43, "I must preach the good news of the kingdom of God to the other towns also, because that is why I was sent." In this verse, Jesus made it crystal clear that he should go around and teach the word. May God grant us the shepherd heart of Jesus who takes care of sheep one by one.

Lesson 12

Jesus Calls Simon

Luke 5:1-11
Key Verse: 5:10b

I. EARLY IN THE MORNING (1-3)

1. Describe the scene by the Lake of Gennesaret. What shows the urgency of the crowd? How was Jesus serving them?

2. What were the fishermen doing while the crowd listened? What had they been doing? How do you think Simon felt when Jesus got in his boat and asked him to put out from shore?

II. PUT OUT INTO DEEP WATER (4-7)

3. After Jesus finished speaking with the crowd, what did he tell Simon to do? Think about Jesus' words. What spiritual lesson can we learn from him?

4. Why was Jesus' suggestion difficult for Simon to accept from a human point of view? What was his attitude toward Jesus and his word? What do his actions show about his potential as a disciple of Jesus? As a leader?

5. What were the results of Simon's small act of obedience? What does this teach about Jesus?

III. FROM NOW ON YOU WILL CATCH MEN (8-11)

6. How did Simon react to this miracle? What did he realize about himself? Why? What did he realize about Jesus?

7. What did Jesus tell Simon? Why might Simon have been afraid? What does it mean to catch men? Compare and contrast catching fish and catching men.

8. How did the fishermen respond to Jesus' invitation? Why do you think they could make such a clear decision? What can we learn from their response to Jesus?

9. What can we learn from Jesus and about him through this event?

Jesus Calls Simon

Luke 5:1-11
Key Verse: 5:10b

> "*Then Jesus said to Simon, 'Don't be afraid; from now on you will catch men.'*"

IN THE PREVIOUS CHAPTER, Jesus visited his hometown with the best gift, the word of life. But his hometown people demanded that he perform miracles as he had done in Capernaum so that they might enjoy instant power and glory on earth and drive out the Roman oppressors. When Jesus did not respond to their demands, they rejected him. At the outset of his ministry, Jesus was rejected. But Jesus did not become negative; he saw the vision of world salvation through two Gentiles—a very poor widow and a man sick with leprosy.

In chapter 5, Jesus calls the first disciples: first, Simon the fisherman, and next, Levi the tax collector. What was his purpose in calling them? What kind of people did he call? From this passage, let's think about Jesus who called Simon.

I. Early in the morning (1-3)

Read verse 1. "One day as Jesus was standing by the Lake of Gennesaret…" This lake appears in the gospels many times. It had three names: the Sea of Galilee, the Sea of Tiberias, and the Lake of Gennesaret. It is 3 miles long and 7 miles wide. It lies deep in the earth's surface, 680 feet below sea level. Its low elevation gives it an almost tropical climate, a climate which must have decorated the lovely plain of Gennesaret on the west side of the lake. Nowadays, the area is almost deserted. But this lake remains beautiful forever, for this is the seashore where Jesus called Simon, and it is where the risen Jesus again visited him and cooked a delicious breakfast for him when he was in despair after Jesus' crucifixion.

One day, early in the morning, Jesus was standing by the Lake of Gennesaret, spending the early morning in prayer as was his custom (Mk 1:35). But the lovely calm of the lake was disturbed by a crowd of people. From early in the morning, many people began coming to Jesus. Soon, they formed a multitude, pushing and shoving each other. This multitude of people crowded around Jesus and finally squeezed him out onto the last foot of land on the seashore.

Why did they come to Jesus from early in the morning? Needless to say, people came to him for help. As the gospels narrate, they were mostly the sick and needy. Probably there were those who were distressed or discontented or despairing, as well as all kinds of invalids too pitiful to look at. There must have been men with leprosy secretly following along behind the crowd, wishing that the healing hand of the Messiah would touch them. They were an abandoned mass, and their needs were so urgent that they could not think of anyone but themselves.

But to Luke the historian, regardless of their helplessness, the point is they wanted Jesus' help. Outwardly, they looked wretched and selfish. But they had a deep longing for the Messiah. They needed a good shepherd who would teach them the true way. When we read verse 1b, "… with the people crowding around him and listening to the word of God," we learn that they were enthusiastic about listening to the word of truth. Their coming to Jesus was more than merely an effort to satisfy their own needs. They came to Jesus to see who he was. This is the reason why they came to Jesus from early in the morning.

How easy it is for us to underestimate those whose demands seem endless and whose inner desires seem to be for something disgusting all the time. But like Jesus in this passage, we must see people with a shepherd heart and without prejudice, and see that all people have a yearning for the word of truth. These days, the dominant philosophies among most young people seem to be pragmatism and hedonism. But this is not entirely true. Whatever their lifestyles may be, they long for the word of life in their inner being because they have a soul.

What could Jesus do for such needy people? Practically, Jesus had to meet their immediate needs because they were needy people. But what did Jesus do for them? He taught them the word of God. It seems utterly impractical to teach the word of God to these needy people. In one sense, this is true. But Jesus saw that their real problem was not physical, but spiritual. The problem was that they had no truth in them. Jesus also saw that their real problem was that they had no hope. Jesus taught them the word of God, believing that any kind of person could be healed and recreated if the word of God was planted in his heart. Jesus preached to them the hope of the good news of the kingdom of God, believing that the word of God would open their spiritual eyes to see the hope of the kingdom of God.

The people listening to the word of God became a huge crowd, swelling like the surging waves of the sea, and the intensity of their attention to his words grew more and more. Jesus realized the danger of being pushed into the water. Two boats had been left at the water's edge by the fishermen, who were washing their nets. So Jesus got into one of the boats, the one belonging to Simon.

In that situation, Jesus did not have to say anything to Simon about using his boat. But Jesus humbled himself and asked a favor of Simon, "Would you put out a little from shore?" No doubt Peter said, "Yes, sir." At that moment, Peter's "yes" must have echoed, riding far away on the horizon of the sea. An eternal friendship between them sprang up and took shape. For Peter, it was a moment of divine providence.

II. Put out into deep water (4-7)

Read verse 4. "When he had finished speaking, he said to Simon, 'Put out into deep water, and let down the nets for a catch.'" In the midst of the crowd, Jesus paid close attention to one person, even when he was teaching the large number of people coming to him. Let's see what kind of person Simon was.

First, he was a man who kept trying. Read verse 5a. "Simon answered, 'Master, we've worked hard all night and haven't caught anything.'" He and his co-workers had worked all night and had not caught anything. He was weary, hungry, and tired. But he did not go back home, abandoning everything at the seashore. This might have been just his daily routine as a fisherman. On a day when he had worked all night and had caught nothing, he could have gone home and enjoyed little Peter for a while, eaten and slept, and waited to fix the nets later. But he didn't go back home immediately. Instead, he mended and arranged the nets for a new day's work. He was not lazy; he was a hard-working man. When Jesus said, "Put out into deep water, and let down the nets for a catch," he had no strength to do anything. But he struggled with himself and overcame his tiredness, and in spite of his all-night failure, he tried again. Many a man does not try anymore because of one failure. He lives the rest of his life with a sense of failure. But Peter was not afraid of another failure. Be it failure or success, it did not matter to him. If he could try, that was everything. He was a man of indomitable spirit—a man who kept trying again.

Second, he was a man with a learning mind. Jesus' command, "Put out into deep water," was ridiculous. Night was the time for fishing, and it was now bright morning, unfavorable for fishing. As far as fishing was concerned, Peter was a veteran fisherman and Jesus was a junior carpenter. But Peter did not say, "What do you know about fishing?" Instead, he humbled himself to learn fishing from a carpenter. Although he was an uneducated man, he had a great learning mind. This was the quality that enabled him to grow to be the greatest teacher who has ever lived, one who has been called the teacher of all human beings. A proud mind makes a man mischievous and sarcastic. A proud mind deprives a man of the gift God gives each man—to grow like an oak tree to the fullness of God's image. A learning mind makes a man grow endlessly. A learning mind makes a man wise and generous, after God's own heart. A learning mind gives a man new days and new life every day because to one with a learning mind, everything is new.

Third, he was a man of awesome respect. When Jesus said to him, "Put out into deep water, and let down the nets for a catch," Peter knew that it was ridiculous. But while he was mending his nets, he overheard Jesus' words. And his words overwhelmed this weary fisherman. Even though he acted as if he was indifferent, the word of truth from the mouth of Jesus touched and came into his heart, going deeper and deeper until awesome respect grew in his soul. When Jesus said to him, "Put out into deep water, and let down the nets for a catch," he obeyed by saying, "But because you say so, I will let down the nets." Peter's obedience was remarkable. These days, we see many young people who seem ready to obey. But when someone tells them to do something, they refuse to obey. They seem to be saying, "I want to obey, but because you say so, I don't want to obey, even if I have to suffer much loss." One man looked very obedient outwardly. But he did not listen to anybody while preparing his Genesis lecture. He could not even accept his professors' lectures in school, so he could hardly get good grades or be successful in anything. But through Bible study he was healed. Now he is an influential servant of God because of his obedient mind.

What was the immediate result when Peter obeyed? By obeying Jesus' words, Peter transcended the shallowness of his life, which was splashing in shallow water, and became a man who plunged his life into the deep water of the ocean.

What was the consecutive result when he obeyed? Read verses 6 and 7. "When they had done so, they caught such a large number of fish that their nets began to break. So they signaled their partners in the other boat to come and help them, and they came and filled both boats so full that they began to sink." When Peter obeyed, he could restore his failure. He could experience a great success. He could experience a miracle and abundant, overflowing blessing. He could experience the mighty power of God. Because of his obedience, his companions were also greatly blessed. Peter and his companions were so overjoyed by such a large catch of fish that they could have a shout of joy in their hearts, "What a great catch! What a great success! What bright sunshine!"

III. From now on you will catch men (8-11)

Read verse 8. "When Simon saw this, he fell down at Jesus' knees and said, 'Go away from me, Lord; I am a sinful man!'" In the past, he thought he was a nice man and that he was a little better than John and James. But when he saw God in Jesus, he came to realize that he was a sinful man. Ignoring his prestige among his fellow fishermen, he suddenly knelt down before Jesus and cried out, "Go away from me, Lord; I am a sinful man!" Peter could no longer stand before Jesus.

Why did Peter cry out like this? When Simon saw the great catch of fish, he saw God Almighty in Jesus (8). He saw that at the words of Jesus, even the fish in the sea obeyed. Peter realized that Jesus is Almighty God who rules nature. He also realized that before the presence of God Almighty he was a petty man. He was nothing but a man who worked extremely hard only to solve his petty problem and no more. He was a man of narrow vision, who had seen only his wife and children, the Sea of Galilee and fish, and the market-place. He had no spiritual insight through which he could have seen what God's great purpose for him was and how God was working in history.

We can better understand what Peter meant when he said, "I am a sinful man," in light of Genesis 3:17-19. Struggling, toiling, and perspiring endlessly day after day just to eat is a cursed life and a life of sin. Peter's life was no exception. He was nothing but a descendent of Cain, who wandered on earth in fear and frustration in order to survive. And he was no more than an animal man.

When Peter met Jesus, his spiritual eyes were opened and he could see himself before God. He realized that he was a sinful man. Nobody knows he's a sinner before meeting Jesus personally. Those who do not meet Jesus live a cursed life and die in their sins, only to someday face eternal condemnation.

How did Jesus help him? Read verse 10b. "Don't be afraid; from now on you will catch men."

First, Jesus helped him overcome his fear. Jesus saw his inner man. Inwardly, he was filled with fear. Day and night he wondered, "How long do I have to work in the darkness of the night sea? What am I going to do when I get old?" When he became weary and tired, all kinds of premonitions overpowered him, and he was haunted by terrible nightmares of shipwrecks and of his body being torn to pieces after falling prey to a large group of sharks. Contrary to his big mouth, he was a man of fear, especially when he saw himself before God. He was really a corrupted and selfish man. Jesus said to him quietly, "Don't be afraid." Jesus comforted Peter's crying soul.

Second, Jesus gave him the meaning and purpose of his life. He went on to say, "From now on you will catch men." The gospel writers Matthew and Mark used the words, "fishers of men," for the words, "catch men" (Mt 4:19; Mk 1:17). When Jesus said, "You will catch men," he wanted to give Peter a new life direction, giving him meaning and purpose of life. To Peter, hard work on the sea only to eat and sleep did not give him any meaning. He was merely existing, not living the life of a human being, because he had no purpose and meaning of life. He could not but despair. But when Jesus said to Peter, "You will catch men," he uplifted him from a cursed life to a life of mission. Jesus wanted Peter to participate in his suffering for the glorious work of redemption instead of suffering for the life of sin. God did not create man just to work hard to eat and then die. Up until now, Peter had lived a selfish life only for himself. Thus far, he suffered so much without any meaning and purpose of life. But Jesus helped him to live for the glory of God.

When Jesus said to him, "You will catch men," he elevated Peter from the level of an animal man—a man whose entity is nothing but flesh—to the level of a normal man—a man who is both flesh and soul.

Third, when Jesus said, "You will catch men," he had a great hope for Peter to be changed from an average fisherman to the greatest teacher who ever lived. Jesus saw in him a greatness of God. Jesus also saw in him an unlimited potential, possibility and dynamism to be raised up as a great leader of the world, as well as a great servant of God in the future. Praise Jesus who is the God of hope! Though at that time his name was Simon, a man of sand, Jesus wanted to raise him as Peter, a rock, firm and immovable as a leader. Jesus wanted to raise him to be his top disciple.

How did they respond to the Lord's calling? Verse 11 says, "So they pulled their boats up on shore, left everything and followed him." Peter and his companions found new meaning and purpose of life in Jesus and made a decision of faith to follow him. So they left everything and followed him. It was not easy for them to leave everything behind in order to follow him. But this was possible for them when they met Jesus personally. Overcoming the pain of losing everything, they accepted God's calling. To follow Jesus and become a man of mission is indeed painful, yet it is indeed glorious in the history of God.

Now let's think about why Jesus chose the first disciples in Luke 5. In short, he wanted to raise them as his disciples for the future gospel ministry. Why then did he not choose them from among the intelligentsia, such as the Pharisees or Scribes? They were too sophisticated and self-glory seeking to be raised up to be sacrificial servants of God. They were men of brains, but not men of heart.

How then did Jesus want to educate such ordinary men like Simon, a fisherman, and Levi, a tax collector? He wanted to help them open their spiritual eyes so that they could not only see through men's hearts, but also see the secret of the kingdom of God. Jesus is the God of hope. Jesus loves those who have a learning mind. May Jesus call you personally by saying, "Don't be afraid; from now on you will catch men."

Lesson 13

Authority on Earth to Forgive Sins

Luke 5:12-26
Key Verse: 5:24a

I. JESUS' MERCY ON A MAN WITH LEPROSY (12-16)

1. What is significant about Luke's describing the man as being "covered with leprosy"? What do you know about leprosy? How is it similar to sin?

2. Put yourself in this man's place. How do you think he felt about himself? About others? What was his attitude toward Jesus? Why did he say, "If you are willing?" What did he believe about Jesus?

3. What did Jesus do and say in response to his plea? What is significant about Jesus' touch? How does Jesus show the Messiah's mercy and compassion? What was the resulting change in the man's life?

4. What instructions did Jesus give this healed man? How might these instructions help him solve his problem of re-entering normal society? What does this show about Jesus?

5. Why did the crowds throng to Jesus? Why did Jesus need to withdraw and pray frequently?

II. FRIEND, YOUR SINS ARE FORGIVEN (17-26)

6. Who was present when Jesus was teaching? Why had they come? How did God show his presence and his blessing on Jesus' ministry, in spite of the critics?

7. How did some men try to help their friend? What problems did they have? How did they overcome? What can we learn from them?

8. What did Jesus see in their actions? What were his first words to the paralyzed man? What does this tell us about the man's real problem? About who Jesus is and why he came?

9. Why were the Pharisees so negative toward Jesus' gracious words? In what respect was their thinking about the nature of forgiveness correct?

10. How did Jesus answer them? What did he teach about himself? Why is this important for us?

11. How did the man who was healed react? What was the response of the crowds? What can we learn from them?

Authority on Earth to Forgive Sins

Luke 5:12-26
Key Verse: 5:24a

"But that you may know that the Son of Man has authority on earth to forgive sins ..."

A S WE KNOW, THERE are four gospels, each with a different emphasis. Matthew is theological; Mark is practical; John is spiritual; and Luke is historical. It is interesting to note the words each gospel writer used most frequently. Matthew used the word "fulfill" most frequently. For example, Matthew 21:4 says, "This took place to fulfill what was spoken through the prophet." Mark used the word "immediately." Before conversion, Mark had been a city man, lazy and speculative. So he marveled at Jesus' immediate actions. John used the word "believe." Perhaps John, the philosophical man of thought, had had difficulty believing. But Luke used the word "mercy," acknowledging that Jesus' mercy was extended even to the Gentiles, who the Jews considered subhuman. In today's passage, we learn what sin is like, and how great is the grace of forgiveness of sin by Jesus, the Messiah.

I. Jesus' mercy on a man with leprosy (12-16)

Read verse 12. "While Jesus was in one of the towns, a man came along who was covered with leprosy." The Synoptic Gospels deal with this event as one of the most important events of Jesus' ministry, in order that the mercy of the Messiah might be fully appreciated. Mark described him simply as a "man with leprosy." But Luke the physician described him more carefully as a man who was "covered with leprosy." In the RSV translation, he is a man "full of leprosy." Of all the ills that can afflict the body of a man, leprosy is the most severe. It affects every part of the constitution simultaneously. It brings sores and decay upon the skin, corruption into the blood, and rottenness into the bones. It is both disfiguring and fatal. Lepers were quarantined (Lev 13:46). To prevent accidental contact with others, they were required to cover their faces with rags and to call out, "Unclean, unclean!" (Lev 13:45).

This man might already have lost several fingers, and the rest of them must have looked like a wooden rake. He probably came to Jesus limping, due to the numbness of his legs. He must have looked at Jesus with rotten eyes, oozing with pus, barely supported by their sockets. A leper is so pathetic even to think about that these days people call them "men with leprosy" instead of "lepers."

What could the man with leprosy do in his fateful condition? Probably, as he sat down watching his fingers fall off one by one, he cursed the day of his birth. Each time one fell off, he would go to a sunny place and bury it in the dirt, then return to the place where he could lie down and nurse his sorrow. Who could imagine that this man's psychological disorientation was even worse than his physical distress?

To him, another part of destiny which made him endlessly sorrowful was his loneliness. As sociologists have observed, man is a social animal. This man with leprosy must have had a strong desire to live among men and be accepted and recognized by others. Probably, to refresh himself, he secretly ran out of the quarantine and walked around. He saw many students who were passing by, laughing and gossiping. He saw many lounges and hamburger houses. But he could not go in because he was a man with leprosy. When he became gloomy, the sky also became dark. Then heavy showers poured down. But he had to stand still like a stone under the roof of a house to escape the heavy showers until they passed by. On the way back to his quarantine, he might have decided to commit suicide. But he could not. He was still a human being with the same desires and feelings as others, whose life was brightly shining as the stars in the night sky. He was condemned and isolated because of his leprosy. Nobody could help him. He had nowhere to go. He was a man with leprosy and he was a lonely man.

One day he heard the good news that Jesus welcomed anybody. It was really good news to him. But it was not easy for him to come to Jesus. He was afraid of people stoning him. More than that, he was too deeply withdrawn into himself to go to Jesus. But when he heard the good news of Jesus, he was compelled by the good news and came to Jesus anyway. It was an act of faith. It was the moment of God's mercy on him. Nevertheless, when he came to Jesus, he was so ashamed to stand with his disfigured body before Jesus that he buried his face in his rake-like fingers and humbly knelt down and begged him, "Lord, if you are willing, you can make me clean" (12). He was a man with leprosy. He was a sick man with an incurable disease. But when he came to Jesus, he believed that Jesus could heal him. "Lord, if you are willing, you can make me clean." He was a man of despair because of his leprosy. But when he had faith in the Messiah, he could overcome his despair and have the hope of a new life. Through this we learn how to overcome human dilemmas as well as human despair.

What did Jesus do to this wretched man? Read verse 13a. "Jesus reached out his hand and touched the man." First, before thinking or saying anything, Jesus reached out his hand of mercy and touched the man with leprosy to heal him. Even if this were a fictitious story, it is indeed marvelous. In human history, there was no one who dared to reach out his hand and touch a man with leprosy. Once I saw a student who brushed his teeth and washed his nose again and again. I asked him, "Why are you washing up so many times when you have to prepare for final exams?" He answered, "I happened to pass by a man with leprosy, and his smell still remains on my body." In the past, Jews despised Gentiles, thinking themselves superior to them. They felt unclean even to look at a Gentile. A few decades ago, ordinary Americans disliked Jews. They hated them and segregated them unconditionally because Jews were regarded as aggressive economic animals. At the front desk of many a hotel was a signboard, "No dogs. No Jews." Human integrity is partial and extremely prejudiced and insolent. We like people we like; we abhor people we do not like.

Jesus is quite different from other human beings because he is the Messiah. Through this we learn that the love of the Messiah is universal. He does not segregate. He does not discriminate. He loves all the more the one whose condition is the worst. The hand of the Messiah touched the man's face as a father caresses his lovely child. Jesus not only touched the man with leprosy, he also said, "I am willing" (13). Nobody was willing even to look at him. Jesus was willing to look at him. Jesus was willing to listen to him. Jesus was willing to touch and to cleanse him. Jesus was willing to heal him so that he could become a normal man. Jesus was willing to bring him back to his kingdom. When someone is asked to do some favor and he doesn't like it, he usually says, "Let me see what I can do for you," and then forgets about it because he is unwilling. But Jesus was willing. This is the mercy of the Messiah. We children of God must learn the mercy of the Messiah and must always be willing to serve others.

When Jesus touched him, a miracle happened. Verse 13 says, "And immediately the leprosy left him." His skin became as lovely as that of a baby. When the hand of the Messiah was laid on the man with leprosy, he became a new creation. How much the young people of this generation are in need of the hand of the Messiah!

Read verse 14. Jesus knew what this man's problem was. It was his social life. So Jesus ordered him to go first to the priest and offer sacrifices and get a certificate of recovery so that he might live a normal life in society.

In the Bible, leprosy is frequently compared to the symptoms of sin. Just as leprosy eats into the body, sin eats into the very constitution of the soul. It corrupts man's mind and heart. It decays man's conscience and will. It makes a man dirty. It wounds and bruises and forms pus in one's inner man. But the strange thing is that while leprosy disfigures man's body, it does not cause any pain. The more leprosy spreads in and corrupts one's body, the more he feels no pain. Because of this numbness, many a man commits sin without hesitation saying, "I am okay." But he is not okay. He is in the tragedy of sin. A sin-sick man becomes like a man with leprosy. Some days he feels unclean both in his body and soul. This uncleanness makes a man most miserable. The most miserable person in the world is the one who cannot experience the holiness of God. When a man does something through which he can experience the holiness of God, he is very happy. This is the reason why many a person lives a life of faith, even though it involves sacrifice, suffering, and persecution from ungodly people.

Just as leprosy is contagious and harmful, a sin-sick man is most harmful to others. He corrupts another's beauty and innocence. He corrupts another's conscience and spirit. Such a person should be condemned and ostracized from society. But Jesus welcomed a man with leprosy and stretched out his hand of mercy to him. Anybody who comes to Jesus is healed and recreated. Through Jesus' healing of a man with leprosy, we learn that our God is the God of mercy who causes the sun to rise on the evil and the good and sends rain on the righteous and the unrighteous (Mt 5:45). Our God wants us to be merciful because he is merciful.

II. Friend, your sins are forgiven (17-26)

Read verses 17-19. One day Jesus was teaching the word of God. Some men came carrying a paralytic on a mat. They tried to lay him before Jesus. When they could not get near him because of the crowd, they did not step back. They went up on the roof and made a hole in it, and then lowered the man on his mat through the tiles into the middle of the crowd, right in front of Jesus. Humanly speaking, they were rude and violent because they devastated another person's property. But to Jesus' eyes, they had great compassion for their sick friend. Their compassion made it possible for them to overcome the impossible situation before them. Their compassion united them into one spirit to bring their paralyzed friend to Jesus.

What did Jesus say to them? Read verse 20. "When Jesus saw their faith, he said, 'Friend, your sins are forgiven.'" Jesus was greatly moved by their faith, and he healed the paralytic. In this we learn that to have faith that pleases Jesus, we must meet two conditions. First, we must have absolute faith in Jesus that he can heal a person who is paralyzed both in body and spirit. Second, we need compassion toward our sick friends. How easy it is for us to make use of someone when he is successful, pretending to be his friend, and then abandon him when he is in need of our help. This kind of selfish friendship cannot please our Lord.

Read verse 20 again. "When Jesus saw their faith, he said, 'Friend, your sins are forgiven.'" It is amazing that Jesus identified with the friends who had brought him. Next, Jesus said, "Your sins are forgiven." The Bible teaches us that faith cannot be inherited, nor is forgiveness of sins bestowed by another's merit. The forgiveness of sins and personal salvation is an absolutely personal matter between a man and his God. The paralytic seems to have had no personal faith in Jesus. But his coming to Jesus was everything, even though he came carried by his friends. Anyway, the paralytic came to Jesus for healing, just as he was. Had he refused to come, his friends could not have brought him. Jesus welcomes those who come to him and credits their coming as the expression of their faith.

But the main point of this passage is that Jesus has authority to forgive sins. Jesus saw that the paralyzed man's real problem was not his paralysis, but the sin in him, which paralyzed him and made him powerless. So he said, "Your sins are forgiven," instead of, "Your paralysis is healed."

Many people in history have recognized that sin is the root of all the troubles of mankind. They have tried to do many good things to find a solution to this problem. But their efforts have been in vain. These days, many people want to analyze the sin problem psychologically, or try to ignore it. Those whose consciences are not totally corrupted acknowledge the sin problem, but most of them try to escape from the wages of sin instead of coming to Jesus for healing. These people are clever, but not wise. In history, Jesus is the only one who said, "Your sins are forgiven."

Read verse 21. The Pharisees asked among themselves, "Who can forgive sins but God alone?" They said, "Who is this fellow who speaks blasphemy? Who can forgive sins but God alone?" They were critical because of their jealousy. However, in their criticism, they admitted that no one has ever had the authority to forgive sins. When they were before Jesus, the one who has the authority and power to forgive sins, these religious leaders together put pressure on him in order to hinder his messianic ministry. They did this because their organizational leadership was immensely challenged by Jesus' spiritual authority and the power of the Spirit. So they grumbled to one another, "Who is this fellow who speaks blasphemy?"

Nevertheless, Jesus quietly appealed to their consciences and asked, "Which is easier: to say, 'Your sins are forgiven,' or to say, 'Get up and walk'?" (23). In this verse, Jesus taught them that the forgiveness of sins is more important and fundamental than the healing of a man's paralyzed body, for the flesh is mortal, but the spirit is immortal. They should have acknowledged the importance of the forgiveness of sins. But they did not.

Did Jesus give up on them because of their jealousy? No. Jesus wanted to teach them that he has the authority to forgive man's sins. He said to the paralytic in verse 24b, "I tell you, get up, take your mat and go home." Verse 25 says, "Immediately he stood up in front of them, took what he had been lying on and went home praising God." He could stand on his own two feet. He was no longer a man who depended on others. On the way home, he praised God with a loud voice.

Read verse 26. "Everyone was amazed and gave praise to God. They were filled with awe and said, 'We have seen remarkable things today.'" Why were they filled with awe? As an immediate result, they were filled with awe because they saw with their own eyes that the paralytic was healed and jumping around, praising God with the very mouth he had used to complain and grumble. But the real reason they were filled with awe was that they had seen the mercy of the Messiah. Furthermore, they were filled with awe because they had seen the one who has authority to forgive man's sins. When they saw Jesus who exercised the authority and power to forgive sins, they were filled with awe and shouted with one voice, "We have seen remarkable things today."

This is the reason why Luke lays such stress on the praising of God by both the paralyzed man and the onlookers. To the eyes of the historian Luke, God's love in sending Jesus the Messiah, who has the authority to forgive sins, was truly amazing. It was like the discovery of the medicine to cure cancer. Ever since Adam sinned, people have become helpless because sin makes man very sick. Sin makes man doubt the love of God. Sin fills man with fear and hatred. Sin makes man heartless and violent. Why did Luke lay such stress on the grace of the forgiveness of sins? It is because God sent his one and only Son to solve man's sin problem. God sent him as the Lamb of God to be the atonement sacrifice for sin. The people of Israel had to sacrifice the Passover lamb for their sins. In order to forgive us of our sins, Jesus hung on the tree and was cursed and condemned in our places. Finally, Jesus shed his precious blood on the cross for our sins.

Lesson 14

Jesus Calls a Man, Levi

Luke 5:27-32
Key Verse: 5:27

I. A MAN NAMED LEVI (27a)

1. Who was Levi? How were tax collectors regarded in Israel at that time? Why might a man become a tax collector? In what respect might Levi be called selfish ?

2. What can you guess about his life and his inner conflicts from the context of this event?

II. FOLLOW ME (27b-30)

3. Describe Jesus' calling of Levi. What do you think Jesus meant by his invitation, "Follow me"? What can we learn from Jesus who called such a man as Levi to be a disciple?

4. How did Levi respond? What does his apparent lack of any calculation show about him? What would this decision mean practically in his life?

5. Describe the banquet in Levi's house. What does this event reveal about the change in Levi's life which meeting Jesus brought about?

6. Why did the Pharisees complain to Jesus' disciples? What does this reveal about the Pharisees? How were they different from Jesus?

III. I HAVE COME TO CALL SINNERS TO REPENTANCE (31-32)

7. How did Jesus answer to their criticism? What did he teach about himself? About his mission?

8. How is a disciple of Jesus different from a Pharisee?

Jesus Calls a Man, Levi

Luke 5:27-32
Key Verse: 5:27

> *"After this, Jesus went out and saw a tax collector by the name of Levi sitting at his tax booth. 'Follow me,' Jesus said to him."*

FROM THE OUTSET OF his earthly ministry, Jesus calls his first disciples. In chapter 5, Jesus calls disciples on two occasions. The first is the calling of Simon (5:1-11); the second is the calling of Levi, a tax collector. Jesus was not negative, but positive about the future of the world. He wanted to raise twelve disciples and make them true spiritual leaders and shepherds for the future so that the world salvation plan of God might be fulfilled. In today's passage, Jesus chooses a disciple by the name of Levi. He was a social outcast and a public sinner. It is amazing that Jesus chose such a man to be his disciple.

I. A man named Levi (27a)

Read verse 27. "After this, Jesus went out and saw a tax collector by the name of Levi sitting at his tax booth. 'Follow me,' Jesus said to him." The opening words, "After this," refer to the two events in the preceding chapter: Jesus healed a man with leprosy, saying, "I am willing. Be clean," (5:13), and Jesus healed a paralytic brought by his friends, saying, "Your sins are forgiven" (20). These two events well display the mercy and glory of the Messiah.

After this, Jesus went out, as was his custom, to find a place to pray. On the way, he saw a tax collector named Levi sitting at his tax booth. Jesus did not bypass him as others had. Jesus knocked on the door of the booth, greeted him and met him personally. This was a meeting between God incarnate and a man who was wretched. In this meeting, a wonderful thing happened.

Who was Levi? Levi was a selfish tax collector. Tax collectors were local Jews employed by Roman authority. As a class, the tax collectors were hated by their fellow Jews because they represented the foreign domination of Rome. Their methods were unnecessarily inquisitorial. They often overcharged people and pocketed the surplus. In the Synoptic Gospels, they were bracketed with "sinners." (Mt 9:10; Mk 2:15; Lk 5:30) By the ordinary Jews, they were considered to be renegades who sold their services to the foreign oppressors to make money at the expense of their countrymen.

There are innumerable stories about the cruelty of imperialists when they controlled people in the colonies. Generally, the conqueror attached a great price to signs of submission or respect on the part of the conquered. At the same time, they oppressed the conquered with heavy taxation. At that time, the people of Israel were oppressed and bled dry by the Roman imperialists. Still, they had not compromised, even in the midst of their suffering, and had kept their racial pride and national identity. But this man Levi, for the sake of small benefits, betrayed his suffering people and became a quisling. Levi was a more detestable person than the cruel imperialists. This creature, for his own benefit, became a renegade and a collaborator with the oppressors. He was a most despicable person. He was the one who brought panic to the hearts of his suffering people.

Levi was a slave of money. Most people living under oppressors are crushed and become losers in life. But Levi was strong and able, able enough to withstand any adverse situation. Probably he was able to do many things without exerting much effort. What a pitiful story! Why did this able and promising young person turn out to be such a notorious tax collector? It's hard to understand. But one thing is clear. He was determined to make money. Probably his family was very poor, and he thought that he should make money to support them. Probably he had seen many rich people who lived without much suffering even in the midst of extortion and oppressive tactics under the imperialists. Probably he was confident that he could go back to school after making a lot of money. Therefore, all of his abilities went into making money. When he got a taste for money, greediness grew and grew in his heart uncontrollably. He became a person who used all available means to achieve his aims. If it meant making money, he could turn away from his suffering people without any remorse. For money, he could sell even his national identity, though to a Jew, this was a matter of life and death. He could swallow any kind of humiliation for money. For money, he could give up his dreams, his humanity, and his conscience. The more money he made, the more he hardened his heart and inflicted damage on others to extort money from them.

Was he happy with a lot of money? No! He only became selfish and fearful. Instead of being happy, he was overwhelmed by a sense of shame and guilt. He was overpowered by a sense of punishment which accompanies an act of crime. He was driven by the fear which dogs the heels of an evildoer. He was like Adam who hid himself among the trees after stealing fruit from the forbidden tree (Gen 2:17). He became like Cain who was chased by fear and punishment after he killed his younger brother and ran away from God. Romans 2:8-9 attest to this: "But for those who are self-seeking and who reject the truth and follow evil, there will be wrath and anger. There will be trouble and distress for every human being who does evil."

His selfishness made him spiritually sick, like a man with spiritual leprosy. A man with leprosy is not happy, even if he could wear a three-piece suit. Likewise, Levi was unhappy all the time like a leper rotting away. Man is most happy when the holiness of God grows in him and the image of God is formed increasingly in his inner man. But this man Levi lost the image of God and became like a smelly leper because of his inner corruption.

Moreover, Levi was more miserable than one could say. Whenever he wronged others or acted as an evildoer, an evil spirit came into his heart and began to torment him day and night. Levi lived in a luxurious house, but in reality, he was imprisoned in the dark dungeon of Satan.

God had given Levi much ability to do good as a steward of God's world. But he only used his ability for himself, and he became a man with spiritual leprosy. He is the kind of person who should not exist in human society. He should be condemned and punished and sentenced to life imprisonment.

II. Follow me (27b-30)

What did Jesus do with this man who was so perverted and wretched?

First, Jesus saw him with the hope of God. To the eyes of his fellow Jews, he was a quisling, but to the eyes of Jesus the Messiah, he was a precious child of God—lost and misguided. When Jesus saw him, his heart went out to him, thinking that he was misusing his ability and committing the sins of fraud and extortion due to his spiritual sickness. Jesus knew he was tired and weary. Jesus knew that all the townspeople frowned at him, saying, "What a despicable creature. He really is no good. He is washed up." But Jesus did not think so. Jesus thought that he was a precious child created in the image of God. Not only that, Jesus knew that in him was the greatness of God, with a sense of honor and desires for recognition. As all women of the world want to look beautiful, Levi must have wanted fame and recognition. Jesus knew that he had dreamt of getting a PhD in Ancient Philosophy and a standing ovation at his piano concert. But the reality of his life was that he was a despicable tax collector and a quisling and an outcast. However, Jesus had compassion on him. Jesus wanted for him what he really dreamt of for himself, to be a truly great man. To Jesus' eyes, he was great leadership material. Why? It was because he was able and so selfish! Generally, we can have hope in a man when we see that he is a promising person. But Jesus had hope in Levi even though he was the last person in the world one could have hope in. Levi was able and selfish, ruthless and wretched. But in the eyes of the Messiah, he was a man of heart, a man who could do anything if he was determined to do it. Jesus saw him as leadership material and put hope in him to be raised up to be a great man.

Of course, Jesus knew very well how difficult it would be to help this clever and selfish man to be changed into a normal person and be raised up as a great man. He was the last man Jesus could have hope in. But from the beginning, Jesus had great hope that he would learn how to use his ability in God and be raised up as the best man who ever lived in the world. We can imagine how Levi repeated his old habits and faults endlessly in the course of growing from a tax collector to St. Matthew. But Jesus bore with him in everything and prayed for him. As Jesus hoped and believed, Levi became the best man in God, a man who could write the Sermon on the Mount: "You are the light of the world" (Mt 5:14).

Through this, we learn that Jesus is more than a man. He is really the Messiah and the Savior of the world. We also learn that we must see people like Levi with God's eyes and put hope in them to be changed into great men and women of God. We praise and thank God that there are many like St. Matthew among young students.

But it is not easy to put hope in such people. Dr. Abraham Kim took care of two young college students like his own sons during the time of his PhD studies. I wanted to bring his ministry to fruition. So I invited one to Chicago first, and then the other. The first man began to live with a Korean missionary. After three months, I discovered that he had gained much weight. On the other hand, the missionary lost much weight and looked like a refugee. Later, I found the reason was that he paid very little money, but ate everything, and the missionary paid most of the expenses, but ate little. I wondered how he could be raised up as a sacrificial servant of God. But I prayed that God would enable me to bear with him for five years as Dr. Kim had done. Then I gave him a prayer topic, "Speak a few words while eating." To our surprise, these days he has given his heart to the study of Luke's Gospel and he is beginning to see Jesus. While I was studying this passage, I repented of my negative view of men and the world.

Second, when Jesus said, "Follow me," it was an invitation to come to his home, the heavenly kingdom. Up until this time, people did not associate with Levi, much less invite him to their homes. But Jesus invited him to his home. Levi was condemned and cast out by the people of the world. But Jesus embraced him and welcomed him. In spite of Levi's wretchedness, Jesus saw that he was both body and soul. In Jesus' eyes, he was lost and wandering like the prodigal son, wearing the mark of Cain and longing to come home. In this case, Jesus is like the father who watches his son who is delirious with a serious sickness, and his heart is broken.

When Jesus said, "Follow me," he was knocking at the door of Levi's heart to invite him to the heavenly feast so that he could eat with him and he with him. Jesus' home is the heavenly kingdom where the heavenly feast had been prepared for him. Revelation 3:20 describes this, "Here I am! I stand at the door and knock. If anyone hears my voice and opens the door, I will come in and eat with him, and he with me."

What was Levi's response? Read verse 28. "And Levi got up, left everything and followed him." This verse tells us two things about Levi.

First, Levi shows sincere repentance. There is an episode about St. Augustine. He was an intellectual hedonist. But he met Jesus through Romans 13:13-14: "Let us behave decently, as in the daytime, not in orgies and drunkenness, not in sexual immorality and debauchery, not in dissension and jealousy. Rather, clothe yourselves with the Lord Jesus Christ, and do not think about how to gratify the desires of the sinful nature." After that, when he saw one of his street girlfriends, he turned around and ran away to avoid looking at her. Likewise, Levi turned from his life as a public sinner and became a student of Jesus when he left everything and followed him.

In the past, for the sake of money, Levi lost everything. He lost his country and his people. He lost his humanity and his conscience. But after meeting Jesus, he found himself in Jesus. He also found the Messiah. Nothing was more important than to be in Jesus. In the past, money was everything to him. But now, Jesus was everything to him. In this, we learn that true repentance is self-discovery in Jesus. Levi was lost in sin. But now he was found.

Second, Levi wanted to be one of his disciples. In this way, he acknowledged that the things of the world only made him deceptive and fearful. In other words, he wanted to start a new life in Jesus by learning and obeying his words. How was it possible for him to do so? At the moment he met Jesus, a new desire to live in the world arose in his heart. Especially at the moment when Jesus accepted him as a human being with respect and love and hope, his heart was moved with tears of thanksgiving. So he left everything and followed him.

Levi could restore his joy of life. In the past, when he lived for money, he had no joy of life. He had no appetite to eat, even though he had everything. But since he met Jesus, joy began to overflow in his heart and his stomach began to growl for food. Why? Because he met the Messiah. Read verses 29 and 30. He was so joyful that he held a great banquet for Jesus at his house. He invited a large crowd of tax collectors and others to eat with them. This time, the penny-pincher spared no expense. He bought lots of food and invited all his tax collector friends and enjoyed having fellowship with them over a meal. This eating scene draws a sharp contrast between the selfish life and the life in Jesus. The mood of the banquet was carefree and exuberant. The disciples, Peter, James, and John, were there, eating with much gusto and with huge appetites, as were Levi's fellow tax collectors. They were sinners. But it was the heavenly kingdom because Jesus was there with them.

Read verse 30. The Pharisees and the teachers of the law complained to Jesus' disciples, "Why do you eat and drink with tax collectors and 'sinners'?" The Pharisees were religious leaders of the times. They thought they were righteous because they kept all kinds of ritual, and that the tax collectors were sinners because they could not practice religious rituals. Jesus and his disciples ate together with tax collectors. Therefore, Jesus and his disciples were sinners. They condemned Jesus and his disciples as sinners.

III. I have come to call sinners to repentance (31-32)

Jesus heard their complaining and knew that they did not have God's mercy in their hearts. So he said to them in verses 31 and 32, "It is not the healthy who need a doctor, but the sick. I have not come to call the righteous, but sinners to repentance." Jesus' reply reveals the nature and purpose of his mission. The nature of his mission is to heal the sick with the love of God. Romans 3:23 says, "For all have sinned and fall short of the glory of God." All men are sinners. Each person is suffering from his kind of sin-sickness. Each person must come to Jesus to be healed, and each person must have a confession of faith showing what kind of sinner he was and how he was healed.

The purpose of Jesus' mission was to call sinners to repentance with the words of God. Jesus came to preach the good news of the kingdom of God so that people might repent of their sins and come to God. Those who think that this earth is the end of everything soon despair and do all manners of evil things to enjoy themselves until they die. But those who put hope in the kingdom of God can be faithful to Jesus to the end.

Jesus' reply is also a rebuke of the Pharisees. As Romans 3:10 says, "There is no one righteous, not even one." But the Pharisees were self-righteous and condemned others.

In this passage, in Jesus' eyes, selfish people are leadership material. We also learn that discipleship training is most important in this dark generation.

Lesson 15

Jesus Chose the Twelve

Luke 5:33-6:16
Key Verse: 6:13

I. NEW WINE INTO NEW WINESKINS (5:33-39)

1. Read 5:33-39. How were Jesus' disciples different from the disciples of the Pharisees? Why did the disciples of the Pharisees criticize Jesus' disciples? Why did Jesus compare himself to the bridegroom? And why can't the disciples fast or weep while they are with the bridegroom? To what did Jesus compare the feast at Levi's house? (Lk 15:6-7)

2. Why can't an old patch be put to a new garment? Why can't new wine be put into old wineskins? Jesus said, "New wine must be poured into new wineskins." How would you interpret this verse?

II. THE SON OF MAN IS LORD OF THE SABBATH (6:1-5)

3. Why did Jesus' disciples pick grain and eat the kernels? What does this suggest about Jesus' disciples? (What kind of men were they?)

4. Why did the Pharisees rebuke them? (cf Ex 20:8-10)

5. What did Jesus teach them from David's example? (1Sa 21:1-6; Lev 24:9) How is Jesus' view of the law different from that of the Pharisees? What can we learn from Jesus about the spirit of the law?

6. What do Jesus' words, "The Son of Man is Lord of the Sabbath," mean?

III. JESUS RESTORES A MAN'S SHRIVELED HAND (6-11)

7. What problem did Jesus encounter in the synagogue on another Sabbath? Think about the agony of the man with the shriveled right hand.

8. How did the Pharisees see this man? How did they try to use him? Why were they so opposed to Jesus? How was Jesus' view of the man different from that of the Pharisees?

9. How did Jesus respond to the challenge to his Messianic ministry? Why did he not heal the man privately on some other day? What did he teach the religious leaders about good and evil and the use of the Sabbath?

10. What did it cost Jesus to help this one poor, useless man? What do we learn from Jesus?

IV. JESUS CHOSE THE TWELVE (12-16)

11. After the conflict in the synagogue, what did Jesus do? Why? What might he have prayed about?

12. Why did he choose twelve of his disciples and designate them apostles right from the beginning of his ministry? What does this suggest about Jesus' purpose in choosing them?

13. Who were the men he chose? What kind of men were they? What do you think his criteria were for selecting those he would train?

Jesus Chose the Twelve

Luke 5:33-6:16
Key Verse: 6:13

> *"When morning came, he called his disciples to him and chose twelve of them, whom he also designated apostles."*

THE FIRST FIVE CHAPTERS of Luke's Gospel mention mainly how the birth of Jesus came about and how he began his earthly messianic ministry. At the time the Savior of the world was born, the world was dark—so dark that it was tangible. In this dark world, the people of Israel suffered unbearably under the Roman imperialists. What was worse, they suffered all the more when religious leaders wielded over them ecclesiastic power and authority by lording it over them both mentally and spiritually.

In today's passage, Jesus, notwithstanding the dark world situation, did not despair. Jesus prayed and chose twelve disciples for the future gospel ministry so that the world salvation plan of God might be fulfilled through them.

I. New wine into new wineskins (5:33-39)

The teachers of the law criticized Jesus' disciples: "John's disciples often fast and pray, and so do the disciples of the Pharisees, but yours go on eating and drinking" (33). Jesus' disciples were not used to ritualism. Especially, Jesus' disciples might have been very reluctant in keeping fasting rituals. Originally, the practice of fasting began with a sincere longing for the holiness of God. It began as a way of true repentance. But in Jesus' time, fasting was hypocritical. They say that modern hypocrites get up late, around 12:30 p.m., and then are idle until sunset. After sunset, they eat a $300 dinner all night. Likewise, the religious leaders of Jesus' time were just like contemporary hypocrites. Those hypocrites came to Jesus and said, "How come your disciples don't fast, but eat so much?"

How did Jesus answer? Look at verse 34. "Jesus answered, 'Can you make the guests of the bridegroom fast while he is with them?'" Jesus was implying that the disciples' mood should be as joyful as a wedding feast. Jesus compared his disciples to the guests of the bridegroom at a wedding feast and compared himself to the bridegroom. This very verse implies that Jesus is the Messiah who restores the joy of a wedding, which was established by God in the Garden of Eden as the supreme happiness of mankind. To our sorrow, this happiness of a wedding was ruined by one man's disobedience to the holy command of God (Gen 2:15-17). As long as they were with Jesus, the Messiah, they could eat a lot and really rejoice to their hearts' content. It is amazing that Jesus compared the banquets of sinners to the kingdom of God (Lk 15:7).

Jesus is our eternal Bridegroom. We have true happiness in Jesus. The Pharisees were leaders of their people, but they did not shepherd God's flock of sheep under their care. They were very unhappy because Jesus' people were very happy. So Jesus said to them, "Can you make the guests of the bridegroom fast while he is with them?" (34). In this verse, Jesus implies that as long as they are with the Messiah, it is not necessary for them to be sorrowful and fast out of depression. "But the time will come when the bridegroom will be taken from them; in those days they will fast" (35). This verse suggests that after Jesus' crucifixion and burial, the entire flock of God would fast out of unbearable sorrow. Jesus was very sorry that the Pharisees, who were the shepherds of his people, had no shepherd heart or God's mission. Jesus came to the conclusion that they were useless, like old wineskins.

Jesus told them a parable. Read verse 36. "No one tears a patch from a new garment and sews it on an old one. If he does, he will have torn the new garment, and the patch from the new will not match the old." The meaning of this verse is very simple. For example, there was an old woman who had a fixed materialistic idea. She had piled up two barns with old newspapers. But she had no idea to throw them away. In this parable, Jesus is teaching them that the Pharisees' idea was so fixed in legalism that they were useless, like moth-eaten cloth. If a man sews a moth-eaten piece of cloth on a new piece of cloth, both become useless. What is worse, they do not match. Simply speaking, the Pharisees looked good, but they were as useless as moth-eaten cloth. Still, the Pharisees did not understand Jesus' words. So Jesus told them another parable. Look at verse 37. "And no one pours new wine into old wineskins. If he does, the new wine will burst the skins, the wine will run out and the wineskins will be ruined." The Pharisees' spiritual condition was as weak as that of worm-eaten wineskins which have no capacity to contain explosive new wine. Why were they like old wineskins? There were many reasons. They were proud, lazy, habitual, and selfish.

But when we carefully study the Bible, the main problem was their self-righteousness.

This is the reason Jesus chose uneducated disciples. Despite their shortcomings, they were humble—humble enough to learn from Jesus. In addition, the disciples were young and elastic and dynamic, like new wineskins, in achieving success as well as in making many mistakes. Jesus did not hesitate to conclude: "New wine must be poured into new wineskins" (38). Many leaders of mainline churches say, "The mainline church leaders are very corrupted." We must remember Jesus' words, "new wine into new wineskins." Jesus warns us in verse 39 not to be corrupted like old wineskin Christians.

II. The Son of Man is Lord of the Sabbath (6:1-5)

Read verse 6:1. "One Sabbath Jesus was going through the grainfields, and his disciples began to pick some heads of grain, rub them in their hands and eat the kernels." In the previous chapter, we saw how the disciples enjoyed eating the delicious food prepared by the tax collector Levi. Soon, the disciples were hungry again, just as hungry as if they had skipped several meals. As soon as they saw ripened heads of grain in the field, they began to pluck them, rub them in their hands, put them in their mouths, and swallow them.

By this time, the bigoted Jewish leaders who opposed Jesus' ministry, in their anger and jealousy, had reached the point of a head-on collision with Jesus. They were jealous of Jesus' Messianic ministry through which he demonstrated power and authority from above. His power fascinated people in every strata of society. The religious leaders were looking for some faults and mistakes in Jesus' people to accuse them of their guilt. The Pharisees saw them when they were eating up a corner of the field. They snapped their fingers and said, "Why are you doing what is unlawful on the Sabbath" (2). The Pharisees charged them with violating the Sabbath law by working on the Sabbath. They regarded plucking corn as working. So the disciples were guilty of many sins. By plucking corn on the Sabbath, they were guilty of reaping; by rubbing it in their hands, of threshing; and by flinging away the husks, of winnowing.

Jesus knew that the Pharisees were critical because they did not know the true meaning of the Sabbath. So Jesus said to them in verses 3 and 4, "Have you never read what David did when he and his companions were hungry? He entered the house of God, and taking the consecrated bread, he ate what is lawful only for priests to eat. And he also gave some to his companions." Jesus told them about David, referring to the incident recorded in 1 Samuel 21:1-6. In this story, Jesus tells us three things.

First, the Sabbath is made for man, not for the Sabbath itself. When God made the Sabbath hallow on the seventh day of creation, he wanted his people to come to him and take rest in him apart from the daily burdens of life. This included animals also. David and his comrades, while they were running for their lives, were very hungry. So they entered the house of God and ate and rested (Lev 24:9). In this case, David, when he was in need, ignored the ritual law and ate consecrated bread which was lawful only for priests to eat. But he did not violate the true meaning of the Sabbath. Sabbath means rest. David and his comrades came to God's house and took rest when they were in need.

Second, laws must be practiced with the spirit of the law. Laws themselves are good. Man is not made for the law; the law is made for man. For example, the foundation of all laws is the Ten Commandments, and the core of the Ten Commandments is love—love for God and love for others. Moreover, the law is not to condemn people, but to encourage them to live according to God's law. Therefore, if the law is practiced without the spirit of the law, there is a danger of damaging people instead of helping them.

See how Jesus manifests the spirit of the law! When Jesus saw that his disciples were accused of violating the Sabbath law, he immediately defended their cause, though he knew that they had made another mistake. By doing this, Jesus did not abolish the law of the Sabbath, but he demonstrated how to practice the law with the spirit of the law. Psalm 68:5 attests to this well: "A father to the fatherless, a defender of widows, is God in his holy dwelling."

The Pharisees' failure was that they practiced the law without mercy, obliterating the spirit of the law. When they practiced the law without the spirit of the law, they became the most abominable people before God's eyes. In 1917, when the communist revolutionaries were marching into Moscow, the priests were fiercely arguing over what kind of finger motions to use when giving the benediction. They did not care at all about the poor situation of the populace in their suffering. Finally, they were devoured by the communists. Jesus rebuked the religious leaders in Matthew 23:23, "Woe to you, teachers of the law and Pharisees, you hypocrites! You give a tenth of your spices—mint, dill and cumin. But you have neglected the more important matters of the law—justice, mercy and faithfulness."

Third, the Son of Man is Lord of the Sabbath. Here the phrase, "Son of Man," in verse 5 invariably refers to Jesus. This phrase, however, explains Jesus' Messianic function. In other words, if David could override the law without blame to feed himself and his comrades, how much more can the Son of David, the Messiah, do so? In verse 5, when Jesus said, "The Son of Man is Lord of the Sabbath," he meant that he is the Son of God who is ready to save them by defending the cause of the weak.

We praise and thank God that he did not criticize or condemn us by the standard of his law, but sent his one and only Son to defend our cause. Thank and praise God that he is our advocate, and that he bore our iniquities and transgressions. In this way, God saved us instead of destroying us.

III. Jesus restored a man with a shriveled hand (6-11)

Let's think about another event which happened on another Sabbath. As usual, Jesus went into the synagogue and was teaching, and a man was there whose right hand was shriveled. Uniquely, Luke the physician mentioned that it was his right hand that was shriveled. This man had a serious life problem because his right hand was shriveled. He could not get a proper job. He could not dream of doing a piano concert. He must have formed a habit of keeping his shriveled hand hidden behind his back or in his pocket. Because of his shriveled hand, his heart must have shriveled also. This unimportant man, in deep resignation of life, was sitting quietly in a corner seat of the synagogue.

As soon as Jesus saw the man whose right hand was shriveled, he was ready to help him, even though it was a Sabbath day. On the other hand, when the Pharisees saw the man with a shriveled hand, they immediately decided to use him as bait. They used the weak to accomplish their purpose to trap Jesus. The Pharisees also made use of the law to trap Jesus.

What could Jesus do in this situation? Read verse 8. Jesus knew the evilness of their hearts. To Jesus, this was a great moment of testing. As the Messiah, he was at a crossroad where he had to decide whether to help the helpless or not. To heal or not to heal was the question. But Jesus did not give up the man with the shriveled hand. He was determined to help him. So he said, "Get up and stand in front of everyone." The man got up and stood there.

Jesus was also determined to challenge those corrupted religious leaders. He said in verse 9, "I ask you, which is lawful on the Sabbath: to do good or to do evil, to save life or to destroy it?" In this verse, Jesus appealed to their conscience. But their consciences were too corrupted to respond to Jesus' appeal. They were so evil that they had no discernment between good and evil. To them, something beneficial was good and something that hurt their pride was evil. They were malicious and their intentions were fiendish. Nevertheless, Jesus taught them they should have clear conscience and discernment to see good and evil.

What did Jesus do next? Read verse 10. "He looked around at them all, and then said to the man, 'Stretch out your hand.' He did so, and his hand was completely restored." Jesus restored his hand at the cost of his own life. Jesus did not think about his future ministry or his own life. He cared much about this poor man with the shriveled hand. In this way, he revealed the glory and mercy of the Messiah. To do evil is easy. On the other hand, to do good involves great sacrifice. Here we learn that without suffering loss, we cannot really help the flock of God.

IV. Jesus chose the Twelve (12-16)

Read verse 12. "One of those days Jesus went out to a mountainside to pray, and spent the night praying to God." Jesus had ample reason to despair over fulfilling the work of world salvation. His enemies were increasing. One day they would kill him. What could he do? He prayed. He prayed all night. Through prayer, he decided to choose the twelve among many disciples and train them as future leaders and shepherds of the world.

Read verses 13-16. At daybreak Jesus called his disciples. What was the purpose of choosing the Twelve? Verse 13 says two things. First, Jesus wanted to make them his disciples. A disciple is a learner or a student. In the early centuries, students studied spirit and principles more than subjects. They studied under a teacher both the subject and the teacher himself. Therefore, a disciple of Jesus is a learner of Jesus. Second, Jesus designated these twelve disciples as apostles. The term "apostle" is derived from the Greek verb "to send," and means, "a messenger." When Jesus chose the Twelve, he had already appointed them as the apostles, the true leaders of the whole world.

What kind of people were they? In most ways, they were ordinary men. Jesus preferred to work, then as now, through perfectly ordinary people. Luke recorded their names two by two.

Peter and Andrew. Read verse 14. "Simon (whom he named Peter), his brother Andrew." Peter is the first in the list in all four Gospels. Peter was a hard-working man. Peter, even though he had failed fishing the night before, was mending the nets while a large crowd of people were pushing and shoving one another to hear the word of Jesus. In the Gospel narratives, Peter is known as a man with a big mouth. Once Peter insisted emphatically, "Even if I have to die with you, I will never disown you" (Mk 14:31a). But he disowned Jesus three times. Even if he disowned Jesus, we cannot deny the fact that he opened his mouth and said, "I will never disown you." Peter was impetuous (Jn 21:7). In spite of all this, Peter was a man of heart. Jesus met him first on the lakeshore of Galilee and called him by saying, "From now on you will catch men" (5:10). He did not calculate. From his heart, he left everything and followed him.

Andrew led Peter to Jesus. He seems to be an older brother to Peter. Andrew was not included in the top three disciples. In many ways, he appears to be vague. But Andrew was a man of possibility. Once, Jesus wanted to feed 5,000 people. Nobody dared try to feed five thousand people out of nothing. But Andrew looked around, then took five loaves and two fish away from a little boy, and brought them to Jesus and made a big smile.

James and John were the sons of Zebedee. They were passionate and ambitious young men. If we say that Peter was like a lion, James and John were like venomous snakes hidden in the grass, waiting for the chance to bite. They were called, "Sons of Thunder" (Mk 3:17). Once Jesus and his disciples wanted to stay overnight in a Samaritan village, but the people there did not accept them. When James and John saw this, they asked, "Lord, do you want us to call down fire from heaven to destroy them?" (Lk 9:54) They wanted to push Peter aside and occupy the right and left seats next to Jesus when the Messianic kingdom was established (Mk 10:35-38).

Philip and Bartholomew. Bartholomew was probably the same person as Nathanael in John 1:45. He was speculative and a daydreamer. Philip was a brilliant person who could figure out at a glance how much it would cost to feed five thousand people (Jn 6:7), but he was negative due to his calculating habit.

Matthew and Thomas. Matthew was a tax collector. He was a man of determination. When he was determined to make money, he didn't care about anything, if he only made money. When Jesus called him by saying, "Follow me," he left everything and followed

Jesus (5:27-28). Thomas was a man of doubt (Jn 20:27-29).

James II and Simon II. James was the son of Alphaeus, and Simon was called the Zealot. At that time, James was a most popular name. This is another James among the Twelve, and he was possibly the same person as Thaddaeus, whose presence or absence seemed to have made no difference.

Judas and Judas. Judas was either the brother or son of James. The other disciple was Judas Iscariot, who became a traitor.

These men have many similarities. They were all passionate young men. They were all men. They were eager to eat and slow to understand. They were full of earthly desires. But one thing is clear. With the exception of Judas Iscariot, we can say that they were all men of heart.

On the other hand, each one was quite different. It is obvious that Jesus wanted to raise each of them as the shepherd of a group of people like himself. For example, he wanted to raise Peter as a shepherd for people who have big mouths; Andrew as a shepherd for people who look vague and for whom nothing is possible, and nothing is impossible. In this case, Jesus is like a skilled woodworker who can use all kinds of wood whether it is big or small, straight or curved. In Jesus, everyone can grow up to be generals for the spiritual battle.

There were twelve of them in total, just like the twelve tribes of Israel. They say that the number twelve is a multiple of the perfect heavenly number, three—representing the Father, Son, and Holy Spirit—and the perfect earthy number, four—representing north, south, east, and west. Figuratively speaking, the number twelve represents the whole world. Obviously, Jesus had in mind to save the whole world through the Twelve. Through Jesus who chose the Twelve, we learn three things.

First, the faith of Jesus. The Twelve that Jesus chose were like the "Dirty Dozen" in the movie by that name. They were unruly and full of earthly desires. But Jesus believed that they would all be raised up to be spiritual generals, leaders of all people of all nations, men who would conquer the whole world with the gospel of Jesus.

Second, the hope of Jesus. The world was full of darkness and evil. The world was noisy with the stomping of demons. In this situation, no one could dare do anything good. But Jesus did not despair. He put hope in the Twelve and prayed for them.

Third, the obedience of Jesus to the will of God for world salvation. When we deeply meditate on why Jesus chose the Twelve, we realize that it was not merely to suffer in the course of raising them to be apostles. It was to obey the will of God for the salvation of the whole world. His obedience was absolute, so absolute that there was no despair in him. In obedience to the will of God, he chose the Twelve. He obeyed even to death, death on the cross.

Lesson 16

The Blessed Ones

Luke 6:17-49
Key Verse: 6:20

I. BLESSED PEOPLE (17-26)

1. Where had this large crowd of people who gathered around Jesus come from? Why had they come? Of whom did this crowd consist? To whom did Jesus address this message?

2. From Jesus' point of view, who are the blessed people? How is his viewpoint different from that of most people? What are the rewards of the blessed people?

3. From Jesus' point of view, who are the miserable people and why are they miserable? How is this different from the viewpoint of worldly people?

II. LOVE YOUR ENEMIES (27-36)

4. How does Jesus define "enemies"? How should a disciple show love practically in each encounter with one who has acted like an enemy?

5. What kind of reward should a disciple expect from acting in love toward enemies? Why is it important to know this?

III. DO NOT JUDGE OTHERS (37-42)

6. What are the practical reasons given by Jesus why disciples should not judge others?

7. What is the main point of Jesus' discipleship training?

8. Why are we not qualified to judge others? What must we do in order to have sufficient spiritual discernment to help others? (What does it mean to take a plank out of one's eye?)

IV. A WISE MAN AND A FOOLISH MAN (43-49)

9. What is necessary if a disciple's life is to bear the fruit which Jesus demands? (43-45)

10. What does Jesus' parable about the wise and foolish builders teach his disciples about how to grow spiritually? What must be a disciple's attitude toward Jesus' words (toward the Bible)?

The Blessed Ones

Luke 6:17-49
Key Verse: 6:20

"Looking at his disciples, he said: 'Blessed are you who are poor, for yours is the kingdom of God.'"

THE WORLD WAS DARK. There was no hope in the world. But there was hope in Jesus. He prayed and chose the Twelve in hopes of raising them as apostles of light. Now, in this passage, Jesus teaches them Christian ethics, appropriate for the children of God and unique in character, both in its motives and standards. His teachings are very ordinary, and at the same time, extraordinary. Only those who love Jesus can accept his teachings.

I. Blessed people (17-26)

In verses 17-19, Luke tries to picture the magnificent view of the inauguration of his disciples. It was on a level place on the mid-slope of a mountain. There was a large crowd of disciple candidates. There were a great number of people who came from all over Palestine, most of whom had been told of the healing power of Jesus or had been touched by the Messiah's love. With this backdrop, Jesus called the twelve disciples out to the front of the crowd. Looking at the disciples, Jesus began to deliver his inaugural speech. The gist of his speech was "You are the blessed ones."

Read verses 20-22. The chosen Twelve whom Jesus called blessed looked wretched to the world because they looked unemployed. The people Jesus called blessed, the world would call wretched. For example, Jesus said, "Blessed are the poor," and "Woe to the rich"! Worldly people would ridicule Jesus and say he has no sense. The people Jesus called blessed are inimical to worldly values. However, they are blessed for several reasons. First, they have a goal and destination of life: the kingdom of God. Second, they have a clear meaning and purpose of life: to live for the glory of God. They are blessed because they are the chosen Twelve. They have the privilege of suffering for Jesus' name's sake. Third, they are blessed because they would become historic people who would start a new era of world history and take over the unfinished task of Jesus Christ. Despite their unceasing struggles and conflicts, they were really blessed, as history proves. For example, the names of Peter, John, and James, who were all former fishermen, might have passed away like clouds which appear for a second and disappear in volatility, but instead they are known to Christians throughout history through the gospel records. At present in the twentieth century, 1,433,000 Christians are familiar with their names. Their names will forever be unforgettable as the ones who were used by God preciously at the beginning of a new history.

Read verses 20-23. These verses teach us more specifically why they are blessed ones. These verses tell us that they are the blessed ones mainly because they do not live their lives for their own selfish purposes, but live sacrificial lives of faith for the glory of God. They undergo all the sufferings, joys, sorrows, and agonies of poor life in and with Jesus. They have the privilege of living poor lives, giving up the enjoyment of worldly wealth for his name's sake. They have the privilege of crying many tears, not for their own discontented hearts, but for his name's sake (21). They are considered outcasts of society simply because they belong to Jesus and they are not like others. They are hated, excluded, and rejected, and their names are regarded as evil, simply because they love Jesus from their hearts (22). It doesn't matter how others think of them. Jesus says they are the blessed ones.

Besides, they are blessed because they will inherit the kingdom of God (20). They will be comforted and encouraged by Jesus while on earth. They are blessed because great will be their reward. Verse 23a says, "Rejoice in that day and leap for joy, because great is your reward in heaven." What could be their reward in heaven? When they have fought the good fight as loyal soldiers of Christ, accomplishing many feats of arms, and when they have kept the faith and have finished the race of physical life and go through the pearly gates of the heavenly kingdom with the entourage of heavenly hosts, Jesus the King, slain for our sins, will welcome each one of them, saying, "Well done, my faithful servant." It is the greatest reward for each Christian. We Christians do not want worldly recognition, but we wholeheartedly want to get recognition from our King Jesus because he is our King and Savior and because we love and respect him so much. We must rejoice and leap for joy because on the day when Jesus our King will crown us, he will say, "Well done, my faithful servant."

Read verses 24-26. These verses tell us about the other kinds of people. Theirs are the woes. They have already lived enough for their own pleasure and comfort. So what is left for them are woes. They have already talked enough about delicious food and eaten enough food for their physical pleasure (25). They have enjoyed laughing and gossiping at parties, scorning the children of God. They have already tried hard to show themselves off and gotten the recognition of others by stealing God's glory insidiously for themselves. They themselves have been spoken well of, instead of glorifying God (26). Theirs are the woes. They will go hungry, and they will mourn and weep, for there is no room service in hell (25). They were not mindful of God's flock, but they only lived to gratify their own sinful desires and for their own self-glory. They did not live up to their purpose of life as human beings. They will gnash their teeth on that day in the furnace of the fiery lake of burning sulfur.

This teaches us that there are two kinds of people. One kind sets their hearts on and bends their energies to obtaining the things which the world values, and they obtain them. They take the easy way and the way which yields immediate pleasure and profit. They seem to be getting everything they want and losing nothing. But in the end, they hold nothing in their hands. They only stored up the wrath of God upon their heads. The other kind gives all their hearts to be utterly loyal to God and faithful to Christ. And they run into all kinds of trouble (2Co 4:17). By worldly standards they look foolish because they seem to be losing everything. But they will have joy eternal and will lose nothing. Great is their reward in heaven. They are the blessed ones before God.

Nonetheless, Jesus knew that they would confront many hardships and difficulties as his disciples. But he did not say, "You will be in for trouble." There is no deviation in Jesus. He said that the life of a disciple is really a blessed one and the disciples are blessed ones. We must have assurance that we are the most blessed people in the world.

II. Love your enemies (27-36)

Jesus just taught them the state of beatitude, the blessedness of being his disciples, and now teaches them what the blessed life is. Read verses 28-31. Jesus' teaching about love is extraordinary. When he said, "Love your enemies," his teachings are against our human nature and beyond our human ability. How can we love our enemies? It is too hard for people even to love their wives, as the rising divorce rate attests. It seems impossible to love our enemies. Perhaps the Old Testament teaching, an eye for an eye and a tooth for a tooth (Ex 21:24), seems fairer to us. In fact, we think more cruelly than this and say that it should be two eyes for one eye and two teeth for one tooth. How can we love our enemies who hate us and mistreat us and strike us on our cheeks? It seems impossible.

So, how can we love our enemies? That's a good question. But this is Jesus' command. This is the way to become blessed in the sight of God. To love our enemies is not easy. It is a great spiritual battle. In order to love our enemies, we must die to our sinful nature and we must be clothed with Jesus who died for the sin of the world. If we have the attitude to love our enemies, then we can be called sons of the Most High. When we have the right attitude before God in loving enemies, the Most High God will recognize us as his children.

Read verses 32-34. These verses tell us that our love receives no credit from God if we love only those who love us and are dear to us. Again, our generosity receives no credit from God if we lend only to those from whom we can expect payment. Through these verses, we learn that it is impossible to love our enemies with a sinner's love (33-34). We must learn how to love our enemies with the love of God which is unconditional.

Read verse 35. "But love your enemies, do good to them, and lend to them without expecting to get anything back. Then your reward will be great, and you will be called sons of the Most High, because he is kind to the ungrateful and the wicked." When we have the promise of God in our hearts, we can love our enemies who make endless demands of us. When we know that our reward will be great, our concession to our enemies is not too big. When Isaac conceded his wells to his enemies, he looked as if he were a fool. But when he conceded them in God's promise, God blessed him and made him very rich (Ge 26). When we Christians give in and generously concede, then God recognizes us to be his children. God's children must be as generous as the heavenly princes and must have God's standard in dealing with people.

We can love our enemies when we have the assurance of forgiveness of our sins. Once we were enemies of God. But God forgave all our sins through his Son who shed his precious blood on the cross for our sins. By the immeasurable grace of Jesus, our sins were forgiven. If we accept his grace of forgiveness, his love compels us to love all kinds of people. The love of God enables us to be like God who is kind to the ungrateful and wicked and who equally gives rain to the evil and to the good. Therefore, Jesus commanded, saying in verse 36, "Be merciful, just as your Father is merciful." It's imperative for his people to see others with the love of God.

III. Do not judge others (37-45)

Read verse 37. "Do not judge, and you will not be judged. Do not condemn, and you will not be condemned. Forgive, and you will be forgiven." This verse takes us one step further to teach us how we have to positively love others by not judging them. In this verse, Jesus warns his disciples not to judge or condemn others. When he said this, he had in mind the Pharisees who criticized and condemned others according to their own criteria. They did not know that they were sinners, too. They were spiritually blind. Though we are forgiven sinners, how easy it is for us to judge others or condemn others and not forgive others! We cannot contradict ourselves by judging others. How often we hurt or undercut others by exalting ourselves to the position of judge. The righteous God alone is judge over us, none other. When we do this, we don't pay attention to the plank in our own eye, but say, "Brother, let me take the speck out of your eye" (42). We must learn how to embrace others instead of judging and condemning others.

Jesus also taught his disciples in verse 38 to give. In this selfish world, how can we always give our money and time while others are getting something? However, the nature of Jesus' love is giving and living sacrificially. Jesus said, "It is better to give than to receive" (cf. Ac 20:35). This is true. When one wants to get something, either love or money from others, he becomes miserable, hurting his own pride. But when one gives something to the needy, he feels like somebody. Not only that, great is the reward of those who give generously by giving away what they have, either money or time. Verse 38 is a sure promise to those who give in the name of the Lord. It says, "Give, and it will be given to you. A good measure, pressed down, shaken together and running over, will be poured into your lap." Let's believe his promise and repent of our stinginess. We see many miserly people around us. They lavish their money for their physical pleasures, but are repulsive penny pinchers for God's work. They are like the Dead Sea, which looks like the leper's rake-like hand. For many centuries, the Jordan River has been pouring fresh water into the Dead Sea, yet it is deplorable that it has remained for many centuries a dead sea in which no living thing can survive. It is only full of deadness. Selfish people are like the Dead Sea, or like spiritual lepers.

Read verses 39-40. This parable teaches how one can be a mature Christian and lead other people to a fruitful life. Verse 39 says that a blind man cannot lead a blind man. They will both fall into a pit. This implies that the disciples were like blind men. They should lead others, but they could not because they were the same blind men. So Jesus said in verse 40b, "But everyone who is fully trained will be like his teacher." Without spiritual maturity through disciplined life in the word of God, no one can really lead others or give to others sacrificially. Therefore, we must be willing to be trained in loving others and building up others. Then God will surely help us to do so.

Read verses 43-45. These verses tell us who the truly great men are. In the past, and at the present as well, there have been many who have wanted to be truly great men. But the true greatness of a man does not lie in what he has, but in what he is. King Agrippa came with great pomp and array and entered the audience room to try Paul (Ac 25:23). He was not a truly great man, but a necessary evil. He could not be recognized as a great man because his inner man was full of evil. The truly great man is one who is really fruitful, like St. Paul who was fruitful in spite of his situations. Our Lord wants us to be truly great before him by growing in his image and by bearing much fruit for him.

IV. A wise man and a foolish man (46-49)

No one wants to be a foolish person, but to be wise and great. Each does his best for his own amelioration and success. But there are many who do not know how to be wise. Read verse 46. This parable teaches us that a man is like a home builder. A man's foolishness or wisdom is decided by the foundation he has, whether sand or rock.

Who are the foolish builders? They are the near-sighted. It is said that in Palestine in the summer, many of the rivers dry up altogether, leaving sandy riverbeds empty of water. But after the September rains come, the empty riverbeds become raging torrents. Mostly, these builders are brilliant people who figure out every detail of their plans, but myopia is their fateful problem. They never bother to think about what their chosen house would be like six months afterward. Their nearsightedness makes them sophomoric and lazy.

Who then are the wise builders? They are the far-sighted men. They are men of vision who have at least a 100-year plan. They also have the love of truth in their hearts. They are willing to listen to the word of God. As the Psalmist said, "How sweet are your words to my taste, sweeter than honey to my mouth!" (Ps 119:103). They also have strength to put what they learned into practice. In their awesome respect for the word of God, they are always ready to obey the will of God. Their obedience is not a kind of self-resignation or a blind submission. It is an inexplicable expression of a heart of love toward the most loved one (Jn 14:23). The wise man who builds his life in Jesus is like a man building a house, who dug down and laid the foundation on a rock. When a flood came, the torrent struck that house, but could not shake it. The final victory is his and he is the most blessed one and he will be called a child of God.

May God be gracious to you and give you indomitable assurance that "I am the blessed one." The conception of happiness of worldly people and Jesus' people is quite opposite. Worldly people think they are blessed ones if they have what they want to have, like money, many children, a house, health, and so on. But these are temporal, ever-changing, and meaningless. But being blessed by God involves the way of the cross and much suffering. Still, they are blessed because they can participate in the divine nature (2Pe 1:4). Man is most happy when he experiences the holiness of God.

Lesson 17

The Faith of the Centurion

Luke 7:1-17
Key Verse: 7:9b

I. SUCH GREAT FAITH (1-10)

1. What was the problem of the centurion of Capernaum? What is a centurion? What was this centurion's probable responsibility?

2. What kind of man would one ordinarily expect a centurion to be? What was unusual about his concern for his servant? To what extent did he go to help his servant?

3. What was unusual about his relationship with the Jews who lived under Roman occupation? Why did they think him worthy of Jesus' help?

4. Why did the centurion send someone to Jesus instead of going himself? Why did he then send friends to Jesus to tell him not to come to his house? What do these actions reveal about his character?

5. How did he express his confidence in the power and authority of Jesus' word? How did being a soldier help him understand Jesus' authority?

6. How did Jesus praise this man's faith? Why was Jesus so amazed at his faith? How did Jesus bless his faith? What can we learn from this centurion?

II. HE SAID, "DON'T CRY" (11-17)

7. What contrasts can you find between the two large crowds that met at the town gate of Nain? Why was the woman crying?

8. What did Jesus say to her? What was in Jesus' heart? What does this reveal about Jesus' shepherd heart?

9. How did the crowd respond? What does this event reveal about Jesus' power and identity?

The Faith of the Centurion

Luke 7:1-17
Key Verse: 7:9b

> "... he said, 'I tell you, I have not found such great faith even in Israel.'"

I
N THE PREVIOUS CHAPTER, Jesus delivered the Sermon on the Mount. In that, he taught that the blessed ones are the ones who suffer many things for the sake of the Son of Man (6:17-49). His Sermon on the Mount was in fact his teaching for the disciples on the principles, attitude, and value system they should have as his people. Praise Jesus who did not tell his disciples to take care of themselves, but taught them to live a glorious life in God. In this passage, we want to study in 7:1-17 the quality and elements of faith that Jesus highly credits and get a glimpse of the Messianic figure when he helps a widowed woman.

I.   Such great faith (1-10)

Read verse 1. "When Jesus had finished saying all this in the hearing of the people ..." This verse refers to Jesus' Sermon on the Mount. After this, he entered Capernaum, located on the northwest shore of the Sea of Galilee, which served as Jesus' home base for the Galilean ministry.

Read verse 2. "There a centurion's servant, whom his master valued highly, was sick and about to die." The centurion was a captain of a hundred Roman soldiers and commissioned to keep the Roman peace in a certain area. He was a soldier. As a commanding officer who controlled people with weapons, cruelty must have been one of his essential qualities. Literally speaking, his occupation involved invading, killing, destroying, and oppressing captives. He could naturally do these things with the sadistic feelings of a cruel soldier. He was in a position to ignore slaves as if they were not there.

In the ancient world, people traditionally regarded a servant or slave as a "living tool" and no more. We can read a story in 1 Samuel 30 about the slave of an Amalekite. The Amalekites had raided the Negev and Ziklag and had taken David's people captive. When David came back to his garrison, he found that all his people's family members—women, children, and old people who were left behind—had been taken away. David began to pursue the Amalekites. On the way, he found an Egyptian, the slave of an Amalekite. David's men asked, "Who are you?" "I am an Egyptian," he replied. 'My master made me work hard and when I became ill three days ago he abandoned me." This was the situation of a servant or a slave of the times.

But the centurion did not throw his servant away because of his illness, as others might have done. Verse 2 says, "There a centurion's servant, whom his master valued highly ..." What does it mean "his master valued highly"? Does it mean that he valued him highly like a jeweler who values jewels for market? Yes, exactly and more. The centurion valued him highly not because he purchased him so expensively, but because he had a deep respect for human life. The centurion saw him as a human being. He valued human life highly. Because of this, whenever he saw his servant, he saw him as a human being like himself, as one who had feelings and emotions. This centurion is admirable for two reasons.

First, he had a deep respect for human life. To him, the slave was very dear, like his youngest brother. The centurion greeted him warmly during daily interaction. Then the servant boy in response would make a big smile. But this time, the servant did not respond. Instead, he hid his face between his arms. He was very sick, hovering between life and death. His eyes were filled with high fever and were red. Yet, he looked as if he had no right to appeal for help in his plight. The centurion shouted, "O my God!" But he was helpless. He did not know anything about medicine. Momentarily, he faced a deep humanistic dilemma in himself. He wanted to be a help for him. But he could not. In this situation, he could have refused to do anything for his servant, saying, "No way," shrugging his shoulders.

But he did not do so.

Read verse 3. "The centurion heard of Jesus and sent some elders of the Jews to him, asking him to come and heal his servant." On the spur of the moment, the centurion remembered what he had heard of Jesus. He snapped his fingers with deep gratitude, heaving a sigh of relief. He shouted, "Yeah, Jesus, Jesus of Nazareth." He was compelled to have Jesus come to his house to heal him. At that moment, he completely forgot everything, even the officers' meeting he had called. He also forgot who he was and went to the elders of the Jews whom he had become acquainted with. He humbled himself and asked them, "Could you please go to Jesus and ask that he come and heal my servant?" His "could you please" did not allow them to catch their breath. It was quite a surprise for the Jews. They were too startled to say anything. Then the centurion again said, "Could you please!" He had a deep love for human life. The elders of the Jews were so moved by his noble humanity that they were eager to help him out. Generally, they were a legalistic people who tried to look dignified. They never acted promptly because they had to think based on the Law and traditions and they had to take time to brush their whiskers or to dress in their long robes for an outing. But this time, they did not care about anything. Probably they came out of their houses in jogging clothes, ignoring their prestige.

As soon as they came to Jesus, they earnestly pleaded with him and said, "This man deserves to have you do this, because he loves our nation and has built our synagogue" (4-5). Their earnest pleading was exactly like that of the centurion. According to the elders' saying, the centurion was a man of integrity. As a Roman officer, he did not exercise his insolent imperialistic disposition. The centurion was a man of good influence. Not only did he love his servant boy, but he also loved people in the colony. He loved the Jewish people like brothers and gave them what they wanted. He built a synagogue for them out of his own expenses. His respect for human life helped him transcend cultural differences. His respect for human life was that which made it possible for him to embrace the bigoted Jewish religious people.

What did Jesus do when he heard their pleading? In verse 6a,

Luke simply says, "So Jesus went with them." This tells us that Jesus was greatly moved by the centurion's noble humanity and is willing to help such a person who has love for human life. Until now, Jesus had encountered many bigoted and malignant religious leaders. They were chosen by God to be his servants, but they did not care for the indigent and their suffering people. Jesus was tired of adamantly withstanding those forces of legalistic people. However, though this centurion was a Gentile, when Jesus saw his love of human life, he was greatly encouraged. Here we learn that basic respect for human life is an indispensible quality in maturing a man in depth and breadth. It is also an essential quality in the process of knowing the Son of Man. High respect toward human life is also essential for one to learn faith in the Son of Man.

Second, he had deep respect for God's word. Read verse 6b. When Jesus was not far from the house, the centurion sent some friends to say to him, "Lord, don't trouble yourself, for I do not deserve to have you come under my roof." When he was overcome by sympathy for the poor slave, at first he was compelled to send the Jewish elders to ask Jesus to come to his house. But he came to a deep realization that he had recklessly conducted himself in asking Jesus to come. So he sent messengers to say to Jesus, "But say the word, and my servant will be healed" (7). He was a Roman officer and Jesus was a country evangelist. But the centurion did not see Jesus' shabby clothes or national background. He saw Jesus' inner man. Not only that, he had heard Jesus' words and acknowledged that his words were full of truth and were life-giving. He also acknowledged that his word had power to heal the sick. He had keen spiritual insight to see through Jesus' person. He had keen spiritual understanding to hear the voices from above.

He said in verse 7b, "But say the word, and my servant will be healed." The centurion had a remarkable faith in the word of God. He put absolute authority in Jesus' word. The ancient heroes of faith believed that by God's word the heavens existed and the earth was formed out of water (2Pe 3:5). Abraham was old and weak when he began his life of faith. But he believed the word of promise absolutely and went, even though he did not know where he was going (Heb

11:8). Finally, he was blessed and he became the source of blessing, whereas Lot became a symbol of human agony. The difference in them came from their attitudes toward the word of God. The centurion was a foreigner. He could be relativistic, oscillating between human thinking and the word of Jesus that he had heard. But there was no doubt about the authority of Jesus' word to him.

How could he have such respect for Jesus' word? Read verse 8. As an officer of the Roman army, he had learned how to submit himself to higher authority. In brief, he was a well-disciplined person who knew how to obey and how to give orders. Through much discipline, he overcame himself. He was not surfeited with pride at being a Roman officer. When the centurion saw his disciplined life, he could see in Jesus the absolute authority, majesty, honor, and power from above. The centurion had authority to order his soldiers to come and go and to his servants to do this and do that. But he realized that his authority was nothing compared with that of Jesus'. Jesus' authority was inimitable. Jesus' coming to his house was more like God visiting his house. Through this we learn that in order to know the truth and the authority of Jesus' word we must have basic discipline.

Read verse 9. "When Jesus heard this, he was amazed at him and turning to the crowd following him, he said, 'I tell you, I have not found such great faith even in Israel.'" So far, Jesus had been dismayed by his own people because they had never believed even though they had seen messianic wonders in Jesus. They had never believed his word of promise. Unbelief was deeply rooted in the hearts of his own people. Because of their unbelief, they brought about the oppression of Satan, as well as the oppression of Roman rule. This unbelief enraged God's anger and their unbelief cast them out of God's protection. But when Jesus heard the centurion, "But say the word, and my servant will be healed" (7), Jesus marveled at his faith. As we know well, to Jesus nothing was great, nothing was frightening (6:11), and nothing was amazing. But the centurion's faith was great that he was amazed and said, "I tell you, I have not found such great faith even in Israel." Why was the centurion's faith so great and amazing? It was because the centurion's faith was based on the authority of Jesus' word. We see many people who are like the centurion. We have been amazed by Dr. Abraham T. Kim's simple faith and fruitful life. He lived in the U.S. the last five and a half years with the faith of the centurion. On the other hand, there are many godless people who scoff at the authority of God's word. Many people ridicule God's promise of judgment, saying, "Where is God's judgment? I am okay even though I have sinned a lot." They don't know God's long-suffering patience. Jesus gave the great command of world mission to his disciples, "Go into all the world and preach the good news to all creation" (Mk 16:15). Down through the generations, innumerable number of saints obeyed this command and sacrificed their lives for this cause. But these days, many deceptive hedonists say that the command was only for the disciples, not for us. They have no respect for the truth and the authority of God's word of promise. I believe that if we learn the centurion's faith from our hearts, we can surely amaze our Lord Jesus Christ.

Read verse 10. "Then the men who had been sent returned to the house and found the servant well." The centurion's faith was blessed in that his servant was healed. Jesus wanted his disciples to have this kind of faith. Jesus wants us to have this kind of faith at this particular time.

II. He said, "Don't cry" (11-17)

Soon afterward, being amazed by the centurion's faith, Jesus went to a town called Nain. His disciples and a large crowd went along with him. It was a procession which paraded the joy of true humanity and the joy of heaven stirred up by the faith of a stranger, the centurion.

Read verse 12. There was another procession. It was a funeral procession. As he approached the town gate, a dead person was being carried out—the only son of his mother, and she was a widow. This tells us that he grew up without a father. He must have been a good child to his mother, and he was the whole world to his mom. It may be that though he was a good child, he grew up sickly, influenced by his widowed mother's sorrowful mind. One day, this child wailed and breathed his last. He died young and he was no more. Now he was being carried out to the tomb. His mother was following, tottering in the rear of the funeral bier, and in back of her was a long line of mourners made up of a large crowd of people from the town. Nothing could be more sorrowful than this funeral procession of this mother for her only son. People, old and young, who followed together in back of the funeral bier, must have felt that man's life is transitory—from nothing to nothing, from one sorrow to another. Beginning with the widowed woman, all were swallowed up by the power of death and became sorrowful and fatalistic. This is a description of human tragedy without the Risen Christ.

What did Jesus do for this widowed woman? Read verse 13. "When the Lord saw her, his heart went out to her." There is a saying, "A tear is a woman's potent weapon." But Jesus was not sorry for her out of sympathy for the tears of a widowed woman. He was sorry when he saw a pitiful widow crying over her only son's death. Jesus was even more sorry when he saw that the woman was overcome by the power of death and was crying endlessly. Jesus was sorry that all the people were overcome by the power of death and were tottering under the power of death. Jesus was seized with great pity for the widowed woman and for the sorrowful procession. So he said, "Don't cry." Jesus wanted to help her believe in the Son of Man. So he said, "Don't cry." To Jesus, she had no reason to cry. But she was crying because she did not know the Son of Man. She cried because she did not have faith in Jesus who is the resurrection and the life (Jn 11:25). When Jesus said, "Don't cry," he wanted her to have faith in the Son of Man who gives eternal life. After saying this, he went up and touched the coffin, and those carrying it stood still. He said, "Young man, I say to you, get up!" (14). The dead man then sat up and began to talk. "Mom, why are you crying? Don't cry. Make a smile. I am hungry." Jesus demonstrated the power of resurrection so that whoever believes in him may have resurrection faith.

Read verses 16 and 17. "They were all filled with awe and praised God. 'A great prophet has appeared among us,' they said. 'God has come to help his people.'" Historically, a prophet was known as a man sent from God to deliver his people. Jesus demonstrated that he was the Messiah who was promised to come among them to save his people from their sorrow and death. When the people saw the messianic work in Jesus, they could not contain their joy. They shouted and shouted, praising God. "God has come to help his people." They were no longer bitter about their lives, but were filled with joy. Jesus also says to us, "Don't cry! Believe."

In the light of this passage, we learn that we must have "say the word and my servant will be healed" faith. We also learn that we have no reasons to cry when we have resurrection faith. May God give you the noble humanity of the centurion and use you to heal young ones who need healing in the United States as well as in Russia.

Lesson 18

Jesus and John the Baptist

Luke 7:18-35
Key Verse: 7:22b

I. JESUS' ANSWER TO JOHN (18-23)

1. When did John's disciples tell him about Jesus, what did he tell them to do, and what did they do? What does John's question mean?

2. Where was John at the time? (Mt 11:2-3) Thinking about John's situation, what may have been his reason for sending his disciples to Jesus with this question?

3. At the time the messengers came what was Jesus doing? What message did Jesus send back to John? What is the significance of this message? How does it answer John's question, and his doubts? (Is 35:5-6; 61:1-2) What can we learn from Jesus here?

II. JESUS' WITNESS ABOUT JOHN (24-28)

4. What were the rhetorical questions Jesus asked the crowd about John? What do these questions reveal about John's life and ministry?

5. What does the quotation from Isaiah teach about John? What did Jesus teach about him? Why is John so great? Why is the one who is least in the kingdom of God greater than John?

III. JESUS AND JOHN WERE REJECTED (29-35)

6. What did John's baptism signify? Who had been baptized by John, and how did this affect their response to Jesus? Why? What did they mean by saying, "God's way is right?"

7. How did the Pharisees and experts in the law reject God's purpose for themselves? Why?

8. To whom did Jesus compare the people of his generation? In what respect were they like children playing in the marketplace? Why did they reject John? Why did they reject Jesus? What does this reveal about them? Who are the children of wisdom? How can we be children of wisdom?

Jesus and John the Baptist

Luke 7:18-35
Key Verse: 7:22b

> *"The blind receive sight, the lame walk, those who have leprosy are cured, the deaf hear, the dead are raised, and the good news is preached to the poor."*

T HESE DAYS, MANY PEOPLE ask, "What's up?" or "What's going on?" They know something is happening and that something is going on but they have a hard time figuring it out. People do not know what is happening in the larger context of world history. These days, even historians have a hard time with this. So, many of them write, "Where is history going?" In today's passage Luke the historian deals mainly with the transitional period from John to Jesus. We learn what to see in history, especially in the work and history of God.

I. Jesus' answer to John (18-23)

Read verse 18a. "John's disciples told him about all these things." During this time, John was in prison (Mt 11:2). Like many plots from fiction, John's life did not have a happy ending, but, humanly speaking, a tragic one. Also at this time, John's disciples' morale was low since their master, John, was imprisoned. They probably wondered why this had happened to their master, John. They must have been distressed, and did not know what to do. They had just gone to see Jesus' work. They saw that Jesus' work was prosperous, and that his disciples were quite happy under his gracious wings. After having seen this, they went back to John in prison. Probably, they told John about all these things through the little window in his dungeon cell. "Master, we've seen Jesus' growing ministry and met his happy disciples."

What was John's response? Read verse 18b. "Calling two of them, he sent them to the Lord to ask, 'Are you the one who was to come, or should we expect someone else?'" This question has worried many scholars, who have thought that there might have been doubt in the mind of John. But when we think of this from Luke's point of view, it is clear that John sent his disciples to the Lord, not because of his personal doubts, but because he wanted to help his disciples because they were in a spiritual crisis. Once, John's disciples had been popular and the main stars of God's work and history. But now they were pushed out and had become mere extras. John knew how they felt. They were envious of Jesus' disciples. They were also fearful because of John's situation and its outcome. But John did not mention his own release or his disciples' future; John only worried about his disciples' spiritual condition. As the best solution to their problem, John sent them to Jesus. He wanted them to know who Jesus really was, for knowing Jesus himself was the complete solution to their problems. Most of all, he wanted them to know Jesus as the Messiah. At that time, people believed that the coming Messiah would be everything to them. But John did not want to satisfy their idle curiosity or pacify their fears of the world. Definitely, he wanted them to know that he was the forerunner of the Messiah, as was prophesied, and that Jesus was the Messiah promised to come.

Read verse 20. "When the men came to Jesus, they said, 'John the Baptist sent us to you to ask, "Are you the one who was to come, or should we expect someone else?"'" The key point of the question was the Messiah.

Read verse 21. "At that very time Jesus cured many who had diseases, sicknesses and evil spirits, and gave sight to many who were blind." So Jesus replied to the messengers, "Go back and report to John what you have seen and heard." Read verse 22b. "The blind receive sight, the lame walk, those who have leprosy are cured, the deaf hear, the dead are raised, and the good news is preached to the poor." This verse is based on Isaiah 35:5-6 and 61:1-2, both of which foretell the work of the Messiah. Isaiah 35:5-6 proclaim: "Then will the eyes of the blind be opened and the ears or the dear unstopped.

Then will the lame leap like a deer, and the mute tongue shout for joy." Where there is the life-giving work of the Messiah, the world is full of joy. Again, Isaiah 61:1-2 proclaims the work of the Messiah: "The Spirit of the Sovereign Lord is on me, because the Lord has anointed me to preach good news to the poor. He has sent me to bind up the brokenhearted, to proclaim freedom for the captives and release from darkness for the prisoners, to proclaim the year of the Lord's favor and the day of vengeance of our God." Luke quoted this prophecy freely in Luke 4:18-19 to introduce Jesus as the Messiah.

In verse 22, although the world was dark and the righteous man John the Baptist was arrested and put in prison, Jesus, who was doing the work of the Messiah, implies that the work and history of God was happening in accordance with God's promises. John came and completed his mission as the forerunner of the Messiah. Now, the work of God was being handed over to Jesus the Messiah.

Indeed, according to the Scriptures, the Messiah had intervened in human history and was doing the life-giving work of the Messiah. "The blind receive sight ..." Life for the blind is very sad because for children who cannot see their mothers' faces, and for parents who cannot see their children's lovely faces. With their eyes they can cry over their sorrowful situation. Our Lord Jesus wiped their tears away and gave sight to many who were blind and made "... the lame walk ..." A person's arms and legs are the symbol of their strength. But lame men are powerless, limping throughout their lifetimes. Jesus restored the lame's dried legs until they could leap like deer. "... those who have leprosy are cured ..." Jesus cured men with leprosy and gave them new flesh and new life. "... the deaf hear ..." The deaf cannot talk with their loved ones. They suffer endlessly in dark silence, and then die. Jesus restored their speech. Jesus raised the dead, and demonstrated the power of resurrection. Jesus preached to the poor the good news of great joy that will be for all the people.

All the work Jesus did was the work only the Messiah could uniquely do. All the work done by the Messiah was a deep expression of God's love toward sinful mankind. The work of the Messiah is evidence that God loves the world deeply and that he is working in history as the Sovereign Ruler.

In verse 22 he replied to the messengers, "Go back and report to John what you have seen and heard: The blind receive sight, the lame walk, those who have leprosy are cured, the dear hear, the dead are raised, and the good news is preached to the poor." This is all he said as an answer, and all the answer they needed to hear. Jesus did not say anything about John's release. He only said, "Good news is preached." To John's disciples, who bore the painful problem in their hearts of their master's imprisonment, Jesus' answer may have sounded incoherent. However, it was not. It was the best answer Jesus could give. It implies that this was a transitional period from John to Jesus. It also implies that the work and history of God was going on and being continued by Jesus. This brief statement, "Good news is preached," eloquently expounds the truth that God is working in history.

According to the promises, John the Baptist came as the forerunner of the Messiah and now he had completed his mission. Jesus was doing the work of the Messiah. This reveals that God is the Sovereign Ruler of history.

From time to time, we feel that the power of darkness rules the world. The work of God seems to be nothing before the power of the world. We fall into doubt and ask ourselves, "What is going on?" because we cannot see God's absolute sovereign rule over history. From time to time, we cannot acknowledge God's deep love living among human beings. In light of this passage, we are like John's disciples, who could not figure out what was going on in the work and history of God.

Even when God was working most powerfully through Jesus and John, the work of God seemed to have been experiencing adversity. John was arrested and put in prison by King Herod. Jesus' ministry of healing and preaching looked poor, like the poor gathering for handouts. Jesus' disciples were too young to do anything. But this was not the case. God works mightily in history. He is working in history to fulfill his world salvation plan. He will work until the kingdom of God is fully restored. The problem is our unbelief. We must repent of our sin of unbelief moment by moment and stand firm in our faith in God Almighty.

In the year that King Uzziah died, Isaiah despaired at his people's corruption. He was fear-stricken because of the possible invasion of foreign armies. One day, by chance he entered the temple and saw God seated on a throne, high and exalted; and the train of his robe filled the temple. Above him were seraphs, calling to one another, "Holy, holy, holy is the Lord Almighty; the whole earth is full of his glory" (Is 6:3). At the sound of their voices the doorposts and thresholds shook and the temple was filled with smoke. In this, Isaiah saw the vision that God Almighty is on his throne ruling over the world. Then he realized that he was a man of unclean lips, for with his lips he had expressed his unbelief and doubts about God's sovereign rule in world history. Since that time, Isaiah proclaimed the message, "Your God reigns!" (Is 52:7).

Many Christians were harassed, thinking that the Christian Church would decline simultaneously with the decline of the Roman Empire, since the Roman Empire had adopted Christianity as her official religion; thereby the church of God was corrupted through riding the political power of the Roman government. But Saint Augustine wrote a book, "The City of God," in which he explained that God is the Sovereign Ruler of history and that the Church of God will never perish until the City of God is fully reestablished, even though the kings and crowns of this world perish.

When the early church was first emerging, most Christians were severely persecuted and scattered. But Apostle John did not doubt God's rule. Rather, he realized in the midst of persecutions was the deep love of God. He was in exile on the Isle of Patmos. There he saw God on his throne, ruling over world history. He saw the glory and majesty of God. He saw the glorious new heaven and the new earth that God was establishing.

When we see the world's situation, we despair. The world is full of deception and manipulation, corruption and evil. It is hard for Christians to discriminate between Christian culture and the Christian faith.

But John's disciples could not understand why such a righteous man as John, who had dedicated himself to God, was arrested and put in prison. To them, the love of God was doubtful. They were ready to fall away from the work of God. But Jesus said to them in verse 23, "Blessed is the man who does not fall away on account of me." In that situation, how could we not? We must see God on his throne ruling the world and history through Jesus.

II. Jesus' witness about John (24-28)

The world is like the surging waves of the sea, on the surface of which there are many ups and downs and many troubles and sufferings. But according to his promises, the history of God is going on like the undercurrent of the sea, which flows quietly and steadily. However, to Jesus the onlookers did not seem to understand who John really was. So, by asking the same question three times to the onlookers, Jesus reminded them of who John really was and how great a man he was.

Read verse 24. The question was, "What did you go out into the desert to see? "A reed swayed by the wind?" Did they go out to see "a man dressed in fine clothes?" Then Jesus asked them the same question a third time, "What did you go out to see? A prophet?" Yes, they went to see the prophet. They went to him and received the baptism of repentance. But they did not know who John was. They missed the point.

In verse 27, Jesus told them clearly who John was. "I will send my messenger ahead of you, who will prepare your way before you." (cf. Mal 3:1) He was the one who was prophesied to come and who came to the world at God's time as the forerunner of Christ. As the forerunner of Christ he lived a pure life, eating locusts and honey in the desert, against the corruption of the world. He preached a baptism of repentance. Once he rebuked Herod to repent because he had taken his own brother's wife. On account of this, John was put in prison. People once wondered if he was the Messiah. But now they wondered if he was a small victim of social evils, who had lived poorly and would finally end in tragedy. Once people thought John was a great man; now they thought he was a small man since he was in prison.

What did Jesus say about John? Did Jesus say that he was a small man and a victim of social evils? No. Read verse 28a. "I tell you, among those born of women there is no one greater than John." Why was he the greatest among men? It was because he was a man of mission and the running mate of Jesus in his Messianic work.

Jesus went on to say in verse 28, "... yet the one who is least in the kingdom of God is greater than he." This statement does not minimize the importance of John. It emphasizes his historical significance. John belongs to the time of Law. The least in the kingdom of God is not smaller than John, because that person belongs to the age of grace.

III. John and Jesus were rejected (29-35)

What were the responses of the people? Read verse 29. Ordinary people and tax collectors responded to Jesus' words and said, "God's way is right." They knew that they were terrible sinners. So, they humbly came to John and confessed their sins and received John's baptism. They received the baptism of repentance from him, beating their chests as the expression of deep repentance. Because they received the baptism of repentance, they acknowledged that "God's way was right" when they heard Jesus' words.

The others were the Pharisees and experts in the law. They knew Bible theology well. They knew who John was and who Jesus was. They also knew what God's purpose for them was. But they rejected God's purpose for themselves as a priestly nation. Why? Luke says that it was because they did not receive the baptism from John. They knew who John was but they did not see John from God's point of view. They saw John with human eyes, rejected him, and, collaborating with the Herodians, put him in prison. They were blinded by their own pride and became useless.

The religious leaders of the times were self-centered. Read verse 32. "We played the flute for you, and you did not dance; we sang a dirge, and you did not cry." They did not care about God's work and history. They did not care about God's flock. They only cared about themselves. Look at verse 32a. They were like children in the marketplace, calling out to each other. They were like people who are greatly interested in groceries in a marketplace.

They condemned whoever they did not like. John the Baptist came and lived a holy life against that corrupt and sinful generation, neither eating bread or drinking wine, and they said, "He has a demon." The Son of Man came and ate and drank with any kind of person, embracing all, and they said, "Here is a glutton and a drunkard, a friend of tax collectors and 'sinners.'" We cannot trust their judgment.

But Jesus was not gloomy because of the hypocrites; he was happy because there were still the children of God through whom the word of God is proved right. Read verse 35. "But wisdom is proved right by all her children." In the Old Testament, wisdom is considered to be God's own character. Here, the children of wisdom refers to God's children. They are those who accepted John and Jesus. They are those who said, "God's way is right." The children of wisdom were those who believed in Jesus.

In this passage we learn that we must have spiritual insight to see how God is working in history (Eph 1:18-19).

Lesson 19

Jesus Anointed by a Sinful Woman

Luke 7:36-50
Key Verse: 7:50b

I. JESUS WELCOMES A SINFUL WOMAN (36-38)

1. Where was Jesus? What was he doing when this woman came in? Describe the woman's actions. What can we learn from this passage about her past life and character?

2. Why did the Pharisee criticize Jesus in his heart? What does his criticism reveal about Jesus' attitude toward this woman and her actions? Why did Jesus welcome her in spite of the criticism he knew her actions would arouse?

3. What was the parable Jesus told, the question he asked Simon, and Simon's answer? What did this parable show about Jesus' understanding of the woman?

II. JESUS REBUKES THE PHARISEE (39-46)

4. What did the Pharisee's criticism reveal about himself? How was his attitude toward Jesus inferior to that of the woman? Why do you think he had invited Jesus to dinner?

5. What was Simon's spiritual problem, and what did Jesus try to teach him?

III. YOUR SINS ARE FORGIVEN (47-50)

6. Why were the people at the dinner party so surprised when Jesus said, "Your sins are forgiven?"

7. What did Jesus teach about the relationship between love and forgiveness?

8. How did Jesus bless this woman? What did he mean by, "Your faith has saved you?" What is the significance of, "Go in peace"?

Jesus Anointed by a Sinful Woman

Luke 7:36-50
Key Verse: 7:50b

"Your faith has saved you; go in peace."

TODAY'S GOSPEL STORY IS about Jesus and two people whom society had classified as a man of standing and a woman of poor reputation; the man was considered good, and the woman was no good. But Jesus who saw both of them from God's point of view saw them quite differently. In this passage Jesus rebuked the Pharisee when he thought he would be admired, and Jesus accepted the woman when she thought she would be rejected.

I.   Jesus welcomes a sinful woman (36-38)

This gospel story took place at the house of Simon the Pharisee (36). They say that at that time the houses of well-to-do people were built around an open courtyard forming a hollow square. In the square was a garden and fountain, and in warm weather meals were served there. At that time in the East, in order to eat, people reclined at the table lying on low couches, resting on the left elbow, leaving the right hand free. They say that in such houses many kinds of parties were customarily given for the enjoyment of social gatherings. All kinds of people came in freely to listen to the wisdom that fell from the lips of distinguished guests. Obviously, the Pharisee was enjoying a luxurious life. As a collector of celebrities, he must have already invited a number of distinguished people into his home. This time, he invited Jesus. Maybe he was an admirer of Jesus and wanted to know more about him, for Jesus had been a man of question throughout the country.

Probably all the guests reclined at the table and stewards were carrying out food to serve. All of a sudden, a woman disturbed the whole atmosphere. What kind of woman was she? Verse 37 says that she was a woman who had lived a sinful life in that town.

How did she come to Jesus? At that time, the work of the Messiah, his merciful healing and hope-giving preaching, had been heard of and responded to widely, from corner to corner. She also had heard of Jesus' Messianic ministry: "The blind receive sight, the lame walk, those who have leprosy are cured … and the good news is preached to the poor" (7:22). When she had heard of Jesus and his good news, something stirred up in her heart. Since then she eagerly wanted to see Jesus. One day, she learned that Jesus was eating at a Pharisee's house. The aristocratic Pharisee's house was not a place that she could dare approach. But it did not matter. She dashed into the Pharisee's house where dinner was already taking place. Though her interruption ruined the atmosphere of the night and damaged the reputation of the Pharisee, she was not aware of it. She was an obnoxious woman. However, Jesus saw her with the eyes of the Messiah. Jesus was ready to help her. How did he want to help her?

First, Jesus welcomed her as she was. Read verse 37. As we have seen, she was a woman who had lived a sinful life. How was it that she was known in that town as one who had lived a sinful life? At that time there were two kinds of public sinners— tax collectors and town prostitutes. This woman must have been a town prostitute, a woman who made money by selling her youth. How could it be that she became the town prostitute? If she were the sister of Lazarus, she might have done it to support her family. If she were Mary Magdalene, she might have done it to support her sinful desires. One prostitute counselor said that some become prostitutes to make money, but 99% of them become prostitutes in order to satisfy their curiosity and sinful desires. Usually pimps manipulate them in order to borrow and use money freely, until the girls become such debtors that their earnings can't even pay the high interest on their debts. In this way, weak women who become prostitutes become the prey of evil men. She was a woman who had lived a sinful life. Many people of the town used her as a prostitute. They satisfied their sinful desires through her. They made her such a miserable person. But when they met her on the street they would turn their faces so as not to look at her. They were ashamed of her. They used her but never welcomed her. So she could not go anywhere.

Anyway, she came to Jesus. As we know, she was a town prostitute. To her, even visiting family members must have been a painful thing. When she thought of her parents, and of her brothers and sisters who had once had respect for her, she must have felt so painful. This kind of woman would be so self-conscious and would never dare to appear on the public scene. But she moved her feet, one step after another, toward the place where Jesus was. When she arrived at the Pharisee's house she saw that his house was too elegant to approach for one who had snuck out of the prostitutes' quarters. But she didn't mind. She came to Jesus. She believed that as he had welcomed others, so he would welcome her.

When she came to Jesus, she cried endlessly. In spite of her tragic past, her tears did not dry up. She lived a wild life as if she did not care about her sin. But she was very conscious of her sins. To her, sinful life seemed to demonstrate her freedom. But in reality her sinful life did not make her free. Rather she was endlessly sorry for what she was doing. While living a wild life, she lost her purity, which is considered the same as a woman's life. She misused her best gifts, such as her beauty, health and smiles, endowed to her from above. As a result she became a shameful woman. She could have made many excuses, or justified herself saying, "I am a human being just the same as all others," or resigned everything to fate. But she did not. She admitted that she was wrong. Physically she was corrupted and smelly. But spiritually speaking she was not totally corrupted, because she admitted that she was wrong, and because her tears were not dried up. When she came to Jesus, she cried endlessly. She was still a precious human being who could cry. She cried endlessly as the expression of her deep repentance for her past sins.

Mostly wayward women are spendthrifts and full of debts. But this woman had saved enough money to buy an alabaster jar of perfume. Probably she had determined to make money, and made enough money to buy an expensive alabaster jar of perfume. It must have been her treasure among her property. When she came to Jesus, she brought it and broke her alabaster jar of perfume, and as she stood behind him at his feet weeping, she began to wet his feet with her tears. Then she wiped them with her hair, kissed them and poured perfume on them. She knew she was a dirty sinner. She knew that she was not worthy to come to Jesus in this way. But she came to Jesus and poured her heart out to him for his mercy. Jesus wholeheartedly welcomed her and left her alone to cry before him. To worldly people, one prostitute's coming to him seems to be nothing. But there is no greater joy in heaven than the joy of a sinner's coming to Jesus.

Second, Jesus regarded her pouring perfume as anointing. Read verse 38. "… and as she stood behind him at his feet weeping, she began to wet his feet with her tears. Then she wiped them with her hair, kissed them and poured perfume on them." When she came to Jesus, he welcomed her. He forgave all her sins, even before she asked. She was so grateful. She could not but cry. At that moment, Jesus saw her as a daughter of God who was lost, who was deeply wounded and tired, and who needed the Messiah's healing and forgiveness of sins. When Jesus welcomed her, she immediately recognized the healing touch of the Messiah and his grace of forgiveness of her sins flooded into her soul. She was grateful, so she cried many tears until his feet were wet with them. She wiped his feet with her hair. Paul said that long hair is a woman's glory (1Co 11:15). But she wiped his feet with her hair. This was the expression of her respect and love and thanks. She broke her alabaster jar and poured perfume on Jesus' feet.

How did Jesus accept her alabaster jar of perfume, which was bought with money earned by prostitution? Jesus accepted it as her expression of gratitude for his forgiveness of sins. Jesus knew that she had bought the perfume with money she had earned from prostitution. But it did not matter; he accepted her perfume most meaningfully as the anointing for his burial. Jesus is full of grace and truth toward sinners. John described his grace as follows, "The Word became flesh and made his dwelling among us. We have seen his glory, the glory of the One and Only, who came from the Father, full of grace and truth" (Jn 1:14).

II. Jesus rebukes the Pharisee (39-46)

What was the Pharisee's response? Read verse 39. When the Pharisee who had invited Jesus saw that a woman was disturbing the dinner with her claimant demand, he was upset and said to himself, "If this man were a prophet, he would know who is touching him and what kind of woman she is—that she is a sinner." He was presumptuous and judgmental because he did not know the Father's mind in heaven.

Jesus knew what was on Simon's mind, and he wanted to help him spiritually. He said to him, "Simon, I have something to tell you" (40). "Tell me, teacher," was his response. Perhaps he expected a kind of compliment about his house and rich table, as other gusts may have. To his surprise, Jesus told him the story in verses 41 and 42. "Two men owned money to a certain moneylender. One owned him five hundred denarii, and the other fifty. Neither of them had the money to pay him back, so he canceled the debts of both. Now which one of them will love him more?" Simon replied in verse 43, "I suppose the one who had the bigger debt canceled." "You have judged correctly," Jesus said.

Read verses 44-46. "Then he turned toward the woman and said to Simon, 'Do you see this woman? I came into your house. You did not give me any water for my feet, but she wet my feet with her tears and wiped them with her hair. You did not give me a kiss, but this woman, from the time I entered, has not stopped kissing my feet. You did not put oil on my head, but she has poured perfume on my feet.'" This story tells us that Simon did not know two things about himself.

First, he did not know that he was a debtor. Simon had a position in the society in which he lived. He was rich. He thought he was a pretty good person because he went to the synagogue regularly. He owed money to no one. So he did not know that he was a debtor. Biblically speaking, a debtor refers to a sinner. Simon did not know that he was a sinner in three ways: a moralistic sinner, an ethical sinner, and a spiritual sinner. The woman is an example of a moralistic sinner. Saint Francis of Assisi is an example of an ethical sinner. Once he was very sick due to malnutrition. One of his disciples brought him a cooked hen. He ate it. Then his conscience was stricken when he thought that he had eaten a hen when Jesus had not. He ordered one of his disciples to tie a rope around his neck, and to drag him along the street as he shouted, "This chicken eater is the most wretched and miserable sinner!"

St. Augustine became known to all as a holy saint to the world down through the generations, especially to the Christians in the past and at the present. Why was it so? It was because he knew he was a sinner and Jesus was Christ the Lord. In other words, he made great efforts in knowing that he was a sinner so that he could know how great was the grace of Jesus who was condemned for his sins. He made great efforts to know that Jesus was Christ, the Creator God, so that he might know the meaning of existence in God. In brief, he was aware that he was a sinner, morally, ethically and spiritually. It was amazing to know that such a great scholar and Christian thinker admitted he was a sinner. It was certain that his spiritual humility made him grow to be one of the most influential and holy of saints.

St. Paul is also a good example of one who acknowledged that he was a spiritual sinner. He worked harder than all the others. But he was sorry that he was still a sinner because he had to go to bed, leaving unfinished the tasks God had assigned him. What he received from God was too great to count. But what he gave to God was too small to notice. Even though he worked harder than any other apostle, he could only find himself to be a sinner in the sight of God. Each is a sinner who works 24 hours a day because there are only 24 hours in a day.

This Pharisee was a moral sinner in that he criticized both the woman and Jesus. Second, he was a sinner before the people, for he was not mindful of the needy. He enjoyed parties for his own pleasure. Third, he was a sinner before God. He did not live for the glory of God, but for himself.

Second, he did not thank God. God is the Creator of our lives and the Ruler of our destinies. So we must thank God for the privilege of enjoying God's life. God gave man his life. God gave this man all the things he needed. But he thought that his life was his own, God gave him his one and only Son to cancel his unpayable amount of debt. He was not thankful for that. Rather, he thought that he was rich because he was able. He did not live a spiritual life even though he was supposed to be a spiritual leader. He had lived, but he lived an animal's life.

Simon the Pharisee was a man of standing and rich. He was an object of envy to the people of his society. Because of his human situation, he had a patronizing contempt even for Jesus. But from God's point of view, he was a self-seeking person. According to Romans, the final destiny of self-seeking people is horrible beyond description. As Romans 2:7-9 describes it, "To those who by persistence in doing good seek glory, honor and immortality, he will give eternal life. But for those who are self-seeking and who reject the truth and follow evil, there will be wrath and anger. There will be trouble and distress for every human being who does evil."

III. Your sins are forgiven (47-50)

Read verse 47. "Therefore, I tell you, her sins have been forgiven—for she loved much." This verse teaches us God's love toward mankind is the forgiveness of sins.

Read verse 48. In this verse, we remember that Jesus did not say, "Don't cry," or even, "You will be okay." He said, "Your sins are forgiven." It sounded quite impractical to her in her present situation. But on the part of Jesus, he offered her the best love that he could, for the forgiveness of sins was the only thing that could save her from her suffering.

Sin takes away man's happiness. In one of Tolstoy's novels, Katyusha was a very pretty and happy girl even though she was a housemaid in a duke's family. But she became ugly and miserable after she committed sin with the young Duke Nekhlyudov one Easter Eve. Later, in her anger and frustration, she committed many crimes, and finally was transported to Siberia as a criminal. Sin also has power like the horns of a bull. Satan scatters his bait here and there, and anyone who he catches taking his bait, he impales and makes crippled. Then that person suffers throughout lifetime because of this wound. This woman must have been tragically wounded because of sin. But Jesus forgave her sins.

Sin gave her many thorns and briers in her life and made her cry all the time. To this woman, "Your sins are forgiven" was the best expression of Jesus' love. Jesus carried all our sins and shed his blood as the ransom sacrifice for our sins. Jesus welcomes anyone who comes to him for the grace of forgiveness. When she came to Jesus, he said, "Your faith has saved you; go in peace" (50). Her coming was a great act of faith which Jesus admired. When she came to Jesus, her sins were forgiven, and the peace of God was bestowed upon this woman.

In this passage we learn how we can love Jesus, and how our sins are forgiven. How can we love Jesus? That is a good question. We can best love Jesus when we come to him with our sins to be forgiven. The more we come to realize the forgiveness our sins, the more we can love Jesus. Jesus said in verse 47b, "But he who has been forgiven little loves little." This brief statement attests that the love of God is the grace of forgiveness of sins.

Lesson 20

The Parable of the Sower

Luke 8:1-15
Key Verse: 8:15

I. THE GOOD NEWS OF THE KINGDOM OF GOD (1-3)

1. What was Jesus' message as he traveled about from one town and village to another? What do you think this means?

2. Who traveled with him? How did those with him share in his ministry? In what respect were they good soil for the gospel? What can we learn from them?

II. THE SECRET OF THE KINGDOM OF GOD (4-10)

3. To whom did Jesus tell this parable? What happened to the seed the farmer sowed? Why did he call out, "He who has ears to hear, let him hear"?

4. Why did Jesus' disciples ask him the meaning of the parable? What does this reveal about the attitude of a disciple? What did Jesus teach them about the special privilege of a disciple? Why can only a disciple know the secrets of the kingdom of God?

III. THE MEANING OF THE PARABLE (11-15)

5. Think about the meaning of the parable. What does the seed represent? How is this parable descriptive of Jesus' ministry? What can we learn here about the importance of believing Jesus' words?

6. What happens to those with hearts like a path when they hear the word? What do you think it means to be like a path?

7. What happens to those whose hearts are like a rock when they hear the word? Why is the shallow soil so deceptive? What causes rootless people to fall away? What is the relationship of perseverance to faith?

8. When the word of God falls on hearts that are like thorny soil, what happens to it? What are the thorns that keep the word from bearing fruit in a person's life? What can we do to get rid of them?

9. What is a good and noble heart? How can we be good soil? What kind of fruit do you think Jesus wants?

The Parable of the Sower

Luke 8:1-15
Key Verse: 8:15

> *"But the seed on good soil stands for those with a noble and good heart, who hear the word, retain it, and by perseverance produce a crop."*

N THIS PASSAGE, JESUS, with the parable of the sower, teaches the secret of the kingdom of God to those who were coming to hear him from many towns. In this parable, we also learn the greatness of a man. Man has great potential and possibility, like a seed. God made man like fruit trees to bear much fruit—thirty times at minimum, sixty times on average, or above average at one hundred times more than what was sown. But there is a problem—how can we bear good fruit?

I. The good news of the kingdom of God (1-3)

Read verse 1. It starts with the words, "After this." This refers to the event of Jesus' healing of a sinful woman in Simon the Pharisee's house. After this, Jesus traveled about from one town and village to another, proclaiming the good news of the kingdom of God. We see here the eagerness of Jesus to evangelize all the towns and villages. Ultimately, Jesus wanted to evangelize all nations.

What was the context of his message? It was the good news of the kingdom of God. Jesus had begun his ministry with the words, "The kingdom of God is near. Repent and believe the good news!" (Mk 1:15). He was now halfway through his ministry, but the key point of his message was still the good news of the kingdom of God. At the last moment on the cross, when one of the criminals hanging there said, "Jesus, remember me when you come into your kingdom," Jesus promised him that day he would be with him in paradise (Lk 23:42-43). Jesus' last message from the cross to this wretched man was also the message of the kingdom of God.

The sixty-six books of the Bible can be summarized in two words: paradise lost and paradise restored, paradise being the kingdom of God. Jesus came to this world to save us from the kingdom of Satan and to take us back to his kingdom. Sometimes we teach others about many good things, but omit the kingdom of God. This is an incomplete message.

While Jesus traveled about, the Twelve were with him, as well as some women who had been cured of evil spirits and diseases. They represented a train of Jesus' attendants. Compared to David's mighty men (2Sa 23:8-39), they were like a handful of poor people. But to Jesus, they were indispensable characters in the redemptive history of God.

First, the Twelve were called to be his disciples and he also designated them apostles. They were ordinary people. Peter, James, and John were fishermen; Matthew was a tax collector; Simon called the Zealot was a member of the national radicals. The rest of them were mere tagalongs. They were by nature unattractive. They were young and vigorous, and they liked to eat. They were clumps of earthly desires. Their hopes were earthbound. In many ways they were unproductive. Their future prospect as apostles did not seem to be promising.

Still, their heart soil was good and they doggedly followed Jesus. They didn't have much hope of being future apostles, but they could have hope because Jesus had hope in them. To Jesus, they were his hope; they were his glory; they were precious jewels to his ministry, now and for the future. To Jesus, they were the future cornerstones of redemptive work and history. They were future history makers who planted the first seeds of the gospel.

It is really surprising to us that Jesus had such hope in them. But when we study this passage prayerfully, we learn that Jesus had hope in them because he believed that they would be makers of a new history due to their good heart soil. All they had to do was open their spiritual eyes to see the secrets of the kingdom of God. For this reason, Jesus had them accompany him wherever he went to preach the kingdom of God. In other words, from first to last, Jesus helped them open their spiritual eyes to see the secret of the kingdom of God so that they might grasp all other things. In this, we learn that we must help others to open their eyes to see the secret of the kingdom of God before trying to inculcate them with other things.

Second, when Jesus traveled about, there were also some women with him. They were the women who had been cured of evil spirits and diseases. Once they were unclean women. Mary Magdalene was possessed by seven demons. Maybe she was possessed by a selfish demon, a marriage demon, a laziness demon, a talkative demon, a party demon, a drug demon, and a sex demon. She had simulated the ugliest woman in the world because of her demon possession. She had once been a beautiful woman, but she became wild and ugly. Joanna was the wife of Cuza, the manager of Herod's household. She must have been an able woman, and she married a rich man. After that, she became so disgusted with living among corrupted and rich fools in the aristocratic stratum of society that she became very sick. There were also Susanna and many others. Once they had been demon possessed and diseased women, but they were healed by Jesus and became useful women in God's work and history. Sometimes we wonder what we can do when we see many wild women. But when we study about the women around Jesus, we learn that all women are very useful and beautiful if they are healed by Jesus. Verse 3b says, "These women were helping to support them out of their own means."

At that time, women were considered inferior to men, but the historian and evangelist Luke put these women in a prominent place in Jesus' life and ministry. As we know, Jesus was poor. When he began his earthly ministry, he was so busy that frequently he had no time to eat, much less make money to support his company. Jesus was occasionally invited to meals by various people. But this could not be sufficient for his daily bread. Judas Iscariot was the treasurer of Jesus' company. But they had no regular income source. It may be that these women fed Jesus and his company regularly. Once they had been selfish and evil women, but after receiving his healing, they sacrificially supported Jesus' ministry by cooking food for them and washing their clothes and socks. These women followed Jesus everywhere he went. Because of their love, they were not afraid to stand beneath the cross of Jesus while all the men were cowering, trembling for their lives.

Their ministry extended beyond Jesus' death. They brought spices with them early in the morning to anoint him. Among them, Mary Magdalene met the Risen Christ first and became the first witness of the resurrection of Christ Jesus. They loved Jesus and his people to the end. This handful of faithful women played the role of mothers at the time of travail for the birth of a new era of a new history.

When we study Luke's Gospel, we learn that Elizabeth spent her whole life in prayer for the birth of her son, John the Baptist, and Mary paid the high price of being the mother of Jesus. Faithful and prayerful women have always been the key factor in the life and growth of the Christian church. We are obliged to pray for the young women of our times, that they may somehow come to know Christ personally and grow up to be pure and sacrificial and prayerful women of God.

II. The secrets of the kingdom of God (4-10)

Read verse 4. "While a large crowd was gathering and people were coming to Jesus from town after town, he told this parable." Innumerable crowds of people from every town were thronging around him. Jesus had compassion on them because they were like sheep without a shepherd. When Jesus saw them, they were filled with all kinds of problems. Their problem was a heart problem. They did not know that the human heart is like a fruit tree or a seed.

In a matter of time, the hearts of most of them became like a path. Some came whose hearts were full of rocks. Some of those who came were willing to accept the words of life. Still, their hearts were cluttered with thorns in which no word of life could grow. Among all the people who were coming to him, there were a few who had good heart soil in which the words of life could grow and bear fruit—thirty, sixty, or a hundred times what was sown. This was the reason why Jesus told them the parable of the sower. "A farmer went out to sow his seed. As he was scattering the seed, some fell along the path; it was trampled on, and the birds of the air ate it up. Some fell on rock, and when it came up, the plants withered because they had no moisture. Other seed fell among thorns, which grew up with it and choked the plants. Still other seed fell on good soil. It came up and yielded a crop, a hundred times more than was sown" (5-8a).

Basically, this parable teaches how the heavenly kingdom grows in one's heart (Mk 4:26-29). When one accepts the words of life into his heart, the seeds in his heart grow night and day, whether he sleeps or wakes. The seed sprouts and grows though he does not know how. In this way, the kingdom of God grows in one's heart.

This parable also teaches us that a man's center is his heart, and his heart either can nurture the seeds of the kingdom of God until he comes to know the secret of the kingdom of God, or he can burden his heart with rocks and thorns and be endlessly miserable.

Many people think that one's heart condition makes up one's character. Therefore, they think that there is no way for them to change their character or inborn characteristics. Those who think like this are very fatalistic, as if they were doomed to be crooked or perverted. But this parable teaches us that one's heart soil or character can be cultivated or ameliorated. Romans 5:3-4 supports this truth: "Suffering produces perseverance; perseverance, character; and character, hope."

Read verse 10. When his disciples asked him what this parable meant, he said, "The knowledge of the secrets of the kingdom of God has been given to you, but to others I speak in parables." In spite of all their shortcomings, Jesus' disciples had good heart soil, so the knowledge of the kingdom of God was planted in their hearts and was growing.

On the other hand, in the souls of many who were coming to him, there was no knowledge of the secrets of the kingdom of God. So Jesus told them of the knowledge of the secrets of the kingdom of God by various methods and approaches. But they did not understand it. This time, Jesus told them of it in a parable so that somehow the knowledge of the secrets of the kingdom of God might be planted in their hearts. Still, they did not understand.

Read verse 10b. "...though seeing, they may not see; though hearing, they may not understand." This is a quotation from Isaiah 6:9, and it is a prophetic description. The people of Isaiah's time heard the messages of hope in God repeatedly, but they did not understand—as if they had decided not to understand. The heart of the prophet was broken because of his calloused people. When Jesus quoted this verse, his heart was broken because of the people who had no knowledge of the secret of the kingdom of God, for they did not accept the word of life from his lips.

III. The meaning of the parable (11-15)

In this parable, the seed is the word of God which can grow in one's heart as the seed of the secrets of the kingdom of God.

First is the heart soil of the path. Read verse 12. "Those along the path are the ones who hear, and then the devil comes and takes away the word from their hearts, so that they may not believe and be saved."

There are many whose heart soil is like a path. The characteristic of the path is hardness. These people are busy-minded. They are filled with worldly desires. Many plans and ideas fill their hearts and minds so that they have no room for anything other than calculating, then re-calculating. They are like unproductive business men. Some are busy trying to satisfy their marriage desires all throughout their youths. Some are busy with their money-making businesses. The seeds which are scattered are good seeds, but they lie bare on the surface of the hard path and cannot stick there long enough to have a chance of germinating. As soon as the sower turned his back to go to the next furrow, the birds that fluttered behind him would come down and take the seeds away. Those whose hearts are like a path can be considered part of a slave class. They are slaves of their desires and passions. They hear the words, but the words never get further than the drum of their ears since they are stuffed full of low desires. Satan comes and takes away all the life seeds scattered around them.

Second is the heart soil of rock. Read verse 13. "Those on the rock are the ones who receive the word with joy when they hear it, but they have no root. They believe for a while, but in the time of testing they fall away." They are those who love the word of truth. They know the word of God is life-giving. But their heart soil is like rock.

The underlying rock has only a thin skin of earth over it. Its shallowness helps the seed to germinate quickly. So with undesirable rapidity, growth begins and shoots appear above the ground before there are enough roots below to nourish the plant. They like the words of life, but because of their other desires, they cannot take root in God.

They are uncommitted people. They are not like trees by streams of water, but are like chaff blown by the winds. The gospel has not really touched the depths of their natures, so they shrivel up when they have to face the toil and self-sacrifice inherent in the Christian life. When they have to grow in spite of many temptations and trials, they fall away from God because they have no truth in their hearts. The commitment problem is the most serious problem of this age. Because of no commitment, there are so many runaway fathers in this country.

Third is the heart soil of thorns. Read verse 14. "The seed that fell among thorns stands for those who hear, but as they go on their way they are choked by life's worries, riches and pleasures." It is interesting to think about what kinds of worries these people have. They worry about riches and pleasures. They worry too much about how to make more money. They become slaves of money. They also worry too much about how to enjoy worldly pleasures. Man is created to do the work of God. But pleasure-seeking people do many ugly things before God. They know they have to be changed into new men and women of God, overcoming their desires for pleasure. At the same time, they don't want to be changed or to lose any pleasures they enjoy. Their hearts are full of the thorns and conflicts of guilt because of their hedonistic ideas. They enjoy pleasures, but in reality, they feel like they live in a thorn bush. In the course of seeking worldly pleasure, they fall into deep sin and live under Satan's control. Money does not make them happy because money and pleasure only hinder them in seeing the kingdom of God.

Fourth is the good heart soil. What is good soil? Verse 15 says that good soil stands for those with a noble and good heart. Good soil is well characterized by one whose aim is noble and whose desires are pure and who is willing to serve God's purpose. He is the one who loves the truth of God's word. As common sense tells us, "The sorer the process, the nobler the result." One who has good soil must fight and resist many things that would draw him away and persistently keep on the course.

How good it is to have a noble and good heart! But it is not easy at all to keep our hearts noble and good. It requires spiritual battles to keep our hearts noble and good. Isaac, the father of faith, seemingly looked weak, conceding everything to his enemies. But he was the one who had fought fierce spiritual battles with the enemies of God. He could be a warrior of prayer (Gen 25:21). He could keep his heart pure and undisturbed. He could keep God's blessings and pass them to his descendants.

We must remember that during the time of much patient labor and self-suppression, the seed sprouts, and the blade becomes the ear, and the ear a full crop. The seeds that fall on good soil, come up and yield a crop, a hundred times more than was sown. May God help us to have fruitful lives when we prepare good heart soil.

Lesson 21

Jesus' Mother and Brothers

Luke 8:16-21
Key Verse: 8:21

I.   A LAMP ON A STAND (16-18)

1. What is the purpose of a lamp? What is done with a lamp to enable it to fulfill its purpose?

2. Why does Jesus say such an obvious thing about a lamp? How is this related to verse 17? When and how do you think the hidden things will be revealed?

3. What does it mean to "consider carefully how you listen"? Why is it necessary to receive God's word and retain it and persevere in obeying it? (18) How else might this parable be applied?

II. JESUS' MOTHER AND BROTHERS (19-21)

4. What was Jesus doing when his mother and brothers came to see him? What may have been their reason for coming? (Mk 3:20,31-35) Why couldn't they get near him?

5. What was the implication of the message someone brought to Jesus?

6. What was Jesus' answer? Was he repudiating his own mother and brothers? (Jn 19:26) What does Jesus teach about priorities in our lives?

7. Who are Jesus' true mother and brothers? What two things are required of us to qualify in being part of Jesus' family?

8. How does Jesus' teaching here (21) emphasize what Jesus had just been teaching? (8:4-15,18)

9. What difference should it make to know who our true family is?

Jesus' Mother and Brothers

Luke 8:16-21
Key Verse: 8:21

> *"He replied, 'My mother and brothers are those who hear God's word and put it into practice.'"*

THE PARABLE OF THE lamp on a stand in verses 16-18 is closely linked with the parable of the sower. While the parable of the sower emphasizes how to retain the word in our hearts, the parable of the lamp on a stand emphasizes how to listen to the word (18).

Verses 19-21 speak of Jesus' mother and brothers. The other gospels placed this little incident before the parable of the sower. But Luke placed it after the parable of the sower, likely as the conclusion of the parable of the sower, and it urges us to put what we have learned into practice.

In today's passage, we learn that we must have an absolute attitude toward the word of God and obey it as our spiritual life principle.

I.   A lamp on a stand (16-18)

Read verse 16. "No one lights a lamp and hides it in a jar or puts it under a bed. Instead, he puts it on a stand, so that those who come in can see the light." This verse teaches us a self-evident truth that even a little child can understand. No one hides a lighted lamp in a jar or puts it under a bed. The purpose of a lamp is to shine so that those who come in can see it.

These days, most people live without the meaning of life. Moreover, they live without life standards, principles, and truth. They just live according to the consensus of the world. The purpose for their study or work is their future security, which cannot be the purpose of human life. The purpose of human life should be noble and meaningful, and it must clearly be based on the truth of God. The purpose of a lamp is to shine forth so that people in the darkness can see.

Allegorically speaking, the lamp light is Jesus. God sent Jesus as the true light to shine in the darkness (Jn 1:5). No one can hide in the darkness when the light shines in the darkness. God puts the lamp on a stand so that each person can see it and come out of the darkness. Here, the lamp light can also be analogous to the word of God's promise (Ps 119:50,105). God's words of promise concerning his salvation and judgment were given by his servants and by the prophets time and again so that everybody could hear and repent. On the day when the words of promise will be completely fulfilled, everything will be disclosed and brought out into the open. Read verse 17. "For there is nothing hidden that will not be … brought out into the open."

Many people scoff and say, "Where is this 'coming' he promised? Ever since our fathers died, everything goes on as it has since the beginning of creation" (2Pe 3:4). They think everything is okay. Nothing changes. What difference does God's promise make? They are blind spiritually because they suppress the truth of God by denying it, as if they have no conscience or truth of God in their hearts. God will fulfill his promise just as he promised. "The Lord is not slow in keeping his promise, as some understand slowness. He is patient with you, not wanting anyone to perish, but everyone to come to repentance" (2Pe 3:9). Jesus said in Matthew 5:18, "I tell you the truth, until heaven and earth disappear, not the smallest letter, not the least stroke of a pen, will by any means disappear from the Law until everything is accomplished." On that day, all they have done will be disclosed before the word of God's promise. "For there is nothing hidden that will not be … brought out into the open" (17). Those who do many evil things in dark places will be exposed red-handed. Those who have secretly committed adultery will be exposed in the very act of committing adultery. Those who were ashamed of Jesus before worldly people will be greatly shamed by Jesus.

Read verse 18a. "Therefore consider carefully how you listen." This is a warning for those who have a poor attitude toward God's word.

Noah is a good example of one who obeyed the word of God absolutely. While others lived according to their sinful nature, completely ignoring God and his word, Noah believed the promises of God. They enjoyed sinful pleasures and ridiculed those who lived on the promises of God. They enjoyed teasing Noah saying, "Why on earth are you doing such foolish things? How long are you going to keep building that monstrous ark?" Maybe Noah said to himself, "How stupid you are! How impractical and unproductive you are!" When we study about Grandpa Noah, he gives us the impression that he's stupid, and at the same time, he inspires some kind of awesome respect, not because he was an old man with a bushy beard, but because he had an absolute attitude toward the promise of God. Before the flood, he was told to build a huge ark. Noah did everything just as God commanded.

Abraham is our father of faith. When we study the life of Abraham, we discover in him human weakness which we also have. But he had an absolute attitude toward God's promise that was superior to anybody's. When he had no child at the age of 75, he believed God's promise that he would have sons and daughters like the sands on the seashore and like the stars in the sky (Ge 15:4-5). He lived in a time of anguish because of 2,000 kinds of torturous superstitions, but he was not completely overcome by cultural sophistications. When the word of God came to him, he simply believed (Ge 15:6).

On the other hand, Lot had a presumptuous attitude toward the word of God. He thought he was smart enough to enjoy both the cultural life of Sodom and God's word of promise. Seemingly, he was smart, but his life was full of anguish and fear like that of an acrobat walking a tightrope between two deep valleys. Because of his bad influence, his sons-in-law took God's word lightly. They scoffed at the word of God concerning the destruction of Sodom and Gomorrah, and they were destroyed when Sodom and Gomorrah were destroyed. His daughters saw him relatively and came to a conclusion that they should be practical. Since no man was there, they decided to sleep with their father to leave children to their family. Therefore, as Jesus says, we must consider carefully how we hear the word of God. Our attitude determines whether we can bear the fruit of life.

Read verse 18b. "Whoever has will be given more; whoever does not have, even what he thinks he has will be taken from him." God has given each of us the capability to bear fruit—thirty, sixty, and a hundred times. He who bears much fruit by having a right attitude toward the word of God will glorify God's name and his joy will be complete (Jn 15:11). But one who does not bear fruit because of his poor attitude toward the word of God will be considered a rebel against God's truth, and everything he thought he had will be taken away from him; he will be put into eternal darkness to gnash his teeth forever.

II. Jesus' mother and brothers (19-21)

Read verses 19 and 20. One day Jesus' mother and brothers came to see him, but they were not able to get near because of the crowd. Until now, Jesus had been an obedient and hard-working son as a carpenter apprentice under his terrestrial father, Joseph. Security-wise, he was the labor power and income source for his family. But when he came to the golden age of manhood, all of a sudden, to their dismay, he left home and went around preaching the kingdom of God. In traditional society, this was unforgivable behavior for the eldest son of a family, who was supposed to inherit the heritage and inheritance of the family. Jesus ignored the deep-rooted Jewish tradition, which was believed by the people to be the truth. Mark 3:21 tells us how his relatives came and tried to persuade him to give up his public ministry and tried to restrain him and take him back home, for they believed him to be out of his mind.

One day, Jesus' mother and brothers put aside their work and decided to go to Jesus and talk about the basic duty to one's family. Perhaps they thought the deepest relationship in life is the blood relationship, for they grew up under the influence of Judaism, which stressed family unity and community relations. They probably expected at least a certain kind of apology or promise for the future from Jesus. But they were not even able to get near him. They were treated equally with others. They were upset when they had to get in line and wait their turn to see him.

Someone saw Jesus' mother and brothers waiting for him. He thought they should be given first priority so he said, "Your mother and brothers are standing outside, wanting to see you" (20).

How did Jesus reply? He said in verse 21, "My mother and brothers are those who hear God's word and put it into practice." His words sound as though he ignored blood relations and family ties. But this does not mean that family ties are unimportant or can be ignored. Jesus had a great affection for his family, especially for his mother. At the time of his crucifixion when he hung on the cross, he was in anguish and pain. But at that moment, he did not think of his own pain. He saw his mother standing near the cross weeping, together with his mother's sister, Mary the wife of Clopas, and Mary of Magdala. "When Jesus saw his mother there, and the disciple whom he loved standing nearby, he said to his mother, 'Dear woman, here is your son,' and to the disciple, 'Here is your mother.' From that time on this disciple took her into his home" (Jn 19:26-27). This story tells us how much Jesus cared for his mother. He was mindful even of the room and board.

What then does it mean when he said, "My mother and brothers are those who hear God's word and put it into practice"? This verse tells us two things about the standard set for God's family members.

First, to hear God's word. This means that the word of God must be the standard for God's family. Why is this so? It is because only the word of God remains forever, and everything in the world, even the family, vanishes. After a few generations pass, nobody remembers the mothers or fathers from previous generations. But the word of God remains forever. "All men are like grass, and all their glory is like the flowers of the field; the grass withers and the flowers fall, but the word of the Lord stands forever" (1Pe 1:24-25).

Read verse 21 again. "He replied, 'My mother and brothers are those who hear God's word and put it into practice.'" This verse not only teaches us how we can be Jesus' true kindred, but also draws a clear dividing line between the children of God and the children of Satan. There are many parables about the kingdom of God and its family members. Matthew 25:31-33 says, "When the Son of Man comes in his glory, and all the angels with him, he will sit on his throne in heavenly glory. All the nations will be gathered before him, and he will separate the people from one another as a shepherd separates the sheep from the goats." There is another interesting parable about this. "Two women will be grinding with a hand mill; one will be taken and the other left" (Mt 24:41). On the last day, we want to be with someone we like, but this doesn't help, for each person must go to his own place—some to eternal condemnation, some to the kingdom of heaven through the pearly gates. This is the reason why we have to set the standard of life on the word of God.

Second, we Christians must put what we learn into practice. Read verse 21 again, "He replied, 'My mother and brothers are those who hear God's word and put it into practice.'" What does it mean to put it into practice? Literally, it means to obey the word of God. Obedience involves sacrifice, love, and loyalty. These days, many people seem to have been born rebellious. Rebellious lifestyles and secular humanism, which promotes perversion and rebellion against the truth, are highly developed and accepted. It is not easy to obey God's word living in this crooked and perverse generation. Who can obey God's word? How can we obey when others are all enjoying worldly ways of life, and when one who obeys the word of God is considered to be an old grandfather like Noah, the object of ridicule? That's a good question! We must learn how to obey.

It is quite a surprise that so many people cry out in their hearts that they are willing to obey and do the right things, but in reality, they cannot obey God's word because the circumstances in which they live are too terrible, not to mention the difficulties of a life in obedience to the word of God. As a result, they live under a burden of sin. The problem is that they did not learn how to obey. Obedience does not come naturally. It requires learning. We must learn how to obey God's word as diligently as we study our school subjects.

One man was a super momma's boy. He was the youngest son, but he studied well and knew how to please those senior to him. He was a most beloved one, the joy of his family. After studying Genesis with Dr. John Lee and Jimmy Rhee, he made a decision to make the word of God his life principle and standard. In the past, he was always willing to listen to his mother because he loved his mother most. But after studying the word of truth, he adopted the word of God as his life principle and gave first priority to obey the word of God. As a result, he was greatly misunderstood, as if he were intentionally disowning his family traditions. They began to treat him as a stranger.

We can obey God's word when we love God. John 14:21 says, "Whoever has my commands and obeys them, he is the one who loves me. He who loves me will be loved by my Father, and I too will love him and show myself to him." Jesus obeyed God's will unto death, even death on the cross, because he loved God. There is no fear in love (1Jn 4:18).

There are clouds of witnesses who died in obedience to God because they loved God so dearly. Polycarp, an early church father, was martyred at the age of 83 because he would not deny the name of Jesus. Pastor Sohn, the director of a large leper colony in Korea, loved men with leprosy so much that he ate and slept together with them. One day, some radical communists came to his house and took his two sons, Tong Jin and Tong Shin, and beat them to death with the butt of their rifles. Later, the men who had killed his sons were arrested by the police and brought to Pastor Sohn. Instead of demonstrating vengeance, he adopted them and made them his own sons. Once he came to my church and confessed that it was possible for him to make them his sons because Jesus loved him first and he loved Jesus more than himself. This is the reason why we have to honor our fellow Christian friends as our own family members. This is the reason why we have to make God's word our standard and principle of life and obey his word absolutely.

But we know how much our Lord had to sacrifice in order to obey the will of God. In order to obey the will of God to accomplish his redemptive work, Jesus gave up the power and glory and all the privileges of the heavenly kingdom. He came down to this world in human form. He emptied himself and took the very nature of a servant. He obeyed God's will to death, even to death on the cross. The obedience of Jesus became the source of salvation for all people (Php 2:6-8). Obedience is spiritual exercise. When we don't obey after hearing the word of God, then we do not grow spiritually. How wonderful it is to know that Jesus showed us a great example of obedience through his life. Hebrews 5:8 says, "Although he was a son, he learned obedience from what he suffered."

Lesson 22

Jesus Calms the Storm

Luke 8:22-25
Key Verse: 8:25a

I. LET'S GO OVER TO THE OTHER SIDE OF THE LAKE (22-24a)

1. Think about the busy life of Jesus and his disciples. What might have been the disciples' mood as they got in the boat with Jesus to cross the lake? What does Jesus' falling asleep in the boat show about him?

2. What unexpected event happened as they crossed? Why was it surprising that the disciples couldn't handle the boat? What does this suggest about the intensity of the storm?

3. What did the disciples do when they reached their human limits? What did they believe about Jesus? What reveals their fear and desperation? What were they afraid of?

II. WHERE IS YOUR FAITH? (24b-25)

4. What did Jesus do and what do his actions reveal about him?

5. How and why did he rebuke the disciples? What does this teach about faith and fear?

6. What was the response of the disciples to Jesus? What is the answer implied by their question? What difference should it make in their lives to believe that Jesus is Almighty God, Creator of heaven and earth? What difference does it make to you?

Jesus Calms the Storm

Luke 8:22-25
Key Verse: 8:25a

> *"'Where is your faith?' he asked his disciples."*

N THIS PASSAGE, JESUS calms the storm. It is a story about a hot summer day. Summer is a dynamic season. Green foliage flourishes vigorously. Especially, the summer sea is boundlessly wide and beautiful. Let's go to the Sea of Galilee and enjoy an old, old story of one summer night long ago. The story develops between Jesus and his disciples on the Sea of Galilee. In this story of a summer sea, Jesus teaches us what kind of faith his people must have. This story helps us open our eyes to learn how to overcome the fear of all kinds of storms of life. Especially, this passage helps us open our eyes wide to see Jesus as the Almighty God who rules over nature.

I.   Let's go over to the other side of the lake (22-24a)

The long-awaited work of the Messiah had begun when Jesus left his carpentry housework and began to minister to the needy. Mark 6:31 describes that Jesus had been so busy that he did not even have a chance to eat. Since Jesus went all out for his earthly ministry, he had no time to see about his family. So his hometown people and his relatives thought he had gone too far. Once they came to take him back home, by force if necessary, for they thought that he was out of his mind.

All Jesus did was shepherding, discipleship training, and prayer. All day long he ministered to all kinds of people, one by one, until dusk fell and it was too dark to minister to them anymore. On the road, or while traveling, or as time permitted, he did his best to plant faith in the hearts of his disciples. In this way, Jesus wanted to help open his disciples' spiritual eyes to grasp the secrets of the kingdom of God.

We can draw three concentric circles as a diagram of Jesus' daily life. The biggest circle represents Jesus' time with the general public. The bigger circle inside the biggest circle represents time with his disciples. The smallest circle in the center represents his personal quiet time with God.

Compared with our daily lives, Jesus had little personal time. But he did have time for himself. It was usually only in the morning before dawn or in the middle of the night while his disciples were enjoying sound sleep. This was the time for him to meet God in prayer. When we examine Jesus' daily routine, we cannot but say that he is more than a man. His life itself reveals that he is the Holy God.

One day Jesus said to them, "Let's go over to the other side of the lake" (22b). It meant, "Let's go to eat and refresh ourselves." This was beyond the expectations of the Twelve, for they thought that Jesus was born to work with no vacations. The disciples were dog-tired even when hanging around him, for they were not spiritually mature enough to welcome the needy who were coming and going ceaselessly. We can easily imagine all of the Twelve shouting, "Let's go!" in unison and the mountains across the horizon echoing, "Leeesgooouu!" No sooner had Jesus said, "Let's go," than they hurriedly prepared a boat and said, "Sir, the boat is ready." Soon Jesus and his disciples got into the boat and began to launch forth, splashing the gentle water of the lake. That night the moonlight was exceptionally bright in the night sky. It was their first vacation. They were overjoyed at this occasion, like students who had just finished their finals and gone on summer vacation. They were happy because for the first time they could go boating with their Master. How excited they must have been when they got into the boat, and how nice the summer evening.

Read verse 23a. They were fisherman. They knew how to handle the boat. They really enjoyed rowing the boat. When their faces were touched by the cool breath of the summer sea, and when waves of the sea crashed on the bow of the boat and smashed into pieces like particles of silver, they began to sing, "Hallelujah, Hallelujah, Hallelujah." While they were enjoying the summer sea, Jesus fell asleep. Now they were some distance away from shore. The boat was gliding on the sea of glass, and Jesus, in his weariness, had already fallen into peaceful sleep.

This sea is surrounded by plateaus, beyond which rise great mountains. Rivers flowing from the mountains over the plateaus into the sea carve out deep ravines. These ravines play the role of funnels, drawing down cold wind from the mountains and thus, causing a sudden storm to arise. A storm on the sea is unpredictable. This is characteristic of the lake which is also called the Sea of Galilee.

What did Jesus do while they were enjoying boating? Jesus continued to sleep on during the storm. Jesus could sleep in a boat even during the time of an angry storm. Jesus was sleeping, pillowing his head on the stern of the boat. Jesus' one movement or one word is full of truth and grace. In this case, Jesus' sound sleep reveals that he is a great God who could sleep in the storm. On the other hand, many people have sleeping problems. Many people want to sleep well because they forget everything while they sleep, and they can rest up. A good night's sleep refreshes one to work hard the next day. But many people cannot sleep well for many reasons. Many people do many evil things to get some sleep. One girl once said to me, "I have a serious problem. I can't sleep well at night." I saw that under the surface, her head was full of gray hairs.

Read verse 23b. Suddenly, "a squall came down on the lake, so that the boat was being swamped." Waves beat into the boat, and it began to fill with water. Yet they had no problem, for many of them were skilled fishermen and men of the sea. They had had to brave many a storm, and they steered the boat right to prevent it from sinking. But everything was in vain. They were in great danger of drowning. They felt like they were dying because the boat was being swamped. So they went and woke Jesus, saying, "Master, Master, we're going to drown!" (24a).

II. Where is your faith? (24b-25)

What did Jesus do when his disciples cried out for help?

First, Jesus rebuked the wind and the raging waters. Read verse

24b. "He got up and rebuked the wind and raging waters; the storm subsided, and all was calm." It is amazing that Jesus rebuked the wind and raging sea. Julius Caesar once met a stormy sea on the voyage to battle. He struggled hard with the stormy sea until his ships were completely wrecked. He had never imagined that he could rebuke the stormy sea and make it calm. But Jesus rebuked the wind and raging sea. At his command, everything was at once calm, and the surface of the water was again motionless and unruffled.

This seems to be a small event. However, it was a mighty revelation of Jesus as Creator God! Jesus demonstrated that he is God who controls heaven and nature. This plainly tells us that Jesus is God who created the heavens and earth with his one word. The God who created the heavens and earth is God Almighty.

When Jesus rebuked the wind and the raging storm, in reality, he rebuked the power of Satan. Undoubtedly, the powers of Satan conspired to nullify the work of salvation. While the wearied Jesus was lying asleep, Satan was trying to make the boat sink by means of a violent storm so that Jesus and his disciples, the main members of the redemptive work, would drown. Satan is so subtle and deceptive. In order to destroy the work of God, the work of salvation, Satan uses everything. Satan's work is intensive, incessant, and destructive.

Second, Jesus rebuked his disciples. Read verse 25a. "'Where is your faith?' he asked his disciples." Jesus rebuked them because they had no practical faith. Instead they were gripped with fear. Jesus' main teaching thus far had been how to have faith in God Almighty. What they had learned was to have faith in God in any situation. They had seen Almighty God in Jesus. By this time, they should have been peaceful and quiet like sleeping Jesus in the storm, as one who totally committed his life to the hand of God. But the disciples could not imitate Jesus in his quietness and peace. They were terrified and overcome by fear. They did not solve their fear problem at all because they had not opened their hearts to learn how to have faith in God. They were still slaves of fear. They feared a small storm and felt like they would die by drowning.

I understand them very well. One summer night at a conference, I wanted to go out to the beach to write a poem while the other conference members were sleeping. When I went to the beach, the waves of the sea were violent and a strong gale stirred up a whirlwind here and there. It was the darkest dark everywhere because there was no moonlight. I went back to my camp terrified.

Most of them were fishermen. Maybe they had left their fishing jobs already because they were afraid of drowning to death. But now their boat was being swamped, and they were in real danger of drowning. Perhaps the stormy sea reminded them of past death struggles on the stormy sea. Perhaps they were harassed by the memory of many horrible stories of sea monsters that crushed all the bones of those who drowned. Perhaps they remembered the sorrowful stories of the widowed wives of their former fellow fishermen.

Jesus saw that they were having a hard time. But he did not say, "Now, now it's okay. You can enjoy the food and the vacation." Instead he rebuked them, saying, "Where is your faith?" It was time for them to examine themselves to see if they had practical faith in God Almighty. They saw the work of the Messiah: "The blind receive sight, the lame walk, those who have leprosy are cured, the deaf hear, the dead are raised, and the good news is preached to the poor" (7:22b). They saw in Jesus that he is the Living God and the Sovereign Ruler of history.

And in Jesus, the disciples were the main history makers in God's redemptive work and history. In order to be the history makers of a new era, they should have solved their inner fear problems through life together with Jesus. But they had not solved their fear problems at all. So they forgot everything when confronted by a storm that made things difficult. In Mark's Gospel, they bitterly complained that Jesus did not care about their drowning, but was only sleeping. The surging waves of the sea drove them into terror and the sinking boat made their hearts melt like water. Their main problem was that they did not have faith in Jesus. They needed the faith that Jesus is Almighty Creator God who controls man and nature.

In the past, all the men and women of God were mighty powerful because they had faith in God Almighty. When they confronted unbearable storms of life, they did not look at the situations or circumstances they were in. They looked at God Almighty, overcame the storms of life, and rendered victories to God. Isaiah lived through many crises of political transitions. He had many things that made him despair. But he encouraged his people because he had faith in God Almighty, and he wrote a poem in Isaiah 45:12 which says, "It is I who made the earth and created mankind upon it. My own hands stretched out the heavens; I marshaled their starry hosts."

The end of verse 24 says that all was calm. This teaches us a spiritual lesson. Where Jesus the Almighty God is, all is calm, as the Christmas carol says. There are many kinds of invisible storms in our lives, such as the storms of temptation. When the storm of temptation arises in our hearts, we are filled with doubts and frustration and become fearful. At that moment, we must hear Jesus' rebuke, "Where is your faith?" From time to time, we are sick with Satan's doubt. At that moment, we must hear Jesus' rebuke, "Where is your faith?" There are storms of hardships where it seems impossible for us to do something for God. At that moment, we must hear Jesus rebuking us, "Where is your faith?"

When Jesus said, "Where is your faith?" he wanted them to have faith in God. He wanted them to depend on God, overcome everything, and do everything. Jesus did not want them to be feeble young men, trembling before a small storm. Jesus wanted them to be strong young men who could wade through all kinds of life storms, grow in faith, and render victories to God. This is the reason why Jesus gave them storm training. In our life of pilgrimage, how much we all want to sail on a sunny and glassy sea all the time! But we cannot always expect to sail under favorable circumstances. In our voyages of life, there are many kinds of storms to overcome.

After the ascension of Christ at the Pentecost, the Holy Spirit came upon 120 disciples who were praying. For the time being, the work of God prospered. Soon afterward, however, the hand of Satan was laid upon them. There was no other way, so all the early Christians had to scatter all over the Minor Asian countries, separating from their loved ones and abandoning all their property. Probably they originally thought that they would gain something if they believed in Jesus. But in reality, they lost everything. All of them became like criminals to the cultural Jews and to the Roman imperialists simply because they believed in Jesus and because they lived pure and holy lives in Jesus. Their pure lives made them look different.

The early Christians thought they would be secure if they believed in Jesus. But they were not. They were plunged into a violent storm. They were drowning. They did not know what was going on. In this situation, their leader Peter said in 1Pe 1:6, "In this you greatly rejoice, though now for a little while you may have had to suffer grief in all kinds of trials. These have come so that your faith—of greater worth than gold, which perishes even though refined by fire—may be proved genuine and may result in praise, glory and honor when Jesus Christ is revealed." Peter was happy, thinking that fiery trials made their faith strong. God was also happy to refine their faith through unbearable hardships. God wanted to use the early Christians to be Gospel preachers to the whole world. But he did not leave them alone to take care of themselves. He put them in a fiery furnace so that their faith might be refined.

It seems like King David was born a man of faith. But this was not the case. From time to time, his heart melted like wax because of fear and troubles. Humanly speaking, David was a man of troubles and anguish. Nevertheless, the more he was in trouble, the more he believed that God was his refuge, rock, and fortress of salvation. God gave him such hard times because he loved him deeply. God's love is deeper. Throughout history, God trains his people so that they may not be overcome by the stormy situation, but may overcome any kind of adverse situation by faith and prove that they are the children of God who have faith in God Almighty.

How often we tremble in fear before the storms of life! Our lives are tragic if we have the fear of storms. Not only that, if we have the fear of storms, we cannot please God, for fear comes from unbelief. We must listen to Jesus' rebuke, "Where is your faith?" With faith we must overcome our inner fears moment by moment.

Through this passage, we learn that storm training is a required course for the children of God. Not only that, storm training is the expression of God's deep love. Hebrews 12:10 says, "Our fathers disciplined us for a little while as they thought best; but God disciplines us for our good, that we may share in his holiness." This is the reason why Jesus rebuked them, "Where is your faith?"

Read verse 25b. "In fear and amazement they asked one another, 'Who is this? He commands even the winds and the water, and they obey him.'" Through storm training, the disciples' spiritual eyes were opened wide, and they began to see that Jesus is the Almighty God. This realization drove all fear out of their hearts and filled them with divine power and wonder, and they cried out, "Who is this?"

Lesson 23

Jesus Heals a Demon-Possessed Man

Luke 8:26-39
Key Verse: 8:30

I. HOW JESUS SAW A MAN POSSESSED BY DEMONS (26-29)

1. Review what happened during the time of sailing. What might have been their physical condition after struggling with the storm?

2. Describe the man who met Jesus when he stepped ashore. What does his peculiar lifestyle suggest about him?

3. How had others tried to deal with him? Why? What do these verses reveal about his relationships with people?

4. What was his reaction to Jesus? (28) Why do you think he acted and spoke this way?

5. How did Jesus respond to the man from the beginning? (29) Why?

II. WHAT IS YOUR NAME? (30-31)

6. How was Jesus' treatment of this man different from others' attitudes and actions? Why did Jesus ask him, "What is your name?"

7. How did the Gerasene man answer Jesus' question about his name? What does his answer mean?

III. AND HE GAVE THEM PERMISSION (32-33)

8. What request did the demons make of Jesus? What was Jesus' response? What happened to the pigs? What does this suggest about the characteristics of demons?

9. What did these pigs mean to the townspeople? Why do you think Jesus allowed their destruction?

IV. TELL HOW MUCH GOD HAS DONE FOR YOU (34-39)

10. How did the townspeople react when they went out to see what had happened? Why? What does this show about their value system?

11. How had this man been changed outwardly and in his relations with others?

12. What mission did Jesus give him and why? How did the man respond to Jesus' mission? What can we learn from this event about the grace and mercy of God?

Jesus Heals a Demon-Possessed Man

Luke 8:26-39
Key Verse: 8:30

> *"Jesus asked him, 'What is your name?' 'Legion,' he replied, because many demons had gone into him."*

THIS PASSAGE TEACHES US that the real enemies of mankind are not social structures or hostile environments, but demons. According to this passage, Jesus is the only one who can solve man's basic problem because he is the unique one who subdues the power of demons.

I. How Jesus saw a man possessed by demons (26-31)

As we studied, Jesus knew that the disciples needed a time of retreat. He also needed a time of close communion with God in prayer. So Jesus and his disciples sailed to the region of the Gerasenes. It was across the lake from Galilee. It was one of the ten towns of the Decapolis, located on the west side of the Jordan. At one time, Greek immigrants had colonized this area. And the 14th Roman Legion occupied this territory in the name of the Roman Emperor. In light of this, the country of the Gerasenes was a nice place for a vacation. After a day of hard work disseminating the seeds of the kingdom of God, Jesus and his disciples left the other side of the lake. It must have been early evening when they departed. The country of the Gerasenes was only six miles away across the Sea of Galilee. They could have arrived earlier, but because of a squall which came down on the lake, they were delayed. Jesus and his disciples probably arrived there in the middle of the night or in the early hours of the morning. It was the time when they were the most tired and sleepy.

Read verse 27. "For a long time this man had not worn clothes or lived in a house, but had lived in the tombs." Verse 27 gives the impression that he sought unlimited freedom. He most likely lived according to his feelings and enjoyed unlimited human freedom. He probably got out of his home as soon as he passed the age of legal protection. He probably changed his job many times a year because his bosses seemed to bother him, telling him to do this or do that. All kinds of regulations and laws of the town seemed to bother him, so he moved around to all ten towns of the Decapolis. Finally, he found nowhere to go except the graveyard. When he had left home, he was probably wearing blue jeans cut to the buttocks and a T-shirt with his name inscribed on it. Later, he threw these away, for he felt they were bothering him. What happened when he lived as he wanted?

First, he became an outcast of human society. Read verse 27b. "For a long time this man had not worn clothes or lived in a house, but had lived in the tombs." This verse describes well what kind of man he was. In short, he was a free man. He was as free as a bird in the sky. Nobody bothered him in the graveyard. For this reason, he left home and society. He even threw away his clothes which seemed to bother him. But there was a problem. He could not get out of himself. When Jesus stepped ashore in the early hours of the morning, this man had not slept until that time. Of course, he must have wanted to get some sleep. But he could not sleep because something bothered him terribly when the wanted to sleep.

Read verse 28. "When he saw Jesus, he cried out and fell at his feet, shouting at the top of his voice, 'What do you want with me, Jesus, Son of the Most High God? I beg you, don't torture me!" When he cried out and fell at his feet, he seemed to be paying obeisance and entreating for help. At the same time, he rejected violently, as a tiger repulsed by a hunter. It seems that his personality was torn in two. It seems that he loved Jesus, and at the same time, he hated Jesus. Something was bothering him. He could not control himself, much less enjoy human freedom. Something drove him, and he was tormented by something until he could not but shout at the top of his voice like a badly wounded animal. He got out of everything. But he could not get out of himself. Psychologically speaking, he was a crazy man. He was out of his mind.

Second, he became a troublemaker. Read verse 29b. "Though he was chained hand and foot and kept under guard, he had broken his chains and had been driven by the demon into solitary places." Obviously, he had been a troublemaker among his people. He inflicted much damage on others. Finally, people beat him up and put him into prison, shackled and chained. Then he would disturb whole towns, shouting and cursing others.

Third, he was possessed by demons. When he lived according to his feelings, the demons took chances. They came into him, one by one, riding his feelings, until 6,000 demons came in. With the power of demons, he was goaded on from vice to vice and from one profligacy to another. He wanted to be the master of himself, but the demons did not leave him alone. Here we learn that men cannot be masters of themselves.

Finally, he became a cursed man. In the course of living in his own way, he cut all human relationships. In cutting his relationships with others, in reality, he was cutting his relationship with God. Many people think that cutting relationships is a light matter, so many break away from their home lives and run away. Many people think, "I don't have to see him or her." But this is not so. According to the Bible, cutting relationships is a serious matter. Cutting is the first cause of sin. The Bible defines sin as separation. The character of sin is cutting, breaking, or separating. When Adam sinned, as a result, his relationship with God was broken; he was a cursed man. Indeed, the man in the tombs was a cursed man. But Jesus did not see him as a cursed one. He saw him as a most dear one and as one who was created in the image of God. Jesus really wanted to help him.

II. What is your name? (30-31)

It is amazing to see how Jesus helped him.

First, Jesus cast the demons out of him. Even if he was a character in fiction, his story would be too eerie to hear. If we had confronted this dolorous and cadaverous-looking man, wailing in a beastly voice, most of us would have been too frightened even to look at him. When Jesus saw the man, though stunned for a moment, he did not blame him because of his damaged life. Immediately, Jesus commanded the evil spirit to come out of him, for he knew that his problem was demon-possession. Jesus saw his problem as a spiritual problem. Demons are Satan's agents, also called unclean spirits. Demons attacked him and subdued him and made him their prisoner. Demons controlled him with absolute command. When Jesus saw him, he commanded them to come out of him. Jesus did not see him as a crazy or abnormal man. He saw him as a man created in the image of God. He saw him with great compassion because he was possessed by demons and became a prisoner of demons. Jesus saw him spiritually and cast out the demons in him. Jesus liberated him from the imprisonment of demons.

When we see people who do horrible things, we can only despair, not knowing what's going on in them. That was the case of the townspeople. When this man became abnormal, they treated him as a psychiatric patient. They adopted the old psychiatric treatment of beating and torturing and put him in prison. Nowadays, though methods and approaches are different, treatment of abnormal men is basically the same as in ancient times. People see such persons only medically and scientifically and dose them with heavy drugs. It is just another kind of torture.

Second, Jesus asked him his name. When he asked him, "What is your name?" he wanted to remind him of himself. Biblically, a name symbolizes one's whole man. A name represents one's inner character. When Moses asked God, "What is your name?" he replied, "I AM WHO I AM" (Ex 3:14). When Jesus asked the Gerasene man, "What is your name?" he could not answer. It was because he had forgotten his name in his oblivion. More than that, his whole man was lost, and his character was demolished by demons. Physically, he existed, but he had no sense of self left. So, he could not tell Jesus his name. If he had said his name, he would have said 6,000 names or "My name is many," for he was possessed by 6,000 demons.

When Jesus asked him, "What is your name?" he could not say his name. Then the demons answered on behalf of him, "Legion," which is a unit of Roman soldiers. When he began to live according to his sinful nature, demons began to enter his heart one by one, one after another. Many unclean spirits came into his heart, like cockroaches which creep around the kitchen when the darkness of the night comes. Then, in his great anguish, he cried out at the top of his voice. At first, the curiosity demon came into his heart; next, the selfish demon; next, the immoral demon; then the amoral demon, marriage demon, fatalistic demon, hedonistic demon, sarcastic demon, divorce demon, etc. Finally, all kinds of demons came into his heart, all in rows.

Like the man possessed by demons, there are many whose inner man is occupied by many demons. A young man I know wants to improve himself with the word of God. He wants to repent of his proud mind and physical desires. But he cannot because he is under the control of a proud demon and a physical desire demon. He is himself, but the components of his inner man seem to be pride and physical desires because of the demons' deception. If he repents, then he feels like his whole being would crumble. If we study Mark's Gospel, a demon penetrated the heart of a teenage boy through the symptoms of epilepsy, and this demon pretended to be an epileptic patient. Likewise, demons penetrate a man's heart through various channels. Demons enter man's heart through all kinds of sicknesses. Demons can enter through all kinds of sinful desires and arrest each person as their prisoner. Only Jesus can help those who are possessed by demons.

Third, when Jesus asked him, "What is your name?" he wanted to restore him to his original being, created in the image of God. When God made man in his own image, he wanted him to be the steward of the world. God expected him to grow like an oak tree to the fullness of God's standard. But he did not live according to God's truth. He lived according to his sinful nature and became the possession of demons and the object of God's wrath. When Adam sinned, he lost the meaning of his existence. Then he hid himself in the trees. God visited him and called him, "Adam, where are you?" Likewise, Jesus, by calling his name, wanted to restore the meaning of his existence before God. At this moment, we must hear God's voice, "What is your name?"

III. And he gave them permission (32-33)

Read verse 29. Jesus had commanded the evil spirits to come out of him. Then they begged him repeatedly not to order them to go into the Abyss, and they wanted to make a deal with Jesus. Read verse 32. The demons looked around and saw a possible captive. They saw a herd of many pigs feeding there. The demons begged Jesus to let them go into them. The demons were so pragmatic that they did not want to release their prisoner free of charge. They made a big demand, not of money, but of the lifeblood of 2,000 pigs. Jesus gave in to their demand, for he knew they only demand blood as a ransom price. He gave them permission to take the pigs. These pigs were not his own, but belonged to foreigners. Nevertheless, in order to save one man, he immediately gave them permission. He valued one man's life more than the whole business of the Gerasa region.

The inverted order of the universe today—first, mammon; second, man; and third, God—is one cause of the depreciation of human value. However, no matter what the consensus of the world might be, the truth is that one person's life is more precious than the whole universe. The people of the world see people's lives according to situational ethics. But Jesus valued one man's life more than anything else in the world. This story is a prologue of Jesus' own ransom sacrifice for many (Mk 10:45).

What happened to the pigs? Read verse 33. When the demons came out of the man, they went into the pigs. When the herd of pigs was possessed by the demons, they pigs stopped eating, which was their only joy. They suddenly became crazy and rushed down the steep bank into the lake. They lost the joy of life and committed mass suicide.

IV. Tell how much God has done for you (34-39)

Read verses 34-36. People from all over the countryside and towns came and saw the situation. All the pigs had drowned, and the man Jesus had healed was there, sitting at the feet of Jesus, dressed and in his right mind. To their eyes, he looked very presumptuous. They were upset over the fact that the man who had been such a disaster had been healed. Moreover, their businesses were ruined within a few hours of one early morning. They became very fearful of further damage or loss. So they asked Jesus to leave them. So he got into the boat and left. Their vacation ended up in this way. His disciples only met a sea storm and a demoniac storm. It was not a good vacation. However, they could see the mind of God in Jesus.

Read verse 38. "The man from whom the demons had gone out begged to go with him." The man healed was too grateful to Jesus for his healing. He experienced God's love through Jesus. He could not miss Jesus. He wanted to follow Jesus wherever he went.

What did Jesus say to him? Read verse 39. "Return home and tell how much God has done for you." In this verse, Jesus teaches him two things.

First, Jesus taught him to become a man who knows the grace of God through his Son, Jesus. In the past, he did not thank God at all. Unthankfulness was the cause of all his problems. Those who do not know how to thank God are all blind men, men groping in sheer darkness, not knowing God's grace, though God's grace for them is countless. Those who do not know how to thank God are lower than animals in their level of existence, for the donkey knows his owner's manger, even though his master drives him hard, and a dog wags his tail for his master as a sign of gratitude. Those who do not know how to thank God are those whose spiritual conditions are like that of the man possessed by 6,000 demons. It was because his root problem was unthankfulness toward God. But through the healing, he could tell exactly what Jesus had done for him. "You know, I was a Gerasene demoniac. But see, now I am okay!" He had a clear testimony in Jesus.

We also must have a clear testimony in Jesus. Otherwise, we have no personal relationship with God. The blood of Jesus is inefficient for such a person. Paul was always very clear about what kind of sinner he was and what kind of grace he had received. He said, "Christ Jesus came into the world to save sinners—of whom I am the worst" (1Ti 1:15). But by the grace of God, his sins were forgiven, and he became an apostle of light. So he said in 1 Corinthians 15:10, "But by the grace of God, I am what I am."

Second, Jesus established him as a man of mission. Read verse 39 again. "Return home and tell how much God has done for you."

This verse also tells us that Jesus gave this man a mission to become a spiritual director of the Decapolis. In the past, he was able and energetic. But he used all his abilities and strength to enjoy sinful pleasures. As a result, he was captured by demons. Because of this, he had ruined his youth and looked too terrible to do anything, much less become a spiritual leader. But with faith, Jesus appointed him as the director of the Decapolis (Ten Cities). He became a man of mission from God, to proclaim the grace of God and to win people to God. Jesus not only restored his whole being, but also his mission and the meaning of his existence.

"So the man went away and told all over town how much Jesus had done for him" (39b). Maybe his testimony sounded something like this. "I was a crazy guy because of demon-possession. I looked like a sea monster. But see, now I look handsome, and I have become a man of mission."

Lesson 24

Jesus Heals a Dead Girl and a Sick Woman

Luke 8:40-56
Key Verse: 8:50

I. JAIRUS, A RULER OF THE SYNAGOGUE (40-42a)

1. Where had Jesus been and why did the crowd welcome him?

2. Who was Jairus and why was he so eagerly waiting for Jesus? What can we learn about him from his actions and words?

II. DAUGHTER, YOUR FAITH (42b-48)

3. What hindered Jesus' short journey to Jairus' house? How was the woman who touched his cloak different from the crowd that pressed him?

4. Describe the woman's condition. How was she different from Jairus humanly? How was she like him? What was the result of her touch and what does this reveal about Jesus?

5. What were the pressures which Jesus had to overcome in order to meet this woman?

6. Describe the woman who came forward to acknowledge Jesus' grace. Why was it necessary for her to put aside her shame and embarrassment and reveal what had happened? How did Jesus bless her?

III. JUST BELIEVE (49-56)

7. How might this incident with the woman have affected Jairus? What might have been his mixed feelings? Why might he have been afraid?

8. What happened while Jesus was still speaking? What advice did the messenger give Jairus? What counter advice did Jesus give?

9. How did Jairus respond to the messenger and to Jesus? How could this seemingly unfortunate turn of events be used to plant faith in Jairus?

10. Describe the general atmosphere of Jairus' home when Jesus arrived. How might these well-meaning neighbors impede Jairus' faith? How did Jesus create an atmosphere of faith? What does Jairus' silent cooperation show about him?

11. Describe the healing of the girl. Why did he tell them to give her something to eat? Why did he order them not to tell what had happened?

Jesus Heals a Dead Girl and a Sick Woman

Luke 8:40-56
Key Verse: 8:50

"Hearing this, Jesus said to Jairus, 'Don't be afraid; just believe, and she will be healed.'"

TODAY'S PASSAGE CONTAINS THE story of Jairus' dead daughter and a woman with a bleeding problem. All three synoptic gospels have the healing of the bleeding woman in the middle of the Jairus' story. The story of Jairus' dead daughter teaches us how we can overcome our inner fear with faith. And the story of a woman with a bleeding problem teaches us how to overcome human hopelessness with faith. Most importantly, this passage teaches us that Jesus is the healer of all kinds of people, even a dead person.

I. Jairus, a ruler of the synagogue (40-42a)

Jesus returned from Gerasa, where he had healed a man possessed by demons. "When Jesus returned, a crowd welcomed him, for they were all expecting him" (40). They needed a shepherd who could take care of them. They were like sheep without a shepherd (Mk 6:34).

Just then, "a man named Jairus, a ruler of the synagogue, came and fell at Jesus' feet, pleading with him to come to his house because his only daughter, a girl of about twelve, was dying" (41-42). A crowd of people were pressing Jesus, each with his own demand. But Jesus chose to go to Jairus' house to see his dying daughter. Obviously, Jesus saw in Jairus something worthy to be favored. What kind of person was he?

Jairus was a leader in his community, a ruler of the synagogue.

Probably because of this, among the crowd, the first priority to see Jesus was given to him. The fact that he had many servants shows that he must have been a rich man. No doubt, Jairus had made a great effort to climb the ladder of earthly recognition and prestige. With success, he married. Perhaps he wanted to have five sons and seven daughters. But he had only one daughter. She must have been a blessing to her family. As a girl of twelve, she must have looked beautiful, like the bud of a Rose of Sharon about to bloom. To Hebrew people, a family heir meant a lot. Jairus had no male heir to take over his inheritance. But as long as his daughter was with him, he did not care about these things. Even when he was upset and angry, his anger subsided as soon as his daughter appeared before his eyes. He was happy with his only daughter. One day, his daughter suddenly got sick and was dying. He could not believe his eyes. He felt like the whole world was crumbling in darkness. He felt like he was dying when he looked at his ailing and dying daughter. He was engulfed with sorrow when he thought about his future life without his only daughter. He became ashamed when he thought about his neighbors criticizing him for having no son as an heir, but only a daughter, and now that his daughter was dying, he had no blessing from God. All of this made him very fearful. It was a time when he could have given in to his own scheming and become fatalistic. In his situation, he could do nothing. But he came to Jesus.

Was it easy for him to come to Jesus? It was not easy because of his social position as a ruler of the synagogue. Since Jesus was branded as a cult leader and a dangerous heretic, even before having examined him, all the Jews had prejudice against Jesus. When Jairus came to Jesus, he had to overcome prejudice and misunderstanding, not to mention the peer pressure of traditional Jews and public opinion. Despite all this, he took a chance and came to Jesus for his one and only daughter's healing.

It was not easy for Jairus to come to Jesus because early Jews were known as being stubbornly proud and prejudiced. Jairus must have been among them. I know one professor who loved his only daughter so much that he would give almost anything to her. But he did not attend his daughter's wedding simply because something hurt his pride. But Jairus came to Jesus. He could not come to Jesus unless he overcame his pride.

When Jairus came to Jesus, he fell at Jesus' feet, pleading with him to come to his home. At that time, Jesus was nothing but a country evangelist and Jairus was the ruler of the synagogue. But he knelt down at Jesus' feet for his mercy on his daughter. He was a humble man. I pray that all American fathers can come to Jesus and humbly kneel down before Jesus for their children's sake.

Why did he fall at Jesus feet, asking for his mercy? Luke comments, "… because his only daughter, a girl of about twelve, was dying" (42a). He could risk his social position, if only it might help his daughter. He could curb his pride. He could even beg for anything. There are many fathers who run away because they love themselves more than their children. But this father loved his daughter more than himself. When his daughter was dying, he became hopeless. Then in Jesus, he found hope and came to Jesus for his dying daughter. Jairus had a broken shepherd heart for his daughter. In short, he had the image of God as a good shepherd. When Jesus saw his shepherd heart, he was most pleased.

II. Daughter, your faith has healed you (42b-48)

As Jesus was on his way to Jairus' house, the crowds almost crushed him. Jesus waded through the crowds of people and moved one step after another to reach Jairus' house where his dying daughter was lying. Jesus wants to help those who have humble faith like Jairus. Jesus wants to help one person at the cost of crowds of people. I remember one handsome American evangelist. He liked mass evangelism. Wherever he went, a great crowd of people gathered to hear him. With every big evangelistic meeting, he hoped for an even bigger one. As a result, he could not take care of his wife. Their relationship got worse. Finally, he divorced his wife and died soon after that. Jesus did not care about the crowds of people. He honored the faith of one person more. He cared more for one person's problem. This event teaches us that Jesus cares for each of us. We must believe this from our hearts.

Look at verse 43. "And a woman was there who had been subject to bleeding for twelve years, but no one could heal her." On seeing this woman, Jesus' heart went out again to this woman. He took time with her on the way to Jairus' house. No one can bypass Jesus. This happened in the hubbub of the crowd. But Jesus spoke to that woman and treated her as if she were the only person in the world. The crowd seemed to have been completely ignored. She was a poor, unimportant sufferer with an unclean body. But Jesus gave all of himself.

Who was this woman? She had suffered from bleeding for a long time. This woman had been sick with bleeding for twelve years. During those twelve years, many people had been born, and at the same time, many people had passed away, and the world in which she was living had changed into quite another world. She had spent all her youth in suffering. The woman's malady was not only distressing to her, but it had also made her a social outcast by making her ceremonially unclean (Lev 15:25). It is said that this type of hemorrhage causes fretting wounds within and intractable sores which nothing can heal. Mark recorded that she had suffered a great deal under the care of many doctors and had spent all she had (Mk 5:26). But Luke omitted these details maybe because he did not want to gibe at doctors since he was a doctor himself. This woman had done all she could. All she could do now was give in to her ill fate, awaiting the day of her sorrowful death. But she did not give up. She came to Jesus.

When she decided to come, there were many obstacles to overcome. For this weak woman, these obstacles were insurmountable. As verse 42b says, the crowds almost crushed even Jesus. She had a fear of mingling with the crowd because she was a sickly woman. But she penetrated the crowd and finally reached the place where Jesus was. She had a fear of getting close to other people because of the offensive smell coming from her bleeding. But she overcame her fear of people and came to Jesus. Her coming to Jesus was a courageous act of faith. Faith is not speculation. Faith involves action.

Look at verse 44. "She came up behind him and touched the edge of his cloak." She had spent all of her youth in dark privacy because of her bleeding. She had been so withdrawn into herself that she could not stand in front of Jesus. So she came up behind him, believing that she would be healed if only she touched his cloak. What could have happened by her touching the edge of Jesus' cloak from behind him? Her act appeared to be a most simple one and utterly inadequate to produce any great result. But the effect was most marvelous. It was but one touch. However, when Jesus' divine power of healing went into her, the poor sufferer was completely healed and Jesus' love and life flowed through her body. Her bloodstained body was cleansed as white as snow. In a moment, as soon as the vestiges of her suffering were gone, liveliness and the beauty of a woman preserved in her blossomed. She became completely new. She looked beautiful. Now she could have the hope of a happy wedding. When she came to Jesus, she was recreated into a new person.

Read verse 45. "'Who touched me?' Jesus asked. When they all denied it, Peter said, 'Master, the people are crowding and pressing against you.'" Peter protested. Maybe he was very tired because the night before, he had stayed up all night, watching his master struggle with a man possessed by demons. Maybe he thought that Jesus was lingering too long on this matter. But Jesus said in verse 46, "Someone touched me; I know that power has gone out from me." Jesus asked again and again about this matter. Jesus did not allow her to retire from the crowd unheeded.

First, Jesus wanted to heal her spiritually. She was healed physically by his grace, but she needed to be healed spiritually. If she went back unnoticed, she would forget God's grace and become worse than before. There is a story about a man who had suffered from paralysis for 38 years. When he was healed, he completely forgot about Jesus and betrayed Jesus to the Jews who were seeking a charge against him. There is a story about a tiger. Once upon a time, a man saved a tiger from drowning in a lake. As soon as the tiger was pulled out from the water, he wanted to devour the man who saved him. Jesus knew that it was not easy for her to confess what kind of woman she was and what Christ had done for her. But it was necessary for her to make a confession of faith so that she might not forget God's grace and might be saved (Rom. 10:9-10).

Second, Jesus wanted to make a personal relationship with her. At the moment the people were crowding and pressing against him, Jesus had to hurry to go see Jairus' dying daughter. But Jesus again asked about this woman. It was because Jesus wanted to know her and have a personal relationship with her.

"Then the woman, seeing that she could not go unnoticed, came trembling and fell at his feet. In the presence of all the people, she told why she had touched him and how she had been instantly healed" (47). By making a confession of faith, she could have a clear testimony: "I was a smelly woman, but by God's grace, I am now a beautiful woman with many beautiful dreams!" Then Jesus said to her, "Daughter, your faith has healed you. Go in peace" (48). Jesus called her, "Daughter"! Jesus accepted her as his own daughter when she had a confession or faith. Her act of faith simply explains the whole meaning of Christianity. Her coming to him was marvelous faith. There are many people who are spiritually bleeding and smelly because of their corruption and sin-stained life. They are helpless and are dying. If only they came to Jesus, they would be healed.

III. Just believe (49-56)

Let's come back to Jairus' story. Read verse 49. "While Jesus was still speaking, someone came from the house of Jairus, the synagogue ruler. 'Your daughter is dead,' he said. 'Don't bother the teacher any more.'" The messenger thought that everything was over. Unintentionally, he planted the doubt of Satan in Jairus' heart. He made Jairus stumble in unbelief.

Read verse 50. "Hearing this, Jesus said to Jairus, 'Don't be afraid; just believe, and she will be healed.'" How could he just believe she would be healed when he had just heard the news of his daughter's death? But Jesus wanted him to overcome the fear of his daughter's death by faith, instead of being overcome by fear. To our surprise, he just believed Jesus' words. What kind or faith did Jairus have?

First, he had patient faith. On the way, Jesus was stopped by the bleeding woman. Jesus healed her and waited for her until she made her own confession of faith. To Jairus, one minute was precious because his daughter was dying moment by moment. Jairus must have been very impatient and upset and beat his chest. He could have been angry with Jesus because his pride was greatly hurt, but he waited on Jesus very patiently until Jesus healed her and helped her to make a confession of faith.

Second, he had faith that overcomes doubt. Read verse 49. "While Jesus was still speaking, someone came from the house of Jairus, the synagogue ruler. 'Your daughter is dead,' he said." To Jairus, everything was over. He felt that he was hearing the tolling bell of his daughter's death. It was the moment of Satan's attack. He could have bitterly complained about Jesus' delay. But when Jesus said to him, "Don't be afraid; just believe," he battled and defeated Satan's doubts. He just believed that his dead daughter would be healed. There are many young people who want to study well and succeed. But most of them fall when they hear Satan's voice, "Why do you have to work so hard? Relax! Enjoy!" Finally, they become useless.

Third, Jairus had faith that just believed, that overcomes fear of losing one's most precious one. To Jairus, his daughter was most precious. Even if he should have to lose everything, he could not lose his daughter. But in reality, he faced the situation in which he would lose his daughter. In this situation, he must have been overwhelmed by human thinking, many good ideas, or ominous premonitions. But when Jesus said "Don't be afraid; just believe," he simply believed Jesus' word. He had tremendous inner power to control himself. He had tremendous respect for Jesus' word. Just believing is not easy at all. It requires self-control, obedience, and respect. In this case, Jairus is like Abraham who offered his one and only son Isaac when God told him to offer his son Isaac as a burnt offering on the Mount of Moriah.

When Jesus saw Jairus' faith, he was ready to raise his dead daughter. But he did not want to demonstrate his resurrection power to those who were unprepared. So on arriving, he took Peter, John, and James, the three top disciples, and the child's parents with him into the house. On the way, he saw people who were wailing and mourning for her. "'Stop wailing,' Jesus said. 'She is not dead but asleep'" (52). Jesus said this because there is no death in him.

How did the mourners respond to Jesus' words? They began to laugh at him, for they knew that she was dead. They thought that facts are facts. In the midst of an unbelieving atmosphere, Jesus took her by the hand and said, "My child, get up!" Her spirit returned and at once she stood up. Then Jesus told them to give her something to eat. Jesus knew that teenagers are always hungry and want to eat. This happy work of God was possible when Jairus listened to Jesus' words, "Just believe." Her parents were astonished to see their daughter eating. They were even more astonished to see the resurrection power of Jesus.

These days fear is the greatest enemy of mankind. In this passage, we learn that we can overcome our inner fear when we come to Jesus with faith. In Christian theology, we learn that faith is a personal matter. But it is remarkable to learn that a teenage girl was healed from the dead because of Jairus' "just believing" faith. May God heal all teenagers and young college students through our "just believing" faith.

Lesson 25

Jesus Sends out the Twelve

Luke 9:1-9
Key Verse: 9:2

I. HE GAVE THEM POWER AND AUTHORITY TO DRIVE OUT DEMONS (1)

1. What equipment did Jesus give the Twelve before he sent them out? Why was this necessary? What does this suggest about their mission?

II. TO PREACH THE KINGDOM OF GOD AND HEAL THE SICK (2)

2. What was the mission he gave them when he sent them out? What does this mean?

III. TAKE NOTHING FOR THE JOURNEY (3-9)

3. What did he tell them not to take, and why? (What was he seeking to teach them?)

4. What kind of relationships were they to make with the people in each town? Why did Jesus tell them to shake the dust off their feet when they left towns that did not welcome them?

5. Why was Herod perplexed? Why did he try to see Jesus?

6. What does Herod's beheading of John and his attitude toward Jesus reveal about the times and the needs of the people? About the danger to Jesus and the apostles?

Jesus Sends out the Twelve

Luke 9:1-9
Key Verse: 9:2

> "And he sent them out to preach the kingdom of God and to
> heal the sick."

CHAPTER 9:1-2 MARKS THE turning point in the public ministry of Jesus. He was at the very peak of his popularity in
the district of Galilee, and this was his golden chance at a
successful long-term business. To our surprise, Jesus almost gave up
his public ministry just when it was beginning to be most fruitful.
It's human nature that everybody wants to make a success of his life;
no one wants to be a failure. Even when success doesn't mean much,
one still wants to be successful. In light of this, Jesus' giving up of
this great opportunity for success is hard to understand. He did so
in order to give more of his time to intensive discipleship training.
This tells us that discipleship training is more significant than showy
mass evangelism.

Today's passage is about fieldwork training. Jesus teaches them
to be equipped with his power and authority in order to be sent out.
When they are sent out, they must preach the kingdom of God and
heal the sick. He also teaches them that they should have a right
attitude toward the message they preach and toward the people to
whom they go.

There are many who are willing to do God's work, who want to
become great servants of God someday and help others while enjoying the popularity and honor of being great servants of God. But
doing God's work in God's way is not some exotic thing, as many
young people think. It is having and practicing the mentality which
Jesus commands. What, then, would be several things which one

should keep in mind when he is doing God's work?

I. He gave them power and authority to drive out demons (1)

Read verse 1a. "When Jesus had called the Twelve together …" Until now, Jesus himself mainly taught and healed, and the Twelve participated in his work, observing this and that. They had really enjoyed watching Jesus' marvelous signs, and many a time their mouths hung wide open in amazement, and they exclaimed, "Wow!" It had been a time of overflowing "wows." Not only this, but their life together with him was the time for them to see the divinity or Jesus. Thus far, they had been called disciples—Jesus' students. Now, Jesus sent them out. In other words, they were promoted from disciples to apostles for the world—"apostle" means "to be sent out." The Twelve were not really good enough to be promoted; rather, they should have been demoted because of their poor records. But Jesus promoted them with the hope of raising them as apostles of the light.

Read verse 1b. "He gave them power and authority to drive out all demons and to cure diseases." Jesus' disciples were still weak and spiritually immature. They were like the "dirty dozen" in the movie by that name. They were not able to do anything for others. They could only suffer enough to take care of themselves. They were not fully qualified to be apostles of light and shepherds for suffering people. But Jesus appointed them to be so. He could do that because he gave them power and authority to drive out demons and cure diseases. In this context, we learn that everyone can do a great work of God if he is humble enough to depend on God's power and authority. On the other hand, no one can say "I am too weak to do God's work." We also learn that the gospel work is a spiritual battle with demons and diseases. We cannot ignore that battle. We have to decide either to fight or to yield to the devil or disease.

These days, many people admit the presence of the Holy Spirit. But most of them try to deny the existence of demons because demons are too horrible to think about. Generally, most people ignore the existence of demons simply because they want to ignore the spiritual reality of their inner lives so that they can live freely according to their sinful desires. What is worse, they don't want to expose their miserable inner lives which are in continuous torment from demoniac powers. But the Bible teaches us of the existence of demons just as it teaches us the presence of the Holy Spirit. They are so deceptive that they have many names—the Old Serpent, demons, evil spirits, unclean spirits, the devil, or Satan.

Demon possession is a horrible thing. In the previous chapter, we studied about a man possessed by demons. He had tremendous power with which he could wrench iron chains off like a spider web. But he did not use this power for doing good, like cleaning his room or doing his homework. He used this power to hurt or damage others and to torment himself. He did this, not because he meant to, but because he was driven by the power of demons. He was always miserable because he wanted to do good, but what he actually did was always bad.

King Saul is an interesting example in understanding the existence of demons. He was a handsome young man, a shy and obedient country boy, standing a head taller than anyone else. When he was filled with the Spirit of God, he became a national leader in the time of national crisis, and a king full of spirit, passion, and anger. But when he became arrogant toward God's law, the devil discovered vulnerability in him, and attacked and possessed him. When he was possessed by demons, he became strange. He became very fatalistic about his future kingship and felt an inferiority complex toward a mere boy, David. He loved David because of his loyalty and his distinguished service; simultaneously, he hated him so much that he tried to pin him to the wall with a spear. He once threw his spear at his son Jonathan because of his friendship with David. So many times he tried to be in control of himself, but he failed, for he was beside himself, driven by the power of demons. Saul was a king, so he felt he had to show himself off to others as a "cool guy." But he failed to do so. The more he wanted to be a "cool guy,'" the more he became a crazy guy, for he was recklessly driven by the power of demons. One is clothed either with the Spirit of God or with the evil spirit.

II. To preach the kingdom of God and to heal the sick (2)

Read verse 2. "And he sent them out to preach the kingdom of

God." The main point of their message is the kingdom or God. It is surprising that the main point of their message was the kingdom of God because preaching the kingdom of God sounds impractical to suffering people. When I was in Korea, I thought that Koreans had been suffering because of the deep-rooted fatalism which arose from being the people of a weak nation, situated amid powerful nations. Koreans enjoyed singing sorrowful folk songs, crying out of self-pity, and depending on powerful countries for mercy. When I studied the Bible, I found that this was wrong and that they were spiritually very sick people. I gave my heart to plant in them the spirit of the gospel and gospel faith in an attempt to change the course of Korean history from passive sentimentalism to the spirit of conquest. After being sent to the United States, for the first three years, I suffered from cultural shock. After that, I learned that hedonism is the worst enemy of this country. It makes young Americans very fatalistic until they say, "Let us eat and drink, for tomorrow we die" (1Co 15:32). Since then, I believe that fighting hedonism is doing God's work. Of course, we must admit that one man cannot accomplish all of God's work. God uses each man according to the needs of his generation. God used Moses as a deliverer. God used Samuel as a king raiser. God used David as a shepherd and king in uniting the people of Israel into a kingdom. Each person must serve the counsel of God in his own generation. Still, the kingdom of God must be the main point of our message and ministry.

The kingdom of God is good news for all mankind, because it gives a living hope. People who put their hope in the world sigh endlessly and finally despair, knowing that they get too little, compared with the effort they put into making it. Moreover, men become fatalistic when they realize that they are going nowhere.

It is the good news of the kingdom of God that opens an outlet to each man to get out of Satan's dungeon. Those who only look down toward the ground see only distress, fearful darkness, and gloom, and they will be thrust into utter darkness (Isa 8:22). On the other hand, one who believes the good news of the kingdom of God can open his spiritual eyes and become a spiritual man who can see the mystery of God's kingdom and its glory. He can understand the spiritual world. As soon as he sees the kingdom of God, his sinful desires begin to diminish and gradually disappear, and he is filled with new spirit and new desires.

Jesus knew that all men in the world need to hear the good news of the kingdom of God. Mark 1:15 indicates that Jesus himself is the kingdom of God. It is true that where Jesus is, there is the kingdom of God. Jesus is the king who rules each person's soul with love and peace. He supplies each of us each new day with new life and new spirit. He creates us anew with new joy and a new heart. He rules each of our families with truth and grace. He makes us grow in love each day until we come to know the depth and width and height and length of God's love. He anoints each of us with the Holy Spirit when we are wounded and broken. He encourages us to live holy lives, lives worthy of being God's children in this complicated world.

Jesus also sent them out to heal the sick. Healing is not the main point of the gospel work. It is a warming-up exercise for the good news of the kingdom of God. However, it is very necessary. For example, the tax collector, Levi, immediately followed Jesus when Jesus called him. But there is an impression that he was still so sick with selfishness that he never spoke even a word during mealtimes, in order to concentrate on eating. He seems to have been so engrossed with himself and indifferent toward others, like a man with leprosy. He is scarcely mentioned in the Gospel narratives of the Twelve. But after meeting the Risen Jesus, his spiritual eyes were opened and he could grow enough to write the Sermon on the Mount, in which is recorded, "You are the light of the world" (Mt 5:14). James and John were politically-minded young men. They were still sick and made many people sick because of their dirty sins. But after meeting the Risen Jesus, John wrote, "God is love" (1Jn 4:16) and "This is how we know what love is: Jesus Christ laid down his life for us. And we ought to lay down our lives for our brothers." (1Jn—3:16). We are saved by the blood of Jesus. But still, we have to be healed continuously and grow to the full extent of the image of God.

Who can deny the fact that Jesus is the greatest physician in the world? But when we study the Gospels in terms of discipleship training, we learn that Jesus was the best healer because he was the best babysitter. There is an impression that he spent most of his time during his earthly ministry babysitting his twelve disciples until they were completely healed, and until their spiritual eyes were wide open to see the spiritual world and its ultimate goal, the kingdom of God.

III. Take nothing for the journey (3-9)

Verses 3-6 teach us what to depend on, and what should be the attitude of apostles of Jesus when they are sent out for healing and preaching.

First, Jesus taught them what to depend on when they were sent out. Read verse 3. He told them, "Take nothing for the journey—no staff, no bag, no bread, no money, no extra tunic." In the time of Jesus, people had great joy in offering hospitality to strangers. Literally speaking, his teaching, "take nothing for the journey" is impossible to practice. However, the spirit of the teaching is still most effective. In doing God's work, if we depend on staff or bag or bread, we can do nothing. When one young man went out fishing, depending on his good looks and gentle-voiced "hello," nobody responded to his invitation. In doing God's work, we must depend on God. This means that God is the Almighty One who can do everything. It also means that our faith in God is all powerful. We can do nothing by ourselves, but we can do all things in him who strengthens us. More specifically, we must depend on the power and authority of God's word. We must believe that the word of God can pierce the hearts and thoughts of all kinds of people and inspire them to believe in God. Therefore, we must speak to a non-Christian, depending on the power and authority of Jesus.

Second, Jesus taught them to identify themselves with people in their mission field. Read verse 4, "Whatever house you enter, stay there until you leave that town." Gospel workers must be grateful in any situation. They must be satisfied with whatever house they have to stay in, even if they have to stay in a dark basement room. They must be thankful even if the menus are unchangingly peanut butter sandwiches and carrots. In this way, they must adapt to the customs of the people in the mission field with them and they can identify with the people. They have to make friends with the members of the family and help them take root in the word of God. American Peace Corps workers in President Kennedy's day enhanced international friendship of the United States with the people of other countries when they lived in the houses of people in the respective countries. Missionary Sarah Barry's ministry was abundantly blessed by God when she identified herself with many sickly and poor Koreans by living in a Korean house, eating spicy Korean food.

Third, Jesus taught them not to compromise. Read verse 5. "If people do not welcome you, shake the dust off your feet when you leave their town, as a testimony against them." This verse teaches us that gospel workers must believe that the gospel of Jesus is superior to all the knowledge in the world. They also must have the attitude of a father of faith and shepherd when they preach the kingdom of God. When people do not accept the gospel of Jesus, gospel workers should not be daunted or hurt. They must have an absolute attitude toward the gospel of Jesus and must shake the dust off their feet when they leave that town as a testimony against them, so that they may know that they are responsible for their own blood. The gospel is absolute. "Whoever believes and is baptized will be saved, but whoever does not believe will be condemned" (Mk 16:16).

How did they respond? Read verse 6. "So they set out and went from village to village, preaching the gospel and healing people everywhere." The result was remarkable.

Read verses 7-9. In these verses, Luke tells us how their field work affected people in the entire land. Let's see the example of King Herod. He had taken his brother Philip's wife Herodias. When he was drunk, he had beheaded John the Baptist in order to please his wife Herodias, even though he recognized John as a righteous man. Since then, his suffering was like that of Raskolnikov in Crime and Punishment. Since that time, he had been tormented by demons. Outwardly, he was king, but in actuality, he was a slave to fear and nightmares. At night, he eagerly awaited the morning; in the morning, he eagerly awaited the night.

Herod had not attended the disciples' evangelistic meetings. But when he heard about all that was going on, he was greatly puzzled and perplexed. When someone came and reported that John had been raised from the dead, Herod felt like he was sinking down into the earth. When others reported that Elijah had appeared, he became spiritless. He said, "I beheaded John. Who, then, is this I hear such things about?" (9). And he tried to see him, hoping that the news he heard was not a reality, but just another nightmare.

The times of Jesus were so evil that a righteous man was beheaded by a lawless man. They were so evil and fearsome that all the people could only sigh and despair. Nobody could offer any solution.

But there is no despair in Jesus. He sent out the Twelve for field-work training with true hope that would conquer the power of the darkness of the world. It was mere fieldwork training. But look! The vision and faith of Jesus have been fully fulfilled and the Twelve have conquered the world.

Lesson 26

Jesus Feeds the Five Thousand

Luke 9:10-17
Key Verse: 9:13a

I. HE WELCOMED THEM (10-11)

1. Where had the disciples been? What kind of reports did they probably make? Why were the Twelve called "apostles" here?

2. Why did Jesus withdraw, taking only the Twelve with him? Why did they find it impossible to be alone?

3. What was Jesus' attitude toward the uninvited guests? What does this teach us about Jesus?

II. YOU GIVE THEM SOMETHING TO EAT (12-14a)

4. When did the Twelve run out of patience with the crowd? What was their suggestion and why was it so reasonable?

5. How did Jesus answer his disciples' request? Why was his command seemingly unreasonable? What was he seeking to teach his disciples through this command? (13a)

6. What were the practical resources available to the Twelve? What is the implication in their response to Jesus? (13b)

III. HAVE THEM SIT DOWN (14b-17)

7. What is the significance of having the crowd sit down in orderly groups? Why might this have been a little difficult to do?

8. What did Jesus do to feed the multitude? How did the disciples participate? What did they learn about God's work?

9. What was the result? What does this event teach us about Jesus' power and love? What do you learn about being his disciple?

Jesus Feeds the Five Thousand

Luke 9:10-17
Key Verse: 9:13a

"He replied, 'You give them something to eat.'"

J ESUS' FEEDING OF THE five thousand is recorded in all four Gospels, and all of them present it as a great climax in Jesus' public ministry, for this event demonstrates well Jesus as the Messiah of the world. Mark described this event to tell what Jesus' shepherd heart is like. Mark 6:34 says, "When Jesus landed and saw a large crowd, he had compassion on them, because they were like sheep without a shepherd." John recorded a valuable supplement to show the spiritual aspect of this event by quoting Jesus' words, "I am the bread of life." Luke, the historian and evangelist, abbreviates many small details so that he can say more effectively that Jesus is the Messiah. He also connects this event directly with Peter's confession, "The Christ of God." In this passage, we learn the Messianic view of man.

I.   He welcomed them (10-11)

Verse 10 says, "When the apostles returned, they reported to Jesus what they had done." Here, the Twelve are conspicuously called "apostles." They had been his disciples or students. More intimately, they were his sheep, or his beloved spiritual children. They had been greatly satisfied to share life together with Jesus. They must have felt as if they were living in the kingdom of God because in Jesus, they had seen wonders and the awesome power of God. In Jesus, they had experienced the compassion of the Messiah and renewal of spirit every day. When Jesus first told them about the evangelistic journey, they must have been fearful. And they must have been even more fearful when they were sent out to preach and to heal. By God's grace, they returned safely, and they were having a joyful report session. As the Gospel story narrates, at the time of the fieldwork training, Peter was not quite sure that he himself put his hope in the kingdom of God. Nevertheless, he was sent out to preach the kingdom of God. As he reported, he most likely said, "Lord, when I preached the kingdom of God, many made decisions of faith to put their hope in the kingdom of God." Bartholomew, whose presence or absence seemed to make no difference, and who never spoke in public, may have spoken a few words, "Lord, when I laid my hand on the sick, many were healed." They were excited to report to Jesus about the power and work of God.

Read verse 10. "Then he took them with him and they withdrew by themselves to a town called Bethsaida." At that time, the Twelve were extremely tired because they were excited by the new experience of the evangelistic journey and because they forced themselves to do something that they didn't really understand. They needed time to take a deep breath and think it over and put things together. Moreover, Jesus was approaching Jerusalem, where suffering and crucifixion awaited him. Before the crucifixion, he had to have enough time with them to explain the meaning of this suffering, death, and resurrection. So he took them with him, and they withdrew by themselves to a town called Bethsaida, which was situated north of the Sea of Galilee and east of the Jordan River (10). John describes the locality as being in the mountains, the highland on the other side of the lake from Capernaum. This time, Jesus preferred a secluded place where the mountains might possibly conceal them from the searching eyes of the crowd.

Was this retreat possible? No. Read verse 11. "But the crowds learned about it and followed him." What could an ordinary leader do with such an inconsiderate crowd of people? He could have said, "Please call me first before you visit me." The other day, I saw a sign for a house sale which said, "Welcome, but only by appointment." But what did Jesus do with them? Luke says in verse 11b, "He welcomed them." It is really amazing that he welcomed them. Jesus welcomed the crowd even in the place where he had hoped to have a quiet time with the Twelve.

Jesus welcomed them. This one phrase reveals the grace and truth of the Messiah, Jesus. There were a large crowd of people. Their demands were endless. They had no personal relationship to make such demands on Jesus with their personal problems. They had no right to come to Jesus when Jesus was having a staff conference. It might have been a conference on the entire plan and strategy for world salvation. But they did not see it that way. They felt they had an inalienable right and an absolute privilege to come to Jesus. Why did they have such a feeling? Theoretically, they had no reason to feel this way. But they believed that he would welcome them anytime, anyplace. They believed that Jesus was the one on whom they could make endless demands. They believed that Jesus was the only one who could satisfy their needs. They believed that Jesus was everything to everybody. They believed that Jesus was the Messiah who came to save them from the miseries of their sins. And Jesus also welcomed them as his most precious ones. Jesus welcomes those who come to him. Jesus welcomes everybody with his outstretched hand.

Jesus not only welcomes, but also invites anybody to come to him. Once, when Jesus went to Jericho with his disciples, a blind man named Bartimaeus was begging by the roadside. When he heard that Jesus of Nazareth was passing by, he began to shout, "Jesus, Son of David, have mercy on me!" (Mk 10:47). Jesus stopped and healed his blindness. Jesus wiped tears from his eyes and gave him his sight. In Jesus, everyone finds his needs satisfied. Matthew was once a tax collector with the name Levi. He was so selfish that no one wanted to talk with him. No one invited him to dinner. He was lonely. He was lost in sin and found by Jesus when Jesus called him, saying, "Follow me" (Lk 5:27).

Luke, the historian and evangelist, tells us specifically what Jesus did for the desperately needy crowds of people. Read verse 11b. "He welcomed them and spoke to them about the kingdom of God, and healed those who needed healing." Jesus knew that they were needy and suffering. Jesus knew that they had come to him to solve all kinds of agonies and miseries of life. But Jesus didn't try to solve the side issues of their lives, such as material problems or political problems. Jesus determined to solve their fundamental life problems, that is, their goal and destination of life. In order to solve their fundamental life problem, he taught them about the kingdom of God. Their real problem was that they did not know where they were going or what they were doing. They did not know the way. Without Jesus, they were wandering in endless restlessness and fear of death. They were groaning under the curse (Ge 3:16-19). They were writhing in Satan's dungeon without any hope of release. To Jesus, what these people really needed was liberation from their unbelief and from bondage in Satan's dungeon. They needed to believe that God so loved the world that he gave his one and only Son to save people from the hand of Satan and bring them back to God. To Jesus, what they really needed was not money or the satisfaction of carnal desires, but direction and destination of life—that is, the kingdom of God. Jesus also healed the sick. This tells us that Jesus not only showed them the ultimate goal of life, but he also met their immediate need for healing. In order to heal the sick, he waded into the crowd, laying his hand on each of them for healing. Many were healed from their sicknesses and demon possession, and many were filled with joy. Jesus was so happy to shepherd them that he did not know the day was wearing away, along with the endurance of the Twelve.

II. You give them something to eat (12-14a)

When the western horizon was turning from red to dusky purple, the Twelve came to him and said, "Send the crowd away so they can go to the surrounding villages and countryside and find food and lodging, because we are in a remote place here" (12). The disciples thought that they had no way to provide food and lodging for the crowd. So they suggested that he send the crowd away so that they could be responsible for themselves. In contemporary terms, they said, "Send them away so they can take care of themselves." Maybe the Twelve were ready to say to the crowd, "Please go away. Take care of yourselves."

In the past, when people parted, they said, "Goodbye," meaning, "God be with you." In their farewell greeting, they included God, man, and the world. It was a three-dimensional greeting. Lately, people say, "Take care of yourself." This phrase is an expression of the fearful and selfish mind of modern man. No one wants to be responsible for others. "Rugged individualism" was once the backbone and jawbone of America. No one expected that individualism would promote self-ishness and the denying of necessary responsibility for a society or a nation. The Twelve were just like the young people of these days. They said to Jesus, "Send the crowd away so they can go to the sur-rounding villages and countryside and find food and lodging." They must have added, "The earlier the better, sir." Their suggestion was reasonable. Their situation did not allow them to take care of five thousand mouths and provide places for them to sleep. They were also tired and hungry.

What did Jesus do when the Twelve said, "Send them away"? He said, "You give them something to eat!"(13a) In this command, we learn several things about Jesus, the Messiah.

First, when Jesus said, "You give them something to eat," he was urging them to have a sense of responsibility. To Jesus, whether or not they could feed the five thousand did not matter. What mattered was whether or not they had a sense of responsibility. Jesus did not allow the Twelve to be irresponsible simply because they were not capable of feeding the crowd. So he said, "You give them something to eat." A sense of responsibility makes a man great. Dr. John Jun was a medical student when God began UBF work in Korea. He had such a strong sense of responsibility that he once said, "Even if Samuel Lee and Sarah Barry run away, I will not run away." At that time, he was burdened with his medical studies and TB treatment. But God blessed his stewardship and enabled him to overcome the adverse situation and made him a great man of God.

Who can be the men and women responsible for this generation and the generation to come? To our sorrow, there seems to be no one who has a sense of responsibility. Everyone seems to be irresponsible and extremely rebellious. Who can be responsible for this generation and for the generation to come? It is the people of God.

Jesus commands us, saying, "You give them something to eat." You must be responsible for the souls of teenagers and young col-lege students. Jesus urges us to have a sense of responsibility for this generation and pray.

Second, when Jesus said, "You give them something to eat," he wanted to teach them faith which is all-powerful. Let's see how the Twelve responded when they heard Jesus' words, "You give them something to eat." They answered, "We have only five loaves of bread and two fish—unless we go and buy food for all this crowd" (13b). They only calculated and despaired. They habitually came back to their propensity for calculation. When they calculated, they despaired because they had too little for the 5,000. They became hopeless when they looked at the five loaves and when they looked at the dried-up eyes of the two fish.

They did not find resources in God, but only looked in themselves. They had no faith in God who is all-powerful. Each of them said, "I can't," instead of saying, "Yes, I can do it by faith." Jesus wanted them to believe that they could feed the 5,000 by faith. Jesus wanted them to say, "Of course we can't, but God can feed the 5,000 through us." Jesus wanted them to obey his command by faith, "You give them something to eat," so that they could experience the power of faith. Jesus wanted them to master this faith training. This is the reason why God did not give his people Israel the promised land free of charge. But he told them to fight and conquer innumerable enemies in the promised land by faith so that they might learn that faith in God is all-powerful and experience the power of faith.

The world is fearsome so escapism seems to be the best way of life. But it is not. Each person must experience the power of faith in one way or the other by overcoming impossible situations by faith.

Third, when Jesus said, "You give them something to eat," he wanted them to learn the shepherd heart. What is a shepherd heart? It is the mind of the Messiah, Jesus. It is to have compassion on others. Mark 8:1-3 illustrates Jesus' shepherd heart very well. "During those days another large crowd gathered. Since they had nothing to eat, Jesus called his disciples to him and said, 'I have compassion for these people; they have already been with me three days and have nothing to eat. If I send them home hungry, they will collapse on the way, because some of them have come a long distance.'" Mark 6:34 also illustrates this well: "When Jesus landed and saw a large crowd, he had compassion on them ..." No matter what their motives or demands might be, Jesus didn't criticize them. Rather, he had compassion on them. This is the shepherd heart.

There have been innumerable great men in history, but many people would agree unanimously that throughout the generations, Moses stands out as the most eminent. Why? Because he had a shepherd heart for his people. Moses' task in God's history was to deliver his people from bondage in Egypt and lead them to the entrance of the promised land, then die. Despite his forty years of hard work, God did not give him the privilege of entering and enjoying the land flowing with milk and honey. God only showed him the panorama of the land once—that was all (Nu 27:12). But he did not feel sorry for himself. He was helpless when he thought of his people who had a slave mentality. Moses said to God, "May the Lord, the God of the spirits of all mankind, appoint a man over this community to go out and come in before them, one who will lead them out and bring them in, so the Lord's people will not be like sheep without a shepherd" (Nu 27:15-17). Moses was great, but he was not great enough to be even a shadow of Jesus.

There must be a thousand names of Jesus which describe the character of his Messiahship. Of them all, "Shepherd," must be the best title for Jesus. Jesus said in John 10:11, "I am the good shepherd. The good shepherd lays down his life for the sheep." How important it is to raise 561 full-time shepherds who can lay down their lives for the sheep! What is a more urgent task than raising many shepherds with our prayers?

III. Have them sit down (14b-17)

Read verse 14b. "But he said to his disciples, 'Have them sit down in groups of about fifty each.'" This time, Jesus wanted to show them the power of faith when they obeyed his command, "Have them sit down." When the Twelve heard, "Have them sit down," they must have looked at each other and tried to figure out exactly what he meant. Why did he say that? Reality is reality, and they had not prepared food for 5,000 people. Maybe the smartest guy, Philip, repeatedly said to himself, "This is ridiculous. Ridiculous." Anyway, to the disciples, Jesus' command, "Have them sit down," was not easy to obey, for they knew it was not necessary to prepare a table when there was no food to put on it.

Read verse 15. "The disciples did so, and everybody sat down." Luke described briefly the response of the disciples. Here we learn the greatness of their obedience. They simply obeyed Jesus' words, going beyond their mathematical reason. They obeyed Jesus' words exactly. The location was a hilly place. So they could have had them sit down in groups of 30 or 120. But they had them sit down in groups of exactly 50.

What happened? Read verse 16. "Taking the five loaves and the two fish and looking up to heaven, he gave thanks and broke them." When we read this verse carefully, we can see an act of faith in Jesus. When Jesus took the five loaves and the two fish, he did not look at the small amount of food. He looked up to heaven. He presented the five loaves and the two fish to God. Then a miracle happened. He broke them and gave them to the disciples to set before the people. They all ate and were satisfied. The shepherd heart of Jesus and his act of faith brought forth a miracle. The story ends with the words, "And the disciples picked up twelve basketfuls of broken pieces that were left over." The power of faith produced more than a miracle. The power of faith not only fed the 5,000; it also made it possible for the blessing of God to overflow into the whole world. This event shows us that the people of the world can only be satisfied when they experience God's overflowing blessing through the Messiah, Jesus.

Lesson 27

Peter's Confession of Christ

Luke 9:18-27
Key Verse: 9:20b

I. THE CHRIST OF GOD (18-20)

1. What were the two questions Jesus asked his disciples? How were these questions similar and how were they different? What might Jesus have been praying about?

2. Look at the answers to the questions of Jesus. What is the difference between the crowd's and the disciples' view of Jesus? Think about Peter's confession. What were the implications of this confession?

II. THE SON OF MAN (21-22)

3. Why did Jesus warn them not to tell anyone? What was it that they were not to tell?

4. What must Jesus do in order to become the Son of Man, the Messiah? Why? What was the good news in this impending tragedy?

III. IF ANYONE (23-27)

5. What does it mean to "deny himself," "to take up his cross," to "come after me"? What does the word "daily" imply?

6. What does Jesus mean by "save" and "lose" in verse 24a? How do people today try to save their lives?

7. What does it mean to lose one's life for Jesus? Why is this the real way to save one's life?

8. Can you think of any example of a man who has tried to gain the world and has lost his "very self"?

9. What does it mean to be ashamed of Jesus and his word? What are the consequences of being ashamed of Jesus?

10. What is the implied promise to those who are not ashamed of Jesus? What promise does Jesus give to his disciples in verse 27? What does it mean to see the kingdom of God?

Peter's Confession of Christ

Luke 9:18-27
Key Verse: 9:20b

"Peter answered, 'The Christ of God.'"

"THE CHRIST OF GOD." This is Peter's confession of Christ. In human history, Peter was the first person who saw God in Jesus and made a confession of faith that Jesus is the Christ of God. But according to Matthew, this was not Peter's own idea, but it was the heavenly revelation of God. Those who have this confession of faith can have the keys of the kingdom of heaven. While in the body, they can see the kingdom of heaven and enjoy the peace that passes all human understanding.

This passage falls into three distinct parts which link closely together: First, Peter's confession, "The Christ of God" (18-20); second, the necessity of Christ's suffering as the Messiah of the world (21-22); and third, three basic requirements as his people (23-27). Compared with Matthew, Luke wrote this passage simply, omitting Jesus' compliment of Simon, son of Jonah. But he retains the main emphasis of this event. May God help us to understand the meaning of Peter's confession of faith, "The Christ of God."

I. The Christ of God (18-20)

Matthew and Mark located this incident in the vicinity of Caesarea Philippi, near the foot of Mount Hermon. It is known that this is heathen territory. Jesus had withdrawn from Herod's dominion and from the crowd that had been thronging around him. Here he wanted to talk quietly with his disciples in order to bring them to a definite confession of faith. This is one of the most crucial moments in the whole life of Jesus. But he did not care about himself much.

He cared much about his disciples. Somehow Jesus wanted them to make personal confessions of faith. What did he do when he came to a quiet place with his disciples?

Read verse 18. He prayed in private, even though his disciples were with him. I don't know what his disciples did, but Jesus prayed first. No doubt he prayed for his disciples that they might somehow know his person and his work, though they were still earthbound in their spiritual condition. Jesus also prayed for himself to obey the will of God for the salvation of the world, though it meant betrayal, rejection, suffering, and dying on the cross.

After prayer he asked them, "Who do the crowds say I am?" This was an objective question. They replied, "Some say John the Baptist; others say Elijah; and still others, that one of the prophets from long ago has come back to life." The people of the times said many things about Jesus. But all of them acknowledged Jesus as one of the prophets. A prophet is known as a man from God or deliverer of his people from their miseries. Abraham, David, Samuel, and Jesus were all known as prophets. People in Jesus' time all knew that Jesus was a man from God. The blind beggar called him Jesus, Son of David (Mk 10:47). A man possessed by demons acknowledged Jesus as the Most High God (Lk 8:28). Ironically though, even the government agents who investigated Jesus thoroughly to report to King Herod could not overcome the general ideas of the people that Jesus was one of the prophets, a man of God. They gave him the highest spiritual position they could give.

People paralleled Jesus to the most prominent prophets, John the Baptist and Elijah, known as men of God in their own generations. Why was he so? It was because the spirit of Jesus was like that of John the Baptist and Elijah, for the Holy Spirit was upon him.

Read verse 20. "'But what about you?' he asked. 'Who do you say that I am?'" This was a subjective question. Nobody appointed Peter as their spokesman, but he answered spontaneously, "The Christ of God." Usually, Peter's answers were incorrect, but this time, he was very correct, and he got an "A$^+$" on his midterm. Biblically speaking, the Christ of God is the Messiah promised to come. He is our Prophet, Priest, and King. Still, we have to think more about this.

First, "The Christ of God." Human logic fails to explain what it means to be the Christ of God. But according to Isaiah, the Christ of God is everything to everybody. In brief, the Christ of God is the Messiah. Isaiah 9:6 says, "For to us a child is born, to us a son is given, and the government will be on his shoulders. And he will be called Wonderful Counselor, Mighty God, Everlasting Father, Prince of Peace." This means the promised Messiah is everything to everybody. The Messiah is a Wonderful Counselor. No one can speak everything in his mind, or reveal the secret meditations of his heart, even to his mother. So many people say, "You just don't understand me." But Jesus listens and understands and tells the truth. He is the Mighty God who created the heavens and the earth with one word, and who raised Jesus from the dead. He is almighty, therefore, he can protect us from the mischief of Satan. He is the Everlasting Father. The father is the symbol of protection and service. When we are young, we need earthly fathers who take us around holding our hands. When we are grown up, we need the Heavenly Father who will lead us into the path of life. Jesus is the Everlasting Father to each of us.

Jesus, our Messiah, is the Prince of Peace. Everybody who lives in the world wants some undisturbed rest. Everybody wants peace. So many people work hard to save money to enjoy vacations with the money they have earned. They come back home with empty feelings. Ever since Satan waged war against the power and authority of God, there is no peace in the world. But there is peace in Jesus.

We can see many examples of Jesus that he is everything to everybody. Jesus became a husband to the disgusting and smelly Samaritan woman, saying, "I who speak to you am he" (Jn 4:26). Jesus treated her as though she was a heavenly princess and his own beloved daughter. He became a friend to Levi, a lonely tax collector. Because of his selfishness, he turned out to be a social outcast and a quisling. People treated him as though he were a man with leprosy. But Jesus saw in him the greatness of God, called him to be one of his disciples, and helped him until he could write the Sermon on the Mount. He became a kind brother to sorrowful Martha and Mary.

One day, when Jesus came to Jericho, a blind man called son of Timaeus was crying aloud in the street, saying, "Jesus, Son of David, have mercy on me!" (Mk. 10:47). Tears gushed out from his blind eyes. Jesus wiped his tears from his eyes and gave him sight. He was a physician who passed his hands over the sick one by one and healed them. Jesus is everything to everybody.

Second, "The Christ of God" is the Savior of the world. The angel's message to Joseph explains this more clearly. "She will give birth to a son, and you are to give him the name Jesus, because he will save his people from their sins" (Mt 1:21). Jean Jacques Rousseau thought that human tragedy was caused by the inequality of men. But from God's point of view all human miseries come from sin. Sin makes man sick. Sin makes man deceitful and inhumane and finally leads to eternal condemnation. Jesus came to the world as the Savior of the world. Paul, who knew the grace of God, exclaims, "Christ Jesus came into the world to save sinners—of whom I am the worst" (1Ti 1:15).

Third, "The Christ of God" is the Lord's anointed King. In the past, kings were anointed at the time of their inauguration. Jesus was anointed to be our King to rescue us from Satan and rule us with love and peace. King David is the image of the Messiah. He liberated his people from all their enemies and ruled them with peace and love. After him, the people of Israel longed for a king like David to come and rule over them. But David was merely a shadow of the Messiah. He liberated his people from their enemies, but he could not save his people from the bondage of sin. Jesus is the Mighty King who destroys the power of Satan and delivers us from Satan's hand. He destroys the power of death and sin and takes the sting of death from mankind. Jesus is the Eternal King who was slain as the Lamb of God for the sins of the world. He is worthy to be our Lord and God, to receive glory and honor and power (Rev 5:12).

Jesus is our King of Peace. Whoever comes to him for help or opens his heart, Jesus comes into his heart and heals, then rules his heart with peace.

II. The Son of Man (21-22)

Read verse 21. Jesus warned them not to tell anyone because there were many secular Jews who wanted to establish a political messianic king through Jesus, or otherwise, destroy him.

Read verse 22. "And he said, 'The Son of Man must suffer many things and be rejected by the elders, the chief priests and the teachers of the law, and he must be killed and on the third day be raised to life.'" Peter's confession, "The Christ of God," explains the person of Christ, who Jesus is. Verse 22 explains the work of the Christ, what Jesus does. This verse tells how he becomes the Christ of God.

The worldly rulers come to power by defeating political opponents and rule people with their power and authority. There is a story about how Julius Caesar was killed and Anthony came to power. There is a story about Judas the Galilean who led a rebellion against Rome. He raided the royal armory at Sepphoris, four miles away from Nazareth. The Roman vengeance was swift and sudden. Sepphoris was burned to the ground; its inhabitants sold into slavery; and two thousand rebels were crucified on crosses which were set in lines along the roadside so that these might be a dreadful warning to others who were tempted to rebel.

But Jesus is quite different. Read verse 22 again. Jesus calls himself, "the Son of Man." This title, "Son of Man," is the title given to Ezekiel, a suffering servant. "Son of Man" meant a suffering servant, and "son of a carpenter, Joseph." Jesus began his kingship from the position of a "Son of Man."

Read verse 22 again. "The Son of Man must suffer many things." In this verse, the word "must" is on the lips of Jesus. "I must," Jesus said. Jesus was the one who knew that he had a specific mission to die for the sins of the world. In order to solve the sin problem, the Son of Man must die on the cross. In order to bring his people to God, he must shed his blood as a ransom sacrifice on the cross. When he said, "The Son of Man must suffer many things," he knew what this suffering meant. But he did not try to avoid it. He said, "The Son of Man must suffer many things."

What Jesus did was heal the sick and preach the good news of the kingdom of God. But those who envied the spiritual authority of Jesus manipulated public opinion to view Jesus as a blasphemer of God. They made him look like a criminal who should receive capital punishment. In the end, secular Jews despised him, condemned him, and ultimately crucified him.

Isaiah cries, "Who could believe that he should receive such great suffering!" (Isa 53). Because of our sins he was despised and rejected by men. Because of our sins, he became a man of sorrow. He took up our infirmities and iniquities. He was smitten and afflicted, all because of our sins. Finally, he died on the cross. In this way, he became our Messiah. He is our spiritual King. Secular Jews said that he is a criminal. But God made him our Eternal King.

III. If anyone (23-27)

Read verse 23. "Then he said to them all: 'If anyone would come after me, he must deny himself and take up his cross daily and follow me.'" This verse tells us of three requirements for his people in following the Messiah.

First, one must deny himself. "Deny himself" has a familiar ring to Christians and it sounds good. But it is not at all easy to deny oneself. God gave each person a special talent, individuality, and creativity so that each man might discover himself and live in his own way. Moreover, these days, secular humanists regard denying oneself as inhumane behavior and severely accuse Christians of their self-denials.

Then what does it mean to "deny oneself"? In the first place, it means to deny one's sinful nature. St. Augustine was an intellectual hedonist. He really enjoyed the life of sin and sarcasm. He knew that he should change his lifestyle, but when he thought of changing his lifestyle, he felt like he was losing all the joy of life. One day, he read Romans 13:13-14: "Let us behave decently, as in the daytime, not in orgies and drunkenness, not in sexual immorality and debauchery, not in dissension and jealousy. Rather, clothe yourselves with the Lord Jesus Christ, and do not think about how to gratify the desires of the sinful nature." He was greatly moved by these words and he could overcome his hedonistic lifestyle.

In the second place, to deny oneself means, basically, to respect God's word more than one's own idea. But it is not easy to respect God's word more than one's own idea. Many choose Matthew 6:33 as their life direction, "But seek first his kingdom and his righteousness, and all these things will be given to you as well." But many of them do not follow the promise. But see, the forefathers of America denied their own ideas and obeyed this word, and then, God showered his blessings upon this country until it became a world power.

Second, he must take up his cross. The cross is a mission which involves obedience, pain, and suffering. Jesus took up the mission of world salvation and obeyed God's will unto death, death on the cross. In following Jesus, we must take up our own cross of mission and follow Jesus. There are many false prophets who say, "You can follow Jesus without the cross of mission." In light of the Bible, they are liars. In this passage, Jesus teaches us to take up our own crosses. It is because God made man to do the work of God. Those who do not know their mission from God are like the unemployed. Each person must discover his specific mission from God and take it absolutely, for only the life of mission gives a deep satisfaction to each person.

Third, Jesus' people must live their lives for Jesus (24-26). In verses 24 and 25, Jesus teaches us a most fundamental truth of God—not to live a selfish life, but to live for the glory of God. "For whoever wants to save his life will lose it, but whoever loses his life for me will save it." When God created the world, he did not make man to live a selfish life, but made man to live for the glory of God and receive eternal life as his reward. Nevertheless, many people live selfishly according to the consensus of the world. But as history proves, selfishness only leads a man to self-destruction. However, when a man lives for Jesus' name's sake, God does not guarantee that he will enjoy quiet happiness. Still, we must live for the glory of God because it is the truth of God.

Read verse 26. "If anyone is ashamed of me and my words, the Son of Man will be ashamed of him when he comes in his glory and in the glory of the Father and of the holy angels." This verse teaches us more specifically how to live for the glory of God. To live for the glory of God is not to be ashamed of Jesus in any circumstances. According to God's promise, Jesus will come again in glory and power. Those who were not ashamed of him and lived for his glory through much suffering will be rewarded and accepted into the eternal kingdom of God. On the other hand, those who were ashamed of Jesus and his words will be shamed and condemned.

Read verse 27. "I tell you the truth, some who are standing here will not taste death before they see the kingdom of God." This verse plainly tells us that those who accept Jesus as the Messiah and deny themselves and take up the cross of mission experience the joy of the heavenly kingdom, instead of tasting agonies and anguishes, before they see the kingdom of God.

Lesson 28

The Transfiguration

Luke 9:28-36
Key Verse: 9:29

I. JESUS TRANSFIGURED (28-29)

1. What had Jesus been talking about 8 days prior to this event? Which of his disciples did he take with him and why only these 3? Where did they go and what was Jesus' purpose?

2. What happened while Jesus was praying? What does this suggest about the importance of prayer in Jesus' life? In our lives?

3. What was the significance of the change in Jesus' appearance? Why did Jesus want his disciples to see this glorious sight? What was the contrast between this and their usual observation of Jesus?

II. JESUS TALKS WITH MOSES AND ELIJAH (30-31a)

4. Who were Moses and Elijah? Why might they have been the ones chosen for this meeting with Jesus? What did they have in common with each other? With Jesus?

III. THEY SPOKE ABOUT HIS DEPARTURE (31b)

5. What did they talk about with Jesus? How might this conversation have strengthened Jesus? What did it teach the disciples and what does it teach us about Jesus?

IV. LISTEN TO HIM (32-36)

6. Why did Peter react as he did in verses 32 and 33? Why were the disciples so spiritually unprepared?

7. What did the voice of God teach them about Jesus? Why was it necessary for them to be told to "listen to him"?

8. How did this event end? What immediate effect do you think it had on the disciples? What was the long-term effect? (2Pe 1:16-19)

The Transfiguration

Luke 9:28-36
Key Verse: 9:29

> "As he was praying, the appearance of his face changed, and his clothes became as bright as a flash of lightning."

THIS EVENT IS COMMONLY called "The Transfiguration of Jesus." This event lifts a corner of the veil which hangs over Jesus who was supposed to bring to fulfillment God's will for world salvation. Jesus' transfiguration and his talking with Moses and Elijah throw light on some of the deep truths of Jesus: his suffering, crucifixion, and resurrection. Though this event, Jesus wanted to help his disciples to catch a glimpse of his original image of God so that their spiritual eyes might be opened to see a preview of the glorious resurrection and so that they might not be swayed at the time of his crucifixion.

I. Jesus transfigured (28-29)

Read verse 28a. "About eight days after Jesus said this ..." This refers to Peter's confession of faith, "The Christ of God." After this epoch-making confession in history, Jesus gave Peter and the other disciples a period of eight days so as to meditate on the confession of faith they had made. After this, Jesus took the three top disciples Peter, John, and James with him and went up onto a mountain to pray. On what mountain might such a glorious event have happened? Traditionally, Mount Tabor has been understood as the place where the transfiguration occurred, but this place is too far away from Caesarea Philippi. Mount Hermon seems to be the more likely place, but this also seems to be far from certain.

Matthew and Mark do not seem to pay much attention to why

Jesus went up onto the mountain. Luke the historian only emphasizes the fact that Jesus went up onto the mountain to pray. Usually many people go up onto a mountain to escape the agony-filled mundane world even for the time being, or to see flourishing foliage or beautifully colored autumn leaves. Many people enjoy seeing the grandiose mountain ranges. Most people are overwhelmed by the mysteriously profound mountain atmosphere and they feel serious about their lives. Some cry; some sing; some think about the transitory and uncertain human life. But Jesus went up onto the mountain to pray. Jesus went up onto the mountain to meet and talk with God.

At that time, Jesus' heart was weighed down by the thought that he was about to set out for Jerusalem, where suffering, rejection, and crucifixion awaited him. His disciples were too young to succeed his work. If he were an ordinary person, what would he do in this situation? He would have gone into his room to cool himself down. But Jesus overcame himself and went up onto a mountain to pray.

Before Jesus climbed the Mount of Transfiguration, he appeared to his disciples as a poor man, a man who was not accepted by men of social standing. He was regarded as an outcast because he identified himself with tax collectors, a despicable Samaritan woman, and downtrodden masses. While shepherding the flock of God, his heart was broken. His face was pain-stricken. When he bore the sorrows and pains of the flock of God, his glorious and majestic image as the heavenly prince was damaged until he looked so humble and lowly like one whom men did not want to look at, but hid their faces from. Before coming up onto the mountain, the powers of darkness surrounded him like angry bulls ready to charge. The whole world seemed to oppose him. In this situation, what did he do?

Read verse 29. "As he was praying, the appearance of his face changed, and his clothes became as bright as a flash of lightning." Jesus was tired and weary and he was burdened with the thought of going up to Jerusalem. But when Jesus met God in prayer, he was strengthened and his face shone as bright as sunshine. His clothes even became as bright as a flash of lightning. When Jesus prayed, he was restored into his original heavenly image. Our Jesus is glorious, but he became like a poor man in order to heal us from sin-sickness and to deliver us from the hand of Satan. John portrayed Jesus' original image as God in Revelation 1:13-16, "… and among the lampstands was someone 'like a son of man,' dressed in a robe reaching down to his feet and with a golden sash around his chest. His head and hair were white like wool, as white as snow … His face was like the sun shining in all its brilliance." This glorious Jesus came to this world to save us. Now Jesus was praying to confirm his decision to go up to Jerusalem to suffer many things and be crucified.

II. Jesus talks with Moses and Elijah (30-31a)

Read verses 30 and 31a. "Two men, Moses and Elijah, appeared in glorious splendor, talking with Jesus." Moses and Elijah died sorrowfully. Their appearance on the mountain should have been doleful and gloomy. But to our surprise, these two men, Moses and Elijah, appeared in glorious splendor. Their sufferings because of their mission did not devastate them at all. Rather, they were ennobled and glorified by the glory caught from the Heavenly Father. Their lives of mission were short in terms of time and space, but their privilege of enjoying the majestic glory of God lasts forever. This conference on the transfiguration mountain was significant. Why, then, do only Moses and Elijah appear in this glorious event regardless of many outstanding prophets such as Samuel, Ezekiel, or Jeremiah? It is because Moses, Elijah, and Jesus had three common factors in fulfilling the will of God.

First, they were deliverers of his people. In fulfilling God's will, deliverance is the first step. God called Moses to deliver his people from slavery in Egypt. This deliverance was not easy because Pharaoh the king of Egypt was a powerful king of the times. On the other hand, the people of Israel had no spirit to resist or fight back for liberation, for they were smitten and crushed, living in slavery in Egypt for the last 430 years. God called Moses when he was 80 years old to deliver his people.

God called Elijah to deliver his people from Baal worship. At that time, the people of Israel were totally corrupted through worshiping the idol of Baal—the god of agriculture. It can be compared to the god of technology or money in modern times. The people of Israel were easy-going and hedonistic. It was not an easy task for Elijah to deliver his people, for his people were completely corrupted by a cultural god, Baal. God called Elijah to deliver his people from Baal worship.

Jesus came to this world to deliver men from their sins. In order to deliver men from their sins, Jesus took the form of a servant and healed the sick and preached the kingdom of God. Jesus came to the world to deliver us from the hand of Satan. But it was not easy for Jesus because the power of sin and the power of Satan were ruling the world. In order to deliver men from their sins, Jesus had to give his life.

Second, they were all suffering servants. In fulfilling God's work, suffering naturally accompanies. Moses suffered endlessly to receive 40 years of palace education and took many exams. He received 40 years of wilderness training to be raised as a humble man of God until he was not able to speak properly. When he was 80 years old, God called him to deliver his people from slavery in Egypt. Moses had to suffer endlessly because his people were broken by hard labor. In addition, their slave mentality was incurable. Moses had to struggle with his people to help them overcome their slave mentality and live according to the Law of God. His suffering lasted for 120 years altogether. He led his people to the entrance of the promised land. But he himself could not have the privilege of entering the promised land, and he died.

Elijah lived in the time of King Ahab. Ahab was the king, but he was a petty man and materialistic. He wanted to have a poor farmer Naboth's vineyard. But Naboth refused to sell it because it was his inheritance from his fathers. So King Ahab went home and lay on his bed, sulking and refusing to eat before his wife Jezebel. Therefore, she had Naboth stoned to death and gave the vineyard to her husband Ahab. She was a cruel and lawless woman. Jezebel had abandoned God Almighty and made Baal the national god. Elijah suffered endlessly all by himself to be a servant of God's word. One day, he said to God, "I have had enough, Lord. Take my life" (1Ki 19:4).

Jesus came to the world to take us back to his kingdom. He healed the sick and preached the good news of the kingdom of God. But the secular Jews despised him and slandered him and punished him endlessly, simply because Jesus was not like them and lived in obedience to God's will. Finally, evil men condemned him as a criminal and handed him over to the Gentile rulers and crucified him.

Third, they were the key members in the fulfillment of God's will. Moses received God's Law at Mount Sinai, and he became the representative of the Law. Elijah became a representative of God's prophecy, for the Israelites thought that Baal worshiping was most beneficial for their earthly lives. Jesus came to this world to fulfill God's Law and prophecy. Jesus needed to talk with them so that he might confirm the meaning of his departure to Jerusalem in bringing to fulfillment the will of God. Therefore, we should not be discouraged when we suffer in the course of doing the work of God.

III. They spoke about his departure (31b)

Read verse 31b. "They spoke about his departure, which he was about to bring to fulfillment at Jerusalem." After the flood, God made a new plan for world salvation. God chose Abraham and David. God began a new world salvation work with one man, Abraham. Next, God confirmed his promise to David that a Savior of the world would be raised from his roots (Isa 9:6; 11:1-2). He is Jesus.

According to God's promises, Jesus came to bring to fulfillment the Law and prophecy. Now he was going up to Jerusalem to fulfill the promises of God. But in Jerusalem, suffering and rejection and crucifixion awaited him.

Moses, Elijah, and Jesus spoke about his departure to Jerusalem. Elijah and Moses obviously spoke to Jesus that he should go to Jerusalem. At this time, Jesus had to make the final decision to go to Jerusalem to fulfill God's will for world salvation. How painful it must have been for Jesus to make the decision! But Jesus made the decision, and they spoke about his departure when he should start on his way to Jerusalem. In this we learn that we also must make a decision to obey God's will. But decision-making is not easy at all because we live in a structure of pragmatism. So generally, people never want to commit themselves to anything, nor do they make any decision. As a result, they live without principle, purpose, direction, or meaning of life, much less with faith. Most people are like Judas Iscariot who betrayed Jesus.

In studying this passage, I was reminded of the early Christians. To conquer the center of the world of the times, Rome, they decided to go to Rome with the gospel of Jesus. Rome was like a den of lions. But they did not run away. They kept their faith in God Almighty. They learned the faith that turns adverse situations into times of God's deep grace and fruitful victories. God blessed their decision and enabled them to conquer the world power, Rome, with the gospel of Jesus.

IV. Listen to him (32-36)

Jesus took Peter, John, and James with him and went up onto a mountain to pray. Jesus took them so that somehow they might open their spiritual eyes to see the preview of his death and resurrection and the world to come in the future. Jesus wanted them to participate in his prayer. What did they do? Verse 32 says, "Peter and his companions were very sleepy." They grappled with their sleepiness, and for a short time, fell asleep. They almost lost the chance to see Jesus in the glory of his transfiguration. They were men of flesh. Like ordinary men, they could have spent nearly twenty years of their lives sleeping, five years eating, and nine years watching T.V.—and then died. They were nothing but clumps of dust. But Jesus prayed for them to the end until they became spiritual men.

Read verse 33. "As the men were leaving Jesus, Peter said to him, 'Master, it is good for us to be here. Let us put up three shelters—one for you, one for Moses and one for Elijah.'" Peter did not say, "One for me, too." But he said it in his heart. Luke comments in parentheses, "He did not know what he was saying" (33b). Peter revealed his desire for his earthly body to enjoy an easy and glorious life without the cross of mission. Even though Peter lived around 2,000 years ago, he had the same desires we have.

Read verse 34. "While he was speaking, a cloud appeared and enveloped them, and they were afraid as they entered the cloud." In the Old Testament, such a cloud represents God's coming to his people (cf. Ex 16:10; 19:9; 24:15; 33:9). A cloud coming down also represents God's glory being revealed (Ex 24:16).

Read verse 35. "A voice came from the cloud, saying, 'This is my Son, whom I have chosen; listen to him.'" This was God's voice when Jesus was baptized by John to begin his earthly ministry. To begin the gospel work all by himself was literally a thorny path, the way to suffering and the painful cross. The voice of God, "This is my Son, whom I have chosen," was again heard when he decided to go up to Jerusalem to bring to fulfillment God's promise. At this crucial moment, God himself spoke to the disciples to understand Jesus and hear his voice. This was God's special revelation. They didn't deserve such a privilege. But there was something in the disciples. They were faithful. It was through this faithfulness that God revealed himself to them.

Read verse 35 again. "A voice came from the cloud, saying, 'This is my Son, whom I have chosen; listen to him.'" In this revelation, God appealed to the three disciples to "listen to him," in other words, to accept his teaching concerning his crucifixion and resurrection. In this we learn, to a physical man, it is not easy to listen to Jesus, even though it is most important.

Read verse 36. When the voice had spoken, they found that Jesus was alone. Moses and Elijah suddenly disappeared. Jesus remained alone. This verse teaches us that Jesus alone remains in the end. This verse also teaches us that life is nothing without Jesus. Men desire many things, but these things are nothing. Francis of Assisi was once tired and the human desire to have a wife and two sons arose in his heart out of nowhere. So he made snowmen and enjoyed them during the night. The next morning, he hoped that they were there and safe, but he saw they were melting in the sunshine, and then he cried.

Verse 36b says, "The disciples kept this to themselves." This experience lasted long in their hearts as the seed of the spiritual world. John was an exile in a cave on the Isle of Patmos as a witness to Jesus' death and resurrection. Yet he was not overcome by the terror of the Roman Emperor. He was filled with the glorious image of Jesus, as well as the glorious view of the kingdom of God, instead of suffering from cruel images of his persecutors. His body was in a cave as an exile, but his spirit was in heaven. To Peter, this glorious transfiguration was the power source to overcome the world in the course of living as a witness of his death and resurrection. He spoke of this glory and honor from the Father in 2 Peter 1:17b. Through the experience at the Mount of Transfiguration, Peter could see Jesus as the Son of God, the Messiah of the world.

The world is anomalous and cruel. Many are wounded by cruel people. Jesus wants each of us to come to him so that we may be healed from the fear and terror of cruel images. Jesus invites each of us to come to him to be imprinted with the glorious image of Jesus as God.

Lesson 29

The Healing of the Boy with an Evil Spirit

Luke 9:37-45
Key Verse: 9:41

I. O UNBELIEVING GENERATION (37-41)

1. When Jesus and three of his disciples came down from the Mount of Transfiguration, who met them? What was going on at the foot of the mountain?

2. What was the problem of the man who called out to Jesus? What did he want Jesus to do? Describe the boy's problem.

3. What was the problem of the nine disciples? Why do you think they failed?

4. To whom was Jesus speaking when he said, "O unbelieving generation"? In what respect were the people at the foot of the mountain unbelieving?

5. What did Jesus tell the father to do? Why?

II. JESUS REBUKES THE EVIL SPIRIT (42-43a)

6. What happened to the boy as he was coming to Jesus? How did Jesus see his problem? How did Jesus help him?

7. How did the people respond? How was God glorified through this event?

III. LISTEN CAREFULLY (43b-45)

8. While everyone marveled at Jesus' work, what did Jesus tell his disciples? Why was it necessary for him to tell them to listen carefully at this time? Why did he talk about his rejection and death?

9. Why didn't they understand? Why were they afraid to ask him about it?

The Healing of the Boy with an Evil Spirit

Luke 9:37-45
Key Verse: 9:41

> *"'O unbelieving and perverse generation,' Jesus replied, 'how long shall I stay with you and put up with you? Bring your son here.'"*

THIS EVENT TAKES PLACE right after Jesus' transfiguration. Jesus again humbled himself to walk this earth as a man. He returned to the yearning, agonizing, and unbelieving world of men to fulfill his work of salvation according to God's will. That day, Jesus healed a boy with an evil spirit. This event occurred because a struggle over the matter of a boy possessed by a demon took place among the crowd at the foot of the mountain. As the last painting by Raphael depicted, this was quite a contrast to Jesus' glory on the mountain.

When he saw the boy with an evil spirit, he lamented in verse 41, saying, "O unbelieving and perverse generation, how long shall I stay with you and put up with you? Bring your son here." As children of God, we want to please God. We don't want to make God lament. Let's study in this passage when and why God laments and see for what we should lament.

I. O unbelieving generation (37-41)

"The next day, when they came down from the mountain, a large crowd met him" (37). They were in a commotion. When they met Jesus, they began to calm down: "Hush! Shh!" On the spur of the moment, a man in the crowd broke the silence and called out,

"Teacher, I beg you to look at my son, for he is my only child" (38b).

What was the man's problem and what was his son's problem? Verse 39 says it was his son's demon possession. Whenever a spirit seized the boy, he suddenly screamed and convulsed until he foamed at the mouth, looking awful and washed-out. It was not just one or two times; it continued time after time. The spirit scarcely ever left him and was destroying him. Because of this, the father had been in great anguish and terror. One day, the father brought his child to the disciples and begged them to drive the spirit out, but the disciples could not.

The child may have been a teenager. When his life should have blossomed, he was sick—too sick to be healed. To this father, his child was dear because he was his only child. His son was the delight of his eyes. The father would look at his son from many angles, rejoicing and laughing with a voice so loud the neighbors could hear him. His life was bound up so closely with that of his son's that they could not be parted unless one died. The father was happy as long as his only child was near him, playing around.

The happiness of parents largely depends on their children. If the children grow well and study well and become successful, parents are very joyful. The joy of life overflows for a parent whose child is outstanding among his classmates or in his society. On the other hand, when the son who was once the hope of his family turns out to be a bad student or seems to be getting worse, his parents' joy is no more. One time a workman came to the Evanston Bible house to install a T.V. antenna on the roof. He was young, but he looked very gloomy. "Why don't you feel good today?" I asked him. "Well, I'm okay," he answered. "You know, I have an only son. He never studies. He is extremely talkative."

Even if this boy was not outstanding among his friends, it would have been too painful for the boy's father to endure. Therefore, how painful it must have been when the father saw his only son fall down to the ground in a convulsion, foaming at the mouth, his eyes rolling back into his head as if he were dying. The father's heart must have been nearly broken. He must have felt as if an iron barb pierced his soul. In pain and anguish, he brought his boy to Jesus' disciples to be healed, but they could do nothing. Rather, the boy's wriggling and twisting in desperate agony only became an amusement and a laughingstock for spectators.

What did Jesus do when he heard about this pathetic boy? Did Jesus immediately try to heal him? No. Contrary to our common sense, Jesus lamented over the people of that generation, saying, "O unbelieving and perverse generation, how long shall I stay with you and put up with you? Bring your son here." Sociologically speaking, the boy was, of course, the problem. He was a great burden, though an unintended one, to his relatives and neighbors. He was the one to blame. But Jesus did not think so. Jesus saw that the boy's problem was caused by the unbelief of that generation, and the root of the problem was their unbelief. The generation was characterized by the word, "unbelieving," and this unbelief made all the people of the times sick, as well as this child. It is really amazing to know that Jesus did not see the boy's problem simply as an illness. He saw the boy's problem as a symptom of the unbelief of the generation. He saw this as a spiritual problem.

In this respect, Jesus was different from most men in terms of dimension. For example, Confucius thought that the fundamental problem of mankind was social order. For this cause, he wrote many books and indoctrinated people to respect the order of seniority. His teaching made a large contribution to the rise of despotic monarchism in China. For the sake of social order, he also strongly forbade men and women to sit together after the age of seven. As a result, he contributed to the debasing of women's rights, bringing them into a state of slavery. His teachings gave birth to the great thought world of China, and it is still matchless. But his teachings did not touch the realm of the spiritual world. He confined himself to the second dimensional world, that is, the physical world.

Jesus saw his generation on the third dimensional plane, and saw that unbelief caused the people of that generation to be very sick spiritually, and as a consequence, this boy was sick with demon possession. To Jesus, the boy was a victim of the unbelieving generation. When Jesus saw the people of that generation, he could not but abandon them in their sin of unbelief. We see in this passage four kinds of unbelieving people.

First, the unbelief of the crowd. There was a large crowd of people. Why had they come, and why were they making such a commotion? Had they come to help the boy? No. Had they come because they were sympathetic toward the boy? No. They had come to watch the boy. They were like spectators at a cockfight or a football game. More candidly, they were like spectators watching a fight between gladiators or a death struggle between a beast and a man. They enjoyed the spectacle more and more when one side was badly wounded and dying. They only watched to enjoy some thrill or suspense and satisfy the lust of the eyes. That was all. They didn't care about anything or anybody. They were an indifferent mob of people who were swayed by the direction of the wind. They lived by their senses and the flesh. They never believed that man is both body and spirit. They themselves were the demonstration of sheer unbelief.

Second, the unbelief of the religious leaders. Luke omitted the argument between Jesus' disciples and the teachers of the law, but according to Mark's gospel, when Jesus and his companions came to the other disciples who were waiting for them at the foot of the mountain, they saw a large crowd around them and the teachers of the law arguing with them. The teachers of the law were the spiritual leaders of the times. They should have prayed for the boy who was lying on the ground in a convulsive fit, foaming at the mouth and looking all washed-out. But they did not pray for the boy. In order to defend their authority and prestige, they only argued with the disciples. Probably, they tested the disciples, asking theological questions about demon possession. Probably, they were checking their licenses to preach and heal. They were shepherds of God's flock. They had a form of godliness, but denied its power. They judged everything by human standards. In order to justify themselves, they perverted everything according to their convenience. This was their main problem. When they saw John the Baptist living an austere life of faith, they said, "He has a demon" (7:33). They saw the Son of Man eating and drinking and said, "Here is a glutton and a drunkard, a friend of tax collectors and 'sinners'" (7:34). In order to justify themselves, they insulted the men of God and the work of God, saying that it was the work of demons.

The teachers of the law studied about God, Christology, the Trinity, the Church eschatology, and so on. But this knowledge did not enable them to know more of God or man. They were like modern theologians who only teach about God, but scarcely ever believe. Paul Tillich, a Protestant theologian, was asked at the end of his life by a student, "Sir, do you pray?" "No, I meditate," he replied. The teachers of the law should have been spiritual men, by they were not spiritual. They did not pray.

Third, the unbelief of the boy's father. The father was desperate because of his son's demon possession. He brought his son to Jesus' disciples to be healed, for he heard that they had cast out many demons and healed the sick. In Mark 9:22, this father said to Jesus clumsily, "If you can do anything, take pity on us and help us." He asked Jesus to heal his son as a man might request something from his congressman. Maybe he expected the answer, "Well, let me see what I can do for you." He wanted his son to be healed, but he only had half-faith. Half-faith is not faith at all.

Faith should be perfect and total. Therefore, James said in James 1:6, "But when he asks, he must believe and not doubt, because he who doubts is like a wave of the sea, blown and tossed by the wind." Half-faith is fortune-seeking faith. Many people believe vaguely, hoping that they might be better off if they believe. Such fortune-seeking is shamanistic. Shamanism has been prevalent in the East for many centuries, but these days, this sickly superstition seems to be more rampant in the West. There are innumerable fortune-seeking Christians in the churches. There are innumerable fortune-seeking pastors who only talk about the welfare of one's life. With such faith, we cannot get any help from God. We also cannot please God.

What did Jesus do for the father when he said, "If you can do anything, take pity on us"? Jesus rebuked him for asking with half-faith using a conditional phrase, "If you can ..." Jesus sternly declared, "Everything is possible for him who believes" (Mk 9:23). From his outward appearance, this boy's father looked like a person who might be eligible for relief goods or food stamps. He was a person who easily could be ignored. But Jesus had great compassion on him. Jesus wanted to heal his disease of unbelief and plant all-powerful faith in him before healing the boy. Jesus was more concerned with the father's unbelief. Jesus saw in him sorrow, despair, pain, and torment. But Jesus believed that all his suffering would be gone if he had faith. So he wanted to plant in him faith in God. "Everything is possible for him who believes." This was the voice of God to this poor man.

There are many problems in the world, but unbelief is the most serious problem. Many people suffer, not because their human conditions are so bad, but because their hearts are divided on account of their unbelief. They suffer most, not because they have no bread, but because of their unbelief.

What was the response of the boy's father to Jesus' rebuke? Mark 9:24 says, "Immediately the boy's father exclaimed, 'I do believe; help me overcome my unbelief!'" We also must exclaim, "Help me overcome my unbelief," whenever we meet impossible situations. There are many things for which we have to be sorry, but in light of this passage, we have to be sorry when we find in ourselves the disease of unbelief.

Fourth, the unbelief of the disciples. The boy's father brought his sick son to the disciples who were waiting for Jesus at the foot of the mountain. They were disciples in the second circle. During the evangelistic journey, when they had depended on the authority and power of Jesus, they had experienced great success in preaching and healing everywhere they went. Even King Herod was perplexed by their power (Lk 9:1-10). But this time, they did not depend on the power or authority of Jesus. They depended on their experience. Maybe Philip and some others confidently stepped out before the crowds and teachers of the law and struck a pose to cast the demon out of the boy. Perhaps it looked for a moment as if they would succeed in driving the demon out. When they ordered the demon to come out of the boy, it only made the demon laugh. In response, the demon drove the boy into a convulsion and showed off his power. They had to learn to depend on God in prayer in whatever they did. But they did not depend on God in prayer. They became presumptuous when they depended on their past experience. Experience works in the material world. In the spiritual world, however, experience only hinders God's work. They should have prayed so that God would rescue this boy, but they did not pray. They hoped that they could show off before the teachers of the law and the crowds of people, and they revealed their unbelief.

Jesus saw that unbelief permeated all the ranks of people and society. Unbelief crept into the hearts of all people. No one could pay attention to this pathetic boy who was suffering from demon possession. Jesus expressed his deep sorrow when he saw the unbelief of the people and the perversion of their thoughts. Jesus can endure all kinds of sins. But he could not endure when he saw the unbelief of the people of his time. So he said, "How long shall I stay with you and put up with you?" (41).

II. Jesus rebukes the evil spirit (42-43a)

Read verse 41 again. "'O unbelieving and perverse generation,' Jesus replied, 'how long shall I stay with you and put up with you? Bring your son here.'" No one could heal the boy, but Jesus could. He said, "Bring your son here." Jesus had great compassion on this teenage boy. Jesus was ready to drive the demon out.

Read verse 42. In this verse, we see the evilness of a demon. First, we see the terror of the demon. Even while the boy was coming to Jesus, the demon, as a last resort, threw him to the ground in a convulsion. Second, the demon is also deceptive. Once a demon, a messenger of Satan, visited Eve and began to coax her to doubt the word of God. Here, the demon disguised himself to be a symptom of epilepsy and entered the teenage boy and controlled him, almost driving him to death every day. The demon also drove the people into restlessness when they saw the boy's deathly convulsions. Third, the demon is very cruel. He was not mindful of beautiful teenagers. Rather, he considered a teenager to be easier to destroy. The demon continually tormented this young boy, seeking finally to destroy him.

These days, most people live as if they were only flesh, ignoring spiritual reality. As a result, innumerable men and women, both young and old, suffer from the torment of demon possession. They go to psychologists to know the reason why they are tormented. But they cannot find the root cause of their troubles. I have asked many times,

"What is wrong with you?" Usually, the answer is, "I don't know. I really don't know." They are right. They cannot know the root of their problems because they do not acknowledge the existence of demon possession. In reality, they are suffering under the torment of demon possession. This passage teaches us the existence of demons, as well as the reality of the spiritual world. A demon is a spirit. But he is an evil spirit and a well-disciplined soldier of his king Satan.

What did Jesus do when the boy coming to him was suddenly thrown on the ground in a convulsion? Jesus did not try to treat the symptoms of epilepsy. He rebuked the evil spirit in him, healed the boy, and gave him back to his father. Many of us rebuke our sheep because of their demonic behavior. We should not do that. Rather, we must accept them as they are. On the other hand, we must rebuke the demons in them, depending on the authority and power of our Lord.

What was the response of the people? Verse 43a says, "And they were all amazed at the greatness of God." Up until now, the large crowd of people stood by indifferently, watching the boy when he was driven into convulsions, foaming at the mouth. They watched to see if the teachers of the law could help him. But they only argued about the theology of demon possession. They watched to see if the disciples at the foot of the mountain could heal him, but they could not. They only exposed their impotent pride. When this large crowd of people watched this event, each of them momentarily felt somewhat unfortunate, as if they would become like this boy.

But Jesus rebuked the evil spirit, healed the boy, and gave him back to his father. And the people saw God working in their midst. When the teenage boy was restored and his eyes began to twinkle with life and sagacity, the gloomy cloud which hung over their souls was lifted by the heavenly sunlight as it penetrated their souls. They saw the great mercy of God revealed in this boy. They could have hope that the mercy of God might be revealed in each of them. At that time, the disciples' prestige, damaged by their failure in healing the boy, was pretty much restored, too. They felt as if they had healed the boy.

III. Listen carefully (43b-45)

Read verses 43b and 44. "While everyone was marveling at all that Jesus did, he said to his disciples, "Listen carefully to what I am about to tell you: The Son of Man is going to be betrayed into the hands of men." Jesus did not speak further. But when he said, "The Son of Man is going to be betrayed into the hands of men," he was saying that he would be lifted up on the cross after his betrayal. Jesus said this right after healing the boy. Jesus saw that the world was full of demons and boisterous devils whose stomping shook the whole world. The people in the world were sitting in darkness. Again, Jesus realized his mission to liberate people from the hand of Satan. How? It was by dying on the cross for the sins of the world. Jesus explained more clearly the necessity of his ransom sacrifice on the cross in John 3:13-15: "No one has ever gone into heaven except the one who came from heaven—the Son of Man. Just as Moses lifted up the snake in the desert, so the Son of Man must be lifted up, that everyone who believes in him may have eternal life."

Right after healing the boy possessed by the demon, Jesus had great compassion on all the people who were rejoicing and praising God after seeing the work of God in the boy. At that moment, Jesus felt the urgency to take up the cross as a ransom sacrifice to free man from the curse. Read Galatians 3:13. "Christ redeemed us from the curse of the law by becoming a curse for us, for it is written: 'Cursed is everyone who is hung on a tree.'"

Jesus healed the boy and gave him back to his father. Everyone was happy and Jesus was very happy to see them happy. So he said, "The Son of Man is going to be betrayed into the hands of men." But they did not understand what this meant. It was hidden from them so that they did not grasp it, and they were afraid to ask him about it. However, Jesus said this so that they would remember it later. Therefore, it is necessary to teach the Bible to everybody as the Lord did so that someday they can understand the word of life.

In light of this passage, unbelief is the most serious problem. Unbelief is the root of all misery and anguish. There are many things for which we have to be sorry, but we must be sorry only when we find unbelief in us.

God chose us to be his servants for this generation. But when our hearts are divided because of unbelief, we cannot be servants of

God working for his lost flock. When our hearts are divided because of our unbelief, we cannot be a blessing to others. Rather, because of our unbelief, we can be a burden and curse. If we despair inwardly because of unbelief and pretend to be a good leader, we cannot be a help to our sheep at all. We only discourage them with our hypocrisy. Above all, we make God very sorry when we are overcome by unbelief.

Let's pray that we may overcome unbelief in us so that we can be called children of God. Let's pray that we may overcome our unbelief and continue to pray for the raising of 561 full-time American shepherds. Let's pray with faith that God may make this country a missionary-sending country through our believing prayer.

Lesson 30

The Greatest in the Kingdom of Heaven

Luke 9:46-62
Key Verse: 9:48b

I. WHO WOULD BE THE GREATEST (46-48)

1. What argument arose among the disciples? What does this argument reveal about the hopes and aspirations of the disciples? Which of the Twelve seemed to be the best contenders for the top position? Why?

2. How did Jesus teach them about true greatness? What does it mean to welcome a child? To do it in Jesus' name? How did the disciples' idea of greatness differ from that of Jesus'?

3. What are the qualities of a child that Jesus wants us to emulate?

II. SONS OF THUNDER, JAMES AND JOHN (49-56)

4. Why did John stop the man who was driving out demons in Jesus' name? What does this show about him?

5. How was Jesus' idea different? Why?

6. Why did the Samaritans not welcome Jesus? How did James and John react? Why? What does this event show about their loyalty to Jesus? Why did Jesus rebuke them?

III. THE COST OF FOLLOWING JESUS (57-62)

7. What did Jesus teach the man who volunteered to follow Jesus anywhere? What do you think Jesus perceived as this man's spiritual problem?

8. When Jesus invited another man to follow him, how did the man respond? What was wrong with his priorities? What choice did Jesus give him? What does this mean to us?

9. What did Jesus teach the man who wanted to go back and say goodbye to his family? What did this man have to overcome in order to be fit for the kingdom of God?

10. Summarize what you learn here about who is fit for the kingdom of God. What does it cost to be a disciple trained by Jesus? Why is it worth it?

The Greatest in the Kingdom of Heaven

Luke 9:46-62
Key Verse: 9:48b

"For he who is least among you all—he is the greatest."

L
UKE 9:51-19:10 IS A description of Jesus' progress toward Jerusalem. This part seems to be Luke's own material concerning Jesus' teachings and it somewhat resembles the particularities of John's gospel. Some scholars call this part, "Jesus' travel records by Luke."

The time setting of this passage is when the thoughts of Jesus were increasingly fixed on Jerusalem, where suffering and rejection awaited him (51). Jesus had repeatedly taught the disciples about the meaning of his suffering and death on the cross. Nevertheless, they did not understand what this meant. They should have prayed earnestly and diligently that they might understand the meaning of his Passion. But they did not. Rather, they engaged in class strife and a power struggle like the main characters in proletariat literature. Their question was which of them would be the greatest. In spite of this, Jesus, without a hint of animosity, taught them what true greatness meant.

On the way to Jerusalem, Jesus was met by several people who expressed their willingness to follow him. They were obnoxious fellows who would dwindle away to nothing after an initial display of greatness. Jesus might have overlooked them because it was unnecessary to spend time with such fellows. But Jesus stopped his heavy footsteps many times and taught them the way of truth concerning the basic requirements of following him. Praise Jesus for his limitless grace and truth even toward such brazen characters.

I. Who would be the greatest (46-48)

Read verse 46. "An argument started among the disciples as to which of them would be the greatest." Probably, they expected the earthly messianic kingdom to appear as soon as Jesus arrived in Jerusalem. When they deciphered his going up to Jerusalem in their own way, they each thought about cabinet members and who would be the greatest among them. Probably, when the three top disciples accompanied Jesus up the Mount of Transfiguration, the nine disciples who were left at the foot of the mountain felt a potential crisis; they might have no chance to seize the top positions. An argument arose among them as to "which" of them would be the greatest. Each one expected to be the greatest, even Bartholomew. No one had any thought of being second. Each of them held a parallel question in his heart: "Am I not the greatest?" Not one of them was beyond the plague of selfish ambition. Jesus had already set the order of precedence and rank. The top three were Peter, James, and John. Among the three, Peter was the top. Philip and Thomas, the men with brains, who frequently seized the opportunity to speak, were in the second circle. Andrew, the brother of Peter, because of his good influence, might have been recognized as a kind of top leader without portfolio.

Outwardly, they seemed to follow the order which Jesus had set among them, but they were too young spiritually to submit to this order. Peter was more than sure that he was at the top now and would be at the top in the future. But James and John had their own ideas. They had negotiated through their mother to obtain the seats to the right and left of Jesus' throne in his kingdom (Mt 20:21). To achieve their purpose, James most likely supported John, and vice versa. But actually, each supported none other than himself. Each thought that the principal place ought to be his unquestionably. Luke the historian understood very well the disciples' human desire to be the top and the greatest.

In order to follow Jesus, they had left their sweet homes. Peter, James, and John had given up developing their fishing businesses. Their sparkling ambitious spirits compelled them to transcend their petty worldly desires and their small pleasures. This spirit compelled them to risk their future security and to readily gamble their future destiny. In one sense, they were like little Jacobs from Genesis. Jacob was always unhappy because he was the younger brother to his older brother Esau. One day, Jacob seized an opportunity to snatch his brother's birthright. So he became the older brother to his older brother. In order to maintain the honor of being the older brother, he had to give up his sweet home and his mother's love and live as a wanderer for more than twenty years.

Why are men like this? It is because God created man in his own image, and God put in men an endless desire to grow in the greatness of God. There is a saying, "If vanity is taken out of a woman, she stumbles; if the sense of honor is taken out of a man, he collapses." Why is this so? Because God made them so. This is the unfathomable wisdom of God. The disciples were not highly educated. But their ambition made it possible for them to grow to be the twelve disciples and as spiritual giants.

Read verses 47 and 48. Jesus, knowing their thoughts, took a little child and had him stand beside him. Then he said to them, "Whoever welcomes this little child in my name welcomes me; and whoever welcomes me welcomes the one who sent me." Here, Jesus teaches them explicitly that he who desires to be great must first be like a child. At that time, children, together with women, were unimportant because they had no labor power. What does it mean when Jesus said that whoever welcomes a little child in his name is the greatest?

First, a child is helpless and totally dependent. Here, a child is compared to the helpless, such as welfare recipients, mental patients, and men possessed by demons. To the helpless of the times, society seems to be nothing but a fierce battleground for the survival of the fittest. There was no piece of ground on which they could stand.

But according to Jesus, the truly great man is one who accepts the helpless in the name of Jesus until they can stand on their own two feet in God. Jesus said in Mark 10:42-44, "Jesus called them together and said, "You know that those who are regarded as rulers of the Gentiles lord it over them, and their high officials exercise authority over them. Not so with you. Instead, whoever wants to become great among you must be your servant, and whoever wants to be first must be slave of all." True greatness is not earthly greatness maintained by applied power, but its antithesis.

Read verse 48 again. "Whoever welcomes this little child in my name welcomes me; and whoever welcomes me welcomes the one who sent me." By syllogism, this verse deduces the truth that one who has the mind of God to accept the helpless can accept Christ. And the one who can accept Christ can accept the Father in heaven. Now the point is clear. The greatest man in the sight of God is the one who has the privilege of knowing Jesus and the one who has the privilege of serving Jesus' children for the sake of his name. The greatest man is the one who knows God very personally. The greatest man is the one who knows God's great purpose for him. For example, Abraham was nothing but a childless old man before knowing God. But he became the greatest of men and a source of blessing for all men when he knew God very personally and discovered God's purpose for him. David was a shepherd boy. But he knew God personally and loved God. Finally he became the greatest of men, not because of his ability as a soldier and a poet, but because he had God in his heart and tried his best to love God as a matter of life and death.

Second, a child is humble. A child has many characteristics which are all beautiful. Generally, a child is innocent; a child can quarrel frequently with other children, but he forgets about everything and becomes friendly again with whom he quarreled. A child is simple. He can simply believe whatever he is told. He can simply trust his parents. A child has a learning mind. A child is obedient. The most beautiful point of all is that a child is humble. One who is humble like a child can grow up to be a great one.

Look at the last part of verse 48. "For he who is least among you all—he is the greatest." This doesn't mean that the disciples in the third circle, such as Bartholomew or Thaddeus or Simon the Zealot, were the greatest. Rather, the most humble person among them was the greatest in the kingdom of heaven. Jesus said, "Blessed are the poor in spirit, for theirs is the kingdom of heaven," and "Blessed are the meek, for they will inherit the earth" (Mt 5:3,5). Moses did not become the greatest among the Hebrews through his 40 years of palace education in Egypt. He became the greatest among his people after 40 years of humbleness training in the wilderness of Sinai.

Paul did not become a great man among his people with his name Saul, which means "the greatest." But he met Jesus on the road to Damascus and came to know what a wretched sinner he was. After this, he humbled himself before God and renamed himself Paul, meaning "a small one." Afterward, he was always humble enough to testify that he was a sinner and that Jesus Christ is Lord. Because of his humility, he became one of the greatest men in human history.

Physically, I am a small man. So I have a desire to become a spiritual giant. I want to be broad-minded like the summer sea so that I can compensate for my smallness and at the same time, embrace every kind of person to my bosom. But so often my proud mind makes me remain as a small man with a narrow mind. I despair about myself and cry for God's mercy.

We thank God because Jesus is the greatest of all who ever lived. He, being in very nature God, emptied himself and came to this world in human form. He humbly served all kinds of sinners as their friend and shepherd.

II. Sons of Thunder, James and John (49-56)

One day, John saw that someone was casting out a demon in the name of Jesus. So John and the other disciples should have been happy. But they were not. John tried to stop him from casting demons out of men because he was not one of them. But the man continued to cast out demons, and John became upset. So he came to Jesus. "Master, we saw a man driving out demons in your name and we tried to stop him, because he is not one of us" (49). The man cast out demons in the name of Jesus. He was doing a wonderful work of God. But John could not accept it because this man was not one of them. When I was young, I saw religious leaders shamelessly condemn each other simply because they belonged to different denominations. We must remember that Jesus rebuked John because of his exclusiveness.

John was spiritually young, but his loyalty was remarkable. He was very clear about being one of Jesus' disciples. He was clear that whoever did not side with Jesus should be punished. When his human loyalty was sanctified and transformed into a spiritual one, he became a most faithful and loyal servant of God.

Read verse 51. "As the time approached for him to be taken up to heaven, Jesus resolutely set out for Jerusalem." Jesus knew well what was before him. The betrayal, the unjust trial, the mockery, the scorn, the crown of thorns, the spitting, the nails, the spear, and the agony on the cross were all undoubtedly spread before his mind's eye like a picture. But he never flinched or shrunk back for a moment from the way he had determined to go, to Jerusalem.

As he traveled toward Jerusalem, Jesus sent his messengers on ahead to a Samaritan village to get things ready for him. But the Samaritans did not welcome him because of their hatred toward the Jews and because he was going to Jerusalem to see the Jews. When James and John saw this, they asked, "Lord, do you want us to call down fire from heaven to destroy them?" (54). They were so passionate, like flashing lightning and roaring thunder. Even if the expression of their feelings was somewhat ornery, imperious, rigorous, and invincibly self-righteous, their loyalty to Jesus was admirable. When they saw that Jesus was humiliated, they were ready to destroy a whole village of people. Because of their loyalty, they could finally become most faithful disciples who took to themselves the remaining suffering of Jesus Christ.

III. The cost of following Jesus (57-62)

A series of stories in verses 57-62 teaches us the cost of following Jesus.

First, in order to follow Jesus, one must commit himself wholly to God. Read verse 57. "As they were walking along the road, a man said to him, 'I will follow you wherever you go.'" The man really wanted to follow Jesus and do the work of God. It was his heart's desire. He wanted to be what a man ought to be; he wanted to be a man of God.

How did Jesus reply? Read verse 58. "Jesus replied, 'Foxes have dens and birds of the air have nests, but the Son of Man has no place to lay his head.'" According to Jesus, this man first wanted to make some money and establish his future security, and then do the work of God. We can understand his problem because the life security problem is deadly serious to everybody. We can also understand his idealism. He wanted to make money, enough to support his family, and then do the work of God. But this kind of person could not be raised up to be a man of God, but in the end, a man like a tax collector. In reality, his problem was not a security problem. His problem was an unbelief problem. Because of his unbelief, he could not commit his future security into God's hand. Because of his unbelief, he could not believe God's blessing was on those who seek first his kingdom and righteousness.

Second, in order to follow Jesus, one must give priority to Jesus. Read verse 59. "He said to another man, 'Follow me.' But the man replied, 'Lord, first let me go and bury my father.'" He wanted to carry out his family responsibilities first, and then obey Jesus' calling. We are not even sure whether his father was dead at that moment. But this man seems to have been one of Confucius' disciples. He thought that a funeral service was gravely important. His priority was his family affairs. By the time he buried his father, he would have children he would need to send to college and support until they could graduate with honors. For him, there were so many important things in the world, each demanding first priority.

The priority problem is not an easy matter. Many people make a vow in their destitution that they will serve God wholeheartedly if God helps them in their hardships. God is generous and credits their crying out prayers. As soon as they get out of their hardships, most of them are filled with future plans for better lives. They forget that they cried to God in the time of hardship. But if we want to follow Jesus, we must choose either to engage in family affairs or to engage in proclaiming the kingdom of God. So Jesus said in verse 60, "Let the dead bury their own dead, but you go and proclaim the kingdom of God."

Third, in order to follow Jesus, one must overcome sentimental feelings. Read verse 61. "Still another said, 'I will follow you, Lord; but first let me go back and say good-by to my family.'" He was a romantic person, one who could cry when he saw falling leaves. He wanted to follow Jesus, but he wanted to first say, "Goodbye, mommy," and "Goodbye, daddy." Such a weak, sentimental person is not qualified to follow Jesus. I know of one U of C graduate who had spiritual desire for campus evangelism. But he has been sentimental ever since he had a girlfriend when he was 12. Since that time, he has been sick with one woman after another. A disciple of Jesus must be one who can overcome sentimental feelings and become like an oak tree, a person of large caliber.

Read verse 62. "Jesus replied, 'No one who puts his hand to the plow and looks back is fit for service in the kingdom of God.'" Here, Jesus' words impinge on our sentimental feelings. The privilege and seriousness of following Christ are of such tremendous magnitude that there is no room for sentimentalism. One who wants to follow Jesus must deny his sinful nature moment by moment and fix his eyes on Jesus all the time. Following Jesus is a matter of heart and demands full devotion and loyalty. Following Jesus is a way of learning truth and a way to eternal life. Therefore, following Jesus is not easy at all. It requires an absolute attitude to his word beyond blind human logic and reason. Following Jesus is the way of the cross, but it is glorious.

Lesson 31

Jesus Sends out the Seventy-Two

Luke 10:1-24
Key Verse: 10:2

I. THE HARVEST IS PLENTIFUL (1-3)

1. Why did Jesus send out the seventy-two? Why two by two? (Compare this with the event in 9:1-9)

2. How did Jesus view the sin-sick world into which he was sending the seventy-two? What prayer topic did he teach them? What imperative command did he give them even though he knew the risks involved? What can we learn about Jesus' shepherd mind and his mission from this?

II. AND TELL THEM, "THE KINGDOM OF GOD IS NEAR" (4-16)

3. What instructions did Jesus give them about equipment? Why do you think he wanted them to travel light?

4. What was to be their greeting to potential sheep? What does this mean? How were they to live in each village? Why?

5. What was their ministry? What was their message? What should this mean to us?

6. In case of rejection, how were they to act and what were they to say? What does the message, "the kingdom of God is near," mean to those who reject the gospel?

7. How were Tyre and Sidon different from Korazin, Bethsaida and Capernaum? Why would judgment on these latter cities be greater? Why is it so serious to reject the servant whom the Lord sends?

III. REJOICE THAT YOUR NAMES ARE WRITTEN IN HEAVEN (17-24)

8. Why were the seventy-two so joyful upon their return? What did Jesus teach them about the source of their power? About the real reason for rejoicing?

9. Jesus was on his way to Jerusalem to be crucified. How could he be so joyful? What was his thanksgiving topic? How did he express his loneliness and his comfort?

10. What did Jesus tell his disciples privately? Why were they so blessed? In what respect can we also be blessed people?

Jesus Sends out the Seventy-Two

Luke 10:1-24
Key Verse: 10:2

*"He told them, 'The harvest is plentiful, but the workers are few.
Ask the Lord of the harvest, therefore, to send out workers into
his harvest field.'"*

"**H**E TOLD THEM, 'THE harvest is plentiful, but the workers
are few. Ask the Lord of the harvest, therefore, to send
out workers into his harvest field.'"
On a previous occasion, Jesus sent out the twelve apostles to
preach the gospel and to heal the sick. But now he sends out a much
larger number of disciples, two by two, to bring spiritual ministration
and to prepare his way in the towns and villages that he still wanted
to visit during the few months before his crucifixion. Luke the historian is the one who, on the whole, avoids doublets, but he allows
these two similar accounts in his Gospel. We must ask why he did
so. Then, we can learn from this passage the permanent principles for
guidance, not only for Christian workers, but for all Christians, that
are embodied in the charge which the seventy-two received. Above
all, we can learn Jesus' view of human beings and his shepherd heart
toward sinful men.

I. The harvest is plentiful (1-3)

Read verse 1. Jesus appointed seventy-two others and sent them
two by two ahead of him to every town and place where he was about
to go. If he had sent them one by one, he could have covered seventy-
two towns and villages and been more seemingly economical. But
why did he send them out two by two instead? Jesus knew that one
individual person, no matter how powerful a person he might be,

is not strong enough to do an evangelistic mission alone. He knew that a man needs support and co-workers. The Chinese character for "man" demonstrates this very well. In making up the character for man, the inventor started with two sticks supporting each other. The character for man looks like this: 人

A one-man show is a poor method in carrying out evangelistic work, much less in doing things of the world. Two people are enough to form a spiritual vessel which can be used by God and which can withstand the power of Satan.

It is interesting to note that formerly, Jesus just sent twelve; now he sends out seventy-two. Twelve had reference to the number of the tribes of Israel, seventy to the number of members of the Jewish Council, a body which represented the nation or a whole world. Through this, we can see very clearly that Jesus, before his crucifixion, wanted to visit all the towns and villages that he could reach. The Twelve were mainly sent for the Jews. The seventy-two were sent to the half-Gentile districts to the east of the Jordan, to the inhabitants of the Transjordan. At that time, they were treated with much indifference by the Jewish religious leaders. This caused them spiritual blindness and intense hatred toward legalistic Jews. But Jesus did not care about racial barriers or human prejudice. He only cared for the people who lived in Gentile territories. To Luke's eyes, it was amazing that Jesus cared for the inhabitants of the Transjordan who were considered half-Gentile. Surely, Jesus was a light to the Gentiles as Simeon had confessed (Lk 2:32). When Jesus sent out the seventy-two, it was more than obvious that he had in his mind to evangelize the whole world.

Jesus was on his way to Jerusalem to be crucified. However, he did not fall into his own sorrow. He was more than willing to save all the people of the world. When we have some problem and the problem seems to be too big to endure, we cannot see others' problems with a compassionate heart. But Jesus was different.

Read verse 2a. "He told them, 'The harvest is plentiful, but the workers are few.'" This verse teaches us Jesus' view of human beings. Once a famous journalist asked someone passing on the street, "What do you think about the world?" "The world is crazy," he answered.

Then he asked him another question, "What about the people?" "They are all crazy," he replied. When we see the people of the world, we despair because they are full of every kind of wickedness. We despair even more when we see ourselves in them.

But the viewpoint of Jesus was different. To Jesus' eyes, their sinful situations were not the problem at all. The problem was a shortage of harvesters. He saw all men as fully ripened crops, golden in color and swaying in a field-like prairie. To farmers who labored so hard for the harvest, a plentiful harvest was very precious. Likewise, to Jesus' eyes, all the people, who were so ugly to look at because of their wickedness and sins, were so precious. To Jesus, they were most precious children of God, created in the image of God. They were like a ripe harvest which needed the hands of the workers of the harvest. To Jesus, they were precious jewels. They were his own children. They were so lovely that he wanted to give them the best gift. Here, we need to learn a right view of men from Jesus. The author of E.T. created in E.T. a creature that no one in the world could love. But the children who found E.T. in their house liked him.

Read verse 2b. "Ask the Lord of the harvest, therefore, to send out workers into his harvest field." This verse tells us how the work of harvesting is possible. In feeding sheep or harvesting, there are several basic requirements and principles. Of all these, prayer is most important because we are not able to change anyone's heart, and we cannot hire anyone to do the harvest work of God. God must work in each person's heart to change it, and God must call those who are willing to do his work. Therefore, we must pray wholeheartedly until God sends us many harvest workers.

Read verse 3. "Go! I am sending you out like lambs among wolves." Lambs surrounded by wolves with gleaming teeth have little chance for life. Jesus knew that it was dangerous to send out his men, but he is always ready to send men out. Jesus, like a commander in a war, commands the seventy-two to go out where deadly peril was awaiting them. In order to rescue his children from the hands of Satan, he was ready to sacrifice his men.

II. And tell them, "The kingdom of God is near" (4-16)

In verses 1-3 we learn of Jesus' shepherd heart for the salvation of the whole world. In verses 4-12, Jesus teaches his apostles the basic attitude of being his men, and he also tells them what their major tasks are.

Read verse 4. "Do not take a purse or bag or sandals; and do not greet anyone on the road." This verse clearly tells us that the apostles should not depend on their purses or bags or sandals, but only depend on the Lord who sends them out. In a spiritual harvest, one who depends on what he has will certainly fail to be a good harvester. A girl who believes in her big smile has not been fruitful. Rather, she has damaged God's work irreversibly many times. A man who gave himself energetically to the pursuit of feeding many sheep had been greatly impeded because he depended on his many abilities. But these days, he has been very fruitful because he has begun to depend on God's power. "Do not greet anyone on the road" does not mean to be impolite or to live in churlish isolation. It means, in contemporary terms, to avoid many parties and other kinds of distractions or social interactions. We Christians are all heavenly princes and princesses, and at the same time on earth, we are soldiers of Christ. As soldiers of Christ, we must not get involved in civilian affairs (2Ti 2:3-4).

Read verses 5-8. These verses teach us how to greet others and what our attitudes should be when we go out to feed sheep. "When you enter a house, first say, 'Peace to this house'" (5). Apostles must bring a greeting which may or may not be received. The great effect of the presence of Christ's servants should be to impart the peace which they themselves possess. All Christians are to be peacemakers in the deepest sense, especially in regard to man's relationship with God. He who accepts this greeting in faith will receive and enjoy this peace and salvation for his own life. But those who do not accept it in faith, their destiny becomes their own responsibility. In verse 7, Jesus tells them that they should not complain about food or go around looking for small conveniences.

Read verse 9. "Heal the sick who are there and tell them, 'The kingdom of God is near you.'" Verse 9 tells us that healing and preaching were the major parts of Jesus' work. We know well that sick people suffer. How great is the suffering of those who are sick with sins! They need healing. But no one can heal sin-sick people except Christ himself. And he works through his servants. Those who are sent out for the harvest must acknowledge that they need healing power. It does not necessarily mean a charismatic way of healing. Healing must come from the broken shepherd heart of Jesus. In healing, one must have the deep compassion of Jesus. Those who do not know the love of God are all very sick with sin or severely wounded by Satan. They are like abandoned children out on the street in the cold winter season. Many sick people go around looking for human sympathy and human love. But these things make them worse by weakening them or spoiling them.

Some people become so rebellious because of their parents' overprotection that they cannot be happy about themselves. Many people become utterly useless in their proud minds because of their many abilities. Because of their sicknesses, they hurt themselves and also wound others. When they do not know God, many able people are liable to become inventors of evil. All people of the world need God's healing hand through Jesus Christ. Each person must know in what respect he or she has been healed. Otherwise, one cannot say that he is a Christian. May God give you his love to heal even one person a year.

Read verse 9 again. The last part of verse 9 says, "... and tell them, 'The kingdom of God is near you.'" This short phrase is the key point of the whole Bible. Through one man Adam's disobedience, all men lost paradise, the kingdom of God. But through one man Jesus' obedience, all men regain the kingdom of God when they believe. How easy it is for us to just believe in order to be better off in the present realities of the world. How easy it is for us to just teach the Bible so as to help people get out of their immediate problems. Healing is good, but it is not enough to make us become real children of God. Each one's Christian faith must focus precisely on the kingdom of God. We must help all our sheep to put their hope in the kingdom of God.

Verses 10 and 11 tell us that Jesus knew that his men would receive much rejection. So he taught them what to do in case of rejection. "But when you enter a town and are not welcomed, go into its streets and say, 'Even the dust of your town that sticks to our feet we wipe off against you. Yet be sure of this: The kingdom of God is near.'" When they are rejected, the apostles must have an absolute attitude toward faith in the kingdom of God. They must not try to moderate the situation or compromise with hostile people. Rather, they should shake the dust off from their feet, and at the same time, tell them that the kingdom of God is near them.

Read verses 12-16. Jesus was sorrowful because of people who rejected the gospel and because of cities that refused the gospel despite the mighty wonders which he had performed in them. Jesus encourages the apostles not to be dismayed when they are rejected because rejection of them is rejection of Jesus himself.

III. Rejoice that your names are written in heaven (17-24)

Read verses 17-19. The seventy-two came back with childish joy, and they almost seemed to have thought that Jesus would be as astonished and excited as they were when they saw proof of the power of his name in them. They must have rejoiced in many ways, but they were most joyful when they could brag about their achievements before Jesus, their Master.

In verse 18, Jesus explains quietly the reason why the demons submitted to the apostles. The mighty power of Satan was already broken when Jesus defeated the temptation of the devil right before beginning his public ministry. Throughout Jesus' public ministry, this victory was revealed in the liberation of those possessed by the devil. To Jesus, Satan was a conquered enemy. When the seventy-two acted, victory was gloriously given. Jesus replied in verse 18 and 19, "He replied, 'I saw Satan fall like lightning from heaven. I have given you authority to trample on snakes and scorpions and to overcome all the power of the enemy; nothing will harm you.'" Jesus promises those who believe in his name glorious victory over the power of Satan and utmost joy in the world.

Read verse 20. "However, do not rejoice that the spirits submit to you, but rejoice that your names are written in heaven." Of course, Jesus knew their minds well. They wanted great power and great recognition. So Jesus said, "However, do not rejoice that the spirits submit to you, but rejoice that your names are written in heaven." Jesus means that it is good to rejoice in power and recognition; however, apostles must find the true grounds for joy in the fact that through the grace of God, their names are written in the heavenly register and the book of life. In this, we must find our real and permanent grounds for joy.

Let's look briefly at verses 21-24. Let's recall Luke 9:51: "As the time approached for him to be taken up to heaven, Jesus resolutely set out for Jerusalem." Humanly speaking, it was time for Jesus to sorrow for himself. But he did not. He rejoiced. What on earth could make him rejoice? He rejoiced in God's way of working in history. He was filled, not only with joy, but with the spirit of praising God, saying, "I praise you, Father, Lord of heaven and earth, because you have hidden these things from the wise and learned, and revealed them to little children" (21). We are in many ways foolish and very much like children. But we rejoice because we receive many small persecutions from people around us and great recognition from our Lord Jesus.

In verse 22, Jesus indirectly expresses his deep human loneliness and the agony of taking up his mission. At the same time, he is overcome by eternal joy and says, "All things have been committed to me by my Father. No one knows who the Son is except the Father, and no one knows who the Father is except the Son and those to whom the Son chooses to reveal him." Those who have engaged in God's work for their own benefits cannot understand what Jesus is praying about. But those who have dedicated their lives for the glory of God and have engaged in God's work can deeply understand what Jesus is praying about. In his deep human loneliness and pain in the course of doing God's work, he rejoices that all things have been committed to him by his Father. No one recognized him or knew who he really was. Rather, he was rejected and despised. But Jesus was very happy because of the fact that God, his Father, knows him and he knows God. Jesus was sure about his close love relationship with God. This was the power source of Jesus, and it was the cause of all his victories on earth.

Read verses 23 and 24. Then he turned to his disciples and spoke privately. The key point of these verses is "You are blessed." Why are the disciples blessed when they receive much persecution and rejection in proclaiming the gospel of the kingdom of God and in shepherding many sin-sick people? Their situation is like that of lambs living among wolves. Nevertheless, they are blessed because they have the privilege of seeing Jesus with their own eyes. Many kings and prophets wanted to see what they saw, but they could not see it, and many wanted to hear what they heard, but could not hear it. From a worldly viewpoint, they were nothing but a handful of shabby-looking low-class people. But to Jesus' eyes, they were the most privileged and blessed people of all times.

Lesson 32

The Parable of the Good Samaritan

Luke 10:25-42
Key Verse: 10:28

I. DO THIS AND YOU WILL LIVE (25-29)

1. What did the expert in the law ask Jesus and how did he answer his own question? What does this show about the man? Why is eternal life related to love?

2. Why did the expert in the law ask Jesus another question? What was the question, and what answer did he probably expect from Jesus?

II. GO AND DO LIKEWISE (30-37)

3. What happened to the man going from Jerusalem to Jericho in the parable? Who were the men who passed by? Why might they have passed by without stopping to help? What does this suggest about the religious leaders of the time?

4. What did the Samaritan think about the injured man when he saw him? How did he serve him? What was his expenditure in money, time, and effort? What is Jesus teaching us here?

5. Why do you think that Jesus picked a Samaritan to be the hero of this story? How does this parable answer the lawyer's question in verse 29?

III. BUT ONLY ONE THING IS NEEDED (38-42)

6. How did Martha receive Jesus and his disciples? How did she show her love for Jesus? What did Mary do? Why?

7. What does Martha's complaint about Mary to Jesus show about her? How is her demand reasonable in itself? Why is she wrong?

8. How did Jesus counsel Martha? Why did he not send Mary to help Martha? What is the one thing that is needed, the thing that Jesus wants the most from those who love him?

9. How do the teaching of the parable and the lesson taught in Martha's house complement each other?

The Parable of the Good Samaritan

Luke 10:25-42
Key Verse: 10:28

> "'You have answered correctly,' Jesus replied. 'Do this and you will live.'"

THIS PASSAGE IS DIVIDED into two parts. The first is the Parable of the Good Samaritan. Jesus is approached by a lawyer who is at least friendly to him. The conversation between them lays stress on the practical application of the command to love one's neighbor (25-37). The second, a story at the home of Martha and Mary, provides something of a counterbalance to the emphasis on practical love by stressing the need for his followers to attend to the teaching given by Jesus (38-42). These two incidents seem to handle the relationships of the disciples to their neighbors, to Jesus, and to God. With the Parable of the Good Samaritan, many unwise attempts have been made to attach many spiritual meanings to the story, but a parable has just one clear teaching. This parable shows how we can be a good neighbor to the helpless. Furthermore, it teaches the true humanity of Jesus.

I. Do this and you will live (25-29)

Read verse 25. One day an expert in the law came to Jesus. "'Teacher,' he asked, 'what must I do to inherit eternal life?'" This is the most important question a person can ask. In the Gospels, this question was seriously put to Jesus on many occasions. Indeed, it was a question that was brewing in the hearts of many people at that time (Mt 19:16-26; Mk 12:28-34; Lk 18:18-27). In reality, it may be assumed that those who are serious about their life problem will ask in their hearts, "What must I do to inherit eternal life?"

The first motive behind the lawyer's question was to test Jesus. He was a teacher of the law. He wanted to ascertain if Jesus was orthodox like himself. This question might have been a kind of intimidation, suggesting that Jesus belong to his denomination or else be considered a heretic. Or perhaps this man wanted to show off his deep knowledge of the law. He was a man of great learning, an expert in the law. To become an expert on a musical instrument, such as the violin, one must fully devote his time and life for more than 18 years. In order to be an expert in something, he must take the pains of total sacrifice, sacrificing everything other than his major. This lawyer was a man who had undergone such a process of life. He was also a man of passion, for he dared to test Jesus in spite of Jesus' overpowering authority over people.

The second motive of his question might have been to get an answer to his own problem. He practiced the commandments meticulously. However, he did not feel life in himself. When he was busy, he was okay. But when he had leisure time, he felt strange. His knowledge of the law and ceremonial practices did not help him overcome his feelings of dread or his deranged spiritual condition. Outwardly, he looked conceited, but in reality, he desperately needed the hand of deliverance.

In verse 26, Jesus said, "What is written in the Law? How do you read it?" Jesus addressed the point where the lawyer thought himself superior. Then the lawyer declared that according to the Law, the requirements for inheriting eternal life are perfect love toward God and perfect love toward one's neighbor (27).

Read verse 28. "'You have answered correctly,' Jesus replied. 'Do this and you will live.'" In helping him, Jesus embraced him as he was by complimenting his knowledge of the Law. It would not be easy for anyone to accept a proud man like this expert in the law. But Jesus was more than willing to accept him so that somehow he might help him. Jesus really wanted to show him the way that he could feel life and the joy of God in himself and have the assurance of eternal life. So he said, "Do this and you will live." Here, the verb "live" can have two meanings. First, it can mean to have abundant life and joy in Jesus. Second, it can mean to have the assurance of eternal life in one's spirit.

This expert in the law was like a man who had eaten an enormous amount of rich food and never exercised, and as a result, became too weak to control his heavy body. Spiritually speaking, he looked like a monster whose head was like that of a lion and whose legs were like that of a sparrow. He needed strength in his body through proper exercise. Jesus really wanted him to be healthy and happy and to feel abundant life flowing in his body and in his spirit.

How did the man respond? He knew Jesus was right. But he did not accept his words simply. Habitually, he justified himself. Then he quickly rode off on another question, "Who is my neighbor?" In this manner, he suppressed the teaching of the Bible and hid his feelings of guilt.

There are many of us who are like him. There are many who have the knowledge of the Bible, but when they have to put into practice what they know, they quickly turn the Bible teachings into theological arguments or denominational differences. To them, Christianity is one thing and life is quite another. They suffer gravely due to a deep conflict and frustration between their knowledge and the voice of conscience. They really want to get out of the powerlessness of intellectualism, yet they remain continuously in their powerlessness because they are not disciplined in simple obedience.

II. Go and do likewise (30-37)

Jesus' answer was so clear and challenging that the lawyer was compelled to acknowledge the truth conveyed by it. No doubt it forced him to a deep realization of himself. However, we are not told whether he reacted to this realization rightly. Luke, as usual, leaves out such detail so that the incident itself and the words of Jesus may speak with full power, personally to each person.

However, Jesus knew that the lawyer did not know how to love God and love his neighbor, so he told him a moving story about a good Samaritan. This parable is well-known, even to non-Christians. But it is not easy to express the exact motif of the parable. The meaning of the parable becomes clear when we compare the priest and the Levite with the Good Samaritan in the story.

First, the priest and the Levite. It is said that Jericho was one of the priestly cities where there were frequent travelers on ecclesiastical errands. The priest was going down the road from Jerusalem to Jericho. The road from Jerusalem to Jericho was a rocky, tortuous road which, through all the centuries, had been a place where robbers all too often attacked travelers. Jerusalem is 2,300 feet above sea level, and Jericho, located near the Dead Sea, is 1,300 feet below sea level. In a distance of 20 miles, the road drops 3,600 feet. This rough geological location is made for dens of brigands.

A priest happened to be going down the road. He saw a man was stripped of his clothes, beaten, and left half-dead. He should have taken care of him, for he was a priest, but he passed by on the other side. Perhaps he had memorized Deuteronomy 6:5, "Love the Lord your God ..." and Leviticus 19:18, "Love your neighbor." Through these Bible verses, he could have learned how to love God and his flock, but he did not. He only remembered that he who touched a dead man was unclean for seven days (Nu 19:11). He feared that if he touched him, he would lose his turn of duty in the temple. He refused to risk missing religious ceremonies. He knew the temple and its liturgy, but he did not know God well. He had much knowledge of God, but he did not do any good work for the helpless. He did not have the life and joy of God in himself. In the course of living the life of a hypocrite, he had lost his humanity, but he disguised himself as a servant of God. He could fool people around him, but he could not fool his own conscience. He was a slave of his wretchedness.

Read verse 32. A Levite also happened to be going down the same road which the priest had passed by. Levites were known as musicians, so this Levite must have had an artistic temperament. Perhaps he had gone over to the man and said, "O you poor guy! How sorry I am for you! Somebody ought to come and help you." He had a compassionate sentiment, but his emotion did not drive the wheel of action. He hardened his heart and trudged on his way. He was just a romantic person.

Second, a good Samaritan. Read verses 33-35. Then a Samaritan came along. This man seems to have been a kind of commercial traveler who was a regular visitor to the inn. Perhaps he was a man whom all the "good" orthodox people despised since he was a breaker of the ceremonial law, and therefore, a heretic. Nevertheless, he alone was prepared to help.

Let's see how he helped the injured man. "But a Samaritan, as he traveled, came where the man was; and when he saw him, he took pity on him. He went to him and bandaged his wounds, pouring on oil and wine. Then he put the man on his own donkey, took him to an inn and took care of him. The next day he took out two silver coins and gave them to the innkeeper. 'Look after him,' he said, 'and when I return, I will reimburse you for any extra expense you may have'" (33-35). First of all, he had pity on him. He did not linger, looking all around him for the bandits, full of fear that they would rush upon him and overpower him. His pity overcame all fear of danger. He did not become helpless because of the man's bruised and bloody body. He acted swiftly. He skillfully applied wine and oil to his wounds. He cheerfully picked him up and put him on his own beast while he plodded along on foot, steadying the wounded man on his donkey. He cared for him at the inn, and his generosity in leaving a great sum of money in the innkeeper's hands to care for him is a sign of true humanity. Humanity is purely a Christian word and a concept never dreamt of before Christ had showed us the unity of mankind.

What is true humanity? True humanity is well revealed in this Parable of the Good Samaritan. First, the Samaritan had pity on a helpless man. Second, he helped him. In order to help him, he interrupted his own business. He gave him a ride while he himself walked. He spent a great sum of money. He even endangered his own life. His pity on a helpless man overcame all his calculations. He lost a lot in order to help the helpless. He seems to be a dummy.

But we cannot say that he was an unhappy man. Rather, the Good Samaritan seems to be the happiest man in the world. Why? It is because he was a true human being. To be a true human being seems to be too costly and impractical. Because of this, many people are inclined to think that selfishness is a shortcut to human happiness. Selfishness may seem to be practical. This parable, however, teaches that selfishness is not the way to happiness; it only deprives a person of his humanity. It makes a person inhumane, heartless, and finally ruthless to others as well as to himself.

Who can be like the Good Samaritan? There is no one. But Christ is the perfect example of that love to every man. In Christ, everyone is our neighbor, and at the same time, everyone is our dear brother or sister whom our hearts go out to and whom we can sacrificially help. Frankly, we lose a lot when we want to maintain the humanity of Jesus. Is that all? No. As a reward, we enjoy the abundant life and joy of Jesus. There are many who are miserable because they have too much Bible knowledge, but lack the true humanity of Christ. To them, all the people of the world, including their own parents, are not their neighbors; they are their enemies. The most urgent problem for each of us is to know who our neighbor is.

Read verse 36. "Which of these three do you think was a neighbor to the man who fell into the hands of robbers?" In verse 37, the expert in the law replied, "The one who had mercy on him." Then Jesus told him, "Go and do likewise." The first time, Jesus had said to him, "Do this and you will live" (28). After telling him the Parable of the Good Samaritan, he said, "Go and do likewise." Jesus earnestly pleaded with him to have true humanity like the Samaritan in the parable so as to somehow save himself from a superficial life.

III. But only one thing is needed (38-42)

As Jesus and his disciples were on their way to Jerusalem, he came to a village where a woman named Martha lived. She opened her home to him. She had a sister named Mary who sat at the Lord's feet listening to what he said. On the other hand, Martha was busy preparing dinner for Jesus and his disciples. Martha loved Jesus because he took away the painful sorrow of her family by raising her brother Lazarus from death. Moreover, Jesus had been a father to her fatherless family. Jesus had visited her house from time to time. His visits were like a father's presence to the children in the family. So Martha wanted to treat him with the best hospitality at this time, too. She thought that the best way was to prepare the most delicious and abundant dinner. She had to prepare much quantity of food because she knew that each of Jesus' disciples could consume more than seven people's portion of food. She became very busy and needed many hands. Martha was hard-working and sacrificial, but she did not understand what Jesus really wanted. She was a one-sided woman. On the other hand, Mary was doing nothing but having one-to-one Bible study with Jesus. Martha became very mad and upset, and she came to Jesus and asked, "Lord, don't you care that my sister has left me to do the work by myself? Tell her to help me!" Martha rebuked Jesus for not really understanding her. Read verses 41 and 42. Martha was like a humanitarian. She was like an orphanage director in character. She was so self-centered that she could not understand Jesus at all.

This story tells us that learning the humanity of Jesus is not enough. In order to become a mature child of God, one must be a combination of Martha and Mary. There are many who give their hearts to God's work, but do not know what to do. Like Martha, many work for Jesus in their own ways. They are very busy and worried in doing many things. Most of them think that if they keep themselves busy, they are good servants of God. I saw one minister who was serving on the board of directors of twelve organizations. He was busy, so busy that he had no time to take care of his three children in prayer. Therefore, all his children all became useless. Moreover, he had no time to study the Bible or to pray. Eventually, he became too weak to minister to the people of his church.

Read verse 42. "… but only one thing is needed. Mary has chosen what is better, and it will not be taken away from her." Here, Jesus tells us that in doing God's work, especially in learning the humanity of Jesus, deep and quiet Bible study is most important. What else can be more important than listening to his words!

The United States of America has been known to the world as being a Good Samaritan country. In the past, this was true. In light of historical facts these days, however, we acknowledge that the people of this land, especially all teenagers and college students, must overcome the peer pressure of the world to be selfish and must renew the fame and position of the US as the Good Samaritan country.

Lesson 33

Jesus Teaches on Prayer

Luke 11:1-13
Key Verse: 11:2b

I. THE LORD'S PRAYER (1-4)

1. What request did one of Jesus' disciples make of him? What motivated him to make this request?

2. Think about the meaning and significance of each of the following petitions of the Lord's prayer:

    a. Father

    b. Hallowed be your name

    c. Your kingdom come

    d. Give us each day our daily bread

    e. Forgive us our sins, for we also forgive everyone who sins against us

    f. Lead us not into temptation

II. THE SPIRIT OF PRAYER (5-13)

3. What does the midnight visitor in the parable want?

4. Why is it so difficult for the one inside to give it to him? Why does he finally do so?

5. What is the main point of this parable? What lesson about prayer must we learn from the midnight visitor?

6. What assurance does Jesus give to those who pray persistently?

7. What will most human fathers do when their sons come asking for something? How is the Heavenly Father like them? How is he better?

8. What should be our main prayer topic as God's children? Why?

Jesus Teaches on Prayer

Luke 11:1-13
Key Verse: 11:2b

"Father, hallowed be your name, your kingdom come."

LUKE THE HISTORIAN EMPHASIZES Jesus' manhood and is ever pointing us to Jesus kneeling in prayer. The prayers of Jesus bring him near to us in his true manhood. The life of Jesus was indeed a life of prayer.

In this passage, Jesus teaches on prayer to his disciples. This prayer is commonly called "The Lord's Prayer." Down through the ages, this prayer has helped innumerable people who were dumbstruck in their desperate situations to say a few words, "Father, hallowed be your name, your kingdom come" (2b). The Lord's Prayer has already been repeated during the past nineteen hundred years by millions of believers in over a hundred languages and in an endless variety of circumstances. This prayer has been a source of comfort to all pilgrims on earth traveling toward heaven. Especially, in this prayer, the entire Christian world through the centuries has a common bond of unity and mutual fellowship. In verses 5-13, Jesus teaches us the basic attitude and spirit of prayer: confidence and persistence.

I. The Lord's Prayer (1-4)

Read verse 1a. "One day Jesus was praying in a certain place." Luke does not say where he prayed or when. Luke, however, emphasizes time and again the fact that Jesus was praying. Jesus' prayer reveals his close personal relationship with God in heaven. It reveals his inseparable love relationship with God the Father. Furthermore, his prayer manifests his absolute dependence on God Almighty.

When he finished praying, one of his disciples said to him, "Lord, teach us to pray, just as John taught his disciples." In the past, because of their low desires, they were harebrained. So whenever they saw Jesus praying, in their absurdity, they shrugged their shoulders and stretched their hands, thinking that Jesus was just too unrealistic. But now, after they saw Jesus' prayer on the transfiguration mountain, their spiritual eyes were opened and their conception of prayer was changed, and in their hearts arose the spiritual desire to pray. In Jesus' prayer, they could see glory and majesty and power. When they realized the necessity of prayer, they realized that they were far inferior to John's disciples in the life of prayer. So one of his disciples said, "Lord, teach us to pray, just as John taught his disciples."

Read verses 2-4. He said to them, "When you pray, say: 'Father, hallowed be your name, your kingdom come. Give us each day our daily bread. Forgive us our sins, for we also forgive everyone who sins against us. And lead us not into temptation.' Jesus gave them a model prayer which contains six major prayer topics: three things in relation to God and three things in relation to our daily lives of faith.

First, "Father ..." Read verse 2. "When you pray, say: 'Father, hallowed be your name, your kingdom come.'" First of all, Jesus teaches them to call God, "Father." Matthew 6:9 says, "Our Father in heaven ..." but Luke more concisely says, "Father." The opening word, "Father," teaches us our basic relationship with God. Just as we have relationships with our fathers, we must have a personal relationship with God until we can call God Almighty, "Father" or "Daddy." In the past, Hebrew people thought that they should not utter God's name with their mouths. So they said God's name using some kind of sign language. Their relationship with God was remote and legalistic. Therefore, Jesus' teaching to call God, "Father," is quite revolutionary. Jesus, the mediator between God and man, opened the way to the conquest of happiness when he taught his disciples to call God, "Father." In reality, man's happiness does not depend on abundant material possessions. Rich material possessions easily make men proud, foolish, corrupt, and deranged. Man's happiness totally depends on how he addresses God. No one is happy until he or she can call God Almighty, "Father."

St. Augustine, as an African boy, had received sufficient financial support from his father for his noble education in Rome. But he was not happy. So he, in search of the meaning of his life, devoted himself to Manichaeism, which taught an extremely ascetic lifestyle based on dualism and Gnosticism. Then he tried rhetoric, oratory, Platonism, and Catholicism. None of these could fill his empty heart; they only made his soul restless until he met God personally and called him "Father." Our God is a loving God, like a father. Our God is like King David. Though he was a king, David cried with a loud voice before his subjects, longing for his son Absalom who rebelled against him to take over his kingdom (2Sa 18:33). Our God is like the father in the Parable of the Prodigal Son. His son who went far away is in his heart, and he waits for his son night and day at the door.

Jesus' teaching to call God, "Father," shows that man's life consists of two kinds of pilgrimages. The first is the pilgrimage from this mundane world to the kingdom of God. The second is the pilgrimage of love, from human love to the Father's love in heaven.

When I was young, I gave my heart to God's work. Because I had one heart, I made my wife very lonely. After a ministry to Kwangju students, I moved to the capital city, Seoul, in 1967 to start UBF work on a national scale. After five months, my family came to Seoul to join me. There at the train station, Little Sarah, my youngest, called me, "Daddy!" Her calling moved my heart to tears. When I saw her, she was wearing an old sweater three sizes too big. Since then, she has been a very dear person to me. How much more is it necessary for us to call God, "Father" or "Daddy," to have a right relationship with him?

To say, "Father," also teaches us the universal brotherhood of mankind. God is the only God in the universe and he is our Father. In him, we are all brothers and sisters. Therefore, those who call God, "Father," in earnest faith and with holy reverence must call others, "brother" and "sister." We must respect and love others with the awareness that in God we are all brothers and sisters. The concept of the universal brotherhood in Jesus is essential in knowing God.

Hebrew people have a habit of using the plural form. For example, they say "the heavens" instead of "heaven." Korean people also like to use the plural form in many ways. They say "our" father instead of "my" father, "our" wife instead of "my" wife. One young man made an excuse by saying, "I could not come to the meeting because 'our' wife was sick." Grammatically, he was wrong. However, his thought of the universal brotherhood was beautiful. To call God, "Father," is not easy, nor is it easy to practice. Still, we must call God, "Father," and his children, dear "brothers" and "sisters."

Second, "hallowed be your name." What does "hallowed be your name" mean? In brief, it means "your name be revered or honored among men in history." To put it in plain terms, God's name must receive the right respect, honor, and praise in our personal lives, as well as in our societies. In order for his name to be respected, we must always recognize his name in any circumstance. Whatever problems we may face, we must do our best to render respect and honor to our God, even though it means persecution and disgrace for us. As children of God, we should be most sorrowful if we cause God's name to be dishonored (Ro 2:24). We must live sanctified lives, not for our personal progress, but for his name's sake. We learn how St. Paul gave all his life to render honor and glory to his name. He says in Philippians 1:21, "For to me, to live is Christ and to die is gain." We must remember Jesus' prayer, "Father, the time has come. Glorify your Son that your son may glorify you" (Jn 17:1). As Paul said in 2 Corinthians 5:20, we must think of ourselves as Christ's ambassadors.

Third, "your kingdom come." To the children of God, this world is not everything.

Our ultimate goal is the heavenly kingdom. The kingdom of God does not refer to a geographical location. Rather, it means where the reign of God is. Therefore, "your kingdom come" might be better rendered, "let your divine rule come." When we look at the world, the kingdom of God seems to be reduced to almost nothing. This is the reason why we must strive to expand the territory of the kingdom of God. "Your kingdom come" is prayer that God's divine sovereignty may more and more attain its rightful place in the hearts and lives of fallen mankind who otherwise are under the rule of Satan.

There are many kinds of people with their own cultures and characters, but actually, there are only two kinds of people. The first is the children of God. The other is the children of Satan. There are more than 233 countries in the world, but spiritually speaking, there are only two. The first is the kingdom of God, and the second is the kingdom of Satan. Therefore, we must pray for our loved ones that the kingdom of God may come and rule their hearts, and that the kingdom of God may prosper in all American campuses.

But Luke abbreviated his statement, omitting "your will be done on earth as it is in heaven" (Mt 6:10b) because "your kingdom come" and "your will be done" are the same in content. God's will is to restore his kingdom so that all his children—even all nature—may be completely redeemed from the bondage of Satan's rule and be brought back to his kingdom where the Lamb of God, who was once slain, rules. Because of this, the children of God are wholeheartedly willing to obey God's will and do whatever is necessary in extending his kingdom. We, the children of God, yearn day and night for the time when God's complete reign will come. Our desire as the children of God is "your kingdom come and your will be done."

Fourth, "Give us each day our daily bread." The second half of the prayer turns to our personal needs. In the early centuries, under the influence of Plato, many thought that the soul is good and material things are evil. They thought that the physical body belongs to the material category, which is evil. This influence permeated the Christian world until Gnostics arose. But Jesus honored man's physical life. In this short sentence, "Give us each day our daily bread," all Christian ethical teachings are summed up.

In verse 3 we learn two important things. In the first place, let's think about the idea of "each day." Why did Jesus not teach us to ask for one or two years' portion of bread instead of asking bread for each day? It was because of fallen man's slave mentality. Fallen man's greediness is endless. For example, when the Israelites were in the wilderness, God told them to go out and gather enough bread for that day. However, some gathered much and kept part of it until morning. But they found the next morning that it was full of maggots and beginning to smell (Ex 16). Therefore, each person must learn what it means to ask for daily bread for "each day." This lesson was so important that God gave the Israelites daily manna for forty years. It was daily bread training through which they might overcome their slave mentality and their material greediness and learn to depend on God. Proverbs 30:8-9 says, "Give me neither poverty nor riches, but give me only my daily bread. Otherwise, I may have too much and disown you." According to these verses, to have just the necessary amount of daily bread is most appropriate.

In the second place, let's think about the concept of "our daily bread." Read verse 3. "Give us each day our daily bread." Jesus did not teach us to pray for "my daily bread," but to pray for "our daily bread." Those who do not pray for others' daily bread are like the rich fool who stored up things for himself, but was not rich toward God (Lk 12:21).

Fifth, "forgive." Read verse 4. "Forgive us our sins, for we also forgive everyone who sins against us." Jesus taught them to forgive others' sins. For the survival of the physical body, we need daily bread. Likewise, for the survival of the spiritual life, the forgiveness of sins is absolutely necessary.

First of all, we must have the right conception of the word "sin." The word "sin" in Greek has the meaning, "to miss the target." In other words, "Sin is lawlessness" (1Jn 3:4). Generally speaking, sin is separation from God. Sin makes man sick morally, ethically, and spiritually. We need God's grace of the forgiveness of sins. As God paid the costly price to forgive our sins, we must learn how to forgive others' sins.

But in the Lord's Prayer, the word "sin" transcends the moralistic level. "Sin" in the Lord's Prayer refers to spiritual sin. In this case, the word "sin" also has the precise meaning of debt. Therefore, "Forgive us our sins, for we also forgive everyone who sins against us," can be put like this: "Cancel our debts as we have cancelled the debts of our debtors." Debts should be paid back. A debt calls for responsibility. From God's point of view, each of us has a debt to his family and society and to his country. Ultimately, each has a debt to God that is unpayable.

To forgive another's sin is not easy. In Matthew 18, in the Parable of the Unmerciful Servant, a certain king canceled his servant's debt of ten thousand talents. But the one whose debt of ten thousand talents was canceled went out and soon found one of his fellow servants who owed him one hundred denarii. He grabbed him and began to choke him, demanding that he pay back what he owed. This parable describes the fallen state of the human mind. We must know that we are great debtors to God and can never pay back what we owe. Paul had a deep sense of debt. He said, "I am obligated both to Greeks and non-Greeks, both to the wise and to the foolish" (Ro 1:14).

Sixth, "And lead us not into temptation." The world is full of evil, so Peter said, "Your enemy the devil prowls around like a roaring lion looking for someone to devour" (1Pe 5:8). Paul said, "So, if you think you are standing firm, be careful that you don't fall!" (1Co 10:12). Nobody can win over Satan's temptations, not even the first man, Adam.

These days, many people use the phrase, "drug culture," in describing the spiritual condition of this country. In this culture, Satan's temptation to enjoy the sinful nature and not to obey God's word has almost become the social consensus. The children of God are helpless in this situation. Therefore, we must pray moment by moment, "And lead us not into temptation."

II. The spirit of prayer (5-13)

Jesus not only gave them a model of prayer, but he also taught them the attitude of prayer.

First, the spirit of prayer. Read verses 5-8. In order to emphasize the certainty of prayer being answered, Jesus first tells a parable. This parable teaches us a persistent prayer spirit when we pray. In this parable, a selfish person wanted to enjoy a good night's sleep with his kids, but a certain friend came in the middle of the night to beg him for some bread for his unexpected guests. The selfish man tried to turn him down by saying, "Don't bother me. The door is already locked, and my children are with me in bed." But notwithstanding the inconvenience to which he was put, he gave in to his friend's persistence and rose to give him what he needed. When we pray, everything seems to be impossible. Prayer seems to be in vain. But this parable teaches us that when we continue to pray, God graciously answers. These days, campus evangelism seems to be impossible. But we must pray persistently until God answers all our prayers. We must pray persistently for 561 American campuses and for 233 countries.

Second, the Holy Spirit. Verses 9-13 teach us what to ask for in our prayers. In verse 9, the verbs "ask," "seek," and "knock" tell us that we must pray to God, asking, seeking, and knocking persistently and urgently. Verses 11-13 teach us for what we should pray so earnestly. We must pray that God may give us the Holy Spirit because all other gifts are included in this gift. Each one must ask for the indwelling of the Holy Spirit who subdues the work of Satan in our hearts and who enables us to bear the fruits of the Spirit.

Through the Lord's Prayer, we learn that God is our Father, and we are all brothers and sisters purchased by the blood of our Lord Jesus.

Lesson 34

On the Way to Jerusalem, Jesus Heals a Mute Man

Luke 11:14-28
Key Verse: 11:20

I. JESUS HEALS A MUTE MAN (14)

1. What does it mean that Jesus was on his way to Jerusalem? What did he take time to do? Why? What is the situation of a mute man? How was his life changed by Jesus? How did ordinary people respond?

II. THE FINGER OF GOD (15-23)

2. Read verses 15-16. What did some doubters say? Who were they? (Mt 12:24; Mk 3:22) Read verses 17-20. What did Jesus teach about Beelzebub? What does his name mean? What did Jesus teach about the finger of God and the kingdom of God? About Jesus' source of power?

3. Read verses 21-23. Who is the strong man? How did Jesus try to help even the crooked religious leaders to believe so that they could enter the kingdom of God? (17-23)

III. EMPTY AND CLEAN HOUSE (24-26)

4. Read verses 24-26. What danger do those who try to clean up their lives without Jesus and without the word of God encounter? Why must a repentant and forgiven sinner hold Jesus' words in his heart?

IV. BLESSED ARE THOSE WHO HEAR THE WORD OF GOD (27-28)

5. Read verses 27-28. What did Jesus teach the admiring woman about what is really important?

On the Way to Jerusalem, Jesus Heals a Mute Man

Luke 11:14-28
Key Verse: 11:20

"But if I drive out demons by the finger of God, then the kingdom of God has come to you."

A S WE KNOW WELL, Jesus was on the way to Jerusalem to suffer much and to die on the cross for the sins of the world. In his humanness, Jesus had to renew his decision at every step toward Jerusalem. Jesus needed to renew God's will for world salvation. For this, he should shed his blood as a ransom for many. For Jesus, going up to Jerusalem was like a lamb going to the slaughter (Is 53:7). In this passage, despite his mission on hand, Jesus did not overlook a helpless person; Jesus healed a mute man. This event shows us that Jesus is the God of compassion. Jesus was severely persecuted by the religious leaders. Mark's Gospel says that they were scribes. Matthew's Gospel says that they were Pharisees. But Luke didn't say who they were. Their persecutions came from their raving madness. Nevertheless, Jesus taught them the way to the kingdom of God so that they might somehow come back to God.

I. Jesus heals a mute man (14)

This mute man was a miserable man. As we know, a mute man is also deaf. There are many people who say, "You are a dummy." It means, "You are mute and deaf and a most miserable person in the world." A man is a man because he can speak. A man is a man because he can sing. How nice it is to sing a song with a beautiful sound! But this man could not sing because he was mute. How beautiful it is to hear Brahams' "Hungarian Dance" from number 1 to 21! When we hear classical music, we feel like our emotions are well balanced and we also feel somewhat like a noble man or woman. This is the reason people buy Handel's "Messiah" or Tchaikovsky's violin concertos. This is the reason many people watch Romeo and Juliet repeatedly in order to enjoy their romantic narrations. It is also mysterious to hear the sound of falling leaves and the sound of flowing streams of water in a brook.

Even if there are many beautiful things in the world, they are beyond comparison to heavenly things. Among them, to hear the story of Jesus is the most beautiful. Down through the generations, millions of people were oppressed and captured by fear. Many people were in distress. Then they recited Matthew 11:28-30: "Come to me, all you who are weary and burdened, and I will give you rest. Take my yoke upon you and learn from me, for I am gentle and humble in heart, and you will find rest for your souls. For my yoke is easy and my burden is light." So many people in history felt empty. Then they heard the word of God which says, "All men are like grass, and all their glory is like the flowers of the field; the grass withers and the flowers fall, but the word of the Lord stands forever" (1Pe 1:24-25a). Through the word of God, they renewed their view of life and the world again and again. In the course of living, people come to the conclusion that man's life is too short and their investment too great. They feel nothingness. But they can hear the word of God in the Bible. John 3:16 says, "For God so loved the world that he gave his one and only Son, that whoever believes in him shall not perish but have eternal life."

One day, Jesus was pressing forward to Jerusalem with his disciples and some other disciples. While Jesus was passing by a certain place, he saw a mute and deaf man. He looked like a wooden log just sitting there with no idea to talk to anybody. He was physically mute and deaf, and he was also spiritually mute and deaf. The worst part of his life was that he underestimated himself increasingly as he got older. He was probably living a life of self-condemnation. At the moment Jesus saw him, his heart went out to him. To Jesus, he was a good boy made in the image of God, and if he were not a mute man, he would have been a successful man with God-given creativity and ability and would have achieved every possible human desire he had. On his way to Jerusalem, Jesus healed a mute man. We praise God!

Jesus saw that his muteness was caused by demon possession, not by closure of the air passage. Because of demon possession, this young man could not call his mother, "Mom," even though he loved his mother as himself. Because of demon possession, this man looked as if he were a piece of wood or a wilted vegetable. He did not ask for Jesus' mercy, but it did not matter to Jesus. Jesus immediately drove out the demon from him. When the demon left, the man who had been mute spoke and the crowd was amazed. He spoke up, "Thank you, Jesus, that you cared for this sorrowful man. You are the God of compassion." Next, he turned toward his mom and cried loudly. Then he said, "Mom, thank you, thank you, Mom." People around him felt as if they were in a paradise. One of them said, "God has come to help his people" (7:16).

II. The finger of God (15-23)

In this part, Jesus teaches the religious leaders the way to the kingdom of God. Read verse 15. "But some of them said, 'By Beelze-bub, the prince of demons, he is driving out demons.'" According to Matthew and Mark, they were the Pharisees and scribes (Mt 12:24; Mk 3:22). When they saw Jesus caring for a mute and deaf man, they despised him, saying, "This man even cares for a dummy! He doesn't know anything about the strata of society. He has compassion, but he does not know anything about politics. He is going to add this dummy to the twelve disciples." But their most serious cynicism was that Jesus drove out the demon by Beelzebub, the prince of demons.

In their minds is the confused picture of Satan empowering Jesus to cast out Satan's subjects. Read verse 15 again. "But some of them said, 'By Beelzebub, the prince of demons, he is driving out demons.'" Jesus saw that they were under the power of sin and death. Their hatred toward Jesus clearly showed themselves as murderers (Jn 8:44). The original meaning of "Beelzebub" may have been "the house." When time passed by, its nuance changed. Beelzebub was known as the lord of oozing flies or heaps of dung. Later, it implied the prince of demons.

Jesus kindly talked with them. Read verses 17-18. "Any kingdom divided against itself will be ruined, and a house divided against itself will fall. If Satan is divided against itself, how can his kingdom stand? I say this because you claim that I drive out demons by Beelzebub." Here, Jesus crystal clearly teaches them that he belongs to the kingdom of God and they belong to the kingdom of Satan. If Jesus works for Satan, as they say, it is to destroy the agents of Satan, demons, and the devil himself. They are not attacking Jesus, but themselves. These religious leaders were suffering from being scatterbrained.

For example, the Egyptian magicians under King Pharaoh could perform, to some degree, some magic before Moses and Aaron. Then King Pharaoh's heart was hardened. He decided to contest God to the end. However, after the plague of gnats (Ex 8:19), Pharaoh's magicians could not perform anymore magic with their secret arts. But Pharaoh, in his delusion, thought that his magicians could do all that Moses and Aaron did. As a result, King Pharaoh liberated the Israelites only after he experienced the death plague, which killed all the firstborn in Egypt. In short, Pharaoh could not distinguish between his witches and Moses and Aaron. In the same way, the Pharisees did not recognize Jesus as the Son of God and called him Beelzebub and said that Jesus' healing of the mute man was done by the power of Beelzebub.

Read verse 20. "But if I drive out demons by the finger of God, then the kingdom of God has come to you." Jesus had mercy on them. So he said, "I drove out the mute demon with the finger of God, not by the power of Beelzebub. And if you believe that I drove out the mute demon with the finger of God, the kingdom of God has come to you." Here, Luke uses present perfect tense. Jesus urges them to repent of their stubbornness and accept the Messiah's work. Then they would see the kingdom of God and could enter the kingdom of God. Jesus was indeed compassionate, even toward the crooked Pharisees and Sadducees.

Read verses 21-22. "When a strong man, fully armed, guards his own house, his possessions are safe. But when someone stronger attacks and overpowers him, he takes away the armor in which the man trusted and divides up the spoils." In these verses, the strong man is Jesus himself. Read verse 23. "He who is not with me is against me, and he who does not gather with me, scatters." It is very clear. Those who don't hear Jesus' word cannot be children of God. The point of this verse is that Jesus is the strong man, the Son of Almighty God. Therefore, they must repent and come to him.

III. Empty and clean house (24-26)

These three verses teach us a very important spiritual lesson. Jesus knew the legalistic and ritualistic Jews of the time. They tried to keep themselves clean by washing the dishes and living a legalistic way of life. Thus, they cleaned their houses. But this kind of legalistic way of life cannot save them from evil.

Jesus tells us a parable here. An evil spirit was bored living in a man-house all by himself. He left the man-house in the afternoon. It became dark. He had no place to go, and he was afraid to go back to the "cleaner place." So he brought several other evil spirits more wicked than himself. They went in and lived there. The final condition of that man was worse than the first (26). One should not be proud that he is a clean-cut young man. Here, Jesus is saying that although man wants to keep himself aloof, self-righteous, ritualistic, and moralistic, and it may work for a few minutes, many demons can occupy him at any minute and the final situation will be worse.

What can we do, then? Jesus strongly urges us to fill up our souls with the word of God so that there is no place left for the devil. In ancient times, many saints memorized Revelation every morning as a warm up for Bible study. Even if we cannot memorize Revelation and Genesis to Leviticus, we must have even one word of God in our hearts. We like St. Augustine. But he did not have much word of God—only two verses of the Bible, Romans 13:13-14. It says, "Let us behave decently, as in the daytime, not in orgies and drunkenness, not in sexual immorality and debauchery, not in dissension and jealousy. Rather, clothe yourselves with the Lord Jesus Christ, and do not think about how to gratify the desires of the sinful nature." When he held on to this word of God wholeheartedly, God raised him as a saint from an intellectual hedonist.

IV. Blessed are those who hear the word of God (27-28)

One woman secretly followed Jesus and saw the great work of God through Jesus. Jesus healed a mute and deaf man and made him sing a beautiful song. Jesus also cared for crooked religious leaders so that they could have eternal life and the kingdom of God as their inheritance. The woman heard that one must hold on to one word of God in one's heart as of first importance, otherwise, a person will be occupied by many wicked demons. This woman really liked what Jesus had done and said, "Blessed is the mother who gave you birth and nursed you" (27). She was a mother herself. She wanted to have a son like Jesus. What did Jesus say? "Blessed rather are those who hear the word of God and obey it" (28). Jesus again emphasized that the word of God is the word of life. Those who hear and obey the word of God have eternal life and the kingdom of God as their inheritance.

In this passage, Luke emphasizes the compassion of Jesus even when he was on the way to Jerusalem. When we think about our sheep, we never like those who are dummies, sophisticated, or who do not trust and obey. But here we learn that we must plant the word of God in them too. May God bless us to do so.

Lesson 35

Practice Justice and the Love of God

Luke 11:29-54
Key Verse: 11:42

I. JESUS REBUKES MIRACLE-SEEKING PEOPLE (29-32)

1. For what did Jesus rebuke the "wicked generation"? Who was Jonah and why did Jesus say that he could give them no sign except the sign of Jonah? How was Jonah a sign to the people of Nineveh? How was Jesus, the Son of Man, a sign to his times?

2. Read verses 31-32. Who was the Queen of the South? Why was she much better than the religious leaders of Jesus' day? Why did Jesus tell them this story? Why were the people of Nineveh saved? How does a sign-seeking mentality keep people from God? (1Co 1:22-23) How is it like a slave mentality?

II. JESUS ENCOURAGES PEOPLE TO HAVE SPIRITUAL INSIGHT (33-36)

3. Read verses 33-36. What is the purpose of a lamp? Why were the religious leaders in spiritual darkness? How could they have spiritual insight?

4. JESUS REBUKES CORRUPT RELIGIOUS LEADERS (37-54)

5. Read verses 37-38. How did Jesus shock the Pharisee who invited him to dinner? Read verses 39-41. What is really dirty and what is the way of cleansing? Read verse 42. What is more important than religious rituals?

6. Read verses 43-54. How did Jesus' humility contrast with the attitude and goals of the Pharisees? (43-45) Why are religious leaders responsible for the godlessness, injustice, and corruption of society? (46-54)

Practice Justice and the Love of God

Luke 11:29-54
Key Verse: 11:42

> *"Woe to you Pharisees, because you give God a tenth of your mint, rue and all other kinds of garden herbs, but you neglect justice and the love of God. You should have practiced the latter without leaving the former undone."*

I N THE LAST PASSAGE, we studied that Jesus healed a mute and deaf man with the finger of God. Moreover, Jesus did his best to win the crooked religious leaders' hearts over to God. Jesus said, "But if I drive out demons by the finger of God, then the kingdom of God has come to you" (11:20). It meant that if you believe in God, you will be members of God's kingdom. In this passage, Luke records Jesus' deep sorrow toward corrupt religious leaders.

I. Jesus rebukes miracle-seeking people (29-32)

We must remember Jesus was on the way to Jerusalem to become a ransom sacrifice for the sin of the world. But the crowd of people did not leave him alone. Read verse 29. "As the crowds increased, Jesus said, 'This is a wicked generation. It asks for a miraculous sign, but none will be given it except the sign of Jonah.'" Throughout Bible history, God gave so many miraculous signs to his people so that they might understand heavenly and spiritual things. But people had no idea about the spiritual world. For example, just a few minutes before, Jesus healed a mute man and enabled him to speak. But they completely ignored such a miraculous sign through which one human being became normal and could have a promising future. They did not appreciate God's deep compassion for one individual person who was once a mute man. They had no compassion on the man who had been healed. They had no thankful mind toward God who had cared for a mute man. Jesus also cared for them and taught them the way to come to the kingdom of God. But they didn't care about Jesus' healing and preaching. They were only interested in miraculous signs. Jesus lamented over the religious leaders' sign-seeking mentality and rebuked them in verse 29b. It says, "This is a wicked generation. It asks for a miraculous sign, but none will be given it except the sign of Jonah.'"

Why did Jesus say that he can only give them the sign of Jonah? It is because Jonah was a nationalistic prophet when he had to be an international prophet. As a result, he disobeyed God's word. God wanted to send him to Nineveh, a Gentile nation, to proclaim the kingdom of God to them so that they might repent of their sins and come to him. When God wanted to send him to Nineveh, the largest city at that time, Jonah attempted to escape to Tarshish by boat. On the way to Tarshish, the sea became turbulent and the sailors cast lots to find out who was the cause of the turbulence. The lot fell on Jonah. No sooner had the sailors thrown Jonah into the sea than a big whale swallowed him up before he landed in the water. Jonah was in the stomach of the whale for three days. He prayed to God earnestly for his rescue. Then God let the whale vomit Jonah out on the seashore of Nineveh. He really didn't want to go to proclaim the message of the kingdom of God to the people of Nineveh because he was afraid that they might repent and not perish. But when Jonah unintentionally proclaimed the message of the kingdom of God, the Ninevites, the most unlikely people, received this message and all came to repent in sackcloth. They received the message of the kingdom of God. Jesus told Jonah's story in the hope that the religious leaders of the time might also repent and proclaim the message of the kingdom of God to people.

Jesus also said that he would speak only the story of Jonah to the religious leaders because they were so wicked. They saw so many miraculous signs, but they did not believe. Instead, they demanded another miraculous sign again and again. In short, they did not repent.

They only wanted to recognize their fabulous idealism through Jesus' miracles. For example, once Jesus saw 5,000 hungry people and fed them with five loaves and two fish to their fill. The next day, they came to Jesus again. This time, Jesus wanted to tell them about the spiritual bread, not the physical bread. But they didn't want to hear about the spiritual bread. When Jesus claimed that he was the bread of life, some argued that Jesus must be a cannibal (Jn 6:52). Then they all left one by one and two by two until no one was left except the twelve disciples.

In his deep grief for the religious leaders, Jesus told them a story in the hope of drawing them to the word of God and proclaiming to them the message of the kingdom of God. At the time of King Solomon, the Queen of the South heard the wisdom of Solomon. She visited King Solomon with many gifts and asked Solomon all the questions she had in her mind. Solomon answered her questions perfectly. Solomon, in his wisdom, expounded all the terrestrial secrets. He also explained the first cause, harmony, and the mysteries of nature. He also knew the innumerable names of the fish in the sea. After listening to Solomon, the Queen of the South repented and accepted the universal truth that God made the heavens and the earth and everything in it. Jesus urged them to listen to the message of the kingdom of God as had Jonah. Jesus urged them so that they might escape the judgment of God. We thank God that Jesus is so kind, humble, and lowly that he could rebuke the religious leaders to repent.

II. A sign-seeking mentality

Paul said in 1 Corinthians 1:22, "Jews demand miraculous signs and Greeks look for wisdom ..." These two trends of the world brought forth Hebraism and Hellenism. These two trends of world philosophy flowed throughout world history. Both trends brought forth many human ideas. These human ideas became the instruments of wicked men for doing evil because they led people not to obey the absolutes of God.

The sign-seeking mentality is especially very wicked. For example, before going into the promised land, God trained the people of

Israel in the wilderness with daily bread training. This training was designed to discipline them to eat three meals a day regularly and depend on God only for their future security. The training could have finished in 15 minutes if they overcame their sinful nature and listened to the word of God, but they really liked daily bread from heaven free of charge. They didn't have to work. They had no future security problem. They didn't have to send out many resumes looking for jobs. This daily bread training was very necessary for the spiritual enlightenment and spiritual leadership of the people living in the promised land, but this bread of heaven made them grow in a slave mentality instead of opening their spiritual eyes.

Nikita Khrushchev, Secretary General of the Soviet Union, really wanted to improve his nation's political climate. Before he rose to power, there was mass murder, and hard labor and oppression was too severe. The political climate of the Soviet Union was not Marxist, but Leninist. He really wanted to practice Marxism so that people might live in peace, as well as in a socialist republic. But when he took a weekend vacation to the Crimea in October 1964, the Presidium voted him out of office and their decision was confirmed by the Central Committee the next day. Nikita Khrushchev's idea to bring about Marxism in the Soviet Union was good, but it was nothing but a sign-seeking mentality in the absolute totalitarian Leninist climate. People with a sign-seeking mentality do not care about the Law of God. They only care about how people see them. As a result, they abandon the Law of God. They become lawless people. As we have experienced, lawlessness is the most fearsome thing to human beings in the world.

III. Jesus encourages people to have spiritual insight (33-36)

Read verse 33. "No one lights a lamp and puts it in a place where it will be hidden, or under a bowl. Instead he puts it on a stand, so that those who come in may see the light." This verse tells us that we must use the light properly and live in the light, not in the darkness.

Read verse 34, "Your eye is the lamp of your body. When your eyes are good, your whole body also is full of light. But when they are bad, your body also is full of darkness." In this verse, the light is compared to the light of men. If one cannot see with his eyes, he is full of darkness and cannot see anything. So Jesus warned in verse 35, "See to it, then, that the light within you is not darkness." This allegorical verse is very simple. If we have no spiritual insight to see man and the world, we are in the darkness. On the other hand, if we study the Bible and receive spiritual insight to see man and the world, we are full of light (36). And we can see what is going on in the world with our spiritual insight. We can see how we should help the flock of God in our generation.

IV. Jesus rebukes corrupt religious leaders (37-54)

The religious leaders of the time were of two kinds. The first was the Pharisees; the second was the Sadducees. The Pharisees were ritualistic in worshiping God and political in helping people. The Sadducees did not care for people. They wanted money and fame and the high priestly office position down through the generations. In view of Bible history, they were both chosen people. But in the time of Jesus, they were so corrupt that they did not even deserve Jesus' rebuke. If Jesus abandoned them like garbage, it would be very proper treatment for them. But Jesus cried sorrowfully and urged them to repent of their sins and come back to God and take care of God's flock of sheep.

Jesus rebukes them to practice justice and the love of God. They were experts of ritualism in worshiping God, but they ignored the holiness of God, that is, the justice of God. They also ignored the love of God. So Jesus rebukes them not to neglect justice and the love of God (42).

A servant of God must be humble and lowly like Jesus. A servant of God must be a wonderful friend like Jesus. But the Pharisees only wanted important seats in the synagogue and people's admiration in the marketplace. So Jesus rebukes them to be humble and lowly (43). Jesus rebukes them because they are whitewashed tombs (Mt 23:27b). Outside everything was beautiful, but the inside was full of dead men's bones and everything unclean. Jesus rebukes them so that they would repent of their corruption due to greediness (44). In addition, they were as proud as they could be.

Jesus also rebukes the experts in the law. While Jesus was rebuking the Pharisees, the experts in the law felt that Jesus was insulting them, too. Then Jesus began to rebuke them also, saying that they spoke well and interpreted the law of God very well, but they abused their authority and loaded people down with burdens and did not lift one finger to help them (45-46).

Jesus rebukes the religious leaders, saying that they had killed so many prophets. Historically, wicked religious leaders killed the prophets. After killing them, they had beautiful funeral services and made for them very beautiful tombs. Jesus rebukes them that they are responsible for the blood of all the prophets from Abel to Zechariah. Good prophets taught the Law of God and rebuked the leaders of nations, especially the religious leaders. Jesus sees that the corruption of the religious leaders is the cause of the miseries of his people.

Jesus rebukes experts in the law because they interpreted the Law of God pragmatically. They took away the righteousness of God and the love of God and the sacrificial lives of God's people. In this way, they led people from keeping the Law of God. They did not have hope in the kingdom of God. They wanted to live in this world permanently. When they did not keep the Law of God, they could not enter the kingdom of God. Moreover, they took away the key to the kingdom of God from people. They were like dispensationalists of these days.

We must live by the Law of God. May God help us to do so.

Lesson 36

Do Not Fear about Your Life

Luke 12:1-12
Key Verses: 12:4-5

I. BE CAREFUL OF THE HYPOCRITICAL PHARISEES (1-3)

1. Read verse 1. Why do you think the people gathered in spite of Jesus' rebukes? (See John 10:14) How committed was the crowd? (Lk. 23:21)

2. What did Jesus warn his disciples? What did he mean by "yeast"? Read verses 2-3. In a world full of betrayal and lies, what is the character of truth? How can we avoid hypocrisy and stand on the side of truth?

II. DO NOT FEAR ANY MAN (4-7)

3. Read verses 4-7. Why should Jesus' people not fear physical death? (Ecc. 3:2) What (Whom) should we fear? Why? (2Cor. 5:10) What difference does it make to know that God is the Sovereign Owner of our lives?

III. CHRISTIAN IDENTITY AND ETERNAL VICTORY (8-12)

4. Read verses 8-12. How should we live if we are not afraid of death? If we trust God for our future security? If we fear God? Can you think of any illustrations from history, life or the Bible?

Do Not Fear about Your Life

Luke 12:1-12
Key Verses: 12:4-5

> "I tell you, my friends, do not be afraid of those who kill the
> body and after that can do no more. But I will show you whom
> you should fear: Fear him who, after the killing of the body,
> has power to throw you into hell. Yes, I tell you, fear him."

OUT OF HIS DEEP sorrow, Jesus rebuked the religious leaders.
It was because religious leaders are supposed to be servants of
God, and they are called to shepherd God's flock. But these
religious leaders were useless to God because they were corrupt, and
their hypocrisy made people feel nauseous badly. Today Jesus speaks
to his disciples several things as warnings and encouragements.

I. Be careful of the hypocritical Pharisees (1-3)

Read verse 1. "Meanwhile, when a crowd of many thousands had
gathered, so that they were trampling on one another, Jesus began
to speak first to his disciples, saying: 'Be on your guard against the
yeast of the Pharisees, which is hypocrisy.'" When Jesus said, "the
yeast of the Pharisees," it meant the "bad influence" of the Pharisees.
Bad influence has one major characteristic. Bad influence spreads too
fast, and it cannot be stopped by human effort.

Jesus said this because a crowd of many thousands had gathered.
There was a danger that they would trample on one another. The
many-thousand crowd of people came to Jesus because they tasted
the healing power of Jesus and they heard the good news of the kingdom of God. So they wanted to hear more about Jesus. This is the
reason why they gathered around Jesus. John 10:14 explains the relationship between Jesus and the crowd of many thousands. It says, "I

am the good shepherd; I know my sheep and my sheep know me." Between Jesus and the people there was a heart-to-heart communication. They do not know much. But they know one thing very clearly, that Jesus is a good shepherd. They want to remain as permanent sheep and be loved and cared for permanently. Despite their stupidity, they have extraordinary knowledge. They know Jesus' voice, just as Jesus knows the Father in heaven.

So Jesus said in the last part of verse 1, "Be on your guard against the yeast of the Pharisees, which is hypocrisy." Jesus prayed that helpless sheep may be kept from the yeast of the Pharisees. Why is bad influence so dangerous? It is because bad influence is like yeast to the dough and like worms to the apple. Especially, it appeals effectively to man's sinful nature not to obey God, but to enjoy the sinful nature.

Originally the Pharisees were chosen to serve God. They were called to teach the peoples of all nations the law of God. They were chosen to raise many Bible teachers and shepherds so that those who were raised by the Pharisees might also be the servants of God. In this way, God wanted to teach the law of God to the people of the whole world. Therefore the Pharisees had to love God with all their hearts and with all their souls and with all their strength. But they did not practice the law of God with their hearts; they practiced the law of God ceremonially. As a result, their hypocritical lives gave bad influence to God's people. When the Pharisees loved the world in their hearts, people also loved the world. When the Pharisees loved money in their hearts, people also loved money. Speedily, both the Pharisees and God's people together loved money more than God. They loved the fleeting pleasures of life more than the law of God. The seed of the Pharisees' bad influence poisoned native people until they forgot all the grace they had received. They began to shout at the top of their lungs, "Crucify him! Crucify him!" (Lk 23:21). It is a totally unbelievable event. It is indeed a sad story. But it was the bad influence of the Pharisees.

There have been many men of bad influence. One of them is Rehoboam, the king of Judah, the son of the great king Solomon. After King Solomon passed away, people came to Rehoboam to plead with him to reduce the quota system of hard labor. Rehoboam should have been like King David, who was humble and cared for his people like his own children. But Rehoboam answered arrogantly and violently, "My father made your yoke heavy; I will make it even heavier. My father scourged you with whips; I will scourge you with scorpions" (1Ki 12:14). Rehoboam's violence in speech planted violence in the hearts of discontented people. The immediate result was the murder of Rehoboam's cabinet member, who was in charge of forced labor. But the principal result was internecine war between brothers. The Bible says, "So Israel has been in rebellion against the house of David to this day" (1Ki 12:19).

Another example is Jeroboam, king of northern Israel. He was afraid that if people went to Jerusalem for an annual pilgrimage, they would be homesick. So he built two idols, one in Bethel and the other in Dan. Lazy people liked it. Jeroboam learned that people followed his political intrigue. Then he built a huge number of little shrines to make people worship God in the shrines just as modern people worship God on the TV screen. Soon people abandoned God. So the Bible repeats that Jeroboam was the worst example of leading his people to sin against God repeatedly. Bad influence is, if anything, compared to setting fire to a beautiful building and burning it down, which was built over a long period of time and with a huge amount of money. Therefore we must be on our guard against the yeast of the Pharisees.

Jesus tells us the character of truth. Read verses 2-3. "There is nothing concealed that will not be disclosed, or hidden that will not be made known. What have you said in the dark will be heard in the daylight, and what you have whispered in the ear in the inner rooms will be proclaimed from the roofs." People can buy sensational media and make sensational stories to discredit good people as bad people. But in the long run, all their deeds done in the darkness will be disclosed as in the daylight. Here Jesus tells them that they should not be swayed by the manipulation of evil men. But stand firm and be on their guard. Moreover, they should prevent the Pharisees' hypocrisy for the sake of God's future blessings on their country.

Jesus said this because he had a broken shepherd heart for his people, who could have been wonderful if they had had a good shepherd to the end. How can we be on our guard against the yeast of the Pharisees? We must read the Bible (Jas 1:5). Then God gives us wisdom to discern good and evil. All other books are one-dimensional or two-dimensional. It is easy for us to know the bad influence of the Pharisees, as a mother knows her babies very well.

II. Do not fear any man (4-7)

As we know well, everyone is burdened by the fear of death. King Hezekiah heard from a prophet that he would die. Then he turned his face to the wall and prayed to God. This shows that even the king had the fear of death. Human beings' best wishes might be to live in this world forever. People in both east and west shouted as their best greetings, "Long live the king! Long live the king, 1,000 years!"

Jesus told his disciples not to be afraid of death. Jesus said this on the basis of the Bible truth that God is the sovereign ruler. God appoints each person to be born in a certain generation and live so many days and so many minutes. To be born at the appointed time is the universal truth. By the same token, to die at the appointed time is also a universal truth. Worrying too much about death is a nagging fear. But it is empty fear. We must thank God for the privilege of living God's life in this generation.

Most importantly, God gave his one and only Son to bear all our iniquities and transgressions. Finally, God crucified him on the cross to shed his holy blood. In this way, God confirmed his promise to send the Messiah from the root of Jesse. More importantly, God promised eternal life and the kingdom of God as the inheritance of those who believe in him. Therefore, we should not fear any man, but fear God who determines eternal life.

One of God's servants thought that he worked so hard when he was young that he would die around the age of 35. But now he is 64. Man's life span is in the hand of God. Not only man, but even the life span of sparrows is in the hand of God. Read verse 6. "Are not five sparrows sold for two pennies? Yet not one of them is forgotten by God." Our God is Almighty God. We have no wisdom to correctly count how many hairs we have, but he knows how many hairs we have. So Jesus strongly encourages his disciples, "Don't be afraid; you are worth more than many sparrows" (7b).

III. God is the owner of our lives

There was a young missionary named John Paton. He was a pioneer missionary to the New Hebrides, a group of islands off the coast of Australia. The name of the island was Tanna, an island inhabited by vicious cannibals. One of his senior pastors strongly encouraged him not to go to the Tanna Island because of the danger that he would be eaten by cannibals. John Paton replied, "You are pretty old, aren't you? Soon you will die and be eaten by worms. I would rather serve the Lord and be eaten by cannibals. What difference does it make, to be eaten by worms or by cannibals?" Soon after they arrived in Tanna, his beloved wife died of malaria. His first son Peter died soon after. John's heart was broken. But he said, "I will not run away from God." He believed God's absolute sovereign rule over man's life. Why should we worry? Why should we fret for nothing? We must learn to trust in God more and more.

One famous evangelist usually spends six months to get many people to his evangelistic campaign. He would not get more than 200,000 people. But John Paul II is beyond comparison to him. John Paul II became pope when he was 58 years old, the youngest pope since 1846. Once, because of his body guard's mistake he was shot badly. But God restored his body very soon. Do you know what he did right after his recovery? John Paul II did not care for his old skin. He realized that he had overcome the fear of assassination. He also realized that the Pope must take care of God's flock. He decided to travel to all the poorest African and Arabian and Latin American countries, not to mention to America. John Paul II was able to do this because he believed that a man's life span is in the hands of God. He endangered his life by traveling to so many countries. Traveling was the worst thing to do as an aged person. But he continued to travel to visit the poor countries and those countries which needed an independent spirit. He loved God. But through his actions, it is very clear that he is an altruist. As a pope, he traveled a lot. Because of his altruism, people loved him so much. One time, in Africa, 3.5 million people gathered to hear him speak. They all cried because of his father-like image. At every meeting, he had an average of 1 million participants. This show how honorable he is and how altruism is so appealing to the thirsty souls who are living at the end of the 20th century. The best example might be Jesus. The religious leaders plotted against him and finally crucified him as a criminal. But Jesus said in Luke 23:34, "Father, forgive them, for they do not know what they are doing." There is no fear of death in Jesus Christ.

IV. Christian identity and eternal victory (8-12)

We are living in the last part of the 21st century. At the present, dogmatic beliefs are fervently denied. Because of this, faith in the absolutes of God has gradually vanished. At the same time, alienable human rights have been riding on high tide. Freedom is good and precious. But there is a problem. Human nature is good and evil. One person was like an angel. Now he is more like the devil. In times like these, it is not easy for anyone to identify that he is a child of God.

Jesus knew his disciples were living under Roman rule. So it was not easy for them to identify themselves as servants of God. So Jesus encouraged them to have a clear identity in verses 8-10, which say, "I tell you, whoever acknowledges me before men, the Son of Man will also acknowledge him before the angels of God. But he who disowns me before men will be disowned before the angels of God. And everyone who speaks a word against the Son of Man will be forgiven, but anyone who blasphemes against the Holy Spirit will not be forgiven." The children of God should not be afraid of those who persecute the work of God. Those who persecute the work of God will not find the way for the forgiveness of God.

When we do God's work, we expect some admiration from others. Such a thing has never happened. When we do God's work, we only receive persecutions. When we receive persecutions, we don't have to think how to answer. The Holy Spirit gives us wisdom on how to answer. We have identity because we believe that Jesus will come again to take us back to his glorious kingdom and to judge the evil and cast them into eternal condemnation. May God help us identify ourselves as children of God.

Lesson 37

The Parable of the Rich Fool

Luke 12:13-34
Key Verse: 12:15

I. A RICH FOOL (13-21)

1. What event motivated Jesus to tell this parable? Why did Jesus refuse to take part in the family fight over property? What can we learn here? (13-15)

2. What happy problem did the rich man in the parable have? How did he decide to solve the problem?

3. What was his belief about life security? Why was he a fool?

4. Why can material things not solve one's life security problem? What is real life security?

II. DO NOT WORRY (22-34)

5. What are the basic things that most people, including disciples, are tempted to worry about? In what respect are these things necessary to life?

6. What does Jesus mean when he says that life is more than food and the body is more than clothes?

7. What is the example of the ravens? What should we learn from them? What is accomplished by worrying?

8. What lesson does Jesus teach from the lilies? What is the basic cause of worrying? (28)

9. What must God's children seek, in contrast to the pagan world? What assurance does Jesus give disciples? (30-31)

10. What is the most precious gift of the Father? How can we claim this gift and be rich toward God?

The Parable of the Rich Fool

Luke 12:13-34
Key Verse: 12:15

> *"Watch out! Be on your guard against all kinds of greed; a man's life does not consist in the abundance of his possessions."*

THESE DAYS, MANY PEOPLE are so anxious to secure their lives by means of material possessions. Most people think that their lives are secure when they have sufficient financial base. If money could solve the human life problem, then the world already would have become the utopia of which many people have dreamt. These days, everything seems to be money-oriented. For money, many people become too practical to maintain their humanity. To get some money, they ruin their whole lives. This passage teaches us that life is more valuable than material possessions. In this passage we learn what it means that a man's life does not consist in the abundance of his possessions.

I. A rich fool (13-21)

Read verse 13. "Someone in the crowd said to him, 'Teacher, tell my brother to divide the inheritance with me.'" Perhaps his father had died a few days before. He was not at all sorrowful for his father's death. He also did not care about what Jesus had been speaking about to the people. Jesus had been warning them against the bad influence of the Pharisees and encouraging them to identify themselves to be children of God before men, an action which would bring the disapproval of the hostile world, and at the same time, the approval and rewards of the Son of Man (1-12). His teaching was serious enough to listen to, but this man didn't care about it at all.

This man had been thinking only of his share in his father's inheritance, and he felt that his brother had cheated him. With a heart full of resentment, he said to Jesus, "Teacher, tell my brother to divide the inheritance with me."

How did Jesus answer him? Read verse 14. "Man, who appointed me a judge or an arbiter between you?" Jesus did not come to this world to act as a judge or arbiter between people over worldly things; he came to bring the revelation of God's salvation. So this unmannerly interruption was very rude to him. If an ordinary man had met such a person, his rudeness would have struck a chill in his heart, and he would have quickly brushed him aside, saying, "Your case is one for the courts." But Jesus wanted to help him. And to help him, he could not but rebuke his foolish request, saying, "Man, who appointed me a judge or an arbiter between you?" Perhaps the man was hurt, thinking that his request was turned down. Perhaps he was as frigid as could be. It did not matter to Jesus what this man thought or did. What mattered to Jesus was that he would somehow come to know why Jesus came into the world.

Read verse 15. Now Jesus turned to the crowd and said, "Watch out! Be on your guard against all kinds of greed; a man's life does not consist in the abundance of his possessions." Jesus saw the deep root of greed in all people in two ways when he turned and spoke to the crowd.

First, greed is something that we must watch out for. In verse 15 when Jesus saw a man with greediness, he turned to the crowd and began to speak. To Jesus, greed was like ever-increasing weed in the springtime. If greed grows in one's heart, it is almost impossible for him to stamp it out, because greed is as vital as weeds, which cannot be rooted out even when the most assiduous weeding is being done. A weed is a useless plant; however, its staying power is remarkable. It can grow back on the sand or on the rock.

Greed is like salt water; the more one drinks, the thirstier he becomes. There is no satisfaction for a greedy man. Finally, he becomes enslaved by his greed. One is overcome by greed and falls into the swift growth of vices. There are many kinds of greed—material greed, sexual greed, and unnatural behavior greed. These things jeopardize a man's life rapidly. One country man omitted his lunch

A STUDY OF LUKE'S GOSPEL

for 30 years in order to save money. As a result, he became rich. Next, he wanted to enjoy an easy life, so he took a second wife. Then one night he lost all the money he had in gambling. Greed is a terrible thing for everybody. So James said, "Then, after desire has conceived, it gives birth to sin; and sin, when it is full-grown, gives birth to death" (Jas 1:15). Jesus saw that men's suffering came mostly from their greed, and that they were helpless before the strength of greed. So he said, "Watch out! Be on your guard against all kinds of greed" (15a).

Second, we learn that life is more than flesh. Man's life does not consist in the abundance of his possessions. This means that abundant material possessions cannot be everything in maintaining one's life. If man's life is nothing but flesh and no more, then abundant material possessions are sufficient for his life. But man is different from animals. Man is soul. Man's life consists in body, mind and soul. This is the reason why man cannot live by bread alone. When Jesus saw the crowd of people as they thought, they seemed to think abundant material possessions would make them happy. Then they would not have any problem in the world. If flesh is everything for a man, there would not be any problem for men in the world. The problem is that man is not only flesh, but also a soul. So he told them a parable.

Read verses 16-20. The man in the parable presents a clear picture of the fatal folly of greed. This rich fool thought that he would find real happiness in earthly abundance. So he worked hard. As a result, he became very rich. He stored harvested crops in all his barns until they were full. Finally, he had to make a happy cry, "What shall I do? I have no place to store my crops?" He thought that if he collected a sufficient quantity of material possessions, he would henceforth enjoy life by eating, drinking and being merry. And he did not make any crucial mistakes. He did not commit any violent crime. He only worked hard to be happy. Judging by worldly standards, he was a yuppie candidate. He was a successful man to whom many a man would look with envious eyes. But he was wrong in two ways.

First, this rich fool was a selfish and self-centered man. There is no other parable so full of the words, "I," "my," "me," and "mine." He considered that everything belonged exclusively to him and that he had a full monopoly to use everything he had for his own pleasure and enjoyment. He never saw beyond himself. He did not regard his possessions as things lent to him by God's grace, to be used by him in the service of God. He had no God. He had no neighbor. He had no mission. He was like a father tiger that eats everything all by himself and leaves nothing for his wife and cubs. He considered himself to have full command over his life, as if he had created himself. But when he had reached the climax of his acquisition of wealth and the zenith of self-satisfaction in material pleasure, God appeared to him and required his soul by means of death. All his plans in connection with the enjoyment of wealth collapsed at once. He could not take even one particle of his riches with him when his soul entered eternity. The people of this world would think that he was a rich man. But to the historian Luke's eyes, he was poorer than the poorest human being and in the kingdom of God as well.

Second, he was a corrupted person. He never saw beyond this world; all his plans were made on the basis of life in this world. He thought he should work hard so that he could enjoy material and physical pleasure. His purpose of life and the point of hard work were to seek pleasure. He had no meaning in life. He could find meaning only in a life of material pleasures. His purpose of life was mean, and there was no nobility in him as a human being. His philosophy of life was "Let us eat and drink, for tomorrow we die" (1Co 15:32b). In his outward appearance he looked happy, but he was not happy at all because no one is happy with just material abundance. His happy cry, "Take life easy; eat, drink, and be merry" (19), was only a camouflage for his unbearable inner sorrow and fear. With much money, he could not change his fate. Whenever he watched millionaires or paupers indiscriminately pass away, he was haunted by the shadow of death and trembled. Whenever the power of death ate away at his soul, he tried to find a way out, an escape. Escapism is the road to death. His luxurious lifestyle and pleasure-seeking activities were nothing but expressions of emotional distress, mental suffering, and moral corruption.

Read verse 21. This verse teaches us that greed makes a man poor in his inner man, as well as poor toward God. "This is how it will be with anyone who stores up things for himself but is not rich toward God." But there is a great danger for a man to fall into sin when he becomes richer because his greed simultaneously grows all the more. When a man's heart is stolen by riches, he gradually forgets about God and his righteous kingdom. He cannot be compassionate toward the poor. He does not depend on God, but depends on his material goods. He does not seek peace in God. He seeks peace by means of material comfort. All these things are basic elements of sin, and these things happen frequently when a man accumulates the riches of the world.

God did not make us only satisfy and enjoy selfish desires. God made each of us the steward of his world. We should be rich toward God as well as toward others. Then God makes one rich both in his physical life and in his spiritual life until he inherits the kingdom of God.

II. Do not worry (22-34)

Read verse 22. Jesus now turned to his disciples and said, "Therefore I tell you, do not worry about your life, what you will eat; or about your body, what you will wear." Here Jesus warns against the anxiety of life, because anxiety is the very expression of unbelief in God. A man of anxiety only tortures himself and proves himself to have the poor man's form of worldliness. Jesus' disciples' concern was not what to do with superfluities, but was how to find food and clothing. The disciples were mostly poor men. They had no regular income and no dormitory. They eagerly wanted to be good disciples of Jesus. At the same time, they could not but worry about their future life.

Read verse 22. When Jesus said, "Don't worry about your life," he knew that they had to worry whether they could eat dinner tonight or not, or what their future lives would be. But he did not want them to remain in the habit of worrying. Most people worry about nothing day and night because of their habit of worrying.

A girl medical student from an extraordinarily rich family had a habit of worrying about everything. Her purpose in studying medicine was to support herself in case she had to get a divorce. She worried about divorce even before she married. She said that she carried sleeping pills with her all the time so that in case she got into a car accident, she could die easily by taking them. She worried very much about her future life after marriage, worrying that she would marry a poor man who could not buy her meat and apples regularly. I really wondered why she worried so much since she was young and rich. Several years later I discovered that her mother had constantly planted fear and anxiety in her heart, until she had formed the habit of worrying.

People of the world worry much about their children's future. They want to raise their children to be strong enough to overcome the world. Despite their good will, most of them do not plant faith in God. Instead they teach worldly wisdom, which makes their children full of fear and anxieties.

Read verse 22 again. Jesus was quite different. When he helped his disciples, he said, "Do not worry about your life." When he said this, he wanted to plant faith in God in their hearts, for God is the Creator and Giver of man's life and body. God the Creator cares even for birds like ravens, which are not able to sow or reap. How much more will God provide for his disciples, who are much more precious than birds? (23-24).

Read verses 25-26. These verses teach that to worry is utterly useless. By worrying, no one can add a single hour to his life. Rather by worrying, one can even reduce one day of his life. One stingy man worked hard in a bank for 25 years. He was rich and rose to be the third man in the bank. He occasionally intimidated me not to teach the Bible to his daughter, saying that she became like a dummy. Actually, through Bible study she was healed of her neurosis caused by a burden of school studies and loneliness. According to the bank rules, he retired at the age of 55 from the bank. He was so anxious to invest his money in real estate, that one day he collapsed on the street. In the hospital it was found that he had a stroke. Then he used up all his money that he had saved in order to heal his paralyzed body. He died leaving no money to his daughter. Worrying did not help this man at all.

To worry is totally useless. One who wants to become successful in the future must listen to Jesus carefully. One who wants to be a servant of God must examine himself to see to it that he has no seed of anxiety in his heart, and no habit of worrying. If he has not solved the problem of anxiety, then he must know that he is a petty man, and that he is a man of anxiety, not a man of God.

In this passage, we learn that there are two kinds of people. The first kind is those who worry about their future lives with their full devotion. The second kind is those who trust in God wholeheartedly, even if nothing is certain. Anxiety only makes a man troubled and cowardly. We must trust in God in all things. How can we trust in God?

Read verses 24-26. Jesus sets his disciples free from anxiety and leads them to ponder on the providence of God, especially on how abundantly he feeds un-anxious lives. The raven is one of the unclean birds and a bird of ill omen. Ravens do not sow or reap, and they have no storerooms; yet God feeds them. How much more will God provide for the disciples, who are worth much more than the birds?

Read verses 27 and 28. It was not easy at all for the disciples to trust in God for their security problem in the face of cold realities. This time Jesus draws their attention to nature. He gives examples of the un-anxious existence of the lilies clothed with beauty. To Jesus, nature itself was a parable. It is a visible manifestation of God. "Consider how the lilies grow. They do not labor or spin. Yet I tell you, not even Solomon in all his splendor was dressed like one of these." If God makes the plants which do not labor or spin grow so wonderfully and endows them with such beauty, how much more will he care for his disciples, people to whom he has granted reason and intelligence and so many other gifts? Here we learn that when we look at present realities, we are pulled into the gravity of worldly anxiety. But when we look at the world and everything God has made, we see that human anxiety makes no more of a difference than the crying of insects or animals. God did not make man to cry all the time and worry about something and then die of worrying. When Jesus saw his disciples who were troubled inwardly, he rebuked them, "O you of little faith."

Read verses 29 and 30. Jesus encourages his disciples not to make the chief aim or passion of their lives the hoarding of material things, for the pagan people run after all such things. What's more, God knows that we have need of food and clothing.

How can they overcome their anxiety about their security problem? Read verse 31. "But seek his kingdom, and these things will be given to you as well." This is the promise of God to them. They must hold onto this promise at any cost and experience God's promise fulfilled through the life of faith.

Read verses 32-34. Jesus taught his disciples how to see his kingdom in detail. First, they must put their hope in the kingdom of God. The disciples were like a small flock of defenseless sheep when compared with the power and glory of the great nations of the world. It was not easy for them to put their hope in the kingdom of God. Still, they must put their hope in the kingdom of God. Second, they must give their hearts to heavenly treasures. To grab and hold something in one's hand is a basic human desire. So unbelievers are all eager to fill up their purses, even when they know that they came to this world with empty hands and must go back with empty hands. But Jesus' disciples must spend worldly treasure for his glory so that they can provide purses that will not wear out—a treasure in heaven that will not be exhausted.

Lesson 38

The Faithful and Wise Servant

Luke 12:35-59
Key Verse: 12:42

I.   A FAITHFUL SERVANT'S READINESS (35-48)

1. Read over the first part of chapter 12, noting what Jesus says about the rich fool (20-21) and about God's gracious provision for his children (31-32).

2. What parable is used in verses 35-48 to illustrate and describe the attitude of God's waiting servants? What kind of attitude does Jesus want his servants to have? What are we to wait for? (40)

3. "It will be good" is repeated in which verses? What is it that will be good for the servants?

4. To what is Jesus' second coming compared in verses 39 and 40? Why? How does this help us to be faithful servants?

5. How did Peter respond to Jesus' teaching about the attitude of a faithful servant? Why did he ask this question?

6. How did Jesus answer? What two kinds of managers does Jesus describe? What reward and punishment does each receive? How does this parable answer Jesus' question?

II.   NOT PEACE BUT DIVISION (49-53)

7. Why did Jesus say he had come? What does he mean by "fire on the earth" and "a baptism to undergo"? (49-50)

8. What did Jesus mean when he said that he did not come to bring peace on the earth, but division? What kind of divisions does he describe in these verses? (51-53)

III.   INTERPRETING THE TIMES (54-59)

9. What kind of signs can most men—especially the Pharisees—interpret well?

10. What do they fail to interpret? Why does Jesus call them "hypocrites"? What warning does Jesus give in the parable in verses 57-59?

The Faithful and Wise Servant

Luke 12:35-59
Key Verse: 12:42

"The Lord answered, 'Who then is the faithful and wise manager, whom the master puts in charge of his servants to give them their food allowance at the proper time?'"

THIS TEXT INCLUDES THREE passages: first, a servant's readiness (35-48); second, not peace but division (49-53); and third, interpreting the times (54-59). When we study this part in contrast with the former passage, "The Parable of the Rich Fool" (12:13-21), we can better understand this text which teaches about a faithful servant who knows what kind of attitude he should have toward his master (35-48). A faithful servant is one who does not compromise his identity as his master's servant at the time of hardship and divisions and who knows how to see signs of the times in which he lives.

I. A faithful servant's readiness (35-48)

In verses 22-34, Jesus taught absolute reliance on God. Verses 31 and 32 say, "But seek his kingdom, and these things will be given to you as well. Do not be afraid, little flock, for your Father has been pleased to give you the kingdom." This is the promise that Jesus will give us the kingdom as our living hope and everything else if we seek first his kingdom. But this does not necessarily mean we should be complacent. We must do our best in fulfilling our duty as his servants while waiting for his coming.

Read verses 35 and 36. "Be dressed ready for service and keep your lamps burning, like men waiting for their master to return from a wedding banquet, so that when he comes and knocks they can immediately open the door for him." In this allegory, Jesus teaches us the fundamental relationship we have with God through the reconciliation of our Lord Jesus Christ. But we must know what is the basic relationship between God and man.

First, a servant's readiness (35-48). Read verse 35. "Be dressed ready for service …" Other versions translate, "Be dressed ready for service," as "Let your belts be fastened around your waists." This description is based on the long Eastern dress. If one wears a long dress, he cannot work effectively because it flops about his feet. He should gather his skirts around him and brace himself. He must be ready with his robe tucked about his middle in order that it may not interfere with his work. This teaches us readiness as his servants. Who is a faithful servant? A faithful servant is one who is always ready. A faithful servant is a "Ready … Go!" man. He is always willing to do something for his master. He is always ready to do something to please him. He is always prepared to go anywhere or do anything for his master. He is like a well-disciplined soldier who tightens his belt in order that he may feel himself all gathered together before he flings himself into the fight for the sake of his commander.

The difference between men that succeed and men that fail in ordinary pursuits is not so much intellectual as it is moral. There is nothing which commands more success than the giving of ourselves with all concentrated power to the task at hand. This concentration and detachment come when we have a basic attitude toward the task.

How much more, then, does Christian service demand a basic attitude of wholehearted devotion and concentration? However, how hard it is to have this basic attitude! When we want a basic attitude which makes us succeed in whatever we do, we must overcome our sophisticated ideas and the deceptive glitter of petty desires.

Second, a servant must keep his lamp burning. Verse 35b says, "… keep your lamps burning …" This requires faithfulness. A servant must keep his lamp burning faithfully. If a servant puts out the light and puts on his pajamas, he cannot welcome his master as he ought to at any hour. It is not easy to keep his lamp burning because it requires constant pulling up of the wick and supplying oil. But when he keeps his lamp burning, he can immediately open the door for his master when his master returns from the wedding banquet and knocks on the door.

Third, a servant's watchfulness. Read verses 37a and 38. "It will be good for those servants whose master finds them watching when he comes." "It will be good for those servants whose master finds them ready, even if he comes in the second or third watch of the night." Read verse 43 also. "It will be good for that servant whom the master finds doing so when he returns." Even though the master does not come until the second or third watch of the night, the servant must wait until his master comes. Why does he have to do this? It is because he is a faithful servant to his master. In order to open the door immediately, he must remain faithful to the end. Readiness, keeping the lamps burning, and watchfulness can all be condensed into one word: faithfulness. To a servant, faithfulness is most important. Paul said in 1 Corinthians 4:2, "Now it is required that those who have been given a trust must prove faithful." Again he said in 2 Timothy 2:2, "... entrust to reliable men ..." How can we remain faithful?

First, we must live before God, not before men. Read verse 37a again. "It will be good for those servants whose master finds them watching when he comes." Read verse 38 again, "It will be good for those servants whose master finds them ready, even if he comes in the second or third watch of the night."

Second, we must desire God's recognition. By nature, human beings want recognition from others whether they admit it or not. But recognition from others who have the same agonies and burdens of life cannot satisfy a man. Man needs God's approval and recognition. A faithful servant is really a happy man because he knows that he has God's recognition.

This allegory is given so that we may always be ready because we do not know when Jesus will come back. He comes like a thief (39). Read verse 40. Jesus warns his disciples saying, "You also must be ready, because the Son of Man will come at an hour when you do not expect him." In truth, those who wait for the Lord's coming remain faithful and joyful always, because they know what they are waiting for and what they are doing faithfully. But those whose faith is not based on the second coming of Jesus can easily remain unfaithful because of their lack of life direction.

How did his disciples respond to his teaching? Read verse 41. "Peter asked, 'Lord, are you telling this parable to us, or to everyone?'" Peter was a little bit upset. He thought that he was most watchful and faithful. He hoped that the parable was for others, not himself. I can understand Peter well. Two years ago, I was sick in bed, but I tried my best to explain the secret to success to a young man. I said, "If you want to be successful in the future, you must overcome yourself toward women and money." Then he talked back to me saying, "Are you talking to me?" Jesus did not rebuke insolent Peter. Instead, he taught about a faithful servant and an unfaithful servant in verses 42-48 and their consequent reward and punishment.

Read verse 42. "The Lord answered, 'Who then is the faithful and wise manager, whom the master puts in charge of his servants to give them their food allowance at the proper time?'" As we have studied, we are servants of God. But according to verse 42, to the world, we are managers. In brief, the children of God are stewards in charge of his children to give them their food allowance at the proper time. When we think about the role of a manager, we learn that the burden and responsibilities of Christians are too heavy to carry. In light of this verse, we, the children of God, are the real leaders of the world, no matter what our present positions may be.

What will be the reward for a faithful servant? Read verse 43. "It will be good for that servant whom the master finds doing so when he returns." The best reward for a faithful servant is the master's recognition, "Good." Read verse 44. "I tell you the truth, he will put him in charge of all his possessions." Our Lord's reward is not a bonus or vacation. He gives more work and more responsibility. We learn that from this gospel capitalist thought took form.

On the other hand, punishment for the unfaithful servants will be severe. Read verse 42. "The Lord answered, 'Who then is the faithful and wise manager, whom the master puts in charge of his servants to give them their food allowance at the proper time?'" To the servant who ill-treats his children and indulges in his own pleasures, calculating, "My master is taking a long time in coming," the master will come on a day when that servant does not expect him and will cut him to pieces and assign him a place with the unbelievers (45-46). The servant who knows his master's will and does not get ready or does not do what his master wants will be beaten with many blows. But the one who does not know and does things deserving punishment will be beaten with few blows.

God's way of dealing with men is not democratic. It is based on his absolute sovereign rule. However, his relationship with man is not relative, but absolute. He is our King, and we are his subjects. He has authority to demand. Read verse 48b. "From everyone who has been given much, much will be demanded; and from the one who has been entrusted with much, much more will be asked."

II. Not peace but division (49-53)

Jesus is the King of peace. He came to the world to give peace to men and glory to God. Before Jesus' coming, men were servants of Satan and sin. Satan uses men to oppose Christ and the Holy Spirit. The peace of Christ does not come from compromise for mutual benefits or conciliatory measures. The peace of Christ comes from God. The peace of Christ is the struggle with Satan.

Read verse 49. "I have come to bring fire on the earth, and how I wish it were already kindled!" Here, "fire" is the fire of the Holy Spirit. The fire of the Holy Spirit does the work of judgment. The fire of the Holy Spirit comes from heaven to the earth to purge men's sins. But this fire had not been kindled yet.

Read verse 50. "But I have a baptism to undergo, and how distressed I am until it is completed!" Jesus came to this world to baptize men with the Holy Spirit, but before this he had to undergo a baptism of suffering—that is, death on the cross. Jesus had to first defeat Satan's temptations, "Save yourself," and "Don't obey God's will to die on the cross. Isn't it too terrible?" Jesus' distress is unutterable until he completes the will of God on the cross. When he completes the will of God on the cross, he is no longer poor Jesus of Nazareth; he is King and Judge over all men.

Read verse 51. "Do you think I came to bring peace on earth? No, I tell you, but division." It is inevitable. Where there is the work of the Holy Spirit, there is the work of Satan. Wherever Jesus went, there was division between him and the Jews (Jn 7:43; 9:16; 10:19). Those who are afraid of this division cannot be called faithful servants of God, nor can they inherit the kingdom of God.

Read verse 53. "They will be divided, father against son and son against father, mother against daughter and daughter against mother, mother-in-law against daughter-in-law and daughter-in-law against mother-in-law." Humanly speaking, the family is most precious. But when division arises because of faith, a faithful servant of God cannot compromise on this. In the past, Asians were family-centered. These days, rich people in America try to find meaning in a family-centered life. However, faithful servants of God cannot compromise with those who do not put their faith in God. In the whole world, wherever or whenever the gospel of Jesus is preached, the kingdom of God is near. And at the same time, there is division between those who can enter the kingdom of God and those who cannot. The preaching of the gospel is God warning mankind, pressing us to make a decision to believe or not. By the gospel, mankind is standing at the crossroads of life and death, where we should not linger even for a few minutes.

III. Interpreting the times (54-59)

People of the world know many things about the world and talk a lot about them. They know especially well about the food and the weather. So Jesus said in verses 54-55, "'When you see a cloud rising in the west, immediately you say, "It's going to rain," and it does. And when the south wind blows, you say, "It's going to be hot," and it is.'" They know how to prepare themselves according to the weather forecasts. If the crowd knew how to interpret the weather, they could also interpret the times in which they lived. But they did not interpret the times. When they looked at the times, they immediately knew that the time in which they lived resembled the time of Sodom and Gomorrah, a time to be judged by fire. But nobody dared interpret the times because they were afraid of people's criticism. They were afraid of not being accepted. Most of all, they were afraid of exposing their hidden sins. They were afraid of repenting of their sins of worldly desires. So Jesus said in verse 56, "Hypocrites! You know how to interpret the appearance of the earth and the sky. How is it that you don't know how to interpret this present time?"

Jesus rebuked them for being hypocrites. They knew what was right and wrong. They saw all kinds of evilness, violence, adultery and idolatry. But they pretended not to see. They saw all kinds of blasphemy and godless behavior. But they pretended not to see. They never rebuked young and growing people because of their lives of sin, for they did not want to hurt them humanly. They were very permissive of their children's sinful lives, for they had no spiritual strength to rebuke them.

These days we see many hypocrites. Most of them say that they are Christians. But they never rebuke, even when they see their children's immoral lives. They just want them to be accepted by worldly people. I saw one of our Bible student's parents. They never cared about their daughter when she was being consumed by her wild living. They pretended not to know anything about her. But when she began to find her life direction through Bible study and wanted to live a changed, new life, they began to persecute her. At the present time, many bad things are ruining young souls. Young people's immoral lives, amoral lives, homosexuality, and demon worship make this country hopeless and futureless. But leaders in neither the spiritual realm nor the political realm are so serious that they want to make the spiritual life of this people a national issue to be discussed. They only talk about money, food, and weather and no more.

They also do not say what is right. Read verse 57. "Why don't you judge for yourselves what is right?" This is another kind of hypocrisy. Most people these days discipline themselves in deceiving their consciences so that they say "Right!" when something is beneficial to them and "No!" when they seem to lose something—even if they have to suppress the truth.

Through this we learn that Jesus wants us to interpret the present time from God's point of view and see the future through the present time's situation. Jesus doesn't want us to conform to the pattern of the times, but have prophetic vision by seeing the signs of the times. Jesus wants us to be prophets and priestly people of the times in which we live. Otherwise, we are hypocrites before his eyes.

Read verses 58 and 59. This is an allegory about a man who had to be reconciled with his adversary so that he would not be dragged to the judge to be judged and condemned. Likewise, those who know it is the time that they must reconcile with God must come to Jesus and repent of their sins and believe in Jesus.

Lesson 39

Jesus Urges for Repentance

Luke 13:1-17
Key Verse: 13:5b

I. UNLESS YOU REPENT (1-9)

1. What terrible thing did Pilate do to some Galileans? Why did some of the people present tell Jesus about it?

2. What did Jesus teach them about the relationship between sin and suffering? What warning did he give? Why?

3. What other tragic event did Jesus mention? How did he reinforce his previous teaching? What should we learn?

4. Why did the man plant a fig tree in his vineyard? How long did he wait for fruit to appear on the tree before saying anything? Why? What instructions did he give his gardener? Why?

5. What was the gardener's plea for reprieve? What was Jesus teaching in this parable?

II. YOU HYPOCRITES! (10-17)

6. When and where did this event take place? What was the woman's problem?

7. How did Jesus help her? What did she do? What does this reveal about Jesus?

8. Why was the synagogue ruler indignant? In what respect was his criticism reasonable? What does this reveal about his way of thinking? About Jesus?

9. Why did Jesus call them "hypocrites"? What did they not hesitate to do on the Sabbath? Why?

10. How did Jesus interpret what he had done for this woman? What did he teach about himself and about the work of God?

11. Why were the people delighted, while his opponents were humiliated?

Jesus Urges for Repentance

Luke 13:1-17
Key Verse: 13:5b

> *"But unless you repent, you too will all perish."*

THIS TEXT INCLUDES TWO parts. The first is a grotesque story which made those who heard it fatalistic. As a solution to human fatalism and sin, Jesus urges them to repent. We will see later what to repent of. The second is Jesus' healing of a crippled woman on the Sabbath. At this, the ruler of the synagogue became indignant, because he thought Jesus had violated Sabbath law. Jesus told him to repent of his hypocrisy. In this passage, Jesus urges those who are weary and tired to repent. It's because repentance is the first step to the Christian faith and salvation and the starting point of our pilgrimage to the kingdom of God. We must learn the importance and deep meaning of repentance.

I. Unless you repent ... (1-9)

The scary story in verses 1-5 is unique to Luke's gospel. Read verse 1. "Now there were some present at that time who told Jesus about the Galileans whose blood Pilate had mixed with their sacrifices." Some who had seen this terrible event came and told Jesus the story, stammering and trembling in terror. Apparently, while some Galileans were preparing the blood sacrifices of animals, Pilate saw them and did not like what they were doing. In his megalomania, Pilate killed them and mixed their blood with their sacrifices. We don't know why Pilate committed such a mischievous crime. But nobody could protest against the Roman governor Pilate's crime. They saw the national situation and became fatalistic. But the best way for them was to remain in acquiescence.

According to verse 2, the people who came to Jesus thought these Galileans were killed on account of their sins. This tragic event corresponded to their own problems, and they became fatalistic. Probably they had many sins, apparent or hidden, and when they saw this tragic event, they felt they would die someday just like that. Since they lived in the time of the Law, their way of thinking was based on cause and effect. They were haunted by the process of crime and punishment, as well as by the imagination that they would die tragically someday.

When they had to really repent of their sins in light of many warnings through many tragic events, they did not repent. They comforted themselves, thinking they were lucky to still be alive. They thought they were not killed because they were a little better kind of sinner, while the worse kinds of sinners were killed.

Both in the past and present, the world has been filled with these kinds of fatalistic people. People who live without God cannot see the spiritual world, the kingdom of God. They only see the world which is so filled with anguish and distress. They live in the world where there is no mercy for the weak and broken. All these people cannot but despair. They despair even more in themselves when they see their inner lives of sin without God.

People who live in the modern culture say that it is a drug culture. It is quite understandable why they have to abuse so many drugs at the cost of their finances and lives. The reason is simple. They do many perverse things either to overcome their despair or to express their despair. People in many fields express their despair in many ways. There are many kinds of musicians who express despair professionally. Literature, philosophy, and painting express man's despair at random. Even the theologians express man's despair by describing the dark side of man. Many people think that they are most unfortunate because they live in the last part of the 20th Century, the time of despair, and they become fatalistic. But when we study man's fatalism, the problem has been there from the beginning.

What did Jesus say to them? Read verses 2 and 3. "Do you think that these Galileans were worse sinners than all other Galileans because they suffered this way? I tell you, no!" Jesus opposed their idea that the Galileans were killed on account of their sins and that they themselves were not killed because they were somehow better kinds of sinners. Jesus went on to say, "But unless you repent, you too will all perish."

In order to lead them to repentance Jesus told them a similar story. Jesus told them about an accident he had heard of a few days before in which eighteen laborers had been crushed to death while getting a water system installed (4-5). What a tragic story! These eighteen laborers who had barely maintained a hand-to-mouth existence were crushed by an unexpected accident. To people, it was a very unfortunate accident that seemed like an ominous sign. But to Jesus, it was no more than an accident. Jesus was not concerned about those who had died in an unexpected accident. Rather, Jesus was concerned about their unrepentant hearts.

When Jesus saw the people of the times despair because of unbelief and become fatalistic, what kind of solution did he suggest? Jesus repeatedly emphasized repentance. "I tell you, no! But unless you repent, you too will all perish" (3,5). How on earth can repentance be the solutions to man's fatalism problem? What is repentance?

First, true repentance is to see men and the world with God's eyes, and to recognize God in every situation. In other words, we must include God in our thought world as well as in our practical lives, for man became fatalistic like a cut flower when he began to leave God out. Most people in the world think that this world is everything. They live without God. In the long run, when they find human limitations, they are frustrated and become very fatalistic. Finally, they come to the conclusion, "Let's eat and drink, for tomorrow we die." But one who sees his existence before our Father God can see the world with God's eyes and can find something to do as his mission. He also finds an outlet for this limited world in the infinite spiritual world. Repentance begins when we see man and the world with God's eyes.

Second, true repentance is to have hope in the kingdom of God. These days there are many people who want to live in ease and glory. They have made a leap of progress from a hippie mentality to yuppie desires. They want to be yuppies. But if we ask them, "What is your hope?" they say, "Well, to study hard and get a good job with good pay, have a beautiful wife and several kids, and have a greenhouse and tennis court." In truth, these cannot be a true hope because they are but a piece of cloud in the sky; they will float for a while, then disappear. In the long run, in their despair, such people run away from home or become perverse creatures. Therefore, unless we have hope in the kingdom of God, we cannot but despair and became fatalistic.

The parable in verses 6-9 is only in Luke's Gospel, but these verses have a background in Isaiah 5:1-7 and John 15:1-17. The Parable of the Tenants in Luke 20:9-19 seems to be more closely connected with the parable in verses 6 and 7. Allegorically, the owner of the vineyard is God. The farmer entrusted with the fig tree represents the Israelites. But generally speaking, the farmer can also represent mankind. Read verses 6 and 7. "Then he told this parable: 'A man had a fig tree, planted in his vineyard, and he went to look for fruit on it, but did not find any. So he said to the man who took care of the vineyard, "For three years now I've been coming to look for fruit on this fig tree and haven't found any. Cut it down! Why should it use up the soil?"'"

Third, true repentance is to discover one's mission from God. In this parable we learned what true repentance means. This parable teaches us that God has given each of us a vineyard to take care of. In other words, God has given each of us a mission. Therefore, it is important to discover what is our specific mission from God. Each must find out what is his or her vineyard. So Paul said in Ephesians 2:10, "For we are God's workmanship, created in Christ Jesus to do good works, which God prepared in advance for us to do." God did not make mankind to indulge in his sinful nature; he made each man to do God's work as a steward of God's world. Therefore, those who have a deep sense of God's mission are the men who truly repented before God, and they are the true leaders and history-makers of the world.

The man in the parable could not produce any fruit for the last three years because he did not accept his mission from the owner to take care of the fig tree in the vineyard. But the man was wise. When he was about to be cut out of God's blessing, and when he was in a fatalistic moment, he said to the owner in verses 8-9, "Sir, leave it alone for one more year, and I'll dig around it and fertilize it. If it bears fruit next year, fine! If not, then cut it down." He finally accepted the mission to take care of the fig tree. He decided to work hard so that he wouldn't disappoint the owner anymore. He overcame his fatalistic situation through repentance.

II. You hypocrites! (10-17)

Again, Luke alone records the event in verses 10-17. To this historian and evangelist, the mercy of Jesus the Messiah amazed him. And at the same time, the cavils of the ruler of the synagogue startled him. In this passage, Jesus heals a crippled woman on the Sabbath day. But the main point seems to be Jesus' rebuking of the hypocrites. Jesus' sorrow for Jerusalem in verses 31-35 delineates even more Jesus' rebuking anger toward these hypocrites.

Read verse 10. "On a Sabbath Jesus was teaching in one of the synagogues." The exact time and place of this event is unknown. But one thing is clear: Jesus was teaching the word of life in one of the synagogues. Just as all of the Jews at that time customarily went to the synagogues, Jesus went to the synagogues where the people were. It is like the saying, "A hunter who wants to catch a tiger goes to a tiger's den."

Read verse 11. While Jesus was giving the word of life to those who had gathered in the synagogue, a woman was there who had been crippled by a spirit for eighteen years. The story in verse 4 overwhelms us with a sense of tragedy, but this woman's story seems to be an unsurpassed tragedy. She had suffered for eighteen years after a spirit captured her. To a woman, outward appearance is important. But this woman was bent over so that whenever she made an effort to straighten up, her eyeballs protruded in reaction.

When Jesus saw this sad figure with her eyes fixed on the ground, ashamed to look at anybody or anything, he put his full attention on the woman who had somehow crawled into the synagogue. It was quite a surprise. Jesus' spontaneous sympathy went out to this crippled woman. She could in no manner lift herself up because of her physical malformation and deformity, as well as an evil spirit which had laid a heavy hand on her.

At the moment, Jesus did not care about anything or anyone but the woman. He stopped the Bible teaching. He ignored the audience as if they were not there. Jesus called her forward. This caused a big commotion. Still, she could not come forward because she thought she was not pretty enough. But she came to Jesus by faith. Then Jesus said, "Woman, you are set free from your infirmity" (12). Then he put his hands on her, and immediately she straightened up. She was healed. She was set free from her bondage. There was no gradual period of convalescence; the cure immediate according to Jesus' wishes. Christ's laying on of his hand obliterated all traces of her past infirmity, and new life flowed into her veins and strengthened her muscles and new beauty of a woman blossomed in her whole physical constitution. She praised God, saying, "Thank you, Jesus." Because of this woman's deliverance, God was glorified in the highest and joy of new life overflowed on earth.

But there was an unhappy man. Read verse 14. "Indignant because Jesus had healed on the Sabbath, the synagogue ruler said to the people, 'There are six days for work. So come and be healed on those days, not on the Sabbath.'" The ruler of the synagogue was supposed to be a servant of God, but he was not. He was a hypocrite because he had no spiritual eyes to see the work of God.

Jesus delivered a woman crippled for the last eighteen long years. This was the work of the Messiah, for whom the devout people had long awaited. Jesus' healing of a crippled woman was an event to rejoice over together, both in heaven above and on earth below. This was an event in which the people of the whole world could see the beauty of Jesus manifested as the Messiah. The ruler of the synagogue was indignant because Jesus had healed her on the Sabbath. But this was only an ostensible reason. The real reason he was indignant was that in all likelihood, Jesus had ignored the hour of the Sabbath offering, or disturbed the whole synagogue, in order to help a seemingly useless woman. The ruler of the synagogue was ready to attack Jesus severely, but in his disingenuous cowardice, he attacked the people around him instead. He said to the people, "There are six days for work. So come and be healed on those days, not on the Sabbath." In this way, he indirectly attacked Jesus' healing on the Sabbath.

What did Jesus say to him? Read verse 15. Jesus rebuked him, saying, "You hypocrites!" Jesus did not say, "hypocrite," but "hypocrites." Jesus not only rebuked the ruler of the synagogue, but also all those who were attached to the pedantic adherence to its forms—in brief, religious formalists or hypocrites. Jesus did not treat them harshly, but tenderly. Jesus told them a simple story so that they could see their hypocrisy. "Doesn't each of you on the Sabbath untie his ox or donkey from the stall and lead it out to give it water? Then should not this woman, a daughter of Abraham, whom Satan has kept bound for eighteen long years, be set free on the Sabbath day from what bound her?" (15b-16). According to the minute rules of the Talmud, these sticklers who rigidly observed the Sabbath laws admitted that they untied animals from their stalls to give them water. But they had no rule for untying a woman bound by Satan. This was hypocrisy and contrary to the universal love of God.

At that time the synagogue was supposed to be the house of God. As Isaiah said, "My house will be called a house of prayer for all nations" (Isa 56:7). The ruler of the synagogue should be a man of prayer. Historically, synagogues had been Bible houses. What's more, synagogues of the time were God's houses, in and through which many sick souls were healed and transformed. But the ruler of the synagogue was not happy about Jesus' healing of a woman crippled for the last eighteen years. He was a "genuine" hypocrite. He knew the Sabbath law, but the spirit of the law was debilitated by his hypocrisy.

These hypocrites made rules for animals to be untied and led to water on the Sabbath because animals gave them milk and sausages. But they ignored sick souls bound by Satan because they looked useless. But to Jesus, this one sick woman was a daughter of Abraham. Jesus said, "Then should not this woman, a daughter of Abraham, whom Satan has kept bound for eighteen long years, be set free on the Sabbath day from what bound her?" (16). She was a heavenly princess who deserved all the glory and privileges of the heavenly kingdom, along with Abraham, David, and Jesus himself. Jesus did not care about the Sabbath law because he did not come to keep the Sabbath law. Jesus untied her from what bound her because he came to set free those who were bound by Satan and sin.

What was the result of his healing? Read verse 17. "When he said this, all his opponents were humiliated, but the people were delighted with all the wonderful things he was doing." There were two kinds of people. One kind was the opponents of Jesus' healing ministry. They were under the power of darkness. The other was those who could experience the healing touch of the Messiah. They were the children in the light. Through this we learn that we must repent of the fatalistic elements in our hearts. Satan does his best to make us fatalistic, only to look at man in the world and the things of the world. But we must overcome it with faith. We must also fight against hypocrisy in our hearts every day.

Lesson 40

The Narrow Door

Luke 13:18-35
Key Verse: 13:24

I. WHAT IS THE KINGDOM OF GOD LIKE? (18-21)

1. What are the characteristics of a mustard seed? What was done with the mustard seed in the parable? What happened to it? How is this like the kingdom of God?

2. What do you think the birds and the tree represent?

3. What is yeast? What is it used for? Why is it an apt illustration of the kingdom of God?

4. In what respect are these two parables saying the same thing about the kingdom of God? What do we learn about the kingdom of God from these parables?

II. THE WAY TO ENTER THE KINGDOM OF GOD (22-30)

5. Where was Jesus going? What did he do on the way?

6. What question did someone ask? What might have led him to ask this question?

7. How did Jesus answer the question? How can we make every effort practically to enter by the narrow door? Why will some people not be able to enter?

8. Who might the people be who insist that they know the owner? Why does he call them evildoers?

9. Who will be at the feast in the kingdom of God? Who will be excluded? Who will be included? Where will those excluded be?

III. JESUS' SORROW FOR JERUSALEM (31-35)

10. What advice did some Pharisees give Jesus? Why do you think Herod wanted to kill him?

11. What message did Jesus have for Herod? Who else was this message for? What does it teach us about Jesus?

12. Why was Jesus so sorrowful about Jerusalem? What does this show about Jesus? What promise did he give?

The Narrow Door

Luke 13:18-35
Key Verse: 13:24

> *"Make every effort to enter through the narrow door, because many, I tell you, will try to enter and will not be able to."*

THIS TEXT INCLUDES THREE parts: First, the Parable of the Mustard Seed and the Yeast, which teaches us the essential character of the kingdom of God (18-21); second, the narrow door, which teaches us how much we should strive to enter the kingdom of God (22-30); and third, Jesus' sorrow for Jerusalem, the city of God, which was laid bare as a den of devils and as the object of God's judgment (31-35).

We live in a time when there are many highways and open opportunities. Especially in materialistic societies, there is little conception of a narrow door. But Jesus says, "Make every effort to enter through the narrow door" (24). Let's learn what this means to each of us.

I.   What is the kingdom of God like? (18-21)

Jesus wants us to know the greatness of the kingdom of God. In order to teach them about the kingdom of God, Jesus compared the kingdom of God to a mustard seed and to yeast.

Read verses 18-19. "Then Jesus asked, 'What is the kingdom of God like? What shall I compare it to? It is like a mustard seed, which a man took and planted in his garden. It grew and became a tree, and the birds of the air perched in its branches.'" Proverbially, the mustard seed is a tiny seed. The mustard seed is a symbol of smallness. Mustard is not a garden herb, but a field plant. Though it is the smallest field plant, it does literally grow into a tree a height of seven or eight feet. It is common to see a cloud of birds around such trees, for they love to eat the little brown and black mustard seeds.

As the mustard seed is the smallest among plant seeds (Mt 13:32) but can grow to be a big tree, so it is with the kingdom of God. The kingdom of God seems to be small, but it has in itself a tremendous growing power. Like a mustard seed, the kingdom of God starts from the smallest beginning. But it grows until it becomes bigger than anything else in the world.

When Jesus came into the world, the kingdom of God also came into this world. The baby Jesus laid in the manger was small, as was the kingdom of God. It was too small to compare with the pomp-ous throne of the Roman Emperor. But unlike the kingdom of God, this Roman throne lacked growing power. In the end, this kingdom became just a European tourist attraction. The kingdom of God in Jesus was small like a mustard seed, but his kingdom had infinite growing power, for the life of God was in it. Like a mustard seed, it grews more and more until it occupies the whole world, while crowns and thrones of worldly kingdoms rose and waned.

Jesus' work looked weak and small before the worldly industries. For example, Jesus called several fishermen by the seaside of Galilee to be his disciples. They were all earthbound and emotional. They were the last persons to be picked up or to be trained. Jesus' choosing and training of the twelve disciples looked like a children's soldier game. It did not seem to make any impact on the Roman Empire. It did not seem to grow enough to influence the world. But it grew and expanded more and more until its power and influence reached the whole world.

The kingdom of God began with small events, such as the healing of a crippled woman and the raising of a widow's son. When Jesus healed a crippled woman, the kingdom of Satan was cast out of her heart and the kingdom of God began in her heart. This seemed to be trivial, but it was not. In the eyes of God, it was a great event, for it was the coming of the kingdom of God into one person's heart. And it was the work of the Messiah. The scenes of troop reviews by many national leaders look spectacular. But in truth, Jesus' healing of a crippled woman is far greater than those worldly events because it is the work of the kingdom of God. The work of the kingdom of God will continue in this way, one person at a time, until the whole world is conquered and saved.

Read verse 19b. "It grew and became a tree, and the birds of the air perched in its branches." The mustard seed is the smallest seed, even compared to herb seeds. But it grows into a big tree. In the Bible, a mighty tree is used to symbolize a great empire, and the birds in its branches are subject nations who find shelter and protection within it (Ez 17:23; 31:6). To the historian Luke's eyes, the kingdom of God will grow into a vast empire in which all kinds of peoples and nations will come together to praise God the Father Almighty. This delineates the eternal victory of the kingdom of God. This allegory is also the prediction of the fate of the kingdom of Satan, which will soon perish.

It is amazing that Jesus told this parable. At that time, Jesus' ministry was nothing but a small grassroots movement, and the opposition which he and his disciples experienced was appalling. His fate was like the flickering wick of a lamp, for he would die after three days. But Jesus was not pessimistic at all because he had in his heart the kingdom of God.

Read verses 20 and 21. "Again he asked, 'What shall I compare the kingdom of God to? It is like yeast that a woman took and mixed into a large amount of flour until it worked all through the dough.'" Jewish yeast is a little piece of dough leftover from the last time of baking which can start fermentation in the next batch. Yeast is also used in Jewish thought to represent influence, usually bad influence because the Jews identified fermentation with rottenness. Jesus also said to his disciples, "Be on your guard against the yeast of the Pharisees and Sadducees" (Mt 16:6b). Here, in Luke's Gospel, yeast is used to teach the expanding power and incredible influence of the kingdom of God.

First, the kingdom of God expands. As the work of yeast is unseen but fulfilling its function, so the kingdom of God is expanding and on the way. When yeast gets inside the dough, it changes the whole lump of dough. It makes the whole lump of dough many times bigger. Likewise, when the good news of the kingdom of God is planted in one's heart, the unseen work of God is always going on gradually and steadily until one can see and enjoy the kingdom of God. We are sometimes upset when we cannot see any change in our sheep's hearts. We are upset when we see that the world seems to be getting worse and worse and gospel work seems to be nonexistent. But this is not true. When Jesus came, the work of the kingdom of God began simultaneously. Though it is unseen, the kingdom of God has been expanding more and more. And it will continue to expand until the cursed world is reduced to nothing and a new world with a new heaven and new earth appears. The kingdom of God comes into one's heart mainly through Bible study. This is the reason why Bible study is so important.

Second, the kingdom of God is revolutionary. The work of yeast is unseen, but someday it becomes manifest to all because it turns a lump of dough into a puffy, seething mass. In this way, yeast stands for the disturbing power of Christianity. In Thessalonica, it was said of the Christians there, "These men who have caused trouble all over the world have now come here" (Ac 17:6). Real Christianity is based on the kingdom of God, and Christianity based on the kingdom of God is the most revolutionary thing in the world. It works a revolution in individual lives and in society. Ungodly people call this revolution "mind control." They are those who do not see the kingdom of God. They are spiritually blind. Here we must know that the kingdom of God is Jesus himself because where there is Jesus, there is the kingdom of God.

II. The way to enter the kingdom of God (22-30)

In verses 18-21, we thought about what the kingdom of God is like. Through verses 22-30, we want to think about how we can enter the kingdom of God.

Read verse 22. "Then Jesus went through the towns and villages, teaching as he made his way to Jerusalem." This verse suggests that Jesus was still preaching the good news of the kingdom of God, going through the towns and villages, even when he was on the way to Jerusalem.

Read verse 23. "Someone asked him, 'Lord, are only a few people going to be saved?'" Probably this man had heard Jesus' message, "Repent or perish!" (Lk 13:1-9). Probably he had heard Jesus' rebuking of the Pharisees' hypocrisy. Most probably he was a Gentile who heard about the character of the kingdom of God through the Parable of the Mustard Seed and Yeast and really wanted to enter the kingdom of God. But he assumed that the kingdom of God was for only a few Jews and not for Gentiles like himself. Jesus taught this man about who would enter the kingdom of God.

First, those who make every effort can enter the kingdom of God. Read verse 24. He said to them, "Make every effort to enter through the narrow door, because many, I tell you, will try to enter and will not be able to." In this verse, making every effort involves agony of soul. Many people think that they should make every effort to fulfill their yuppie dreams. But many people think that they can enter the kingdom of God without lifting a finger. But this is not true. That's Satan's deception. To enter the kingdom of God is much harder than entering medical school. Without agony of soul, no one can enter the kingdom of God. The Christian must make every effort, like an alpinist who strives to climb up a mountain pathway toward a peak. The Christian must make every effort to press on, like a good soldier who fights boldly, enduring all kinds of hardships for his commander. The Christian must make every effort, like an athlete who competes according to the rules and receives the victor's crown. The Christian must make every effort, like a good farmer who sows in tears and reaps with songs of joy (2Ti 2:3-6).

Every human being wants to live a life worthy before the Holy God and enter the kingdom of God. Nobody wants to live deceitfully. Nobody wants to be a dirty sinner. Everybody wants to be a holy child of God and enter the kingdom of God. But most people are not able to do so because they give up and end up as spiritual dropouts. Why? Because there are two kinds of doors. One is the wide door by way of the broad road. Those who go through the wide door have their own blueprints of life in this world. They live without self-discipline and without the cross of mission. But finally they find that they are going nowhere. So Matthew said, "For wide is the gate and broad is the road that leads to destruction, and many enter through it" (Mt 7:13).

The other is the narrow door. Those who go through the narrow door are those who have made a decision of faith to participate in the divine nature (2Pe 1:4). They do not live according to their feelings or human reasoning, but by the word of truth (Jn 8:31-32). They do not live for their own glory, but for the glory of God. They deny themselves and take up their crosses daily and follow Jesus. When I had to fill out a customs report at the airport, I found that there were only two purposes of travel: business or pleasure. I did not know which one to select because I could not say I was a businessman or a pleasure-seeker. Those who are going through the narrow door can hardly enjoy worldly pleasures. Those who are going through the narrow door are those who follow the footsteps of Jesus and who lose their lives in the world. They are those who will participate in his glory when Jesus comes again in his glory.

Second, those who enter the kingdom of God must have a sense of timing. Many people think that they must first go through the wide door and by the broad way so that they can have something in their hands, like human achievements or being established in the world, and then after, go through the narrow door. But when they want to return to the narrow door, these people soon find that they have gone too far on the broad way to return. I knew the father of one student who would say, "I want to be a real Christian." But when his daughter asked him, "Why don't you go to church?" he said to her, "I am washed out." He meant, "I am too late." So Jesus said in verse 24b, "… because many, I tell you, will try to enter and will not be able to." Why? Because they missed the time to go through the narrow door.

"There is a time for everything, and a season for every activity under heaven: a time to be born and a time to die" (Ecc 3:1-2a). Likewise, there is a time to go through the narrow door. We must go through the narrow door when we are young. Tomorrow is already too late because time which passes by never comes back again.

What happens to those who miss their opportunity to enter through the narrow door? Read verse 25. "Once the owner of the house gets up and closes the door, you will stand outside knocking and pleading, 'Sir, open the door for us.' But he will answer, 'I don't know you or where you come from.'" They are not recognized by the owner. They insist that they are Christians, saying, "We ate and drank with you, and you taught in our streets" (26). They think that just because they are members of a Christian civilization, all is well. But they are not well. Those who live in a Christian civilization are not necessarily Christians.

What will be the owner's answer? Read verse 27. "But he will reply, 'I don't know you or where you come from. Away from me, all you evildoers!'" Those who come through the wide gate by means of broad ways cannot enter the kingdom of God. Jesus will say to them, "I don't know you or where you come from. Away from me, all you evildoers!" They will weep because of their fate in hell and gnash their teeth because of the pain of suffering in the fiery lake of burning sulfur in hell (28).

Third, those who came through the narrow door will participate in the feast of heaven. Read verses 28 and 29. There will be a time when Abraham, Isaac, Jacob, all the prophets, and all those who went through the narrow door will enjoy the feast of the kingdom of heaven (28b). But there will also be a time when all those enjoying the world and Christian civilization will be thrown out of the kingdom of heaven.

There will be a time when the Gentile people will come from the east and west and north and south and will take their places at the feast in the kingdom of heaven (29). Those who thought they were Christians and didn't do anything but drive the highways of their own ideas and plans will not attain the privilege of participating in the feast in the kingdom of heaven. We must make every effort to enter through the narrow door; otherwise, we will be among those who are thrown out.

III. Jesus' sorrow for Jerusalem (31-35)

God chose the people of Israel out of all nations and made her the people of a Bible teachers' country as well as people of a missionary-sending country. Jerusalem was supposed to be the Holy City where peoples of all nations could come to study the Bible. The people of Israel were chosen to be a priestly nation to shepherd the peoples of all nations so that they might not go by the broad way which leads to destruction, but go by the narrow way which leads to life. But the people of Israel did not accept God's mission. Rather, they enjoyed the highways of other nations.

Herod the king of Israel killed the righteous man, John the Baptist. Now he wanted to kill Jesus. How did Jesus answer some Pharisees who told him about Herod's conspiracy to kill him? Jesus expressed his belief that he would reach his goal by doing what he should do. Even though his life on earth would last only three more days, he wanted to cast out demons today and tomorrow and on the third day (32). In verse 33, Jesus repeated the same thought that in any case, he must keep on going today and tomorrow and the next day, for he could not die outside Jerusalem.

Jesus wept for Jerusalem because of the people's unrepentant hearts that made them ignore God's mission and kill the prophets. Jesus wept for Jerusalem because Jerusalem remained a place of killing prophets, a city doomed to be desolate. Jesus wept for Jerusalem because they would not escape God's wrath and judgment on the day when he comes again as Judge, not as a shepherd (34-35).

Lesson 41

The Great Banquet

Luke 14:1-35
Key Verses: 14:13-14a

I. A PHARISEE'S BANQUET (1-14)

1. Why was Jesus being carefully watched at the Pharisee's banquet? Why do you think the Pharisees invited him, and why did he accept? What did Jesus do when the man suffering from dropsy stood before him? What did he teach? Why were the Pharisees silent?

2. What did Jesus notice about the guests at the banquet? What do their actions reveal about them? What teaching did Jesus give these guests? Why did he teach them?

3. What was the Pharisees basis for selecting the guests he invited to his banquet? What did Jesus teach his host about whom he should invite? Why?

II. THE GREAT HEAVENLY BANQUET (15-24)

4. Why did the man in verse 15 make a remark about the great heavenly banquet? What did he mean?

5. In Jesus' parable, who is the host? Who do the invited guests represent? What were the responses of the invited guests?

6. How do these responses reveal their worldliness? What do they reveal about their attitude toward God?

7. Who did the host send his servant out to invite? Who do these guests represent? What did he finally do to fill his house? Who do these last guests represent?

III. THE WORKERS OF THE KINGDOM OF GOD (25-35)

8. What did Jesus teach the large crowd following him? What does he mean by "hate" his loved ones and himself?

9. What does each of the two parables in verses 28-33 teach about counting the cost of following Jesus? About the importance of making a decision and a commitment?

10. What does salt that has lost its saltiness represent? What is salty salt?

The Great Banquet

Luke 14:1-35
Key Verses: 14:13-14a

> "*But when you give a banquet, invite the poor, the crippled, the lame, the blind, and you will be blessed.*"

CHAPTER 14:1-35 CONTAINS TWO stories about banquets through which Jesus teaches us who can eat at the feast in the kingdom of God (1-14) and who can have the most glorious privilege to occupy the feast table in the kingdom of God (15-24). We can also learn who can be the workers for the kingdom of God (25-35).

I. The Pharisee's banquet (1-14)

Only Luke the historian recorded the account in verses 1-14. One Sabbath, Jesus was invited to a dinner by a prominent Pharisee. He stood out among the Pharisees. He must have been a leader with great wealth and honor in his community. His garden was probably wide enough to keep over 200 trees in full foliage. Probably the interior décor of his house was magnificent. Guests at the dinner were all from the high upper class, for they were the Pharisees and experts in the law. They are equivalent to modern-day PhD graduates. Obviously, this dinner party was just a show. When Jesus went to eat there, he was being carefully watched. They prepared a big dinner, and at the same time, they brought a man with dropsy there. They prepared this kind of atmosphere and invited Jesus to the dinner. And it was a Sabbath. So their motive was clear. They attempted to have a big dinner and satisfy their intellectual hedonism by embarrassing Jesus with the Sabbath law.

What did Jesus do under this circumstance? Jesus did not care about anything but the man suffering from dropsy. Jesus was very sorry that he was suffering from dropsy and that he was being used by them like bait for fishing. Jesus was determined to help him. "Jesus asked the Pharisees and experts in the law, 'Is it lawful to heal on the Sabbath or not?'" (3). They could have said something in response to Jesus' question, but they remained silent because they were frustrated by their inner motives which were evil. As a result, they were dumbstruck. They were doing what they were not sure of.

What did Jesus do next? Jesus took hold of the man, healed him, and sent him away (4b). Jesus did not hesitate even for a few minutes, but healed him even though it would upset all at the dinner party, even though it involved risking his own life. In this way, Jesus demonstrated the true meaning of the Sabbath. The Sabbath is the seventh day set apart for man to rest in God after six days of hard work. But nobody can rest if he is seriously sick. So Jesus healed him so that he could experience the love of God and rest in God. Jesus healed him, set him free from bondage to his sickness, and made him very happy. Jesus sent him away. The man with dropsy flew away like a bird which just got out of a cage. Jesus gave him healing, true freedom, happiness, and rest on the Sabbath. This shows the true spirit of the Sabbath.

Then Jesus explained his act of mercy. Read verse 5. "Then he asked them, 'If one of you has a son or an ox that falls into a well on the Sabbath day, will you not immediately pull him out?'" That's right. It was a self-evident truth, the truth all people of the world should practice. The true meaning of the Sabbath is to practice the truth so as to worship God. In this verse, Jesus teaches them that on the Sabbath, it is better to heal a man with dropsy than to enjoy a dinner party for their own pleasure.

Originally, the Pharisees and experts in the law were assigned to serve God's children. They were highly respected by people simply because they were servants of God. But they did not serve his people. They had no idea how to serve God's people. They took honor and respect for granted. They indulged themselves in rich dinner parties, not caring for the poor and needy. They were really no good before God's eyes.

Their corruption did not stop there. Read verse 7. "When he

noticed how the guests picked the places of honor at the table, he told them this parable ..." They tried to show off their imposing appearances. They tried to make a show of power and dignity. In this atmosphere, Jesus' hungry disciples, who came with him as uninvited guests, did not know where to sit—at the places of honor or at the places for extra members? They were the future pillars of God's church and new history makers, but they stood there like a bunch of beggars.

Jesus told them this parable. Read verses 8 and 9. "When someone invites you to a wedding feast, do not take the place of honor, for a person more distinguished than you may have been invited. If so, the host who invited both of you will come and say to you, 'Give this man your seat.' Then, humiliated, you will have to take the least important place." It is human nature to think, "I am a little better than him." There is no one who does not exalt himself. But the Pharisees and experts in the law were supposed to be the spiritual leaders. Humbleness should have been a basic quality for them. But they only exalted themselves. Those who exalt themselves are truly not great men even if they occupy high positions in society. They have a great danger of being humiliated by more distinguished people.

Jesus admonished them to take the places of the humble. Read verse 10. "But when you are invited, take the lowest place, so that when your host comes, he will say to you, 'Friend, move up to a better place.' Then you will be honored in the presence of all your fellow guests." Those who are called the children of God are all expected to learn how to humble themselves, for God opposes the proud but gives grace to the humble (Jas 4:6). Only humble people can see God. They know they are sinners before God, and they realize that they need God's grace and salvation. Paul was great, not because he had eye diseases and stomach troubles or was short, or because he was well-versed in the philosophies of the East and West. He was great because he was humble before God, humble enough to know that he was a sinner who needed God's grace. In 1 Timothy 1:15b Paul said, "Christ Jesus came into the world to save sinners—of whom I am the worst."

Read verse 11. "For everyone who exalts himself will be humbled, and he who humbles himself will be exalted." Jesus taught them that they should not exalt themselves before people. They should be exalted by God. Those who exalt themselves cannot be members of the kingdom of heaven, and neither are they qualified to eat at the feast in the kingdom of heaven.

Jesus saw that the members of the dinner were composed of the Pharisees and experts in the law and those who shared their own kinds of pleasures and mutual benefits (12). Here, Jesus taught them that it was no good to spend money to enjoy dinner parties among themselves, complimenting each other, "Oh, your puppy is so cute!" or "Your hairstyle is nice!" This was a pleasure-seeking lifestyle in high-class society. Historically, these kinds of pleasure-seeking people have been the nursery of corruption and evil. These kinds of people have ground the faces of the poor and have bled harmless people of all strata. They are the symbols of the power of darkness. What is worse, they have no right to join in the feast of the kingdom of God.

Read verses 13 and 14. "But when you give a banquet, invite the poor, the crippled, the lame, the blind, and you will be blessed. Although they cannot repay you, you will be repaid at the resurrection of the righteous." Jesus wants us to invite those that are so poor that they cannot repay. Jesus wants us to invite those who are in need of God's hand of mercy. This kind of act of mercy cannot be repaid in the present world. But when we do these things, we can please God and be happy in proportion. A Christian's real happiness is there when they serve the poor and needy in the name of Jesus. Surely our Lord Jesus recognizes them. Matthew 25:36-40 tells us this is true. "'I needed clothes and you clothed me, I was sick and you looked after me, I was in prison and you came to visit me.' ... 'When did we see you sick or in prison and go to visit you?' The King will reply, 'I tell you the truth, whatever you did for one of the least of these brothers of mine, you did for me.'" In short, we must have dinner parties for the glory of God instead of for seeking pleasure. Paul said in 1 Corinthians 10:31, "So whether you eat or drink or whatever you do, do it all for the glory of God." Those who have dinner parties for the glory of God, God will reward at the resurrection of the righteous, at the day of Jesus' second coming.

II. The great heavenly banquet (15-24)

Read verse 15. "When one of those at the table with him heard this, he said to Jesus, 'Blessed is the man who will eat at the feast in the kingdom of God.'" This man must have also been one of the Pharisees. When he heard Jesus' teaching, he could comprehend the happiness of those who eat at the heavenly feast of the resurrection of the righteous. Following his cry of wonder, Jesus taught him more specifically who could eat at the feast in the kingdom of God, in brief, who would be the blessed one in the kingdom of God.

Read verses 16-20. "Jesus replied: 'A certain man was preparing a great banquet and invited many guests. At the time of the banquet he sent his servant to tell those who had been invited, "Come, for everything is now ready."'" Here in verse 17, those who had been invited were those who had studied the laws of God and tried to observe them. They refer to the Pharisees and experts in the law. They were the chosen people. They were the most privileged people. They were the most blessed people (Ro 9:4-5). They were the priestly nation and royal priesthood (Ex 19:5-6a). The heavenly banquet was prepared for them. When Jesus said, "The kingdom of God is near. Repent and believe the good news!" (Mk 1:15b), it was his invitation to the feast in the kingdom of God. But his chosen people Israel became the embodiment of worldly desires and rejected God's invitation. They did not realize God's deep love. Rather, they saw the material prosperity of neighboring countries and were enslaved by obsessive jealousy. Because of their materialistic view of man and the world, they could not thank God for his deep love that is spiritual and eternal. In their spiritual blindness, when they were invited to the heavenly banquet, they unanimously refused to come (18-20). They made many excuses, both social and religious. But their immediate problem was their material problem, and their root problem was their rejection of God's love. When the owner ,who is Jesus, kept on inviting them, they crucified him on the cross.

Read verse 21. "The servant came back and reported this to his master. Then the owner of the house became angry and ordered his servant, 'Go out quickly into the streets and alleys of the town and bring in the poor, the crippled, the blind and the lame.'" The owner of the house was greatly discouraged and burnt with anger because his own people, for whom he had prepared the heavenly banquet, rejected his invitation (Jn 1:11). So the invitation was extended to those who thought that they did not deserve the invitation to the heavenly banquet. They were the tax collectors and prostitutes who repented (Mt 21:32). They were the poor, the crippled, the blind, and the lame who thought they were nobodies. When they were invited, they went with great joy. It is surprising that the members of the heavenly banquet are the tax collectors, prostitutes, the poor, the crippled, the blind, and the lame. But they were qualified because they were humble and lowly enough to accept God's love.

Read verses 22 and 23. "'Sir,' the servant said, 'what you ordered has been done, but there is still room.' Then the master told his servant, 'Go out to the roads and country lanes and make them come in, so that my house will be full.'" The owner of the house ordered his servants to go out to the roads and country lanes and make the people come in so that the banquet hall would be filled up. Here, those who are wandering on the roads and country lanes refer to the Gentiles. The owner of the house said, "Make them come in." This does not mean to use violence in bringing them to the banquet. It is the expression of God's burning desire to invite them all to the heavenly banquet. First, he prepared the banquet and called those who had already been invited so that they might come and enjoy the blessedness of those who eat at the feast in the kingdom of God. But they rejected his invitation. The owner was very sorry that they refused to come. But the feast in the kingdom of heaven was not affected. Instead, it was filled by many ordinary people and by the Gentiles. Here we learn that luxurious parties can be stumbling blocks to anyone. Each person must live a self-disciplined life instead of seeking sinful pleasures so that we may not be the "dropouts" among those who can enter the kingdom of heaven. We must invite poor people in the name of Jesus and make them happy just as Jesus invited us to the heavenly banquet, though we are like the sick and needy. We must invite poor people in the name of Jesus so that Jesus can invite us to the heavenly banquet. Each person must get a taste of the heavenly banquet.

III. The workers of the kingdom of God (25-34)

Large crowds followed Jesus, but they did not know that Jesus was going up to Jerusalem where his crucifixion awaited, nor did they know why they were following Jesus (25). Jesus said to them that if they want to follow him, they should meet the required conditions and count the cost as his disciples. More specifically, Jesus teaches them how they can be workers of the kingdom of heaven.

Read verse 26. "If anyone comes to me and does not hate his father and mother, his wife and children, his brothers and sisters— yes, even his own life—he cannot be my disciple." Here in verse 26, the word "hate" means to deny one's natural desires. Everyone who thinks that natural desires are everything cannot be his disciple or a worker of the kingdom of God. The first condition to be a worker of the kingdom is that one must deny himself. It means to deny one's natural desires, such as the desire to enjoy the sinful nature and the desire to love his own family members. The second condition is that one must carry his cross of mission. Read verse 27. "And anyone who does not carry his cross and follow me cannot be my disciple." One cannot be a worker of his kingdom without a specific mission.

Verses 28-33 are recorded only in Luke. Here we find another condition to being a worker in the kingdom of God. A worker of the kingdom of God must count the cost. Read verses 28-30. "Suppose one of you wants to build a tower. Will he not first sit down and estimate the cost to see if he has enough money to complete it? For if he lays the foundation and is not able to finish it, everyone who sees it will ridicule him, saying, 'This fellow began to build and was not able to finish.'" For the task of the workers of the kingdom is like building a tower to watch his vineyard. It demands a lot of labor and sacrifice of time. They must receive the same suffering that Jesus received. When Jesus exposed the sins of the world, the world hated him. A worker of the kingdom must be determined to be hated by the world as Jesus was. It's very costly to be a worker of the kingdom, but it is most noble and worthy. Their labor is not in vain. But they must count the cost; otherwise, they will be a laughingstock when they collapse along the way.

To become a worker of his kingdom is like going to war against another king. In order to win the war against the enemy king, one must prepare enough to defeat the enemy who's stronger than himself (31-33). It is not easy at all for anyone to defeat an enemy who is stronger than himself. In order to defeat the stronger enemy, one must discipline himself. He must also equip himself with the spirit of victory; otherwise, he will be defeated before fighting. These two parables teach us that a worker of the kingdom of God must count the cost of hardships and determine to overcome any kind of hardships or suffering.

Read verses 34 and 35. "Salt is good, but if it loses its saltiness, how can it be made salty again? It is fit neither for the soil nor for the manure pile; it is thrown out. He who has ears to hear, let him hear." The workers of the kingdom must have the flavor of Jesus' grace and truth. They must be a preservative against the corruption of the world. They must be influential so that they can be an encouragement and blessing for the world.

Lesson 42

While He Was Still a Long Way Off

Luke 15:1-32
Key Verse: 15:20b

I. THE LOST SHEEP (1-7)

1. To whom did Jesus tell this parable, and what criticisms was he answering?

2. In what respect is a sinner like the sheep who wandered away?

3. According to verse 4, what does one do when he discovers that one sheep has wandered away? Try to explain the heart of the shepherd who leaves the 99 sheep to go and search for the lost one.

4. What happened when he found his lost sheep? What does this response teach us about God? How does it explain Jesus' welcoming of tax collectors and sinners?

II. THE LOST COIN (8-10)

5. In what respect is a sinner like the coin that rolled away? What does the woman who loses one of her ten coins do? What does this reveal about her character? What does she do when she finds the lost coin? How does this parable reinforce the other in its teaching about the heart of God?

III. THE LOST SON (11-32)

6. Why do you think the younger son wanted to leave home? What does this father's way of dealing with his son teach us about God? (11-12)

7. What happened to the younger son? Why did he decide to go back home? Why is this a crucial and significant decision? With what kind of attitude did he return?

8. Describe the waiting father. What did he do when he saw his son coming? How did he reveal his unconditional love and forgiveness? What does this father teach us about God and God's attitude toward sinners?

9. Why could the older son not understand his father's actions or his father's heart? In what respect was he a lost son too? What is Jesus' message to the critical Pharisees?

10. How did the father counsel the older son? What is Jesus primarily teaching in this parable about God?

While He Was Still a Long Way Off

Luke 15:1-32
Key Verse: 15:20b

> *"But while he was still a long way off, his father saw him and was filled with compassion for him; he ran to his son, threw his arms around him and kissed him."*

U P UNTIL NOW, LUKE has described those who have had opportunities to listen to the word of Jesus. Among these were his disciples. Others were experts in the law and the Pharisees (11:37; 13:31; 14:1) and the crowds (11:14; 12:13; 13:1,4). Luke 15 includes among those listening to him some quite new people—"sinners," called publicans or public sinners simply because they did not keep the Law meticulously. In this event, we can see that Jesus is the light to the Gentiles. The main point of these parables is the shepherd heart of God who saves totally useless sinners if they come to him. Each of the three parables in this chapter metaphorically typifies a kind of sinner. They are lost sheep (3-7), lost coins (8-10) and lost sons (11-32).

One day the tax collectors and the "sinners" were all gathering around to hear Jesus. Perhaps after listening to the word of God, they feasted with great joy. But the Pharisees and teachers of the law were quite different from Jesus. They muttered, "This man welcomes sinners and eats with them" (2). Then Jesus told them three parables consecutively so that they might somehow understand the mind of God.

I. The lost sheep (3-7)

Read verses 3 and 4. "Then Jesus told them this parable: 'Suppose one of you has a hundred sheep and loses one of them. Does he not leave the ninety-nine in the open country and go after the lost sheep until he finds it?'" In the Bible, the people of God are frequently called sheep, and God, their shepherd. Accordingly, the owner of the sheep is God.

When we look at verses 3-5, we find that Jesus did not tell them a story one-sidedly; rather, he asked their opinion: "Suppose one of you has a hundred sheep and loses one of them. Does he not leave the ninety-nine in the open country and go after the lost sheep until he finds it?" This question throws light on the owner's care and pain in searching for what is lost. It is human instinct to take any pains to find something that is lost, quite apart from the consideration of its intrinsic worth. In his desire to find one lost sheep, a shepherd does not care about anything, even about losing the ninety-nine. When he finds it, his joy is endless (5-6). God gave man this desire so that we may be good shepherds.

There is a shepherd. He has a hundred sheep. He lost one sheep out of a hundred. The thing lost is so small in proportion to the things still retained. The shepherd might well have said: "Well, one in a hundred does not matter much. I still have ninety-nine." But he did not; he went to look for it. He left the ninety-nine in the open country and went after the lost sheep until he found it. In the world, people think a minority should be sacrificed for the benefit of a majority. Most people think that it is good to lose one sheep in order to protect ninety-nine sheep. But God's way of thinking is different. God cannot rest until he finds the lost sheep. God does not want anyone to perish, but everyone to come to repentance (2Pe 3:9b). God leaves the ninety-nine in the open country and goes after the lost sheep until he finds it.

In this story, a sheep is lost. It represents a sinner. He did not intend any mischief. But he lived what we call an animal life. Sheep only know where the herbage is abundant and fresh, and this sheep went there. He had no foresight because he was an animal. He had only a rudimentary conscience and instinct. His inclinations were not restrained by any sense of responsibility. So, unwittingly, he wandered further and further from the flock until he found himself in a waterless desert. Many men live like this without any restraint on their appetite or feelings. Living by nature seems to be a small matter. It is natural and human and quite attractive. However, this way of life leads a man to have no sense of direction or purpose of life. Furthermore, for a man who lives this way, his sinful nature becomes the master of his life. And there is danger that he will be led to utter destruction and become an object of God's wrath (Eph 2:1-10).

Read verse 7. "I tell you that in the same way there will be more rejoicing in heaven over one sinner who repents than over ninety-nine righteous persons who do not need to repent." In this verse Jesus teaches legalists that God pours out all his love and affection on one sinner.

II. The parable of the lost coin (8-10)

Jesus continues to teach them with another parable. Read verse 8. "Or suppose a woman has ten silver coins and loses one. Does she not light a lamp, sweep the house and search carefully until she finds it?" To the woman, the ten coins must have been very precious. Each coin was heavy, and so one coin fell. It was round, so it rolled. It was dead, so it lay flat.

In this parable, the coin represents a sinner. Many people, because of their sinful nature, have given up their will entirely and allow themselves to be determined by their circumstances. There are so many people who no longer resist the pressure of circumstances and temptations, like the coin when it dropped from the woman's open palm and trundled away into some dark corner. But for a human being to abnegate the right and power of resisting circumstances is to give up one's own human right which God has crowned people with.

Sometimes two kinds of men are exposed to precisely the same conditions. One of them is overcome by the circumstances and is ruined. The other resists, and is raised and strengthened. To stumble or to stand in the time of adverse circumstances is each one's choice. But the results of the choices are quite different. Here we learn that we must rule over the adverse circumstances instead of letting them rule over us. There is a saying: "Adverse circumstances are a fool's master and a wise man's servant."

The parable of the ten coins teaches us that God values one person's life most preciously. God is like a mother and a father. Parents who have many children still find each child so precious that they can still lavish all their love and devotion on one child at a time. Likewise, to God's eyes, one lost sinner is as precious as all the children he has.

Read verse 10. "In the same way, I tell you, there is rejoicing in the presence of the angels of God over one sinner who repents." The parable of the lost coin represents the value system of God given to mankind. God and all his angels in heaven are happy when one sinner is found.

III. The parable of the lost son (11-32)

Read verses 11 and 12. Jesus continued: "There was a man who had two sons. The younger one said to his father, 'Father, give me my share of the estate.' So he divided his property between them." The younger one wanted to get his share of the estate, and he wanted to use it freely. Freedom was the best gift to mankind given by God in the Garden of Eden (Ge 2:17). The tree of the knowledge of good and evil was the sign of free choice and the symbol of human freedom in the cosmos of God. Therefore, freedom is the grace of God, and at the same time, there is great danger that it can be misused, like a sharpened knife in a little kid's hand. The father in the parable felt that danger for his son, but he did not want to treat his son like a slave or like a dependent child, so he gave him his share of the estate.

The foolish boy was overcome by his desire to become his own master, so he did not care about his father's love and care. He wanted to handle his own money and to enjoy the sense of possession. He had an upsurging desire for independence, and he was impatient to control his life and exercise his self-will. The boy in the parable is the same as the tenants in Mark 12:1-12. They were most blessed people who had the privilege of keeping the master's vineyard. They could enjoy all the harvest of the vineyard and give just a little fruit to the master as the sign of their good relationship with him. But they forgot their position as tenants. They wanted to be the owners of the vineyard. So they seized the servant sent from the owner and beat him and sent him away empty-handed. Finally, they killed the owner's son. It was rebellion against the owner. In the same way, this younger son's false conception of freedom was actually rebellion against his father's love.

Read verse 13. This verse well describes the inner condition of a sinner who has left God. A sinner who leaves God corresponds to the prodigal son. Those who use all their inheritance from God, all their wealth, knowledge, health and so on for themselves, are sinners before God. "Not long after that, the younger son got together all he had, set off for a distant country and there squandered his wealth in wild living" (13). After he had spent everything, misfortune and bad luck came upon him in succession. And so he began to be in need. He wanted to get a job, but he found a pig-feeding job which only made him hungrier. He longed to fill his stomach with the pods that the pigs were eating. He had been a blessed and dear son to his father. But when he made this venture, he was forced to become a slave, doing the last thing he wanted to do. The godless world is a hard taskmaster and it made him a helpless slave.

Verses 17-20 tell us how the son decided to return to his father. "When he came to his senses, he said, 'How many of my father's hired men have food to spare, and here I am starving to death! I will set out and go back to my father and say to him: Father, I have sinned against heaven and against you'" (17-18). When he left his father's love, he was beside himself. When he remembered his father and his richness, he came to himself. He realized that he had been wrong. His realization of his poor situation and his father's richness was the beginning point of knowing himself. Man without God is like an abandoned infant. Man without God is like an orphan whose heart cannot be satisfied by food. Material things cannot replace parental love. It is true. I have seen so many rich people in the world around me. But they are so extremely poor in some areas of their lives that they could not get out of the misery of life. A man can find true richness only in God.

His resolution to go home seems a small thing. But it is all a sinner can do. It is all the responsibility a sinner can take in making a new relationship with God. Coming back is not easy at all. I heard that 95% of runaway teenagers come back within 72 hours. But those who do not come back within 72 hours never come back—mainly because of an unknown force pulling them down. But this boy made a resolution and began to carry it out. His resolution was not weakened by procrastination. As low as the motive was for his return, the fact of his return was more than enough.

The climax of the parable is the father's welcome (20b-24). The rest of the story is but scaffolding. Perhaps the son's heart sank as he came near his father's house. No doubt he hesitated when the old home came into sight, and perhaps all his resolution might have oozed out of his fingertips if he had had to march up alone in his rags and appear before his father's servants, as well as before all the people in his hometown, before making his appearance to his father.

Let's see what the father did at that moment. "But while he was still a long way off, his father saw him and was filled with compassion for him; he ran to his son, threw his arms around him and kissed him" (20b). The son had not discovered his father, but his father recognized him even while he was a long distance away. As soon as he saw his son, he did not hold himself back in his prestige or feeling of seniority. He threw his arms around him, even though he was covered in dirty rags. He kissed him on his dirty face. The father could not adequately express his joy and love towards his returning son. His joy was like a torrent of a stream flowing over the banks of a canal. This reminds us of God's love which is poured out on sinners through his only Son Jesus.

Read verse 21. "The son said to him, 'Father, I have sinned against heaven and against you. I am no longer worthy to be called your son.'" In verse 19b, the son wanted to ask his father to give him a job as one of his servants. But he could not say that. Instead he said, "I'm sorry, Father." His father's beautiful welcome made him talk to his father as a son.

What was the father's reply to his son's confession? Read verses 22 and 23. "But the father said to his servants, 'Quick! Bring the best robe and put it on him. Put a ring on his finger and sandals on his feet. Bring the fattened calf and kill it. Let's have a feast and celebrate.'" Here, the father gives no verbal answer to his son's confession, for his kiss had already answered it. But he issued instructions to the servants to bring the best kinds of gifts for his son.

It is interesting to think about the gifts given to the prodigal son. They seem to represent various aspects of the blessed results of returning to God. These days, in general, salesmen or restaurant managers are the ones who wear decent robes. But the robe, traditionally, was a familiar emblem of character. The father clothed his prodigal son in the best robe. The son was treated like a heavenly prince. His rags were stripped off, and he was clothed anew in a dress of honor. I see here that he was justified, and furthermore, sanctified. The ring is a token of wealth and position and it is the promise of heirship. It is a sign of authority, as well as an ornament for his hand. The father elevated the prodigal son to a position next to himself. The father gave him shoes when he came back footsore and bleeding. Last of all, a great feast was served to celebrate his son's return home. The prodigal son came back to his father for the sake of bread, but he was bathed in the outflow of his father's love feast. The feast is a symbol of the utmost joy which comes from the grace of forgiveness, and it is the rich endowment of honor for the one who comes back to his father.

Read verses 25-30. The older brother came back from working in the field and heard the sounds of joyful music and dancing. He asked one of his servants, "What's going on here?" The servant explained about the feast. Then the older son became very angry and refused to go in. He thought that his younger brother didn't deserve such a big feast, and he thought that his father's treatment of them was unfair. He thought that he had obeyed his father and worked hard while his young brother had rebelled against his father and had squandered his property with prostitutes. Yet his father had never given him even a young goat. His argument is reasonable. But he did not have a love relationship with his father. He had only a legalistic relationship with his father. He did not understand his father's mind. He could not participate in either his father's sorrow or in his father's joy.

Read verses 31 and 32. The father said, "My son, you are always with me, and everything I have is yours. But we had to celebrate and be glad, because this brother of yours was dead and is alive again; he was lost and is found." According to the father, the older son's inheritance was safe. But the elder son did not realize this. What a great inheritance he had! His father's possessions were all his. Furthermore, the father himself was his as his supreme inheritance. He had the great privilege of serving his father while his brother had not had that privilege. But he did not realize this blessed privilege. When he did not realize this privilege, he was full of complaints toward his father and criticism towards his younger brother. People are unhappy mainly because they do not realize their God-given privileges. This parable teaches us clearly that the prodigal son who came back to his father was happier than the self-righteous elder brother who was at home. Happiness does not consist in one's possessions or in morality. It belongs to those who come back to God and abide in his love. This parable also teaches us that God's love is not legalistic, but boundless in finding one lost sheep.

Lesson 43

Be a Wise Manager

Luke 16:1-31
Key Verse: 16:9

I. USE WORLDLY WEALTH TO GAIN FRIENDS (1-18)

1. Why did the rich man decide to fire his manager? How did the manager assess his situation? What did he do to provide for his future security? (What was his purpose in reducing the debts of his master's debtors?)

2. What commendable point did the master find in his manager? What spiritual lesson does Jesus teach from this shrewd manager's worldly wisdom? Of what does your worldly wealth consist? How can we use our worldly wealth to prepare for eternity?

3. What are true riches? How can we be trustworthy in handling worldly wealth so as to be entrusted with true riches?

4. Why can we not serve two masters? Why did the Pharisees sneer at Jesus? What is the difference between the way God looks at men and the way men look at themselves? How is God's value system different from men's?

5. How did people force their way into the kingdom of God during the time of John the Baptist's ministry? Why is keeping the law no small matter? How is marriage a test of trustworthiness? What does Jesus teach about the real motives for divorce?

II. THE RESULT OF A PLEASURE-SEEKING LIFESTYLE (19-31)

6. Describe the respective situations of the rich man and Lazarus on earth. Describe their respective situations after they died.

7. What two requests did the rich man make of Father Abraham? What reasons did Abraham give for refusing each request? How had the rich man failed to be a shrewd manager?

8. How can Bible study help us make preparations for eternity? Why is it important to listen to and obey the teachings of the Bible?

Be a Wise Manager

Luke 16:1-31
Key Verse: 16:9

> *"I tell you, use worldly wealth to gain friends for yourselves,*
> *so that when it is gone, you will be welcomed into eternal*
> *dwellings."*

HERE ARE TWO PARABLES in this chapter: the Parable of the Shrewd Manager (1-18) and the Parable of the Rich Man and Lazarus (19-31). There are many different verses to understand in this chapter, but the point is very clear. In these parables, Jesus teaches his disciples to use worldly wealth to win many friends over to God. When their wealth is gone, they will be welcomed into eternal dwellings. The second parable of the rich man and Lazarus is a good illustration of a man who lived a pleasure-seeking life on earth only to face agony in hell.

I.   Use worldly wealth to gain friends (1-18)

Jesus told his disciples a parable. Jesus' disciples should possess several kinds of qualities. First, they must have a high-level scholarly attitude in learning about God, man, and the world. Second, they have to be leaders who can lead God's children in any adverse situation to victory and success and train them to be strong future leaders. Third, they must have ability as managers or administrators. In this parable, Jesus teaches his disciples to be wise managers.

Jesus tells his disciples a story about a shrewd manager. Read verses 1-7. When this man was proven guilty of wasting his master's possessions, he found that he was in trouble. He was too weak to dig. He was too proud to beg. He was going to be fired. He could have become fatalistic. But he did not. He immediately devised a plan of how to live after being fired. Verse 8a says, "The master commended the dishonest manager." Why did he commend him even when this manager made the master suffer loss by giving his debtors drastic reductions? There are two reasons.

First, he was wise because he made a plan for the future. Read verse 4. "I know what I'll do so that, when I lose my job here, people will welcome me into their houses." The master did not commend him because he was dishonest, but because he was wise—wise enough to think about his future destiny and devise a counterplan. Foolish people work for immediate benefits. Foolish people live for today, not for tomorrow. Furthermore, foolish people do not prepare themselves for their future destiny. Foolish people only live for the physical life and try to please their physical bodies. Foolish people cannot see spiritual realities. Only wise men have the gift of foresight. This dishonest manager was, in a sense, wise despite his dishonesty.

Second, he was wise because he managed to work things out. At that time, the manager could do nothing. But he was not frustrated by his situation. When he thought about his situation, it was dark. But he did not think that he had no way. In a discouraging situation it is not easy for anyone to keep on thinking. But he kept on thinking until he was fully inspired about what to do. When he was inspired, he snapped his fingers and said, "Yeah! That's it!" Finally, he found a way to work out his adverse situation to make the best possible future.

This manager made good use of his authority. He boldly reduced the debts of the debtors of his master. He gave benefits to the debtors at a loss to his master. In this way, he made many friends among the debtors of his master so that when he lost his job he could be helped by those friends whom he made during his time in office. Read verses 5-7. "So he called in each one of his master's debtors. He asked the first, 'How much do you owe my master?' 'Eight hundred gallons of olive oil,' he replied. The manager told him, 'Take your bill, sit down quickly, and make it four hundred.' Then he asked the second, 'And how much do you owe?' 'A thousand bushels of wheat,' he replied. He told him, 'Take your bill and make it eight hundred.'" This manager was very shrewd. He knew how to deal with the situations, be they good or bad. He knew how to get out of trouble. He knew the difficult situation. He used the owner's wealth shrewdly and found a way out of the difficulty. From a worldly point of view, he was a man of wisdom.

Read verse 8b. "For the people of this world are more shrewd in dealing with their own kind than are the people of the light." When Jesus saw the people of the world, they were doing their best. The people of the world do their best to do the things of the world. They are admirable in their zeal, diligence, and desire to fulfill their goals. They do their best. They take drastic measures if necessary to meet the needs in fulfilling their goals. I heard that the son of a bean curd company president delivers the bean curds himself for all the restaurant's orders. He eats only food made of bean curd when he goes to a restaurant with his friends in order to promote the bean curd industry. We see how researchers in every field of scholarship strive to see new results or invent something new. During the last 30-year period, the communists' single goal has been to conquer the whole world with communism. For this, they live up to their own kind of moral standards. They live according to their communist principles. They sacrifice themselves heroically for their ideology.

Jesus told this parable to his disciples so that they might be better and wise managers. The disciples' first and last task is to serve God. Read verse 9. "I tell you, use worldly wealth to gain friends for yourselves, so that when it is gone, you will be welcomed into eternal dwellings." When we hear the word "wealth," most people immediately think of money. But money is just a small part of a man's wealth. To wise men, their health can come before money. To them, higher wealth can be knowledge, potentiality, youth, the spirit of conquest, dreams, idealism, and so on. Jesus teaches them to use their wealth unsparingly in doing God's work. Jesus' saying, "Use worldly wealth to gain friends for yourselves," is similar to the truth expressed in Deuteronomy 6:5, "Love the Lord your God with all your heart and with all your soul and with all your strength." In serving God, we must use worldly wealth and our heart, soul, and strength. But how easy it is for us to serve God habitually.

Jesus himself showed many good examples of how to be a good manager of God's world. Jesus was very popular while he was ministering to the sick and needy. Thousands of people followed him. But he was not interested in the mob of people, nor did he care about his own popularity. He gave his attention mostly to raising the twelve disciples for the future generations. Humanly speaking, he ran an unproductive business. But see how wise he was that he raised the Twelve.

Once Jesus saw a blind beggar crying by the roadside, but he had no way to help this man. Jesus had no medical instruments. But he did have a way. He spit on the ground, made some mud with the saliva, and put it on the man's eyes (Jn 9:1-7).

Another time, Jesus went on a retreat with his disciples. A large crowd of 5,000 people came to him and did not go away. Then Jesus fed them all with five loaves and two fish. Nothing was impossible for Jesus who had the spirit of a wise manager. We see in history many wise managers in God's world.

The early Christians went to Rome according to the world mission command of Jesus to evangelize the whole world. They were persecuted and killed. They had no place to put their feet. They lived in catacombs. But they had a way. They kept their faith. Faith was their wealth. Finally, they conquered the whole world through Rome.

Sometimes we want to serve God wholeheartedly. But we don't know how to serve him. This is the reason why Jesus asked Peter three times, "Do you love me?" Each time when Peter answered, "You know that I love you," Jesus said, "Feed my lambs" (Jn 21). The disciples can serve God when they feed God's flock. They can serve God when they take care of his lost children. This is the best way to serve God.

Read verse 10. "Whoever can be trusted with very little can also be trusted with much, and whoever is dishonest with very little will also be dishonest with much." This verse tells us that those who do their best with small things can do their best with many things, and they are those who are trustworthy and faithful and useful to God our King Jesus. But those who are dishonest with small things can be dishonest in everything. In short, those who do not use small worldly wealth for God are not worthy to enjoy heavenly wealth. They are dishonest before God. What is worse, those who did not use worldly wealth according to God's will cannot gain the wealth of the kingdom of heaven (11). Those who have not been trustworthy with God's property while on earth cannot get God's inheritance in heaven (12).

Many people think that they can serve God and the world at the same time. They hope that they can be wonderful Christians and at the same time, outstanding figures in the world. But this is Satan's deception. Read verse 13a. "No servant can serve two masters. Either he will hate the one and love the other, or he will be devoted to the one and despise the other." Why is this so? Because man has one heart. Those who think that they can serve God and the world at the same time are men of great mistakes and intellectual suicide. Therefore Jesus said in the last part of verse 13, "You cannot serve both God and Money." Jesus' disciples should not make money for the sake of money. His disciples must use money for the glory of God.

What was the response to Jesus' teaching? Look at verse 14. "The Pharisees, who loved money, heard all this and were sneering at Jesus." Why did they sneer? Those Pharisees who heard Jesus' teaching to use worldly wealth unsparingly in establishing the kingdom of God thought that Jesus' teachings were unrealistic and nothing but an empty discussion. They thought if it was realistic, it was only for religious fanatics, like Jesus and his disciples who were penniless. Throughout all generations, worldly people have sneered at faithful Christians who are serious about Jesus' teachings. Christians should not be afraid of them or imitate them. The Pharisees appeared to be most religious and pious. But they were not good managers of God. In their hearts, they loved money more than God. Jesus rebuked them, "You are the ones who justify yourselves in the eyes of men, but God knows your hearts. What is highly valued among men is detestable in God's sight" (15).

Jesus saw that they rejected his teachings blindly. Jesus knew that they rejected his teachings because they did not believe God's promises. Jesus told them how God had continually given them his words. Until John the Baptist, the Law and the prophecies had been proclaimed to them. So they heard the word of God sufficiently. And by the coming of Jesus, the good news of the kingdom of God was being preached, and everyone was forcing his way into it. They heard the word of God in both the Old Testament and New Testament times. They saw with their own eyes that many were eager to repent and were dashing toward the kingdom of God. The Pharisees loved money and rejected his words. They are like those who divorce with many excuses. Their true motive for divorce is to commit adultery (18). But the day will come when they will see that the promises of God are true. Read verse 17. "It is easier for heaven and earth to disappear than for the least stroke of a pen to drop out of the Law."

II. The result of a pleasure-seeking lifestyle (19-31)

Part II is a story that shows the result of a pleasure-seeking lifestyle. Most people do not accept the word of God mainly because they love the pleasures of the world. This was also the Pharisees' problem. But those who waste their money, wealth, and lives for the pleasures of the world must some day give an account.

Read verses 19-21. There was a rich man who lived in luxury every day. He was dressed in purple and fine linen. He enjoyed his pleasures by eating and drinking and chatting endlessly among rich people. Probably his companions were landlords, usurers, and politicians. In contrast, Lazarus, covered with sores, would swallow his saliva while watching them eat deliciously. He longed to eat what fell from the rich man's table. But he could not. He could not get anything from him, not even the leftovers from his table. Probably Lazarus ate by the alms of passersby. The rich man was indifferent toward him. The dogs came and comforted him by licking his sores. But he was never comforted by the rich man who lived in luxury.

When the time came, both Lazarus and the rich man died. The angel carried the beggar to Abraham's side and the rich man to hell. The rich man thought that he would live forever in the world in luxury, enjoying the pleasures of the world. He had never imagined that he would get old and die. He had never realized that he was dashing into eternal condemnation. He was blinded by his corrupted way of life. He didn't know what he was really doing. He thought the pleasure-seeking way of life was the best way, not knowing that it was a most serious crime before God, as one who wasted God's property by indulging in sins. In hell, the rich man was in torment and looked up and saw Abraham far away with Lazarus by his side. In his agony in hell's fire he begged, "Father Abraham, have pity on me and send Lazarus to dip the tip of his finger in water and cool my tongue, because I am in agony in this fire." He had never given anything to Lazarus, but now he wanted Lazarus to run an errand for him.

What did Abraham say to him? Read verse 25. "But Abraham replied, 'Son, remember that in your lifetime you received your good things, while Lazarus received bad things, but now he is comforted here and you are in agony.'" Abraham reminded him of how he had lived a selfish and pleasure-seeking life and what the result of it was: eternal agony in hell. But he couldn't do anything further because he had spent his life in seeking pleasure and his life was now no more. His lifetime, during which he could have done many good things, had passed away. He cannot live his life again. During his lifetime, he could have repented of his sins, but his life passed away. He thought he had everything. But he found that he had lost everything and was in hell. There is a great chasm between those who go through the narrow door and those who go through the wide door, a chasm which cannot be retrieved (26).

The rich man realized that his brothers should not join him where he was. So he said to Abraham in verses 27-28, "Then I beg you, father, send Lazarus to my father's house, for I have five brothers. Let him warn them, so that they will not also come to this place of torment." His begging for pity on his brothers did not move Abraham. Abraham replied, "They have Moses and the Prophets; let them listen to them" (29). Therefore, it was not necessary for Lazarus to go. The rich man's fundamental problem was that he did not believe in the authority of the Bible. He ignored the Bible's teaching about the promises of God because he couldn't see God with physical eyes. He chose to go through the wide door by the broad way, which led him to eternal destruction.

What did the man do next? In his desperation, he begged again. "'No, father Abraham,' he said, 'but if someone from the dead goes to them, they will repent'" (30). He regretted that he did not repent and was perishing in the fires of hell. In reality, his life on earth was a succession of regret, as well as a succession of escape from God's truth. He hoped that somehow he might help his brothers repent by sending

Lazarus from the dead. But Abraham told him that it would not work. Read verse 31. "He said to him, 'If they do not listen to Moses and the Prophets, they will not be convinced even if someone rises from the dead.'" This verse tells us that man cannot truly repent by means of a spectacular advertisement, such as news from the dead.

I heard a story about a woman who rose from the dead one day after she died. She told all her villagers that she had been to hell and heaven and that hell is really a terrible place and heaven is paradise. Then all the villagers decided to attend church. But after one month, the villagers dropped out of church one by one until nobody went to church. Finally, the woman who had been to hell and heaven also decided not to go to church. This sounds funny. But the story tells us that repentance is possible for each person only through the living word of God. Each person must stand before the truth all by himself and choose his destiny in God's word.

Lesson 44

The Kingdom of God Is within You

Luke 17:1-37
Key Verse: 17:21b

I. FOUR BASIC RESPONSIBILITIES (1-19)

1. What is the first basic responsibility which Jesus' disciples must have toward all people? How serious is it to be the cause of someone else's fall into sin?

2. What double responsibility do we have toward a Christian brother who sins? To what extent must we go in rebuking and/or forgiving?

3. How did the apostles respond to Jesus' teaching about these first two responsibilities? Why did they ask for more faith? How can faith be increased? (6)

4. Summarize the parable of the unworthy servant. What basic attitude toward God and what basic responsibility toward duty does this parable teach?

5. Who did Jesus meet on his way to Jerusalem and where did he meet them? What did they want from Jesus and what did he do for them?

6. How was the one Samaritan leper different from the other lepers? What does Jesus teach about a person's basic responsibility to give thanks to God?

II. THE KINGDOM OF GOD IS WITHIN YOU (20-37)

7. When Jesus was asked when the kingdom of God would come, what did he teach about the kingdom? (20-21) What do you think this means?

8. To whom does Jesus refer when he speaks of the Son of Man? What future event is he talking about? What must happen before the Son of Man comes in glory? (22-25)

9. How would the days of Noah before the flood be like the days before the second coming of Jesus? What does this analogy teach us about God? About man? How should we live in light of this teaching?

10. How does the story of Lot reinforce this teaching? What lesson should we learn from Lot's wife? What do you think verse 37 means?

11. What do verses 20-37 teach about the kingdom of God? How should we live in light of this teaching?

The Kingdom of God Is within You

Luke 17:1-37
Key Verse: 17:21b

"... because the kingdom of God is within you."

CHAPTERS 17 AND 18 tell us the basic qualifications of those who can enter the kingdom of God. When we study chapter 17 carefully, we learn that there are two parts: first, warnings to those who are preparing to enter the kingdom of God (1-19); and second, the coming of the kingdom of God is not material, but spiritual (20-37). The kingdom of God does not come idealistically, but it begins in our hearts.

I. Four basic responsibilities (1-19)

In verses 1-19 Jesus teaches his disciples four basic responsibilities to keep as his disciples and as the people of the kingdom of God.

First, we should not cause others to sin. Read verse 1. "Jesus said to his disciples: 'Things that cause people to sin are bound to come, but woe to that person through whom they come.'" In verse 1, Jesus admits that the world is full of temptation and mischief.

Here in verse 1, "cause people to sin" has two meanings. First, it means to cause others to yield to temptation. As we know, human beings are corrupt and curious about sin. And yet, everyone wants to keep his or her genuineness, nobility, and purity in particular. This holy desire might be man's true heart's desire. But because of all kinds of temptations, innumerable people fall into sin. Because of sin, man becomes impure and loses his spirit. Second, it means to cause others to drift away from their faith in the kingdom of God. This sin causes one to transfer his membership from the kingdom of God to the kingdom of Satan, from the sonship of God to slavery to Satan. The sin of causing others to sin grieves God most. "It would be better for him to be thrown into the sea with a millstone tied around his neck than for him to cause one of these little ones to sin" (2).

Second, we must rebuke and forgive. Read verse 3. "So watch yourselves. If your brother sins, rebuke him, and if he repents, forgive him." This is our Lord's command. But these days many people say, "You do your work and I'll do mine. Don't bother me and I won't bother you." Not bothering others seems to be the social consensus of these days. But this is based on irresponsibility and indifference.

The societies in which we live are permissive of sins. Indulgence in the permissiveness of sin is not generosity; it is irresponsibility. Without God's heart, no one can rebuke others. Corrupted people cannot rebuke others; only spiritual people can rebuke others. We must rebuke others if we love God. We cannot abandon our brothers who are falling into eternal destruction. We must follow the example of Joseph in the Old Testament. He is the kind of exemplary good person that God wants to raise up on the earth. He is a shadow of the Christ. He looked too nice to rebuke others, but he rebuked his brothers until they repented. In doing this, he cried many tears. Jesus said, "Those whom I love I rebuke and discipline" (Rev 3:19). If we love our brothers, we must be fully qualified to rebuke them.

Read verse 3 again. In this verse, Jesus commands us to forgive our brother if he repents. Throughout history, there were many heroes who did many great things. But when we read Plutarch's Lives, we find that most of them died harboring enmity for their enemies. They were conquerors, but they could not conquer themselves. They could not overcome their hostile feelings toward others. They were not mature enough to forgive others. But Jesus forgave all our sins, so we must learn how to forgive others' sins. Jesus urges his disciples to forgive seven times a day the one who repents (4). Matthew 18:22 says to forgive seventy-seven times. This means that we must forgive endlessly those who repent.

How did the disciples respond? They were startled by Jesus' teaching. At the same time, they realized that they did not have enough faith to do this. So they said to the Lord, "Increase our faith!" (5). Perhaps they thought they needed more faith in order to forgive others seven times a day. But Jesus taught them that faith is not a matter of quantity, but quality. So he said, "If you have faith as small as a mustard seed, you can say to this mulberry tree, 'Be uprooted and planted in the sea,' and it will obey you" (6). Faith, however small it may be, has absolute power, for God's power works in it. Faith is everything. With our human strength, forgiving someone may not be possible; however, with the power of faith in God it is possible for us.

Third, we must have a humble attitude as his servants. Read verses 7-9. This parable tells us that a servant worked all day long in the field, perhaps from 5:30 a.m. to 7:30 p.m., from sunrise to sunset. But when the day was over, the servant came back home. Then the master said, "Prepare my supper, get yourself ready and wait on me while I eat and drink; after that you may eat and drink (8)." The authority of the master is so absolute that the slave is but, as it were, an animated instrument in the hand of the master. He has no will of his own and no claims to personal rights. But the servant must work no matter what the master demands, and the master does not even have to say, "Thank you." This was the situation of servants in those times.

But Jesus told his disciples this story to teach them the relationship between men and God. Read verse 10. "So you also, when you have done everything you were told to do, should say, 'We are unworthy servants; we have only done our duty.'" This teaches us the basic attitude of a servant of God. Paul said in Romans 1:1, "Paul, a servant of Christ Jesus ..." He meant that he was a slave of God because he had been ransomed by the blood of Jesus from slavery to sin. However, the Christian conception of "slavery" is quite different from that of the secular world. A "slave" of God is one who knows God's love and grace. Therefore, God's "slave" is one who willingly serves God while experiencing his grace and love, not one who is controlled by force. Because of this love relationship, the children of God are faithful all the time.

Fourth, we must learn how to thank God (11-19). The story about ten men with leprosy is a story which most adequately teaches that man must learn how to thank God or his benefactor. Who is a Christian? He is the one who knows how to thank God.

Now Jesus was on his way to Jerusalem. On the border between Galilee and Samaria, he was met by a band of ten men with leprosy. We know that the Jews had no dealings with the Samaritans. Samaritans were Israelites themselves, but since the time in history when they were divided into two parts—Northern Israel (Samaria) and Southern Israel (Judah) — They had become each other's worst enemy. Hostility and enmity grew between them until they had no dealings with each other. There were ten men born in this tragic national background. They were men with leprosy. Because of leprosy, they could not identify themselves as citizens of the country they lived in. They lived on the borderline. But under the common tragedy of leprosy, they had forgotten that they were Jews and Samaritans and only remembered that they were men in need. Surely one of the things which should draw all men together is their common need of God. As Jesus was going into a village, the ten men who had leprosy met him. "They stood at a distance and called out in a loud voice, 'Jesus, Master, have pity on us!'" (12b-13).

When Jesus saw them, he did not cleanse them, but ordered them to go to the priests. Jesus wanted to know if they had faith to obey his words. Jesus also wanted them to get medical certificates from the priests so that they might be accepted into society where they could enjoy normal lives. These men with leprosy obeyed the words of Jesus in their desperate condition.

What happened when they obeyed and went to see the priests? Verse 14b says, "And as they went, they were cleansed." They did not know the reason why they had to go to the priests whom they did not like. But they obeyed his words absolutely. They were healed wholly in consequence of their faith.

It was a great miracle that they were all healed from their leprosy. Therefore, all of them should have come back to Jesus and bowed their faces to the ground in gratitude. But they didn't. Read verses 15 and 16. "One of them, when he saw he was healed, came back, praising God in a loud voice. He threw himself at Jesus' feet and thanked him—and he was a Samaritan." Nine of them who were healed were Jews. They did not come back to Jesus. As soon as they were healed, they went away to do something they wanted to do. Maybe they wanted to see a football game so that they could satisfy their desire to mingle with a mob of people. No story in human history so poignantly shows man's ingratitude. How could it be that they did not remember the grace of Jesus? Why did all the lepers go away while a Samaritan leper showed up before Jesus in exaltation and thanksgiving? Nine Jewish lepers were healed of their leprosy, but they still remained as spiritual lepers.

We can easily see the total depravity of human beings. When we read the book of Judges, the phrase, "The Israelites once again did evil in the eyes of the Lord," is repeated from the beginning to the end. Because of their sins, whenever they became impoverished or lived in distress, they cried out to the Lord again and again. God delivered them whenever they cried out to him. No sooner had they lived in peace and prosperity than they rejected God again. The Israelites had never appreciated God's grace of deliverance.

Nobody can thank God naturally. Each person must learn how to thank God. If one masters how to thank God, he is already a great man. But it is not easy at all to thank God in any circumstance. It requires a lot of struggling. Hezekiah was one of the prominent kings among the kings of Judah. Once he became ill and was at the point of death. He prayed to the Lord, who answered him and gave him a miraculous sign. He should have thanked God, but his heart was proud, and he did not respond to the kindness shown him (2Ch 32:25). When he forgot how to thank God, he became stupid. The most difficult thing in the world for each person is to not forget God's grace and remember it to the end.

Read verses 17 and 18. "Jesus asked, 'Were not all ten cleansed? Where are the other nine? Was no one found to return and give praise to God except this foreigner?'" Jesus was very sorry that even his own people who had been men with leprosy did not know how to thank God when they were cured. But the Samaritan was different. He came back and gave thanks. Jesus said to the Samaritan who had returned, "Rise and go; your faith has made you well" (19). In light of Jesus' blessing on the Samaritan, we learn that thanksgiving to God is the first step in having faith in God.

II. The kingdom of God is within you (20-37)

The Pharisees abandoned the basic life of faith before God, ignoring the problem of sin, belief, and duty as human beings before God. Ironically, they expected the kingdom would come. It was not in accordance with the Scriptures, but based on the political ideology of the earthly messianic kingdom for the people of Israel.

How did Jesus respond? Read verses 20b and 21. "The kingdom of God does not come with your careful observation, nor will people say, 'Here it is,' or 'There it is,' because the kingdom of God is within you." The kingdom of God is not a visible or physical phenomenon that is temporal, but it is a spiritual one that is eternal.

What does it mean, "the kingdom of God is within you?" This explains plainly the character of the kingdom of God. The kingdom of God is like a mustard seed. It grows, becomes a tree, and the birds of the air perch in its branches. The kingdom of God works in men's hearts. It transforms the hearts of men. It works to produce new people. The kingdom of God is right there where Jesus is.

Fanny Crosby was a shy and pretty blind woman. She lived in darkness and sorrow. But since meeting Jesus, light dawned in her heart. She was no longer sorrowful because the joy of the kingdom of God grew more and more in her heart. She became a famous hymn writer. One of her best hymns begins with the words, "I am Thine, O Lord; I have heard thy voice."

Verses 22-37 speak of the second coming of Jesus. Out of this difficult passage we learn two things: we should watch out for false messiahs, and we must live faithfully before God doing our duties.

First, Jesus warns us not to go running after false messiahs. Read verse 22. "Then he said to his disciples, 'The time is coming when you will long to see one of the days of the Son of Man, but you will not see it.'" The world has ever been getting worse. All the people of the world long to see the Messiah, the Savior of the world. Christians especially long for the coming of Christ, for this is the only ultimate solution to men's problems.

Read verse 23. "Men will tell you, 'There he is!' or 'Here he is!' Do not go running off after them." During the 1940s and 1950s, people ran after democracy and communism, thinking that they could be messiahs. These days, since they despaired in looking for messiahs in ideologies, most people live as if pleasure-seeking were their messiah. But the Son of Man does not come, saying, "There he is," or "Here he is." The Son of Man in his day will come suddenly like lightning which flashes and lights up the sky from one end to the other (24). But this could not happen before his crucifixion (25).

Second, Jesus warns them not to indulge in worldly pleasures (26-37). In the last days when Jesus comes and judges, people will be eating and drinking, marrying and being given in marriage, just as in the days of Noah (26-27). In the last days people will be busy buying and selling, planting and building, as in the days of Lot. But the day Lot left Sodom, fire and sulfur rained down from heaven and destroyed them all. All the material wealth they loved burned down (28-29).

When the time is ripe and the Son of Man comes again, people will again be busy eating and drinking, acquiring material things, and buying and selling. But when the Son of Man comes again, their efforts to save any material things will be useless, for it is the Day of Judgment. If anyone wants to preserve anything, he will be like Lot's wife who looked back at Sodom with lingering affection over her private properties and became a pillar of salt. According to Jesus, we must "Remember Lot's wife!" (32).

In the last days, it is not easy for anyone not to be attached to material things and not to try to preserve his life. But verse 33 says, "Whoever tries to keep his life will lose it, and whoever loses his life will preserve it." When the Son of Man comes again, some will be taken and the others left. Read verses 34 and 35. "I tell you, on that night two people will be in one bed; one will be taken and the other left. Two women will be grinding grain together; one will be taken and the other left."

It is certain that the Son of Man will come again, but nobody knows the day when he will come. When they asked Jesus when all this would happen, he answered by quoting a well-known proverb, "Where there is a dead body, there the vultures will gather" (37). This simply means that it will happen when the necessary conditions are fulfilled. God will bring Jesus Christ again in his good time. Therefore, we must spiritually wake up and live faithful lives before God.

Lesson 45

Always Pray and Not Give Up

Luke 18:1-14
Key Verse: 18:1

I. PERSISTENT PRAYER (1-8)

1. To whom did Jesus tell this parable? What did he want to teach them?

2. What kind of person was the judge in the parable? In what respect does he contrast with the image of a shepherd?

3. What did the widow want? What characterized her asking attitude?

4. Why did the judge finally relent and give her what she wanted?

5. How is God's attitude toward his people different from that of the unjust judge? Why should God's people cry out to him day and night?

6. What surprising thing will Jesus find when he comes again? What should this parable teach us about prayer?

II. HUMBLE PRAYER (9-14)

7. To whom did Jesus address this parable?

8. Who were the two men who prayed in the temple? How did the Pharisee pray and what was wrong with his prayer?

9. What was the attitude and prayer topic of the tax collector?

10. What was God's response to each prayer? What can we learn here about prayer?

Always Pray and Not Give Up

Luke 18:1-14
Key Verse: 18:1

> *"Then Jesus told his disciples a parable to show them that they should always pray and not give up."*

T HERE ARE TWO PARTS in this passage. The first is the Parable of the Persistent Widow (1-8) in which Jesus taught his disciples that they should always pray and not give up. The second is the Parable of the Pharisee and the Tax Collector (9-14) in which Jesus taught his disciples that they should be humble before God when they pray.

I. Persistent prayer (1-8)

Luke mentioned the days of the Son of Man in 17:22-37. The days of the Son of Man will be the last days of the world. In the last days, many people will be in great distress because of their sins. Many will long to see the Messiah, the one who can save them from the miseries of their sin. False messiahs who know the weaknesses of men and women will arise to devour them. There will be confusion and frustration because of false messiahs.

In the last days, godless people will only eat and drink and buy and sell, just as in the days of Noah and the days of Lot. They will live without God and become violent and corrupt and live in perversion. According to Genesis 3:19, this kind of life is a cursed life. The Israelites' slavery to the Egyptians is a good example of this. The Israelites were willing to work hard if only they could eat and sleep. In order to eat and sleep, they would do anything the Egyptians demanded.

In their vague anxiety, they are busy-minded and restless. In order to overcome their restlessness and despair and fear, they indulge in many unnatural things, such as sexual immorality and drug abuse. By any available means they want to keep themselves busy; otherwise, they feel very uneasy. But in the last days, the people of God should not be pointlessly busy-minded. Then what should they do? They should pray instead of despairing. In the last days, the most difficult thing in the world to do is to pray while people are going crazy. In the last days, another difficult thing to do is not give up while living in the midst of a despaired culture. But Jesus wants his disciples to pray and not give up.

Read verse 1. "Then Jesus told his disciples a parable to show them that they should always pray and not give up." Jesus told his disciples that they should pray. They should pray, not just for one or two days, but "always." Here the adverb "always" includes both times of happiness and times of discouragement, even times when prayers are not answered. They should always pray without losing heart. In order to teach his disciples to pray persistently, Jesus told them a parable.

Read verse 2. "He said: 'In a certain town there was a judge who neither feared God nor cared about men.'" This judge is not the kind of judge we usually see in the Bible. In Israel, there were always three judges among the elders: one chosen by the prosecutor, one by the defendant, and one independently appointed. The judge in this parable must have been one of the magistrates appointed by the Roman imperialists for the benefit of the Empire. The judge in the parable did not fear God. Psalm 53:1-4 says that those who do not fear God say, "There is no God." They are like fools who cover their eyes with their hands and say that there is no sky. "They are corrupt, and their ways are vile." They devour God's people as men eat bread. This kind of judge is too proud to have an eye for anyone as long as he is in power. This kind of judge is generous to powerful people and mean to weak people. This kind of judge is so insolent and audacious and unjust.

Read verse 3. "And there was a widow in that town who kept coming to him with the plea, 'Grant me justice against my adversary.'" At that time, a widow was a symbol of all the poor and defenseless. She had no hope of extracting justice from such a judge. As a widowed woman, sorrowing over herself and remembering all the good days in the past must have been her habit. Crying many tears must have been her way of comforting herself. She must have been too sensitive to ask anybody to do something for her. She must have been easily hurt and wounded. She must have been a woman who got mad at her neighbor's dog barking at night. But she overcame her human feelings and conditions and kept on going to this judge to get justice. She was a persistent woman.

What did the judge do for this woman? Read verse 4a. "For some time he refused ..." When she visited him at his office for the first time, he refused, saying, "What can I do, ma'am? Well, I will give you a call." When she visited him for the second time he refused again, saying, "Well, please excuse me. I will let you know what I can do for you by mail." Then she met him on the street in front of his office; the next time, in front of his home; the next time, at the restaurant; the next time, at a party.

How did he deal with this persistent woman? Read verses 4b and 5. "Even though I don't fear God or care about men, yet because this widow keeps bothering me, I will see that she gets justice, so that she won't eventually wear me out with her coming!" This judge was a tough man who could ignore God in heaven and men on earth. When he decided something, he didn't consider the situations of others.

But he was worried about her pestering. He said to himself, "Well, I cannot refuse her anymore. What can I do if she comes again in the middle of the night? It has already been seven months, but she never stops coming. What shall I do if she keeps on coming? Even though she did not come yesterday, I met her in my dreams last night all night. It's better for me that she gets justice so that she won't eventually wear me out with her coming." This judge was afraid of her persistence and yielded to her pleading. Her persistence was like mental violence to him. Her persistence was like the saying which goes, "Little strokes fell great oaks."

What did Jesus want to teach his disciples with this parable? Read verses 6-8. "And the Lord said, 'Listen to what the unjust judge says. And will not God bring about justice for his chosen ones, who cry out to him day and night? Will he keep putting them off? I tell you, he will see that they get justice, and quickly.'" Here, "justice" is God's justice. In the Bible, God's justice is always accompanied by his peace and love. Our God is the God of justice and the God of love (Isa 11:4a). To "see that they get justice" means that he will restore his sovereign rule in the world. So it is the prayer of his people that he comes and rules us with justice and love.

In order to pray to bring about God's justice, what should the prayer topics of the people of God be?

First, the Lord's Prayer should be the prayer topic of the people of God. Read Matthew 6:9-13. "This, then, is how you should pray: 'Our Father in heaven, hallowed be your name, your kingdom come, your will be done on earth as it is in heaven. Give us today our daily bread. Forgive us our debts, as we also have forgiven our debtors. And lead us not into temptation, but deliver us from the evil one.'" The people of God must pray in the last days that all peoples of all nations may call God, "our Father," and recognize his sovereign rule in history. The people of God must pray that all peoples of all nations may hallow his name, honoring God as God. The people of God must pray most of all that his kingdom may be expanded more and more. The people of God must pray that God's will for world salvation be fulfilled on earth as it is in heaven. The people of God must pray, not only for their own welfare, but for all the children of God in the world to be provided with daily bread. The people of God must have a sense of debt to all peoples of all nations. The people of God must ask for God's mercy so that God may protect them from the evil one.

Another prayer topic of the people of God is for the second coming of Jesus. "Come, Lord Jesus" (Rev 22:20b). This should be the first and last prayer topic for the people of God, for the second coming of Jesus in glory and power will be the final solution to all the problems of the world. Why is it so? As we know well, people throughout generations have tried to improve the world. They have tried to establish a utopia in which man can be happy. But all of their efforts have been in vain. The world is still getting worse and worse with no hope for the future. But when he comes again, it will be the day when God brings about his justice. There will be no more curses, no more tears. There will be no more pain and sickness. There will be a new heaven and new earth. His chosen people will be changed into the likeness of Jesus, glorious and splendid. At the same time, he judges all the wicked people. This is the day of victory for the saints. But for the wicked this is the day of judgment and punishment.

Second, God answers the prayers of his chosen people. Read verse 8. "I tell you, he will see that they get justice ..." This verse clearly tells us that he answers our prayers. Of course, it is not easy for us to pray that God's will be done on earth while we live among godless people. The world seems to be too dark to do anything for God. The world is filled with people who seek physical pleasures, liars, and those who are proud-minded and who love money. Many people pray for what they can believe, but they do not pray for what they cannot believe. Many people pray for the recovery of a patient in bed or for getting a good job or for buying a proper house. In brief, they pray for better eating or sleeping in this world. But most people do not pray for the will of God to be done. Why do they not pray for this fundamental prayer topic? It is because it seems to be impossible for them to believe that God's will can be done when they see the selfish and sick people of the world. That is not faith that prays.

But we must believe God's promise that he answers our prayers. Before the power of the world, we become helpless. We feel as if we are paralyzed even before beginning to do anything for the glory of God. But we can be courageous because we believe that God hears our prayers. 1 John 5:14-15 says, "This is the confidence we have in approaching God: that if we ask anything according to his will, he hears us. And if we know that he hears us—whatever we ask—we know that we have what we asked of him."

Third, prayer is the most potent weapon for the people of God. Prayer is a measure of faith. We can do nothing. But when we pray, God can do a mighty work through us. One morning, his disciples saw that the fig tree Jesus had cursed had withered from the roots overnight. Peter was surprised at the power of Jesus' word and said, "Rabbi, look! The fig tree you cursed has withered!" Then Jesus said to him, "Have faith in God." Jesus kept on saying, "Therefore I tell you, whatever you ask for in prayer, believe that you have received it, and it will be yours" (Mk 11:20-24).

6

Fourth, the people of God must pray persistently. Read verse 7 again. "And will not God bring about justice for his chosen ones, who cry out to him day and night?" This verse encourages the people of God to pray persistently, day and night. Jesus showed us many good examples. His disciples were nothing but uneducated country boys. They had no hope of being the future cornerstones of his church. But Jesus believed and prayed for them to the end. As he prayed, they all became indispensable characters in his work and history. The disciples of Jesus received the world mission command, "Go into all the world and preach the good news to all creation" (Mk 16:15). They were too weak to do anything. If they had thought about this command logically and calculated how possible it would be for them, they would have despaired even before starting. But they did not calculate. They believed that they could not do it, but that God could do it through them, and they persistently prayed for world mission in one accord. Then God enabled them to do the work of world mission.

Here we see Jesus' sorrow in verse 8b. "However, when the Son of Man comes, will he find faith on the earth?" When he comes again, he will look for those who have faith that prays. But he will not find many. Jesus wants his people to pray persistently to bring his justice on earth until he comes again.

II. Humble prayer (9-14)

Jesus tells the Parable of the Pharisee and the Tax Collector in verses 9-14 to teach his disciples that they should pray with a humble attitude. He introduced a story of two men who went up to the temple to pray, one a Pharisee and the other a tax collector.

Read verses 11 and 12. "The Pharisee stood up and prayed about himself: 'God, I thank you that I am not like other men—robbers, evildoers, adulterers—or even like this tax collector. I fast twice a week and give a tenth of all I get.'" There's no doubt that all that the Pharisee said was true. He fasted. He meticulously gave tithes. He was not like others, much less a tax collector. But he was not right before God.

First, he prayed before men, not before God. Usually the devout Jews prayed three times daily at 9:00 am, midday, and 3:00 p.m. It was especially efficacious if they prayed in the temple. Many Pharisees prayed and fasted on Mondays and Thursdays, the market days on which Jerusalem was full of country people. The Law required fasting one time per week. But they fasted two times per week before men's eyes and prayed with their faces whitened to impress the biggest audience possible. Prayer is secret communication between God and man. But the Pharisee prayed to show himself off to people. He is like a religious prostitute who puts on heavy make-up to attract passersby. His hypocrisy is despicable. These days there are many "religious" people like this man. They never pray in the closet. They only pray before people with the finest language they can make and with dramatic showmanship. They are concerned about how to impress people for their popularity. They do not fear God.

Second, he was proud. When he prayed, he said, "I thank you that I am not like other men—robbers, evildoers, adulterers—or even like this tax collector. I fast twice a week and give a tenth of all I get" (11-12). This Pharisee did not go to pray to God, but he went to inform God of how good he was. He was very proud and looked down on others. He was nothing but a sinner who needed God's mercy and salvation. But he was self-righteous and eager to brag about his own merit. He was a disgusting person because of his proud mind. He did not know how terrible he was. What he did before the eyes of men and what he did behind the scenes were quite different. He was a hypocrite. Man's proud mind is the root of sin. This kind of person neither admits that he is a sinner or repents when he commits a serious sin before God. He does not know what kind of person he is. In reality, no man who is proud can pray. We cannot lift ourselves above our fellow man in prayer. God cannot accept a proud man's prayer.

There was also a tax collector. He stood far off and would not even look up to heaven, but beat his breast and said, "God, have mercy on me, a sinner" (13). He was a notorious sinner whose accumulated sin was greater than the Empire State Building. This man made God sorry because of his selfishness. This man hurt others so often because of his heartlessness. He was a sinner both publically and privately before God and man. He was a man who questioned whether or not he could he come to God in prayer. But what did Jesus say to him? Read verse 14a, "I tell you that this man, rather than the other, went home justified before God." The tax collector was a great sinner. But he was humble, so he was justified. The Pharisee was a good person before man's eyes, but he did not pray. He only exalted himself before God. So he was humbled and went home. This parable teaches us that no man is righteous before God and that anybody can come to God in prayer. When we pray, we must remember that we are all wretched sinners not worthy to kneel before the throne of God's mercy.

Through this passage, we learn that we should pray persistently, not for the welfare of our physical life, but for the will of God to be done on earth. We also learn that to pray for the raising of 561 American full-time shepherds is admirable to God.

Lesson 46

To Inherit Eternal Life

Luke 18:15-30
Key Verse: 18:22

I. RECEIVE THE KINGDOM OF GOD LIKE A LITTLE CHILD (15-17)

1. Why did people bring their babies to Jesus? What did they believe about Jesus? Why did the disciples rebuke the parents?

2. What did Jesus do? What does it mean that the kingdom of God belongs to such as these? Why is it that one who does not receive the kingdom of God like a child cannot enter it?

II. HOW TO INHERIT ETERNAL LIFE (18-23)

3. What do we know about the man who came to Jesus? What was his question? Why did Jesus teach him about "good"? What does his question and Jesus' counter question show about his real problem?

4. Which commandments did Jesus ask him about? Why did he ask him about the commandments concerning the love of neighbors? What does his reply show about him? What was the one thing this man lacked?

5. What was Jesus' invitation? (22-23) Why did Jesus tell him to sell everything and give to the poor? What did Jesus want him to know about loving God and loving neighbors? How did the young man respond?

III. THE BLESSED LIFE OF A DISCIPLE (24-30)

6. What was Jesus' comment about the rich young man? Why is it so hard for a rich man to enter the kingdom of heaven? What was the disciples' question? How can we be saved? What was Peter's response? What does Jesus promise in this age? In the age to come?

To Inherit Eternal Life

Luke 18:15-30
Key Verse: 18:22

> *"When Jesus heard this, he said to him, 'You still lack one thing. Sell everything you have and give to the poor, and you will have treasure in heaven. Then come, follow me.'"*

I N THE LAST PASSAGE, Jesus taught us about prayer. We learned that we must always pray and not give up. Usually we like to have instant food, instant services, and instant answers to prayer. But God does not always accommodate us in this way. Our God is great and he is absolutely sovereign. God answers prayer in his own time and in his own way. He wants us to be persistent in prayer as the expression of our faith in him.

In this passage, there are two events. In the first event, little children come to Jesus for his blessing. Through them, Jesus teaches us how to receive the kingdom of God. In the second event, a rich ruler comes to Jesus asking how he can inherit eternal life. Although Jesus lovingly teaches him how to do so, he fails. This sad event is included in all three synoptic Gospels as a warning to us. On the other hand, Jesus' disciples are found to be members of the kingdom of God who have eternal life. Let's learn from Jesus how to inherit eternal life.

I. Receive the kingdom of God like a little child (15-17)

Our Lord Jesus Christ is the Son of God. Though he came to this world in the form of a man, he is in very nature God. His touch was not the touch of an ordinary man. It was the touch of our Holy God. Miracles happened at the touch of Jesus. When Jesus touched a man with leprosy, he was healed immediately. When Jesus was touched by a woman subject to bleeding, she was healed immediately.

People recognized Jesus as the source of God's blessing. Big and small alike wanted to be touched by Jesus. Read verse 15a. "People were also bringing babies to Jesus to have him touch them." Perhaps it began with one woman bringing her little baby to Jesus. Then other parents began to bring their babies too. Soon, there was a long line of parents with babies around Jesus.

When the disciples saw what was happening, they felt Jesus might be overrun by demanding parents and crying babies. To them, it seemed like a useless burden to their ministry. They probably wanted to protect Jesus. So they began to rebuke the parents, "We are not running a nursery!" They meant well, but their strict, authoritarian manner wounded parent and child alike.

When Jesus saw the little children going away from him with tears streaming down their cheeks, he was heartbroken. So Jesus intervened. Read verse 16. "But Jesus called the children to him and said, 'Let the little children come to me, and do not hinder them, for the kingdom of God belongs to such as these.'" Jesus affectionately called their names one by one, smiling with arms open wide. They lifted up their heads, felt the love of Jesus, and went running to him with new joy and hope. No doubt, Jesus laid his hand of blessing on each one and prayed for them. Perhaps future spiritual leaders were anointed by Jesus that day.

We must know that Jesus welcomes little children. Children are ready to hear the message of the kingdom of God and believe. One five-year old boy heard his father talking seriously about heaven and hell. Because his father believes that hell is real, the little boy was convinced that hell is real. So he became quiet and serious for a few days. Then he came to his father and said, "Dad, if someone says a bad word, will they go down there?" His father told him, "Yes. But if you tell Jesus you are sorry, then he will forgive you and take you to heaven. Do you want to pray to Jesus?" The little boy thought for a moment and said, "Yes." They prayed and he accepted Jesus into his heart. After that, he was no longer serious. The simple joy of Jesus came into his heart, and in a few minutes he was playing happily. Dr. John Rice was an evangelist in America in the middle of the 20th century. He participated in many national conferences. According to his research, about half of those who became Christian did so by age fifteen. He himself accepted Christ at the age of nine. Jesus loves little children. Little children are receptive to Jesus' kingdom.

The disciples made a mistake. Jesus was sorry that they were boorish and harsh. They understood neither his heart nor the hearts of little children. Worst of all, they violated the rule of the kingdom. Jesus invites anybody and everybody to come to him personally and directly. In John 6:37, Jesus says, "All that the Father gives me will come to me, and whoever comes to me I will never drive away." The disciples had no right to hinder little ones from coming to Jesus. They must have great respect for everyone who struggles to come to Jesus. They must be shepherds who know the heart of Jesus and welcome sinners. Moreover, they had something to learn from these little ones.

Read verse 17. "I tell you the truth, anyone who will not receive the kingdom of God like a little child will never enter it." Children know how to receive things properly. When little children are loved by their parents, they receive it simply and respond with loyalty and obedience. We must receive the kingdom of God with the same attitude. We must trust and obey. When we simply trust Jesus and accept him as King in our hearts, he will protect us, provide for us, bless us, and guide us. So we obey him with loyal devotion. When we receive the kingdom of God like this, Jesus is happy to enter our hearts as Savior and King. Let's learn from little children how to receive Jesus.

II. How to inherit eternal life (18-25)

A certain ruler came to Jesus. This man had an important position, responsibility, and authority. He was also a man of great wealth (23). Many people envy rich rulers like him throughout their lifetimes, thinking that they are happy. But this man was not really happy. He came to Jesus with a big problem. He asked, "Good teacher, what must I do to inherit eternal life?" (18). This man had everything, but he could not relax and enjoy his life. The thought of death and the power of the devil had begun to harass him. Desperation was seeping into his heart little by little, day by day. This is the agony of the rich and famous.

How did Jesus answer? Read verse 19. "'Why do you call me

good?' Jesus answered. 'No one is good—except God alone.'" Jesus immediately perceived that this man did not have God in his heart. So his concept of good was based on relative humanism. This man probably thought that Jesus was good because many people followed him and that he himself was good because he graduated with honors and that life was good. Everything was good. It was easy for him to think this way when he enjoyed a privileged life. Those who suffer at the bottom of society amid tragic events would not share his concept of good. The Bible teaches us that man without God is only evil all the time (Ge 6:5). The best man is a mixture of good and evil, being good to the degree that Jesus rules his heart. Jesus said, "No one is good—except God alone" (19). God alone is good.

Therefore, we must learn God's standard of good. Jesus started with the Ten Commandments. Read verse 20. "You know the commandments: 'Do not commit adultery, do not murder, do not steal, do not give false testimony, honor your father and mother.'" It is interesting that Jesus shared only those commandments which deal with loving others. Jesus did not mention the first commandments that deal with loving God. And Jesus left out the commandment, "Do not covet." Perhaps Jesus limited his discussion to make it simple for this man to find his problem. As 1 John 4:20 says, "If anyone says, 'I love God,' yet hates his brother, he is a liar. For anyone who does not love his brother, whom he has seen, cannot love God, whom he has not seen."

How did the man answer? Read verse 21. "All these I have kept since I was a boy." How could he say that? Probably, according to the most cursory understanding of the commandments, it may have been true. The man did not kill anyone or rob a bank or break into his neighbor's house and terrorize the family. But his understanding of the commandments was shallow. He did not know the spiritual meaning at all. As Jesus taught in the Sermon on the Mount, to look at a woman lustfully is sinning in the heart, and hatred in the heart is akin to the sin of murder. This man disregarded motive in practicing the law. He is like some students who decline Bible study, saying, "I am okay," or "It's alright, I'm good," without much thought.

When Jesus heard his answer, he wanted to perform major surgery on the spot. Still, Jesus tempered his words. Read verse 22. "When Jesus heard this, he said to him, 'You still lack one thing. Sell everything you have and give to the poor, and you will have treasure in heaven. Then come, follow me.'" He lacked one thing: treasure in heaven. Jesus taught him how to have treasure in heaven.

First, "sell everything you have." As a wealthy man, he must have had many kinds of treasures among his possessions that he enjoyed and valued. When his heart was set on these things, he had no room for heavenly things. Jesus does not want us to lose our hearts to the things of the world. We must be ready to sell worldly goods for spiritual gain.

One young missionary seriously prayed about how to make his wife happy and serve campus ministry well. He came to the conclusion that he should get rid of his television. So he gave it away. Since then, he has more intimate prayer time with his wife. He has room in his heart for God's word and for his sheep. Now, even though he works full-time, he feeds ten sheep per week and several of them attend the Sunday worship service regularly. By simply getting rid of his television, he gained treasure in heaven.

Second, "give to the poor." Until now, this man seems to have shown no concern for the poor. There were so many needy ones around him. He could have helped them, but he totally ignored them. He was really selfish. Selfishness made him hard-hearted. Selfishness was like cancer to his soul. Jesus said, "Give to the poor," to help him overcome his selfishness.

One young man felt sorrowful all the time because his family situation was unstable. This sorrow consumed his thoughts and energy day and night. But a good shepherd helped him begin to think about others by telling him to make lunch for his roommate every day. At first, it was hard for him. But as he did so faithfully, a giving spirit grew in his heart. Now he has become a most compassionate shepherd. A giving life may seem heard at first, but it is the way to grow as true human beings and to know the heart of God.

Our God is the God who gave his one and only Son to sinners. John 3:16 says, "For God so loved the world that he gave his one and only Son, that whoever believes in him shall not perish but have eternal life." And what about Jesus? 2 Corinthians 8:9 says, "For you know the grace of our Lord Jesus Christ, that though he was rich, yet for your sakes he became poor, so that you through his poverty might become rich." Young people today seem to be really good at selfishness. But selfishness blinds the heart and mind and makes us evil. May God help us to practice a giving life and have treasures in heaven.

Third, "come, follow me." This was a call to discipleship. This was a most precious blessing of Jesus. Implied is Jesus' commitment to raise him in Christian character and to make him a fruitful gospel worker. It would lead him into God's redemptive history and everlasting blessing.

In the 12th century, there was a young Frenchman named Francis who was the son of a successful cloth merchant. For a time, he lived in sin with some unwholesome friends. After seeking fulfillment in romance, business, pleasure, and military glory, he was left empty and meaningless. So he began to seek God earnestly. He read Jesus' words to the ruler, "Sell everything you have and give to the poor, and you will have treasure in heaven. Then come, follow me." He accepted these words and obeyed them literally. He renounced his father's fortune and declared himself a child of his heavenly Father. He began to serve whoever he met sacrificially with whatever he had. He was persecuted a lot for his decision. But through a poor and giving life, he tasted the joy of heaven every day. The love of God grew in his heart. The image of Jesus was gradually formed in his soul. Francis' impact had a great impact on his times. Within ten years, he built a community of faith in which five thousand people began to live poorly and purely for the sake of God's kingdom. He could have lived and died as just another rich man, but when Francis obeyed Jesus' words, he became a most influential member of God's history and a true saint.

Let's return to the rich ruler. How did he respond to Jesus' challenge? Read verse 23. "When he heard this, he became very sad, because he was a man of great wealth." He could not accept Jesus' invitation. This man loved money and was a slave to it. No one can serve both God and money. He knew he should follow Jesus. But when he had to make a right decision, he had no power to do so. So he became very sad.

When Jesus saw this man's failure, he grieved over him. Read verses 24 and 25. "Jesus looked at him and said, 'How hard it is for the rich to enter the kingdom of God! Indeed, it is easier for a camel to go through the eye of a needle than for a rich man to enter the kingdom of God.'" When people hold on to the dust of the earth and forsake eternal blessings, God is really sorry. They become eternal losers. We should not envy the rich, but realize their deep inner misery and pray for them.

III. The blessed life of a disciple (26-30)

Those who heard Jesus' words were surprised and asked, "Who then can be saved?" (26). When we think about human beings, even the best people can be utterly hopeless and a source of despair. This rich ruler's failure discouraged everyone and made salvation work seem impossible. "Jesus replied, 'What is impossible with men is possible with God'" (27). Jesus turned their attention back to God. God can work miracles in any human heart to turn men back to the kingdom of God. When Peter heard Jesus talk about God, new hope came into his heart. He stopped thinking about the miserable rich ruler and began to think about God. With God all things are possible. Peter must have thought about God's work in his own life and in the lives of his fellow disciples. Then he realized that they were not like the rich ruler. They had made definite decisions of faith to leave all they had to follow Jesus. So he blurted out, "We have left all we had to follow you!" In essence it meant, "What is our reward?"

Read verses 29 and 30. "'I tell you the truth,' Jesus said to them, 'no one who has left home or wife or brothers or parents or children for the sake of the kingdom of God will fail to receive many times as much in this age and, in the age to come, eternal life.'" Jesus deeply acknowledged the sacrifices his disciples had made. Their most difficult sacrifices were not leaving behind material possessions, but their homes and family members. Jesus promised them overflowing blessings.

First of all, they would receive many times as much in this age.

This means that they would become members of his family, the church. They may have left behind one mother, but in the church of Christ they would find many spiritual mothers who would love them even more. They may have given up the chance to have children, but they would have spiritual descendants as numerous as the stars in the sky. For example, Mother Barry sacrificed her marriage and chance to have children for the kingdom of God. But in return, God has given her so many spiritual descendants that she is busy traveling all over the world to visit and pray with them all.

The most precious blessing Jesus gives is not in this world. It is eternal life in the world to come. Eternal life is what we really need. When we have eternal life, we have everything. Those who have eternal life are like those who have an unlimited bank account. They can spend freely of their time and energy for others because they have an everlasting supply. Those who have eternal life are the truly rich. They have peace and joy like a river in their souls. When we follow Jesus, we may lose something in the short run. But in the long run, Jesus blesses us exceedingly and abundantly beyond what we can even imagine.

In this passage, Jesus teaches us how to receive the kingdom of God and how to inherit eternal life. We must receive Jesus with simple faith like a little child. We must make a clear decision to sell everything, give to the poor, and follow Jesus. Then we can enjoy God's blessing in this life and eternal life in the world to come. May God help us to do so.

Lesson 47

Jesus Gave Sight to a Blind Beggar

Luke 18:31-43
Key Verse: 18:41

I. JESUS AGAIN PREDICTED HIS DEATH (31-34)

1. What would happen to Jesus in Jerusalem? How did Jesus view his upcoming suffering and death? What was he trying to teach his disciples?

2. What is the message of good news embedded in the painful events to come?

3. Why did the disciples not understand any of what he had told them? Why do you think the meaning was hidden from them? What should we learn here?

II. WHAT DO YOU WANT ME TO DO FOR YOU? (35-43)

4. Where did the blind man live and what was his occupation? How did he know that Jesus was passing by?

5. When he did learn that Jesus was passing by, what did he do? What did he believe about Jesus? What can we learn from him?

6. Why did those who led Jesus' procession rebuke the blind man? Why did their rebuking not have any effect?

7. What did Jesus do when he heard him? How was Jesus different from those who led his procession?

8. How did the man respond to Jesus? How would you respond if Jesus asked you, "What do you want me to do for you?"

9. What did Jesus do for him? What did Jesus mean when he said, "Your faith has healed you"? How would you describe the blind man's faith? What can we learn here about faith?

10. How did the man and the crowds respond to this miracle? What does this event teach about Jesus?

Jesus Gave Sight to a Blind Beggar

Luke 18:31-43
Key Verse: 18:41

> *"'What do you want me to do for you?' 'Lord, I want to see,' he replied."*

THIS PASSAGE IS ABOUT Jesus' going up to Jerusalem. On the way, Jesus again predicted his death (31-34). On the way he was also stopped by a blind beggar. Jesus' footsteps were very heavy. His heart was burdened by the upcoming crucifixion on the cross. In spite of all this, Jesus manifested himself as the Son of God.

I. Jesus again predicted his death (31-34)

On the way to Jerusalem, Jesus took the Twelve aside and told them something. Read verses 31 and 32. "Jesus took the Twelve aside and told them, 'We are going up to Jerusalem, and everything that is written by the prophets about the Son of Man will be fulfilled. He will be handed over to the Gentiles. They will mock him, insult him, spit on him, flog him and kill him.'" Nobody knows about tomorrow. Most people do not know what is going on in the world or where they are going. But Jesus knew who he was and what he was doing. He knew that he came to the world to die on the cross. Now he was on the way to Jerusalem to fulfill the prophecies concerning the Messiah. There he would be handed over to the Gentiles. There they would mock him, insult him, spit on him, flog him, and kill him. On the third day he would rise again (31-33).

Jesus had predicted his crucifixion previously in 9:22: "And he said, 'The Son of Man must suffer many things and be rejected by the elders, chief priests and teachers of the law, and he must be killed and on the third day be raised to life.'" Again in 9:44 he said, "Listen carefully to what I am about to tell you: The Son of Man is going to be betrayed into the hands of men." Therefore, this is his third prediction of his death as a ransom sacrifice. But the disciples did not understand any of this because they did not want to understand. They understood the earthly things very well, but they did not understand the heavenly things at all because their desires were still earthbound.

From the beginning, Jesus had taught them about the kingdom of God, but they neither saw the kingdom of God nor believed in it. In spite of their spiritual blindness, Jesus faithfully taught them the meaning of his death and resurrection so that they might somehow, someday come to know the deep meaning of his work on the cross.

In this we learn that we also must admit that it is not easy to accept the meaning of his rejection, suffering, death, and resurrection from our hearts. But we must learn the Bible teachings from our hearts until we can see the deep meaning of his rejection, suffering, death, and resurrection. We must study the Bible in order to know the deep meaning of his person and work. Paul said in Philippians 3:10-11, "I want to know Christ and the power of his resurrection and the fellowship of sharing in his sufferings, becoming like him in his death, and so, somehow, to attain to the resurrection from the dead." We also must teach his suffering, death, and resurrection to our Bible students until they come to accept the meaning of his cross and resurrection from their hearts so that their suffering may not be due to sin, but for the glory of God.

II. What do you want me to do for you? (35-43)

Verses 35-43 contain a story between Jesus, God incarnate, and a blind beggar, a symbol of human tragedy. Read verse 35. "As Jesus approached Jericho, a blind man was sitting by the roadside begging." On the way to Jerusalem, Jesus passed through Jericho. This event came to pass within a week of his crucifixion. So Jericho, a satellite city of Jerusalem, must have been filled with pilgrims who were going up to Jerusalem for the Passover. As Jesus approached Jericho, it was already full of people who were in the city with various motives. Some people must have been excited by the festive mood. Some must have been distracted by the clothing styles of the crowd of pilgrims. Some people must have been busy with the opportunities of making big sales. Jericho was busy and noisy.

But as Jesus approached Jericho, a blind man was sitting by the roadside begging. He was a human being, but he was the most sorrowful person in the world. In Mark's Gospel, he was called Bartimaeus, which means a son of Timaeus. Everything or every person has its own name, such as Taylor, Smith, Wagonman, Grave, or Hunter. But this man had no name of his own. Nobody valued him as a person who needed his own name. He was a deserted being. He had no value of existence in the eyes of men of the world. He cried many tears with his blind eyes.

He was a beggar. He had no life security. He lived on the mercy of others. He was a slave of his beggar's mentality. He was most sorrowful because he could not see the world. He could not see his mother's face. He could not see the beautiful world. He could not see his friends' faces. He only groped around in darkness. In his darkness, he misunderstood others' words, and with the sensitivity of a blind man, he was easily hurt and wounded. His eyes seemed to have been made only for the purpose of crying many tears.

No one could help him. No one could have mercy on him. Especially during the festival period, no one could pay attention to him. But Jesus had great mercy on him. Not only that, Jesus' heart went out to him, and he asked, "What do you want me to do for you?" (40). To the people of the world, he was considered altogether an annoyance. To Jesus, he was a beloved one who needed the mercy of the Messiah.

What did the blind man do when he met Jesus? He could have acted habitually and rung his blind beggar's bell to draw the attention of someone from whom he could beg. But he did not. Instead he called out, "Jesus, Son of David, have mercy on me!" (38). In this we learn something about him. He knew he was miserable because he was a blind man. Generally, people try to find the cause of their miseries in others. But he did not. He knew he was miserable because of his blindness. He also knew that he needed the Messiah's mercy. Generally, people want some human comfort or financial help or temporal relief when they are in desperate situations. But he wanted the mercy of the Messiah. He knew that no one could help him except Jesus. This blind man knew about Jesus of Nazareth, and he believed that he was the Son of David. He also believed that this Jesus would have compassion on him enough to open his blind eyes.

But when he focused his attention on Jesus, suddenly a big obstacle blocked his way to Jesus. Those who led the way rebuked him, saying, "Be quiet, you blind beggar!" Jesus' disciples and close followers also rebuked him, for they had perceived something extraordinary in the determination and tension which impelled Jesus along the road all the way from Galilee. They were astonished, and those who followed him were afraid (Mk 10:32). When they saw Jesus' gentle lineaments fixed in a new expression of resolution and absorption, they could not come near him. Their parade was solemn and their footsteps were heavy. When they heard this blind beggar pleading, they thought he should not bother their Master. They thought it was not a good time to ask for his help.

It was the time for the blind beggar to yield to the people's rebuke and withdraw into his negative thinking, saying, "I'm really no good. I am a blind man. I cannot see. None of the people of this world are my friends." But he did not. It was the time for him either to give up or to depend on God by faith. At the moment of despair, he made a leap of faith. With the strength of faith, he shouted all the more, "Son of David, have mercy on me!" (39). In this way, he overcame himself and overcame all the obstacles and came to Jesus. Here we learn a lesson. It was not easy at all for the blind beggar to come to Jesus with faith. He did not know what was happening when Jesus' company was coming into Jericho. He could not see. People disparaged him and rebuked him when he wanted to come to Jesus—not one, but all of them. It was easier for him to give up coming to Jesus. But he overcame his feelings. He overcame all the obstacles. He cried out all the more, "Son of David, have mercy on me!" until Jesus was moved by his pleading. We must know that we can come to Jesus in this way.

As for Jesus, the cross was casting its shadow over him. He was bracing himself for the last struggle. It was the time for Jesus to be self-conscious about the agonizing suffering he was about to confront. So Jesus could have been indifferent toward the blind man, as his disciples were. But he was not. What did Jesus do for him?

Read verse 40a. "Jesus stopped and ordered the man to be brought to him." In spite of the heavy weight lying on his heart, with his face set like flint on the road to the cross, he was still sufficiently free of heart to turn to the blind beggar. Jesus had room in his heart for the blind beggar. Jesus did not hesitate to invite the blind beggar into the glorious heavenly kingdom. There was noise enough on the road—the trampling of many feet and the clattering of many tongues. But Jesus had ears to hear the agonizing voice of one poor man sitting in the dust by the roadside.

Look at verses 40b and 41. "When he came near, Jesus asked him, 'What do you want me to do for you?' 'Lord, I want to see,' he replied." Jesus knew he was a blind man. Jesus knew that he was asking for the mercy of the Messiah. But Jesus wanted to hear from his mouth that he wanted to see, for there was a danger that he might ask for something else besides seeing. The blind man was bothered by many people, so he could have asked, "Lord, have mercy on me and rebuke those that despised me." Or as a beggar, his philosophy could have been, "Fill the stomach first. Next, travel to Europe." So he could have asked Jesus, "Alms for the poor and blind. Alms for the poor and blind." Read verse 41. He was very clear about what he wanted. It is surprising that he knew what he really wanted. It is not easy at all for a person to know what he really wants.

Suppose Jesus were to ask you, "What do you want me to do for you?" Suppose that you could only make one request and that your request would determine your future destiny. What would your request be? You would find it difficult to make just one request. You would find it difficult to decide whether or not to ask for some material thing, such as a good car or a large bank account. You would find that you should make a request for something spiritual and paramount. You would find that you really don't know what to ask him. You would find that you have too many things to ask; but in reality, you have nothing to ask him. This teaches us that we must learn what to ask of Jesus.

First, we must ask for God's mercy. We must know that without God's mercy, we are nothing. We are like cut flowers which look good outwardly, but have no life source. They soon wither and dry. Because of sin, man lost the fountain of life and is perishing. Somehow, man must restore a right relationship with God so that he might have a vine and branch relationship with him (Jn 15:1-2). But by man's efforts, it is impossible to restore it. Only by God's mercy and through his one and only Son can this relationship be restored.

Second, we must learn to say, "I want to see." When we see blind men, they look pathetic. But we must know that there are also spiritually blind men. In John 9:41 Jesus said to the Pharisees, "If you were blind, you would not be guilty of sin; but now that you claim you can see, your guilt remains." The Pharisees were religious leaders who should have seen the kingdom of God. But they were, in fact, spiritually blind men. Because of their desires for worldly power and because of their hypocrisy, their eyes were blinded from seeing all the goodness of God. They were entrusted with the word of God to teach all peoples of all nations (Ro 3:2), but they did not see the glorious privilege and blessing in this. They were people chosen to be a priestly nation, but they were not willing to do God's work. They only envied foreign cultures. They were spiritually blind men who did not see all the goodness of God. They did not see the love of God because it was invisible. They did not see the kingdom of God because their hearts were impure. In light of the Pharisees' blindness, we must learn to say, "Lord, I want to see."

Third, we must learn to say, "Lord, I want to be like Jesus." Even though we may have many great human achievements, if our inner man is not like Jesus, we are like blind men. A blind man cannot be happy by wearing dark sunglasses or nice suits. The other day one young man came to see me. He bragged about how he had two cars, one motorcycle, a yacht, and some investments. So I asked him, "Are you happy?" He did not say, "Yes," so I asked him, "Do you eat well?" He then said, "Not really." So I said, "When you didn't have much, you ate everything very well at the Chicago center kitchen, but since you have some money now, you lost your appetite. There is a danger for material things to corrupt your spirit. If your spirit is corrupted, there is no happiness for you in the world."

When Jesus asks, "What do you want me to do for you?" we must be ready to say, "Lord, I want to be holy like you. I really want to be holy." When Jesus asks, "What do you want me to do for you?" we must be ready to say, "Lord, I want to be faithful like you. You are the same yesterday, today, and forever. But I cry because of my unfaithfulness." When Jesus asks, "What do you want me to do for you?" we must be ready to say, "Lord, I want to be pure like you. Because of my impurity, I have suffered more than I can say."

Fourth, we must learn to say, "Lord, have mercy on this country." Personal prayer is good. But if we are educated people, we must know how to pray on the national level. The people of this country have gotten out of a material crisis, but now they are in a moral crisis, as well as a spiritual crisis. Most parents don't say anything even when their daughters have abortions. But they strongly reject their children when their children want to live as children of God. This country is filled with all kinds of contagious diseases, moral corruptions, and perversions. But no one seems to care about them. We are responsible to pray for the future glory of this country, saying, "Lord, raise many young Paul's for this generation. Lord, change the course of history in this country from a hedonistic social consensus to a missionary-sending country once again."

In history, there had been no record of a blind man being healed. Only in the book of Isaiah is there a prophecy concerning the Messiah who would give sight to the blind. Therefore, this blind man could not imagine asking for his mercy. But he transcended his imagination and asked for his mercy, "Son of David, have mercy on me!"

Jesus said in verse 42, "Receive your sight; your faith has healed you." When Jesus saw his faith, he was moved and admired his faith. When Jesus saw his faith, he was willing to wipe away the tears from his eyes and give him new sight. Jesus was willing to give him a new life and a new future. We learn that Jesus heals when one has faith to depend totally on his mercy. Jesus gives when one knows what he wants to have. Jesus praised the blind man, saying, "Your faith has healed you." We must ask for God's mercy on us that we may have this kind of beautiful faith. In order to have this kind of faith, we must humble ourselves before the throne of God.

Let's see how he was healed. Read verse 43. "Immediately he

received his sight and followed Jesus, praising God. When all the people saw it, they also praised God." He was a blind man. He could not see, so he always lived in darkness, incurring the deep prejudicial misunderstanding of others and indulging in self-condemnation. He lived with deep fatalistic sorrow and much ridicule. But when he was healed, he came out of the darkness of the night. Glorious sunshine flooded his sight and his soul. The whole world, with all its beauty, was caught in his sight, and it penetrated his mind until he praised God with joyful songs. Jesus was the whole world to him, so he decided to follow him. His joy was so overflowing that all the people saw it. They also praised God. He was no more a blind beggar. Now he was a heavenly prince, honored and exalted by God's grace.

Lesson 48

Jesus Found Zacchaeus

Luke 19:1-10
Key Verse: 19:10

I. ZACCHAEUS CAME TO JESUS (1-4)

1. Where was Jesus and where was he going when he met Zacchaeus? What might have been on his mind?

2. Who was Zacchaeus? What can you learn from the text about his appearance, occupation, relationships with the people of his community, lifestyle, etc.?

3. What were the obstacles he encountered in going to Jesus? How did he overcome them? What does this show about him?

II. ZACCHAEUS, COME DOWN IMMEDIATELY (5)

4. How is it that Jesus met Zacchaeus? What did he say to him? What is the significance of Jesus' calling him by name?

5. Why did Jesus invite himself to Zacchaeus' house? Why was there such urgency in Jesus' invitation?

III. ZACCHAEUS' REPENTANCE (6-8)

6. How did Zacchaeus respond? Why was he so eager and happy to welcome Jesus?

7. How did the townspeople view Jesus' decision to visit Zacchaeus' home? Why?

8. What does Zacchaeus' repentance show about his former life? How did his meeting with Jesus change him practically?

IV. A SON OF ABRAHAM (9-10)

9. How did Jesus view the change in Zacchaeus? What does he mean by "this man, too, is a son of Abraham"?

10. What can we learn from this event about Jesus? About who are the lost people?

Jesus Found Zacchaeus

Luke 19:1-10
Key Verse: 19:10

"For the Son of Man came to seek and to save what was lost."

ESUS MET A MAN by the name of Zacchaeus when he entered Jericho. Jesus helped him find himself in God from where he was lost. In this passage we learn many characteristics of the Messiah. But particularly we learn what it means to be lost. We have to consider whether we have pity on the lost or whether we envy them.

I.   Zacchaeus came to see Jesus (1-4)

Jesus was on his way to Jerusalem to fulfill the will of God for world salvation. Each Gospel contains long narratives concerning Jesus who was on his way to Jerusalem. All the stories about Jesus on the way to Jerusalem touch the strings of our hearts. All these stories are very sad if they are imposed on an individual person. Nevertheless, they are all beautiful stories about Jesus who called and healed, sought and found all who were in need of the hand of the Messiah. Today Jesus found a man who was wretched and alienated.

Read verse 1. Now Jesus entered Jericho and was passing through. As we know, Jericho was a very wealthy town. She lay in the Jordan Valley and commanded both the approach to Jerusalem and the crossings of the Jordan River, which gave her access to the palm forest and balm groves. Her gardens of roses were known far and wide. All this decorated her with natural beauty and combined to make her one of the greatest centers of taxation in Palestine.

In spite of natural beauty, in time past and present, human beings who live in time and space have not been able to ignore the agonies of life. Man's happiness largely depends on how he digests the agonies of life. When one can see the agonies of life before God and find their meaning, then he can grow up to be a mature person like a big oak tree. On the other hand, when one takes the agonies of life as the burden of life, then his life is only miserable. Whether one wants to or not, each person must fight the battle to preserve human life.

In Jericho, a man was there by the name of Zacchaeus, a name meaning "sinless" or "righteous." Probably his parents named him Zacchaeus hoping that he would be an upright person in the eyes of God. Zacchaeus must have heard from his parents all through his boyhood about how to be an upright person in the world. But when he saw all his friends and relatives around his age wanting to study practical subjects, such as biology, psychology, or business, he also became interested in studying for an MBA. Eventually he became a member of the IRS, and later, the chief of the Jericho IRS.

In short, Zacchaeus was a tough man. At that time, most of the people of Israel were groaning under the yoke of Roman rule. In the Gospels, we can see numerous poor, sick, and crippled people thronging around Jesus. But this man Zacchaeus was not crushed by the hard situation. He withstood all difficulties. He struggled to preserve himself. He struggled to survive in this fight of the survival of the fittest. It is not easy at all for anybody to be the top or chief in any area. But Zacchaeus competed and defeated all the rivals. Finally, he rose above all the tax collectors and became a chief tax collector.

Was he happy with his position and wealth? No, he was not happy because he was not recognized. As we know well, man's desire for honor and recognition is greater than many other desires. Probably Zacchaeus shouted in his heart, "I want recognition!" Probably he wanted to hear from others, "Oh, you are great!" But instead, people whispered behind his back, "Tax Collector!" "Renegade!" "Traitor!" "Quisling!" At first he thought they were speaking to someone else. Later he found that it was him. He never imagined that he had chosen the way that had made him the most hated man in the district, a way that had made him an outcast.

He was not happy because he was not accepted by the people. As we know well, a human being is a social animal, so each person wants to be accepted by others. In order to be accepted by others or by a peer group, many a person does many things that he or she really doesn't want to do. As a human being, Zacchaeus must have had a strong desire to be accepted. But he was not accepted. Jews did not accept him as a fellow Jew, and Romans did not accept him as a Roman. He was not happy because he could not identify himself either as a Roman or a Jew. He was not happy because he had to justify himself as a sinless, righteous man before other people in spite of himself. He was not happy because he could not satisfy his desire for holiness. Without exception, all the people in the world want to be pure and honest. But Zacchaeus lost his purity, honesty, and even more, the holiness of God in himself. He became filthy and useless.

Zacchaeus was not happy because he was no longer himself. When he became vulnerable without God's protection, demons—the disciples of Satan—did not leave him alone. Demons penetrated his meaningless, empty, and dirty heart one by one until it became a living hell. He was helpless because he was controlled by the evil spirit. His daily work seemed to be nothing but being mean to others during the day and condemning himself at night. He was a man of self-condemnation. He was a man who hated himself more than others who hated him.

Zacchaeus was in a hopeless situation. He was completely lost. But he found hope in Jesus. Read verse 3. He wanted to see who Jesus was. What made him want to see Jesus? He had already heard about Jesus, that he welcomed sinners and tax collectors and ate with them. He found in Jesus the Messiah. Jesus was the last hope for a man like him. But there were still several obstacles for him in reaching Jesus.

The first obstacle was the crowd of people. For Zacchaeus, to mingle with the crowd was not an easy thing to do. At that time, people blindly hated people like Zacchaeus. If they saw a person like him, they all became like football players against him. They would nudge, kick, or push him until he was badly hurt. After awhile in the crowd, Zacchaeus might have been black and blue with bruises, and his best suit which he had worn to go and see Jesus must have been torn apart into many pieces.

The second obstacle was his being a short man. In order to see Jesus, he went into the crowd of people. Because he was a short man, he was surrounded and buried by taller people so that he could not see Jesus. There was a danger that he would be pushed down and trodden over. But he did not give up. He did his best to push through the people. When he got away from the people, he looked around and found a sycamore-fig tree ahead of him. It was not easy for him to climb up the tree. As he was a short man, he must have had a chubby body with a stomach that stuck out further than the length of his arms. But he climbed up the tree and hung onto a branch like an old monkey. He was determined to see Jesus.

Through this, we learn that it is not easy at all to go to Jesus. When we want to go to Jesus, there are many kinds of obstacles. The first obstacle is the people around us. Usually people are not interested in us. The second obstacle is our own human feelings. When we cannot overcome our feelings, we cannot achieve anything, much less come to Jesus.

II. Zacchaeus, come down immediately (5)

As soon as Jesus saw Zacchaeus, he called out to him. Read verse 5. "When Jesus reached the spot, he looked up and said to him, 'Zacchaeus, come down immediately. I must stay at your house today.'" In this verse, we learn two things about Jesus.

First, Jesus called Zacchaeus by name. "Zacchaeus, come down immediately." One's name stands for one's inner character. We don't know how Jesus knew his name. Anyway, Jesus knew his name. Jesus knew his inner character. Jesus knew his agonies of life. Jesus knew why he came to see him. To the eyes of worldly people, he was a tax collector and a public sinner and an outcast, despised and hated. Everybody knew that he was a wretched guy. That was all. But Jesus understood him well, that he had done his best to be a good man. But in the course of living by the pattern of the world, he became lost. Above all, Jesus knew that he was created in the image of God and that he was seeking for the truth; he was searching for the Messiah.

Jesus knew that deep down below Zacchaeus' superficial and vulgar curiosity there was something far more noble, something which Jesus could nurture into life and consciousness. Jesus was to him all that he needed.

Jesus called him, "Zacchaeus," in the same manner that a father calls a son who is suffering from an unknown fever. This individualizing personal affection and love are all well expressed in that one word, "Zacchaeus." There certainly is a bond of personal regard, compassion, affection, and purpose of salvation in Jesus' heart in regard to one solitary soul among all the masses of humanity. "Zacchaeus, come down immediately" (5). This was the voice of God. "Zacchaeus, come down immediately." It was the voice of one seeking the lost. It was probably the first time since Zacchaeus had been a child on his mother's knee that he had heard his name pronounced in a tone of kindness. It was the only time Zacchaeus had met a man who wanted to be friends with him.

Second, Jesus invited himself to Zacchaeus' house. "I must stay at your house today" (5). Up until now, no one wanted to go to Zacchaeus' house. Though he was wealthy, he was lonely. Though he was wealthy, he could not but eat all by himself. He was so lonely and sick that one bottle of milk and one bag of bread were enough for a week. Money did not mean anything for his happiness. His hometown people would invite him to many restaurants and public dinners, but they had never invited him to their homes. But Jesus was willing to invite Zacchaeus to his house. But Jesus had a problem in inviting him. He did not have his own house. Jesus found a way. Jesus invited himself to Zacchaeus' house. When Jesus invited himself to Zacchaeus' house, he had in mind the heavenly banquet in the kingdom of God. Revelation 3:20 says, "Here I am! I stand at the door and knock. If anyone hears my voice and opens the door, I will come in and eat with him, and he with me." There Jesus wanted to talk with him and eat with him. Jesus was knocking at the door of his heart. Jesus wanted to treat him as his own pure virgin bride if he would accept his invitation.

III. Zacchaeus' repentance (6-8)

How did he respond to Jesus invitation? Read verse 6. "So he came down at once and welcomed him gladly." His response was immediate, just as Jesus' invitation was immediate. Usually climbing up a tree is easier than climbing down from a tree. I heard Missionary Sarah Barry once climbed high up on a tree and could not come down, so her father and neighborhood people had to come to rescue her with a tall ladder. Zacchaeus came down and was ready to welcome Jesus and his company. There were people there who waited with intense curiosity to see what would pass between Jesus and a tax collector. They began to mutter, "He has gone to be the guest of a 'sinner'" (7). They did not know the love of God in Jesus. People frowned on Jesus that he had gone to be the guest of a sinner. They branded Zacchaeus as a sinner and only made him bitter. They loathed him and made him set his teeth more firmly. They drove him by their contempt to deviltry and made him more lonely.

But when Zacchaeus met Jesus, he was changed into quite a different man. He became a born-again Christian. His way of thinking, together with his lifestyle, was completely changed. He was moved by Jesus' embracing love. Jesus' love made a deep dent in his heart and revolutionized his whole nature. His love turned him inside out and upside down and made a new man of him. We can see two things in his change.

First, he was changed in his value system. Read verse 8. "But Zacchaeus stood up and said to the Lord, 'Look, Lord! Here and now I give half of my possessions to the poor, and if I have cheated anybody out of anything, I will pay back four times the amount.'" The half given to the poor plus the fourfold restored to those whom he had wronged would leave nothing for Zacchaeus himself. But it didn't matter to him. He didn't have to calculate this and that for some small benefits. In the past, material things were everything to him, but to be worthy of Jesus' grace, he could give up all material things. Making a new relationship with Jesus and being together with him was enough for him. He was filled with joy and unutterable happiness.

Second, he was changed from a self-centered to a God-centered person. In the past, whatever he did, thinking or speaking, drinking or eating, he did only for himself. His day began with "I, my, me" and ended with "I, my, me" every day. He had only thought of himself because he was egocentric. He was a victim of self-condemnation. He was a kind of mental patient. But for the first time he began to think of others in Jesus. He thought of the poor and of those who had been wronged by him. Through the love of Jesus, his humanity was fully rehabilitated and the image of God in him was fully restored.

IV. A son of Abraham (9-10)

Read verse 9. Jesus said to him, "Today salvation has come to this house, because this man, too, is a son of Abraham." When he saw Zacchaeus, Jesus' joy was like that of the father of the prodigal son. In the past, Zacchaeus had been a source of anguish to his household because of his lost situation in life. But now he became a blessing to his family members. Through him the door of salvation was opened wide to his household. This is why Jesus said to him, "Salvation has come to this house." In the past, he was excommunicated by the Jews and was not considered a son of Abraham. Rather, he was called a quisling and traitor to his suffering people. But when he was found by Jesus, he was restored as a son of Abraham. Now, he was justifiably a Jew. He was a son of Abraham. He was a child of God and a heavenly prince. Jesus' joy was great to see Zacchaeus' change and restoration to sonship and to his inheritance as a child of God.

To ordinary people, Zacchaeus should have been punished because of his guilt and crimes. But Jesus was happy when he repented. Jesus explained why he was happy in verse 10. "For the Son of Man came to seek and to save what was lost." Here the phrase, "what was lost," has deep meaning. When we see those who are highly educated, we think that they are men and women of high education. When we see rich people, we think they are rich and happy. But Jesus sees people as lost, whoever they may be, if they do not live according to God's truth. They are wanderers in life. They are descendants of Cain. They are gripped with fear and self-condemnation. Zacchaeus was one of them. He had a secure job and a position as chief tax collector. He was wealthy. But Jesus saw him as a lost soul.

Then who are lost? They are those who do not have the truth of God. I know one person whose life key verse is Matthew 6:33, "Seek first his kingdom and righteousness ..." He talks and writes a lot based on this key verse. But in reality, he only pursues human fame and wealth. Now he is rich. But he cannot eat well because of his overweight and blood pressure problems. His wife also cannot eat well because of her stomach ulcer. They are not joyful because they have no meaning in their agonies of life. They are lost. We must not envy lost people. We must teach them the Bible so that they may come to know Jesus Christ. Jesus came to seek and to save what was lost.

There are many tax collectors among young people. They are selfish and mean. But we must realize that they are crying in their hearts, seeking to see the Messiah. They need shepherds like Jesus. There are many who are helpless to help themselves. But in their hearts they want to be children of God. They need Jesus, the Shepherd and the Messiah.

Lesson 49

The Parable of the Ten Minas

Luke 19:11-27
Key Verse: 19:13

I.   PUT THIS MONEY TO WORK (11-13)

1.   Where was Jesus when he told this parable? To whom did he tell it? What reason is given for Jesus' telling this parable? What does this mean?

2.   In the parable, for what purpose did the man of noble birth go away? How does this parable parallel Jesus' life?

3.   What commands did he give ten of his servants before he left? What do you think the minas stand for? What does the command, "Put this money to work," mean?

II.   WELL DONE, MY GOOD SERVANT (14-19)

4.   Who opposed the nobleman's kingship? Who opposed Jesus' kingship? When the king returned, what did he do first?

5.   What reports did the first two of the ten servants give to the king? What can we learn from them?

6.   What is the king's comment and reward? What can we learn here about Jesus' way of rewarding his servants?

III.   TO EVERYONE WHO HAS, MORE WILL BE GIVEN (20-27)

7.   What was the third servant's report? What excuse did he give? What was wrong with his excuse?

8.   How did the king judge him by his own words? Why hadn't this servant put the money on deposit?

9.   How did the king rebuke and punish him? Why did he do this? What does this teach about Jesus? What principle of life does this teach?

10.   What did the king do about the enemies who had opposed him? How was the third servant like the enemies? What does this teach about the kingship of Jesus?

The Parable of the Ten Minas

Luke 19:11-27
Key Verse: 19:13

> *"So he called ten of his servants and gave them ten minas. 'Put this money to work,' he said, 'until I come back.'"*

THE PARABLE OF THE Ten Minas teaches us the relationship between Jesus and his children. Jesus is the King, and his children are his loyal and faithful servants. In this passage, we must learn what Jesus our King expects each of us to do until he comes again in glory and power.

I. Put this money to work (11-13)

Read verse 11. "While they were listening to this, he went on to tell them a parable, because he was near Jerusalem and the people thought that the kingdom of God was going to appear at once." The people who had heard Jesus were so inspired that they wondered if Jesus might possibly be the Messiah promised to come, and they thought that the kingdom of God would come on earth as soon as Jesus entered Jerusalem. Historically, the people of Israel had expected the Messiah's coming ever since the prophecies of Isaiah had been proclaimed. But the Messiah they had expected was not the spiritual Messiah who would suffer and die for man's sins and rise again on the third day and give men a living hope in the kingdom of God. The Messiah they had expected was a political Messiah who would establish an earthly, political messianic kingdom in which Jesus could rule over the whole world after annihilating all their enemies.

The hope of the Messiah's coming had enabled the Jews to endure all kinds of hardships and sufferings and molded them into great people in many ways. On the other hand, the hope of the Messiah's coming made them abstract and poetic and pursue phantoms. Finally, they inclined to be miracle-seeking people.

This tendency has always been prevalent in Christian churches. So Paul said in 1 Corinthians 1:22-23a, "Jews demand miraculous signs and Greeks look for wisdom, but we preach Christ crucified." Miracle-seeking faith is fortune-seeking faith. And fortune-seeking faith is shamanistic faith. Miracle-seeking faith is a way of escaping into spiritual hallucinations. In essence, spiritual hallucination is the same as drug abuse. We see these days that there are many kinds of drug Christians living in a drug culture.

The disciples should have learned the deep meaning of his suffering, death, and resurrection. But because of their sinful natures, their spiritual eyes were blinded and they could not see God's wisdom for world salvation, that he wanted to save people through his Son's suffering, death, and resurrection. His disciples thought they had suffered enough. So they could not accept his teachings of the cross and resurrection. Rather, they hoped like ordinary people that the earthly messianic kingdom would come at once.

Jesus wanted to correct the error of their expectations for a political messiah, and at the same time, he wanted to teach them that the eternal kingdom of God would be established through his cross and resurrection and the perfection of the kingdom of God would be completed when he comes again. Until that time, his servants must live fruitful lives. In order to teach this truth, Jesus told them a parable.

Read verse 12. "He said: 'A man of noble birth went to a distant country to have himself appointed king and then to return.'" Here, "a man of noble birth" refers to Jesus, his going to a distant country to Jesus' ascension, and his returning to Jesus' second coming. Here we must learn why he ascended to the heavenly kingdom. He went back to the heavenly kingdom so that he might come back to this world as King and Judge.

Read verse 13. "So he called ten of his servants and gave them ten minas. 'Put this money to work,' he said, 'until I come back.'" In this verse, his servants refer to his disciples and all Christians. One mina is about three months' wages. He gave his servants the money and said, "Put this money to work." He did not say, "Use the money properly." In this verse, "mina" can be said to metaphorically represent many different things. But when we study this passage carefully, we can liken mina to life in two ways.

First, a mina stands for a man's life. Each man was given one mina. One mina to each person seems to indicate one lifetime to each person. One mina to each person also seems to signify that equal opportunity is given to each person.

Man's life is definitely limited to a certain amount of time. But the element of life in a man is abundant and unlimited. After creating man, God said to him, "Be fruitful and increase in number; fill the earth and subdue it" (Ge 1:28a). The element of life in man is limitless. Man's joy comes when he works hard to make his life fruitful (Jn 15:11). Therefore, each person must put his life to work. One who puts his life to work can live 30, 60, or 100 times more abundantly and splendidly.

Life is like money. We can use up the money we have or we can put it to work and earn a remarkable profit. Those who put their lives to work will be victors of life. Those who use up their lives according to their feelings will be losers in life. In light of this parable, man's lifetime is like a race. Men are all like track runners who are standing on the starting line to compete and win the victory. When we read Hebrews 12, we learned that there had been a great crowd of people who ran the race of life with perseverance and became victors and champions of life. St. Paul was a good racer. He said in 2 Timothy 4:7, "I have fought the good fight, I have finished the race, I have kept the faith."

How then can we be fruitful? We must put our lives to work. For example, Abraham did not use his life like other idolaters. Rather, he gave his life to God by faith. Then God made his life abundant. As God promised, his descendents became as numerous as the stars in the sky and sand on the seashore. Another example is Moses. Moses could have enjoyed all kinds of sinful pleasures of the kingdom of Egypt. But Hebrews 11:24-25 tell us that "By faith Moses, when he had grown up, refused to be known as the son of Pharaoh's daughter. He chose to be mistreated along with the people of God rather than to enjoy the pleasures of sin for a short time." Later he became a power source in delivering 600,000 of his people from slavery in Egypt. Jesus said in John 10:10b, "I have come that they may have life, and have it to the full." Jesus laid down his life for us so that we may have abundant and eternal life in him.

Second, a mina stands for a man's talent. When God made man, he made each person uniquely. Therefore, each person is unique and the best. Also, each person is endowed with a unique talent which is superior to that of anyone else. In this case, we must put our talent to work. If we put our talent to work properly, we can bear fruit 30, 60, or 100 times the original amount.

Again, let's think about what "Put this money to work" means. "Put this money to work" seems to mean, "Work hard and gain some profit without fail." Our King Jesus does not want us to remain helpless, but wants us to make things work out, overcome depression, and make our situations prosperous. But how can it be possible? It is impossible for anyone because man wants to live according to his situation. No one wants to swim against the current of the stream. If all people only want to be happy humanly, then there would be no one to turn the bad situations into flourishing and prosperous situations. It is possible for us to work hard and earn some profit without fail only when we have loyalty and a faithful heart toward our King. Historically, there have been innumerable stories about loyal subjects who died in order to be loyal and faithful to their kings.

But we can see the best example of "Put this money to work" in our Lord Jesus. God gave him one mina to shepherd his flock. He put his mina to work well. Once Jesus saw a blind man by the roadside. But Jesus had no medical instrument with him because he was not a physician. He had no way. But Jesus was loyal, faithful, and willing to the utmost to obey his Father God. So he could find a way. He spit on the ground, made some mud with the saliva, and put it on the man's eyes. "'Go' he told him, 'wash in the Pool of Siloam'" (Jn 9:7a).

Once Jesus went with his disciples to a quiet place for a retreat. But people who carefully watched his movements came to him. They were a large crowd of 5,000 people. Jesus taught them all day long. It was sunset, but they did not go away. They wanted to eat first, and then go away. Jesus had no way. But he found a way to work things out because he wanted to feed his Father's children by any means. He said to his disciples, "You give them something to eat" (9:13). Then Andrew looked around and found a boy with five loaves and two fish. Somehow he took them away from the boy and brought them to Jesus. Jesus blessed the five loaves and two fish and fed the 5,000 people with them.

St. Paul was chosen by God to be the apostle for the Gentiles. Paul wanted to go and evangelize Rome, the center of the Gentile world at that time. Paul wanted to absolutely obey his King Jesus' command, "Go into all the world and preach the good news to all creation" (Mk 16:15). But he had no way to go to Rome, for he was imprisoned because of the gospel. But his loyalty made it possible for him to find a way. He appealed to Caesar the Roman emperor that his case be decided at Rome. The Emperor said, "Your request is granted," and he went to Rome as a prisoner in chains.

In Korea, we were eager to obey the world mission command of our King Jesus. We prayed for world mission for nearly 10 years, but nothing happened. Then one day, we heard that some women were going to West Germany as nurses. We shouted, "Yeah, that's it!" We were determined to persuade them to accept a missionary calling from God. Surprisingly, they accepted God's calling. Some of them received missionary training for one week or for one month, and then they went. In this way, God started campus work in West Germany.

II. Well done, my good servant (14-19)

Read verse 14. "But his subjects hated him and sent a delegation after him to say, 'We don't want this man to be our king.'" This verse teaches us sinful human nature, and at the same time, it teaches us the kingship of Jesus. The illustration in this verse was based in part on an actual historical event. When Herod the Great died in 4 BC, he left his kingdom divided into four parts. Then one of his sons, Archelaus, went to Rome to get this division ratified by Augustus Emperor of Rome. At that time, the Jews hated Herod's son and sent an ambassador to Rome to inform Augustus that they did not wish to have him as king. Like this illustration, the people of the world don't want Jesus to be their king because they want to be kings for themselves.

Read verse 15a. "He was made king, however, and returned home. Then he sent for the servants to whom he had given the money …" This verse clearly tells us of Jesus' coming again whether people of the world want it or not. When he comes again, he will ask each person to give an account in order to see if they had faithfully obeyed his command, "Put this money to work" (15b).

Read verses 16 and 17. "The first one came and said, 'Sir, your mina has earned ten more.'" This servant had put the money to work and earned 1,000% profit. "'Well done, my good servant!' his master replied." How does he reward his faithful servants? The reward the faithful servant received was the master's recognition, "Well done, my good servant!" This reward seems to be too small, but it is everything to his faithful servants. The king will say to those who ran the race of life and won the victory, "Well done, my good servant!" "Well done, my good servant!" are the best words for a faithful servant who has completed his life of mission and is standing before his King Jesus to receive the crown of life.

Another reward of work well done is more work. Our King Jesus does not give his faithful servants a reward they can enjoy by sitting down, folding their hands together, and doing nothing. The one who earned ten minas was put over ten cities so that he could work harder and be more faithful.

Read verses 18 and 19. "The second came and said, 'Sir, your mina has earned five more.' His master replied, 'You take charge of five cities.'" The master gave the servant who had earned five more the same recognition and the same reward as the one who had earned ten more. God sees quality and a faithful heart.

III. To everyone who has, more will be given (20-27)

The Parable of the Minas concludes with one of the inexorable laws of life. To him who has, more will be given; from him who has not, even what he has will be taken away (26).

Read verses 20 and 21. "Then another servant came and said, 'Sir, here is your mina; I have kept it laid away in a piece of cloth. I was afraid of you, because you are a hard man. You take out what you did not put in and reap what you did not sow.'" He was the kind of person who knows who God is and who knows himself. But his problem was that he did not want to put his life or talent to work. In the secret meditation of his heart, he wanted to use them for his own pleasure.

Read verses 22 and 23. "His master replied, 'I will judge you by your own words, you wicked servant! You knew, did you, that I am a hard man, taking out what I did not put in, and reaping what I did not sow? Why then didn't you put my money on deposit, so that when I came back, I could have collected it with interest?'" The master rebuked his disobedience of not putting his mina to work and said in verse 24, "Take his mina away from him and give it to the one who has ten minas." The master's decision seems to be unfair and too hard. So those who were standing by said, "He already has ten!" (25). But this is the law of life. The man who kept his mina laid away in a piece of cloth looks good because he did not use the original capital of one mina. But that's not enough. This kind of person will be considered a part of "those enemies" (27), and what he has will be taken away and given to the one who earns ten more because he did not obey the King's command to put the mina to work.

God does not forgive such servants. Read verse 27. "But these enemies of mine who did not want me to be king over them—bring them here and kill them in front of me." Their problem is that they do not recognize the sovereignty of God and the kingship of our Lord Jesus Christ. They want to live their own lives. They don't want any king over them. They cannot escape God's judgment and punishment.

Lesson 50

Jesus Enters Jerusalem

Luke 19:28-48
Key Verse: 19:38

I.   THE LORD NEEDS IT (28-34)

1. What had Jesus been saying as he approached Jerusalem? What did Jesus do to prepare to enter the city? Why? (Zechariah 9:9)

2. Why might the command he gave his disciples be difficult for them to obey? How did they respond?

3. How did the two disciples answer the owners of the colt when they were caught taking it? What do the words, "The Lord needs it," suggest about Jesus? About his disciples' faith?

II.   BLESSED BE THE KING (35-38)

4. What is the significance of the people spreading their cloaks on the road before Jesus?

5. As they went down to the Mount of Olives, why did the crowd shout so joyfully? Which of his miracles might they have remembered? What did they shout? What did they believe about Jesus?

6. How did the Pharisees respond to the shout of the crowds? Why? What did Jesus mean by his statement in verse 40?

III.   JESUS WEPT (39-44)

7. Why did Jesus weep over Jerusalem? What would happen to her in the future?

8. What was now hidden from her eyes? Why did he say that it was now hidden? In what respect did she not recognize the time of God's coming to her?

IV.   KING JESUS WHO JUDGES (45-48)

9. Where did Jesus go and what did he do after entering Jerusalem? Why was he so angry? What does this event teach us about Jesus?

10. Why did the Jewish leaders try to kill Jesus? Why didn't they succeed at that time?

Jesus Enters Jerusalem

Luke 19:28-48
Key Verse: 19:38

"Blessed is the king who comes in the name of the Lord! Peace in heaven and glory in the highest!"

FROM THIS PASSAGE, WE want to study about Jesus' triumphal entry into Jerusalem (28-44) and Jesus' cleansing of the temple (45-48). These two events reveal Jesus' kingship in two ways. Jesus' entry into Jerusalem reveals the humble King Jesus who saves. His cleansing of the temple reveals the righteous King Jesus who judges. May God help us to know the nature of our King Jesus through this study.

I. The Lord needs it (28-34)

This event opens with the words, "After Jesus had said this ..." In the previous passage (11-27), Jesus taught his disciples about his kingship through the Parable of the Ten Minas. In the parable, Jesus ascends into heaven in order to have himself appointed King. When he returns as King, he will ask his servants to give an account to see whether or not they have put their minas to work.

Read verse 28. "After Jesus had said this, he went on ahead, going up to Jerusalem." Why did he go up to Jerusalem? First, Jesus' entry into Jerusalem was to fulfill the prophecy in Zechariah 9:9 which says, "Rejoice greatly, O Daughter of Zion! Shout, Daughter of Jerusalem! See, your king comes to you, righteous and having salvation, gentle and riding on a donkey, on a colt, the foal of a donkey." His entering into the city as the Messiah had been long planned, promised, prophesied, and long awaited, and now, fulfilled. In order to proclaim the good news of his coming, many prophets and pious people of God had suffered and bled. At last, according to God's promises, he came to this world in human form, giving up all the glory and power of the kingdom of heaven. Now he was entering Jerusalem to fulfill the prophecy of God concerning the Savior King.

Second, Jesus' going up to Jerusalem was to fulfill the will of God for world salvation. The will of God for him was to go up to Jerusalem to die on the cross as the Lamb of God for the sin of the world and to rise again from the dead on the third day to give all mankind a living hope. It was not easy for Jesus to go up to Jerusalem to die on the cross like a criminal. But he was willing to obey the will of God. Through the shedding of his blood as the ransom sacrifice, he was to make peace between God and men. Through his death and resurrection, he was to destroy the power of sin and death and restore his kingdom. The will of God was great and beautiful. But for Jesus it meant painful sufferings and rejection and death on the cross. The will of God for him was to bear on the cross all the loads of man's sins, rebellion, and disobedience. How could Jesus obey the will of God? Humanly speaking, it was impossible. But it was possible for Jesus because he was willing to obey the will of God absolutely. Jesus did not care much about his life. He cared only about the will of God being fulfilled. In this, Jesus shows the example of a loyal subject to the Almighty King.

Jesus, with concentrated determination, impelled his firm steps up the steep and weary road to Jerusalem and arrived at the Mount of Olives, which was situated on the east side of Jerusalem beyond the Kidron Valley, facing the Jerusalem temple. From the Mount of Olives, the whole view of Jerusalem and its temple could be seen. Bethphage was on the west and Bethany to the southeast. Bethany was only two miles from the city and Bethpage was still nearer. Now Jesus was about to enter Jerusalem. But he had no colt. How did he get a colt to ride on?

Read verses 29b-31. "He sent two of his disciples, saying to them, 'Go to the village ahead of you, and as you enter it, you will find a colt tied there, which no one has ever ridden. Untie it and bring it here. If anyone asks you, "Why are you untying it?" tell him, "The Lord needs it.""'

How did the disciples respond? Probably his disciples were surprised by Jesus' transcendental knowledge. He did not see it, but he knew where a colt was and what the owner of the colt would ask when his disciples would untie it. When they were told to untie someone else's colt and bring it, they were probably puzzled, not knowing what to do, because there was a danger for them to be charged as thieves. They could have asked Jesus, "Do you want us to be thieves?" or "Isn't it robbery?" But they did not say such things. To our common sense, Jesus' command to his disciples was too hard to obey. However, it was clear that Jesus was teaching them the kingship of Christ. No one can claim another's property by saying, "The Lord needs it," or "I need it." Ahab, the king of Judah, wanted to possess the farmer Naboth's vineyard. But Naboth refused to give it to him. Then King Ahab went home and refused to eat before his wife Jezebel (1Ki 21:2-4). Only the Almighty King can claim, "The Lord needs it." "The Lord needs it" asserts that Jesus is the King Almighty and the Owner and Maker of everything.

It is surprising that the disciples obeyed his command. Read verses 32-34. "Those who were sent ahead went and found it just as he had told them. As they were untying the colt, its owners asked them, 'Why are you untying the colt?' They replied, 'The Lord needs it.'" Here we learn that the disciples were beginning to learn the kingship of Jesus by obeying a command that only an absolute ruler could make.

How did the owner of the colt react? Probably the colt was very dear to him. His joy of life must have been to stroke the colt on its back two or three times a day and make a big smile. When the owner of the colt saw that the two disciples had in their hearts an absolute attitude toward their Master's command and an absolute loyalty to their Master, he was amazed and became happy to see them and said, "All right. You have my permission. Take it." Suppose the two disciples had disobeyed Jesus' command. Then his entry into Jerusalem would have been immensely hindered. But when the two disciples obeyed his command absolutely, as loyal subjects obey their king for his majesty and glory, the work of God proceeded as was planned.

II. Blessed is the King (35-38)

As a rule, Jesus had avoided public attention. But the time had come for him to reveal himself before Israel as their King, making the triumphal entry into Jerusalem as was prophesied.

Read verse 35. "They brought it to Jesus, threw their cloaks on the colt and put Jesus on it." This verse tells us that the disciples acknowledged his kingship and paid homage to him by throwing their cloaks on the colt. Read verse 36. "As he went along, people spread their cloaks on the road." As a way of paying homage to a king, people frenziedly took off their cloaks and spread them on the road when he came near the place where the road goes down the Mount of Olives. The whole crowd of disciples began joyfully to praise God in loud voices.

Why did they praise God? Verse 37b says it was for "all the miracles they had seen." They had seen beautiful Jesus who went around all the districts of Galilee, healing the sick and preaching the kingdom of God. They had seen Jesus who became eyes to the blind. They had seen Jesus who became a father to the Samaritan woman and a friend to a lonely tax collector. They had seen many miracles done by Jesus to heal the sick and to plant in men the hope of the kingdom of God. They had seen the true Messiah in Jesus. They had seen God's mercy and salvation in Jesus. The miracles they had seen were all Messianic miracles. Jesus' entry into Jerusalem meant to them that the King of salvation was marching into Zion. They praised God, shouting, "Blessed is the king who comes in the name of the Lord! Peace in heaven and glory in the highest!" (38). They called upon Jesus himself as the blessed King, the Messiah. His coming is peace to men on earth and glory to God in heaven. Men needed a king like Jesus who would save them from their sins. They wanted the dominion of a king like Jesus.

Here we learn from the crowd of disciples that we need a king like Jesus because when we have a king like Jesus, we can be loyal and faithful. For example, if we have money, we want to spend it. If one has a girlfriend, he wants eagerly to write many poems and becomes very romantic. If one has a great teacher, he wants to learn something from him. Likewise, if we have a king, we want to be loyal and faithful unlimitedly. Historically, people have been so loyal and extremely joyful to serve their kings. Once when King David was thirsty, his three mighty men broke through the Philistine lines, drew water from the well near the gate of Bethlehem, and carried it back to David. They did not care about their lives as long as they could please their king. Historically, there has been an unquenchable desire in men to be loyal to their kings. Why is it so? It is a mystery. However, it is clear that God made men like this so that men can serve God, the King of kings, as his loyal and faithful subjects.

Paul was loyal and faithful to Jesus because he acknowledged Jesus as his King in his heart. He expressed his loyalty to him in 2 Timothy 2:11-12a, "If we died with him, we will also live with him; if we endure, we will also reign with him." St. John was in exile on the Isle of Patmos. His suffering as a cave prisoner was great, but as his expression of loyalty to his King, he recorded in Revelation 2:10b, "Be faithful, even to the point of death." This loyalty of Christians to their King Jesus has been so invincibly strong that no power of principalities has broken it. The power of the Roman Empire failed to break it. These days, secular humanists want to break the loyalty of Christians in many ways, but they cannot. It is like kicking the goads or dashing an egg on a rock.

What kind of king is Jesus? First, he is a humble king. When worldly kings enter their cities after a victory, they march in, riding on a white horse, followed by innumerable dignitaries, attended by banner-bearers and soldiers armed with weapons, and saluted by the blast of trumpets paying homage to the king. But Jesus, a poor king, made his public entry into the Holy City Jerusalem mounted on a borrowed colt with his followers' clothes for a saddle and attended by a shouting crowd of poor people. For the display of his parade he had palm branches. King Jesus is humble and lowly.

Second, Jesus is the King of peace. Usually kings rode on a horse during wartime and on a donkey in the time of peace. But Jesus rode on a donkey when he entered Jerusalem to fell Satan's invincible fortress. Worldly kings destroy and kill their political enemies in order to attain the power of a king. But Jesus entered Jerusalem to die on a tree for the sin of the world. St. John said that Jesus is worthy to be our king because he was slain for our sins. Revelation 5:12 reads, "Worthy is the Lamb, who was slain, to receive power and wealth and wisdom and strength and honor and glory and praise!" When he is our King, we have true peace.

Third, Jesus is the King of salvation. Zechariah 9:9 reads, "Rejoice greatly, O Daughter of Zion! Shout, Daughter of Jerusalem! See, your king comes to you, righteous and having salvation, gentle and riding on a donkey, on a colt, the foal of a donkey." This prophecy describes the character of the Messiah King as being righteous, gentle, and humble. But his purpose in entering Jerusalem was to destroy the kingdom of Satan and save his children from the hand of Satan. In brief, he is the King of salvation. The crowd in Matthew's Gospel welcomed him, saying, "Hosanna to the Son of David!" (9a). "Hosanna" is a Hebrew expression meaning "save."

Through this, we learn that Jesus is the only King who saves men from their sins. Peter said, "Salvation is found in no one else, for there is no other name under heaven given to men by which we must be saved" (Ac 4:12). Jesus is the King of salvation. Everybody needs Jesus' salvation. We must have a right view of man and the world in Jesus.

III. Jesus wept (39-44)

How did the Pharisees respond to Jesus' coming into Zion? Read verse 39. "Some of the Pharisees in the crowd said to Jesus, 'Teacher, rebuke your disciples!'" At that time, the Pharisees were the religious leaders. From God's point of view they were supposed to be shepherds of God's flock and Bible teachers of his people, as well as of all peoples of all nations. They had been the people waiting for the Messiah King. But because of their petty desires, they gave up waiting for the Messiah King. They became unfaithful to their King. They became political figures. They became spiritually blind. They could not see the glorious revelation of God's promises concerning the Messiah King's coming into Zion. With their establishment power, they wanted to stop the work of God.

What did Jesus say to them? Read verse 40. "'I tell you,' he replied, 'if they keep quiet, the stones will cry out.'" His entering into the city as the Messiah had been the only hope for them. At last, according to God's promises, he came to this world in human form, giving up all the glory and power of the kingdom of heaven. His entry into Jerusalem on a colt is salvation to men and glory to God. It is a glorious revelation to the chosen people. No one can stop this work of God. If men are silent, heaven and nature will cry out for his coming. Even the stones will cry out for his coming to Zion. But the religious leaders wanted to stop this work of God.

Read verse 41. "As he approached Jerusalem and saw the city, he wept over it." Why did Jesus weep? It was because the city of God had become the city of Satan. God had made Jerusalem the city of God, from which the law of God would go out, and where the people of all nations could come and study the word of God. But the city was filled with Satan's rebellion and unbelief. Now the glory of God and the peace of God were being brought to men by Jesus' coming to Zion. But it was hidden from the eyes of the people of Jerusalem.

Jesus wept because horrible judgment was impending on them. Read verses 43 and 44. "The days will come upon you when your enemies will build an embankment against you and encircle you and hem you in on every side. They will dash you to the ground, you and the children within your walls. They will not leave one stone on another, because you did not recognize the time of God's coming to you." This prophecy was carried out in A.D. 70 by the Romans at the fall of Jerusalem. This is just a picture of the future judgment.

IV. King Jesus who judges (45-48)

When Jesus came to Jerusalem, he first entered the temple. But it was full of businessmen selling and buying. On seeing them, Jesus began driving out those who were selling. Thus far, we studied about meek and humble Jesus. But Jesus who drove the merchants out of the temple is quite a contrast to this. We learn here another side of Jesus' kingship. He is not only the King of salvation, but also the righteous King who judges. Jesus drove them out of the temple because they made the house of God a den of robbers. The temple is supposed to be a house of prayer. But the religious leaders did not pray. They used the prayer house as a marketplace. They were already too corrupted to be cured by spiritual medicine.

Here we see the profile of Jesus as the righteous King. Jesus loves people. He saves and heals. But he does not compromise with sin. When he came to this world, he came as a humble King and as the King of peace and the King of salvation. But when he comes again, he will come with the armies of God in power and glory to judge the living and the dead. In this passage, we learn that Jesus is the King of salvation and the King of judgment.

Lesson 51

The Parable of the Tenants

Luke 20:1-19
Key Verse: 20:17b

I. THE AUTHORITY OF JESUS QUESTIONED (1-8)

1. What has Jesus been doing throughout his ministry, and what was he doing now? Why did the chief priests and other Jewish leaders question Jesus about his authority?
2. Where did Jesus' authority come from?
3. How did Jesus respond to them? Why did Jesus ask them about John's authority?
4. What was the discussion they had amongst themselves? What was their conclusion? What does their discussion and conclusion show about them?

II. THE PARABLE OF THE TENANTS (9-19)

5. What did the man who planted the vineyard do with his vineyard when he went away on a journey? What did he expect at harvest time? Why? Who does the owner of the vineyard represent? The tenants?
6. When the owner sent for some of the fruit, how did the tenants respond? What does this show about them? What happened to the three successive servants?
7. What did the owner finally decide to do? Why? What happened to his son? What does this event predict?
8. What will the owner of the vineyard do? Who are the "others"?
9. When the people refused to accept this teaching, suggesting that God would never do such a thing, what Bible teaching did Jesus give them? What does verse 17 mean?
10. What does it mean that "everyone who falls on that stone will be broken to pieces, but he on whom it falls will be crushed"? What should we learn from this parable?

The Parable of the Tenants

Luke 20:1-19
Key Verse: 20:17b

"The stone the builders rejected has become the capstone."

N VERSES 1-8, ALL the rulers of the establishment join together to
denounce the divine authority of Jesus with a concocted question.
It was too malicious a question to answer. But Jesus, pleading with
love, confronts their question, hoping that they might come back to
a spiritual realization. But he did not stop there. He told them the
parable of the tenants, attempting to awaken them to the work and
history of God.

I.   The authority of Jesus questioned (1-8)

What did Jesus do right before Satan's final assault and during
the one week's time before his crucifixion? He planted the trees of
truth and hope in the hearts of lost souls. Read verse 1. "One day as
he was teaching the people in the temple courts and preaching the
gospel ..." It was the time for Jesus when the cross was on his mind,
and he was struggling with it. In spite of this, he was doing what he
should do. He was doing his best to do the will of God. To do the
will of God for Jesus was to plant the word of truth and the hope of
the kingdom of God in the hearts of lost souls. It is amazing that he
taught the word of truth to the people at the beginning of his ministry and was still teaching the word of truth during the last days of
his life and ministry.

One day I met a friend of mine. He looked so gloomy and anxious. So I asked him what was the matter. He said, "I have to go to
court for my parking ticket, so I could not sleep at all last night." But
it is indeed amazing that Jesus could teach the word of truth to the

people who came to him during the last week of his earthly lifetime. Through this we learn that no matter what happens, we must teach the word of God to people who are unlikely to accept the word of God because of their wretchedness.

What did the religious leaders do at this time of the Passover? Read verses 1b and 2. "… the chief priests and the teachers of the law, together with the elders, came up to him. 'Tell us by what authority you are doing these things,' they said. 'Who gave you this authority?'" In these verses we learn that they were amazed by the authority of Jesus, for they asked, "By what authority you are doing these things?" At the same time, they were enraged by Jesus because they thought he was doing night work without a license, for they said, "Who gave you this authority?"

They were religious leaders who were component parts of the Sanhedrin, the supreme council of the Jews. They had seen him riding into Jerusalem like a king. They had seen him cleansing the temple, driving the merchants out. What was even more surprising for them was that he came to the temple regularly from early morning and taught the word of God to the crowd of people who came to the Passover festival. They felt threatened. They felt that they themselves were powerless and crumbling before the authority of Jesus. So they came and said, "Who gave you this authority?" By this question, they cross-examined Jesus to get him to say directly that he did these things with authority from God, so that they might charge him with blasphemy and catch him preaching illegally without a license. They devised a scheme to charge him as an outlaw.

What did Jesus say to them? Read verses 3 and 4. Jesus did not answer them. Instead he asked them a question. He replied, "I will also ask you a question. Tell me, John's baptism—was it from heaven, or from men?" When they heard Jesus' question, they felt they were driven up against a wall. So they discussed it, in defiance of their prestige, among themselves and said, "We don't know!" These miserable creatures confessed their spiritual blindness to spiritual realities, though they were supposed to be spiritual leaders. If they said, "From men," all the people would stone them because the people were persuaded that John was a prophet. If they said, "From God," Jesus would rebuke them because of their unbelief. His words spoke to their consciences. But they refused to face the truth and said, "We don't know where it was from." They knew in their hearts what Jesus was talking about, but they refused to answer. In this way, they deceived themselves and also exposed themselves for who they really were.

Irrationally, they had tried to stop the work of God with their establishment power, but they failed. Probably they had never thought they were hindering the work of God. They had never thought that they were rebelling against God's will. Probably they thought that they were servants of God because they were wearing the robes of priests. But in reality, they were the devils.

The deep motive of Jesus' question was not to drive them into a predicament, but to help them think about how God's work had been fulfilled through John the Baptist and through Jesus himself. According to God's promises, John came and preached the baptism of repentance. He witnessed to Jesus as the Lamb of God, saying, "Look, the Lamb of God, who takes away the sin of the world!" (Jn 1:29). He had fulfilled the role of the forerunner of the Messiah and ended his life in martyrdom (Isa 40:3-5). According to God's promises, Jesus, the Messiah, came and fulfilled the work of the Messiah. He preached the good news to the poor. He proclaimed freedom for the prisoners and recovery of sight for the blind. He released the oppressed and proclaimed God's grace of forgiveness of sin. He preached the kingdom of God to those who had no hope in the world (4:18-19; Isa 61:1-2). The work of God through John the Baptist and through Jesus was self-evident. But these religious leaders did not recognize it.

II. The parable of the tenants (9-19)

Read verse 9. He told them the Parable of the Tenants so that they might open their spiritual eyes to see who they were. The Parable of the Tenants is a poem of God's history. This parable is pleading with and rebuking the leaders of Israel. Through this parable, Jesus showed their position in God's work and history. In this parable, we learn something about fallen man and about God who rules men and history.

First, it teaches of human blessing and privilege. Read verse 9b. "A man planted a vineyard, rented it to some farmers and went away for a long time." In this verse, "a man" refers to God, and "some farmers" to the rulers of Israel. In light of the book of Isaiah, the vineyard stands for the nation of Israel (Isa 5:1-7). God made the world and everything in it, and he gave it to men to take care of and to bear much fruit so that they might render fruit to God and also rejoice with the abundant fruit. Man did not make anything. Everything was made by God, including our very lives. How wonderful it is to enjoy his life in us and the privileges of taking care of God's world as his workmen.

Whether we believe it or not, God gave the best blessing and privilege to each person and to each nation. For example, in his great wisdom, God did not give Israel a materially rich and big, mighty country like Egypt. Instead, God gave them a special mission to be the Bible teachers for all the peoples of all nations. To Israel, their blessing was the best, and theirs was the most blessed privilege. But they despised spiritual blessings. They envied the material blessings of other countries. They were not grateful to God for his blessing to them. They did not accept God's blessing to them as the best blessing of all. They were bitter toward God.

Through this we learn that God blessed each person and each nation in the best way he could bless them. But most people think that those who are rich materially are blessed and that those who are poor materially are not blessed. This is fallen man's way of thinking. For example, children from rich families are not necessarily happy. They never ate bread mixed with tears and sweat. They do not know the deep agonies of human beings. On the other hand, those who are suffering because of their human conditions are not necessarily unhappy. Rather, they are happy because they can better understand the suffering of Jesus as well as the suffering of people.

Whatever the situation we may be in, when we deeply meditate on our life, we can only marvel at God's love toward us. God blessed each one of us in the best way that he could. But it is not easy to realize God's grace upon each of us. Each person can only realize God's grace through our Lord Jesus Christ. Humanly speaking, Jesus was the one who had lived the most sorrowful and tragic life. But Jesus was the one who knew God's grace the deepest. Those who do not know God's grace and blessing as the best are still in the darkness. They are spiritually blind. There is no happiness in the world for such a person. Therefore, each of us must be very sure to know in what respects, "I am the most blessed one in the world."

Second, this parable teaches about fallen mankind. Read verse 10. "At harvest time he sent a servant to the tenants so they would give him some of the fruit of the vineyard." This tells us allegorically that God made men stewards of his world and gave them freedom to care for their own vineyards by their own devices. How great it is to be a steward of God's world.

How did the tenants bear their obligation? Read verse 10 again. "At harvest time he sent a servant to the tenants so they would give him some of the fruit of the vineyard. But the tenants beat him and sent him away empty-handed." The tenants had probably been thankful when the owner of the vineyard entrusted the vineyard to them. So they must have worked hard to produce much fruit. But when they saw the abundant fruit, they went crazy. They were in a welter of confusion. They became greedy and were overcome by their greediness. When the owner of the vineyard sent a servant to the tenants to get some of the fruit of the vineyard, the tenants beat him and sent him away empty-handed. They committed an act of rebellion. They were no more themselves as human beings.

Fallen man always rebels against God when he is most blessed. In my early ministry, I dedicated myself to raise seven young men. They grew up enough to be leaders. Then they forgot God's grace through me and rather wished that I would die soon so that they might take over my leadership. When the tenants beat up the servant of the owner, they did not care what would happen tomorrow. They could send his servant away empty-handed. They thought that they were the owners of the vineyard.

As the history of Israel proves, the Israelites, the chosen people, repeatedly rejected God and his servants. Their rejecting God was a national habit, stretching through the ages. God chose Israel as his own people and trained them in Egypt for 430 years in the hope of raising them as a priestly nation—a nation of Bible teachers. After 430 years of training, God sent them to the promised land. But what did they do? No sooner had they arrived in the promised land than they completely forgot God's grace and his calling to be a priestly nation. They only enjoyed the flowing of milk and honey in the promised land. They became sick with the cultural diseases of the land, which degenrated their spirituality to the animal level. They could not maintain their honor as a priestly nation. Virtually, they were corrupted. They became miserable when they abandoned God, licking the milk and honey of the land. When they became miserable, they called out to God. Whenever they called out to God, God faithfully responded to their prayers and saved them again and again.

Did they get better when God saved them again and again? No, they were just the same. They were like a dog which returns to its vomit (2Pe 2:22). We see fallen man in the people of Israel. A fallen man is one who forgets God and his mission given to him. Hosea lamented over the fallen men of Israel in Hosea 13:5-6: "I cared for you in the desert, in the land of burning heat. When I fed them, they were satisfied; when they were satisfied, they became proud; then they forgot me." Here we learn that forgetting is abandoning.

Third, this parable teaches of God's long-suffering patience and of his judgment. Read verse 10. "At harvest time he sent a servant to the tenants so they would give him some of the fruit of the vineyard." In this verse, "he" refers to God, and "a servant," to the prophets. God sent his prophets with messages to his people so that they might have a right relationship with him. Whenever God sent his prophets, the people mistreated them or persecuted them and killed them relentlessly.

Why did they do so? They wanted to be the owners of the vineyard. When they wanted to be the owners of the vineyard, they could not accept his servants. They were outraged whenever they saw that his servants were sent. However, the owner did not strike at the first sign of their rebellion. He gave them chance after chance to do the right thing. But the tenants treated the servants with increasing contumely and cruelty. Not content with beating the first messenger, they added shameful treatment the second time, and proceeded to wound the third.

What did the owner of the vineyard do to them? Read verse 13. "Then the owner of the vineyard said, 'What shall I do? I will send my son, whom I love; perhaps they will respect him.'" He must have known that he was running a risk in sending his son, but he desired so much to bring the dishonest stewards back to their duty that he was willing to run the risk. This highly figurative expression is meant to emphasize God's longing for men's stewardship of his vineyard, and for the sake of this, he hopes in all things and endures to the end.

The tenants showed contempt for the riches of his kindness, tolerance, and patience. At first they thought they just made a small mistake. The owner did not punish them. Then they thought, "Nothing happened to us." So they said, "We are okay." They presumed on the master's patience. In their miscalculation, they made a terrible mistake. Read verses 14 and 15. "But when the tenants saw him, they talked the matter over. 'This is the heir,' they said. 'Let's kill him, and the inheritance will be ours.'" So they threw him out of the vineyard and killed him." In this way, they rejected God's love, and they thought they could get away with it before the owner.

What did the owner of the vineyard do? Read verse 16. "He will come and kill those tenants and give the vineyard to others." When the owner saw that the tenants did not keep their position as the stewards of his vineyard and did everything they wanted, he took the vineyard away from them and gave it to others.

Fourth, this parable teaches us Jesus' faith in God's history. When people heard of the judgment, they said, "May this never be!" (16b). Jesus looked directly at them and asked, "Then what is the meaning of that which is written: 'The stone the builders rejected has become the capstone'?" In this verse, we learn two things.

In the first place, we learn the judgment of God. This quotation about the stone which the builders rejected comes from Psalm 118:22-23. It is a favorite quotation which the early church applied as a description of the death and resurrection of Jesus (Ac 4:11; 1Pe 2:7). Jesus came to that which was his own, but his own did not receive him; they killed him and threw him away like a rejected stone, for he did not fit into their blueprint. They freely rejected Jesus, but the result was horrible. In verse 18 Jesus said, "Everyone who falls on that stone will be broken to pieces, but he on whom it falls will be crushed." Those who reject Jesus for small benefits or small pleasures will be like this. Therefore, we must live before God.

In the second place, we learn that Jesus is the sure foundation. Even though he was facing the cross, Jesus had the faith that God would raise him from the dead. Jesus laid his hand on the ancient prophecy of the stone rejected by the builders and applied it to himself. He is the stone rejected by his people Israel. To the eyes of people, he became useless, like a stone rejected by the builders. He was abandoned by men. But he believed that God would elevate him to the summit of the building and make him the sure foundation of all human beings. All other things were like sinking sand. When Jesus had to be crucified, the will of God to save the world seemed to be shattered. But Jesus believed that God would fulfill his salvation plan through him, the rejected stone. He believed that God would raise him from the dead and make him the sure foundation of all men.

Lesson 52

He Is the God of the Living

Luke 20:20-47
Key Verse: 20:38

I. TO CAESAR WHAT IS CAESAR'S, TO GOD WHAT IS GOD'S (20-26)

1. Why did the Pharisees send spies to Jesus? (19-20) What was their question? (21-22) Why was this such a controversial issue? In what respects was this question a trap?

2. How did Jesus respond to them? (23) How does this teach man's basic obligations to rulers of the world and to God? What are man's basic obligations to God?

II. WHOSE WIFE WILL SHE BE? (27-33)

3. What was the Sadducees' place in Jewish society? Why do you think they said there is no resurrection? (27) Why do you think they came to Jesus with this question?

4. Notice carefully the main contents of their question (28-33). What does this reveal about their inner way of thinking? Why do you think their inner way of thinking was so tragic? How can they be compared to modern yuppies?

III. THE GOD OF ABRAHAM, THE GOD OF ISAAC, THE GOD OF JACOB (34-40)

5. How did Jesus describe the main concern of the people of this age? (34) Why can't marriage be a solution to people's problems? How did Jesus describe the new age? (35-36) Why is this the true hope for all human beings? What does it mean, "those who are considered worthy of taking part in that age and in the resurrection from the dead"?

6. How did Jesus teach the truth of the resurrection? (37-38) Why did he use the example of the Lord being called "the God of Abraham, and the God of Isaac, and the God of Jacob"? What does this mean? What can we learn from this about human beings? (38) What can we learn from this about God?

IV. WHOSE SON IS THE CHRIST? (41-47)

7. What was Jesus' question to the teachers of the law in verses 41-44? How does this teach his deity and ultimate victory? How

does this reveal that even though they knew many sophisticated things about the Bible, they did not know the main point? According to verses 46 and 47, what kind of people were they?

He Is the God of the Living

Luke 20:20-47
Key Verse: 20:38

> *"He is not the God of the dead, but of the living, for to him all are alive."*

THIS PASSAGE INCLUDES THREE questions: a question about whether the Jews should pay taxes to Caesar or not (20-26), a question about marriage life in the resurrection body (27-40), and a question about how Jesus, one of the descendants of David, can be David's Lord (41-47). The first two questions were manipulated subtly in an attempt to trap Jesus. Nevertheless, Jesus kindly talked to his opponents, hoping that they might open their spiritual eyes to see spiritual things and come to God Almighty.

I. To Caesar what is Caesar's, to God what is God's (20-26)

Three sets of men—chief priests, scribes and elders, and the ruling class of the Jews—asked Jesus by what authority he was carrying out his ministry. Jesus asked them back, "Tell me, John's baptism—was it from heaven, or from men?" (3-4). They were silenced. With great compassion, Jesus told them the Parable of the Tenants, hoping that they might come to realize their original mission as God's chosen people. Instead of acknowledging his compassion, they were determined to trap Jesus in order to hand him over to the power and authority of the Roman governor (20). They sent spies to Jesus who pretended to be honest. They asked him, "Teacher, we know that you speak and teach what is right, and that you do not show partiality but teach the way of God in accordance with the truth. Is it right for us to pay taxes to Caesar or not?" (21-22).

The tax mentioned here was a poll tax. The Jews did not complain about the burden of this tax, for it was less than $5. Nevertheless, Roman taxation was a boiling question among the Jews and had been the cause of incessant rebellion. At that time, the Jews claimed that they had no king but God, and they held that to pay the poll tax to Caesar was treachery to God. If Jesus had said that this tax should not be paid, as surely as the night follows the day, the Pharisees would have reported this at once to Pilate so that Jesus might be arrested. If Jesus had said that this tax should be paid, all the frantic Jews would have stood against him.

What could Jesus do in this situation? Read verse 23-25. "He saw through their duplicity and said to them, 'Show me a denarius. Whose portrait and inscription are on it?' 'Caesar's,' they replied. 'Then give to Caesar what is Caesar's, and to God what is God's.'" Jesus did not try to avoid them by merely giving them a shrewd answer. Rather, he answered them on the basis of God's truth. He said, "Then give to Caesar what is Caesar's, and to God what is God's." This verse teaches us that we have basic obligations to the rulers of the world and to God.

If a man lives in a country and enjoys all its privileges, he must fulfill four basic obligations: paying taxes, national defense, elementary education, and labor. In time of war, all eligible men in their twenties are obliged to be drafted. Everyone should submit themselves to the governing authorities, for there is no authority except that which God has established (Ro 13:1). The authorities that exist have been established by God. He who rebels against the authorities is rebelling against what God has instituted.

Likewise, we, as children of God, have basic obligations to God. Each person is created by God; therefore, each person has basic obligations to God as his child. When God created man, he created him for the glory of God; therefore, each person is obliged to live for the glory of God. God made man to be the steward of his world; therefore, each person has a basic obligation to take care of God's world as a steward. God made man to do a specific mission from God; therefore, each person has a basic obligation to carry out God's mission.

II. Whose wife will she be? (27-33)

After the Pharisees' emissaries left Jesus, the Sadducees came to Jesus with a question. They were wealthy Jews and a politically-minded group. They had a close connection with pagan leaders. Ironically, they controlled the high priesthood at that time, though they were not spiritual people at all. They held the majority of seats in the Sanhedrin. They were largely collaborators with Rome. In order not to risk losing their wealth, comfort, and positions in the world, they used any and all available means. They did not want to believe something that seemed to disturb their establishment in the world. In order to rule ecclesiastically, they accepted only the written law of the Old Testament and set no stock in the prophetic books which urged them to repent. They believed in unrestricted free will.

They asked who would be the husband in heaven of the woman who was married to seven different men. Their question was based on the levirate law. For example, when Er, the firstborn of Judah, died with no heir, his younger brother Onan married his wife Tamar. When Onan also died, Tamar had to wait for Shelah, the youngest son of Judah, to grow up as a man and become her husband (Ge 38:1-11). The Sadducees hoped that this kind of question would make resurrection faith look ridiculous. They were the intelligentsia of the times. They were wealthy. They had political power and their own place in the world. They looked happy. They were the objects of aspiration. In brief, they were the yuppies of their times. But they were tragic in many ways.

First, what they thought of was tragic. Read verses 29-31. They talked about the death of seven brothers who were most unlucky as human beings. All of them did not live long enough. Each died young and childless. This story is gloomy because it contains the death of seven young men. This story also contains a most sorrowful woman who had married these seven brothers and then died herself, unable to fulfill her duty of bearing an heir to the family.

Their question was full of tragedy. They were talking and thinking only about tragic death—the first son's death, the second son's death, and all seven brothers' deaths, and finally, the death of the woman who had seven husbands and died childless.

The gist of their question was, "At the resurrection, whose wife will she be, since the seven were married to her?" (33). In other words, they were really asking, "Who would possess her as his wife among the seven brothers?" The Sadducees had already possessed enough. They had obtained the places of honor in society. Still they were interested in scrounging something. They were not satisfied with what they had. They were weary, not knowing satisfaction. They were tragic, making frantic efforts to possess something. They were sick and tired because of their greediness.

Second, they had no spiritual reality in their thinking. The Sadducees did not believe in spiritual realities, much less in the resurrection of the body. Therefore, what was on their minds were present realities, such as material wealth, marriage, success, and future security. They thought about the things of the world, which were prospering and perishing, boiling and spoiling. They were sick and tired because they always thought about the sick and tired world. Leo Tolstoy wrote so many good things about human beings, but what he really thought about human beings was not so beautiful. When he breathed his last, he cried out, "Tragedies, tragedies!" His last cry must have been what he really felt and thought about human beings.

One man I know wanted to enjoy his life with his great wealth. He thought he would be happy if he could drink little by little, for a long time, throughout his lifetime. But he was always miserable whenever he thought about people better than himself or richer than himself. Whenever he became miserable, he would beat his wife and children. He could not enjoy his great wealth because he died young. Paul wrote in Romans 8:6, "The mind of sinful man is death, but the mind controlled by the Spirit is life and peace."

Those who want to live in this world easily and gloriously cannot understand the deep meaning of human agonies and sufferings because they have no spiritual eyes to see it. For example, through much suffering, man can grow in perseverance, humbleness, love, sympathy, wisdom, courage, and inner strength. John Milton was blinded at the zenith of his life. But in his sufferings due to his blindness, his spiritual eyes were opened and he wrote "Paradise Lost." Only in the darkness of the night can we see the stars in the distant sky. Those who have spiritual eyes can see the deep meaning of human sufferings and agonies and can grow in the image of God, and they are really happy. They can see spiritual meaning in everything, even in death. As a result, they become noble children of God. People like the Sadducees who desire to be easy and happy cannot have a right attitude toward human sufferings and agonies. As a result, to them everything seems to make them suffer. The world is literally a living hell to them.

People like the Sadducees want to enjoy their lives in this world. They become very hedonistic. They corrupt themselves by enjoying sinful pleasures, and they also corrupt others. Their inner man becomes like that of a leper and they become extremely miserable. Furthermore, in their personal lives they make God sorry.

III. The God of Abraham, the God of Isaac, the God of Jacob (34-40)

Read verse 34. "Jesus replied, 'The people of this age marry and are given in marriage.'" Jesus knew what people of this world mainly do. To mankind, birth, marriage, and death are the three main events of life. Men do their best to grow up and get married, and then die. Most women devote a great deal of time in solving their marriage problems. I know one lady who spent eight years of her life only trying to solve her marriage problem. Since the curse came into the world because of one man's sin, women were cursed to only desire for a husband day and night. Because of this cursed desire, many women live in a curse. The people of the world seem to be doing many great things, but they do no more than the people in the terrible times of Noah. They are eating and drinking. They marry and are given in marriage. Most people think that they can solve their life problems if they marry. But this is not true. One boy was stone-faced for the last two and a half years because of his marriage problem. After marriage, he had on big smiles for two or three days. But now he became stone-faced again.

Read verse 35. "But those who are considered worthy of taking part in that age and in the resurrection from the dead will neither marry nor be given in marriage." In the new age, there will be no more serious problems, such as marriage problems or broken family problems. There will be no more businesses, procreation, or death.

Those who are considered worthy of taking part in that age and in the resurrection from the dead will be like angels. They are not angels; they will look like angels. They will look most noble. They will look most pure. They will look most beautiful. They are called God's children. Each one is worthy to be called the son of God or the daughter of God.

The Sadducees declared that they could not believe the resurrection of the body because there was no information about it, still less any proof of it in the books of the Law. But Jesus gave them an answer from the book of Exodus. Read verses 37 and 38. "But in the account of the bush, even Moses showed that the dead rise, for he calls the Lord 'the God of Abraham, and the God of Isaac, and the God of Jacob.' He is not the God of the dead, but of the living, for to him all are alive." These words, "The God of Abraham, and the God of Isaac, and the God of Jacob" are repeated over and over again in the Bible whenever it was necessary to teach that God is living. These verses have deep meaning.

First, these verses teach us that man is an immortal being. "The God of Abraham, the God of Isaac, and the God of Jacob" means that God is not only the father of Abraham, but also the father of Isaac and of Jacob. It also means that before the living God, all three of them are alive. Even though the three of them died bodily, they are alive spiritually. In short, these verses teach us that men are immortal. According to Jesus, this immortal body will be resurrected again in the likeness of Jesus at the time of his second coming. We will all look like Jesus. Man is different from other animals because he is an immortal being. We must remember this truth day and night.

Second, these verses teach us that God is the God of history. Horizontally, God is the God of Abraham and the God of Isaac and the God of Jacob. Vertically, God is the God of Abraham and the God of David and the God of Jesus Christ. Through men and women of faith, God rules the world according to his sovereign will.

Third, these verses teach us that God is not the God of the dead, but of the living. Those who believe in God have no elements of death or tragedy of death in them. There is no fatalism in them. Instead, in their inner persons, they are full of life. They are full of hope. They are full of love. Our God is the Sovereign Ruler. The world is ruled by many politicians. But they are not the real rulers. God rules the world in his sovereign will. His sovereign will is to send his Son again to judge the living and the dead. His sovereign will is to save all people so that they might live forever before him.

The Sadducees asked him, "Whose wife will she be?" This question is based on the death of seven brothers and on the sorrowful woman who died childless. This kind of question is connected with the emptiness of life in this world and with the fear of death. This kind of question is silly. Jesus said that our God is the God of Abraham and the God of Isaac and the God of Jacob, and the God of you and me. In God we live forever.

IV. Whose son is the Christ? (41-47)

Some of the teachers of the law responded, "Teacher, that's right, that's right!" These teachers of the law thought of themselves as religious, so they did not like the Sadducees' atheistic view of life. Jesus saw the hypocrisy in them and asked them a paradoxical question so that they might somehow open their spiritual eyes to see their own spiritual blindness.

Read verse 41. If the Messiah was supposed to be a descendant of David, how could David, this honored king, refer to his own offspring as "Lord"? With their logic, they could not answer this question. Unless Jesus' opponents were ready to admit that the Messiah was the divine Son of God, they could not answer his question. They proved themselves to be ignorant spiritually. They did not know anything about the main points of the Bible. They were self-glory seeking, hypocritical, and they took advantage of the defenseless group of people by fraud and schemes for selfish gain. They were under great condemnation.

Read verses 45-47. "While all the people were listening, Jesus said to his disciples, 'Beware of the teachers of the law. They like to walk around in flowing robes and love to be greeted in the marketplaces and have the most important seats in the synagogues and the places of honor at banquets. They devour widows' houses and for a show make lengthy prayers. Such men will be punished most severely.'"

We see that the hippie generation has passed away and that the yuppie generation has come. But yuppie life without spiritual reality is tragedy itself. We must believe in God who is the God of Abraham and the God of Isaac and the God of Jacob. We must also believe that we are immortal beings.

Lesson 53

Signs of the End of the Age

Luke 21:1-38
Key Verse: 21:8

I. A WIDOW'S OFFERING (1-4)

1. Read verses 1-4. What did Jesus teach his disciples about giving? How does the value system in the spiritual world contrast with that of the material world? (Dt 6:5; Lk 18:11-12)

II. WATCH OUT THAT YOU ARE NOT DECEIVED (5-19)

2. Why did the temple impress Jesus' disciples? How was Jesus' view of the temple and elaborate rituals different from that of his disciples? What shocking thing did he tell them about the temple?

3. What two questions did the disciples ask Jesus? Why did the destruction of the temple seem to imply the end of the age?

4. As the end time approaches, what is the first thing of which Christians must be aware? What are the false messiahs which try to deceive God's people? How can we avoid being deceived?

5. What are some of the earth-shaking events that will happen before the end comes? When they happen, how can we not be frightened?

6. How and why will Christians be persecuted in the last days? Why can times of persecution become opportunities to glorify God? How can we know what to say and have courage to say it when we are persecuted?

7. According to verse 16, what will be the persecution that is most difficult to endure? What does this teach us about our priorities? What promises does Jesus give to those who are faithful to him in every circumstance?

III. THEY WILL SEE THE SON OF MAN COMING (20-38)

8. Jerusalem was destroyed in AD 70. What does Jesus predict about the destruction of Jerusalem? How is this a portent of the future?

9. What are the signs that will appear in the heavens at the time of Jesus' second coming? Why will men be terrified?

10. Describe the coming of the Son of Man. What does his coming

mean to mankind? How can we be sure that the kingdom of God is near?

11. What kind of preparation can we make so that we will be sure to be ready to joyfully greet and stand before the Son of Man when he comes again?

Signs of the End of the Age

Luke 21:1-38
Key Verse: 21:8

"**W**ATCH OUT THAT YOU are not deceived. For many will come in my name, claiming, 'I am he,' and 'The time is near.' Do not follow them" (8).

In this passage, Jesus tells his disciples about the signs of the end of the age. However, Jesus' discourse was neither meant to gratify idle curiosity, nor to supply a timetable in advance, but to minister encouragement and to lead to watchfulness. Whether "that day" (34) is understood as the fall of Jerusalem or as the final coming of the Lord, it will come as a snare upon men who are absorbed with the earthly things which will perish. In this chapter, we learn that we should not be dismayed at the signs of the end of the age, but must have a wary eye to see the signs of the end of the age in view of the promises of God.

I. A Widow's Offering (1-4)

Jesus knew that his disciples were greatly tempted when they saw the rich put their big bundles of money into the temple treasury in the sight of many people. In order to teach his disciples, Jesus told a story about a poor widow. He said, "This poor widow has put in more than all the others" (3). Jesus really wanted his disciples to know that a sacrificial heart is more important than money. The widow's offering reminds us of Deuteronomy 6:5. It says, "Love the Lord your God with all your heart and with all your soul and with all your strength." On the other hand, the rich people's offerings remind us of Luke 18:11b-12 where a Pharisee says, "God, I thank you that I am not like other men … I fast twice a week and give a tenth of all I get." The rich were like the swaggering Pharisees in the temple. Here Jesus teaches his disciples that they must see the things of the world with a spiritual value system.

II. Watch out that you are not deceived (5-19)

Read verse 5. "Some of his disciples were remarking about how the temple was adorned with beautiful stones and with gifts dedicated to God." According to Mark 13:1, Jesus and his disciples had just come out of the temple. They were leaving the temple for the Mount of Olives, which was situated in full view of the temple. It was obvious that Jesus was going there with his disciples to pray about his approaching suffering and crucifixion. Of course, Jesus had decided to accept the cup of suffering and death—even death on the cross. But it was not easy for him. Jesus, as a sheep before her shearers, was silent. But when he had to take up the sin of the world as the Lamb of God, Jesus needed much prayer to overcome himself, as well as the world, so that the world salvation plan of God might be fulfilled.

What was in his disciples' minds? Probably they felt deeply ashamed of their dusty clothes when they looked at the priests in pompous robes using elegant manners. Read verse 5. "Some of his disciples were remarking about how the temple was adorned with beautiful stones and with gifts dedicated to God." The poor disciples bubbled over, looking at the beauty of the massive stones of the temple buildings. The disciples, who were susceptible to the glittering things of the world, reveal their worldly desires. They were amazed by the spectacle of the temple building, adorned with beautiful stones and covered all over with plates of gold of great weight. They also envied rich people who threw big bundles of money into the offering box. Maybe they sighed and said, "When can we have even a small house where we can have dinners and gather and talk?" To Jesus, they were the future leaders of the world who should influence the world to such a degree that the trend of world history would be changed and human culture and civilization would be set on right foundations. But the disciples had no spiritual insight to see the culture.

Jesus understood their surprise at the aggregation of cultural achievements. But he wanted them to have prophetic insight and a sense of history to see through human culture. Jesus prophesied to them concerning the doom of Jerusalem and its temple. Read verse 6. Jesus said, "As for what you see here, the time will come when not one stone will be left on another; every one of them will be thrown down." They were surprised at his words and asked, "Teacher, when will these things happen? And what will be the sign that they are about to take place?" (7).

His disciples were like children playing in the marketplace, so vulnerable to Satan's attack. So Jesus said in verse 8a, "Watch out that you are not deceived." They needed to watch to keep themselves from the cravings of sinful man, the lust of their eyes, and the love of the world. And Jesus continued, speaking of several signs of the end of the age for which to watch out.

First, the rise of false Messiahs. Read verse 8b. "For many will come in my name, claiming, 'I am he,' and, 'The time is near.' Do not follow them." Who are the false messiahs? Those who teach people things that are quite opposite to the truth are all false messiahs. Jesus, the true Messiah, taught us meaningful suffering for the glory of God through the way of the cross and gave us the promise of the glorious kingdom of God. But the false messiahs teach the way of an easy-going life, justification of living according to the sinful nature, and pleasure-seeking lifestyles. They falsely promise peace and security and earthly utopias. They are liars and inventors of evil.

In the past, political ideologies were false messiahs. Communists promised a utopia with a classless society. But they have built an iron curtain, behind which are many concentration camps. Capitalists, in the name of democracy, promised a utopia where people could enjoy freedom and peace. But instead of freedom and peace, people in this social structure suffer from fear and insecurity more than one can say. After the ideological wars ended, materialism became the false messiah. Many earthbound people thought they would be happy if they had much money. So in order to make money, they did every-thing. In the process, they sold their consciences. They even taught their children how to be deceptive and bold at telling lies. But they could not buy happiness with money. Instead, they became more sinful by abusing the power of money.

But these days, hedonism seems to be the most powerful false messiah. The basic idea of most people is to seek pleasure. In this hard world, people want to enjoy fun and relax even for a while. Many people want to go crazy even for a little while. Many people want to enjoy excitement. Many young ones enjoy dark privacy. As a result, their lives become a bad joke.

Hedonism has been the worst enemy of mankind and a most deceptive false messiah. In the past in Rome, many hedonists sadistically enjoyed the bloodshed of gladiators, and history proves that hedonism was the main cause of the destruction of the Roman Empire. We see the bad influence of hedonism in grandfather Noah's time, as in the time of Sodom and Gomorrah. People were eating, drinking, marrying, and being given in marriage up to the very time when the flood came and destroyed them all (Lk 17:27). 2 Timothy 3:4 says these kinds of people are "treacherous, rash, conceited, [and] lovers of pleasure rather than lovers of God."

Hedonism appeals to many passionate young men. But we must know that the basic foundation of hedonism is fatalism. To those who don't believe in God, death is the end of everything. So they say, "Let us eat and drink, for tomorrow we die" (1Co 15:32b).

We have to think about why so many false messiahs arise. It is because people are wandering, not knowing where to go or what to do or why they have to work so hard to survive. People who live without God seem to be free. But they belong to the descendants of Cain, who wandered without destination in an overpowering sense of punishment and fear.

People who live without God are relativistic. They have no absolute truth of God in their hearts. They think about everything relatively. In 1975, I met a female student in Chicago. At that time, she was a freshman. She studied the Bible with Sarah Chang for a while and left. After four years, she visited us on the day she was supposed to get married. I was very much surprised to see her gloomy face. She said, "My boyfriend married another girl." I was very angry and said, "He practically lived with you for the last four years—and he disowned you?" After a while she said, "We shared benefits mutually." What a surprising relativistic idea! What a rebellious idea about God's truth between a man and a woman!

People who live without God are like sheep without a shepherd. They are lost and troubled. They seek guidance. Then the false messiahs arise to devour them. They make use of their vulnerable spots and capture them as their slaves.

Second, man's paralysis with fear is another sign of the end of the age. Read verse 9. "When you hear of wars and revolutions, do not be frightened. These things must happen first, but the end will not come right away." Most people are gripped with fear because of the world's dark situation. In the world, there are continual rumors of war, and the probability of an accidental explosion due to nuclear missiles is real. People are so fearful that they are ready to do anything to overcome their fear. Because of fear, many people practice drugs. According to a cocaine hotline specialist, every day 5,000 Americans try cocaine for the first time. They say that a one-time use of cocaine costs over $100. Nonetheless, people spend money they earned by hard labor seeking to quell their fears even for a moment.

Third, another characteristic of the end of the age is the rise of God-haters. Read verse 12. "But before all this, they will lay hands on you and persecute you. They will deliver you to synagogues and prisons, and you will be brought before kings and governors, and all on account of my name." The immediate cause of the persecution of Christians was the apostasy of Judaism and the resistance to Roman Emperor worship. But the direct cause of the persecution of Christians was Jesus' name.

In the last days, the world is full of haters of God. They think it strange that Christians do not plunge with them into the same flood of dissipation, and they heap abuse on us. But they have to give account to him who is coming again to judge the living and the dead (1Pe 4:4-5). They are tolerant of rock music in a crowded apartment building, but they are intolerant of hymn singing in the same apartment. I saw a mother who didn't care when her daughter was rebellious and mean. But since her daughter became a Christian, she began to persecute her day and night for no reason. I saw a father who said nothing when his son lived a sinful life. But since his son became a Christian, he began to hate his son furiously. But in reality, they do not hate their children. They hate God because they are haters of God. They hate God as much as they are sinful and fearful.

Read verse 13. "This will result in your being witnesses to them." Here we learn that Christians can witness to Christ through much persecution. But Christians do not have to worry about what to say to them (14-15). We may be sure that we are hated because of his name's sake (17). Then God will protect us so that not a hair of our heads will perish (18). All we have to do is stand firm in the words of the promises of God (19).

III. They will see the Son of Man coming (20-38)

In this part, Luke the historian tells us how to see the signs of the last days as Christians. First, Christians must see the world phenomena with God's eyes. For example, the fall of Jerusalem, the Holy City, and the desecration of the Jerusalem temple are too painful to think of. It appeared to be the total decline and fall of God's work and history. Such things as these can discourage God's people for a while. Nevertheless, we must see all the ups and downs of the world as the process of fulfilling all that has been written in the prophecies. Read verse 20. "When you see Jerusalem being surrounded by armies, you will know that its desolation is near." This was Jesus' prophecy, closely related to verse 6, "As for what you see here, the time will come when not one stone will be left on another; every one of them will be thrown down." As Jesus prophesied, in AD 70, Jerusalem fell to the besieging army of Titus, who was later enthroned as Emperor of Rome. At that time, the temple was completely desecrated and demolished so that not one stone was left on another. At that moment, the meaning of this event was inscrutable. However, in view of history, the fall of Jerusalem was a powerful factor in the deliverance of the Christian church from Jewish swaddling bands which hampered its growing limbs. To Jesus' people, all things work for good.

Read verses 20-24. When Jerusalem was besieged and fell, it was so calamitous that no one could escape. This was the time of punishment for the haters of God. At the same time, it was the time of fulfillment of God's prophecy of all that had been written. To a woman, pregnancy is a time of joy and a nursing mother is a symbol of peace. But all these kinds of blessings turn out to be burdens. After the destruction, many people were dragged into captivity in foreign lands. This happened just as it was prophesied.

Second, at that time they will see the Son of Man coming (25-33). At that time, when the Son of Man comes in a cloud with power and great glory, there will be no more need for the sun and moon because the glory of the Son of Man will shine over the whole world.

The Son of Man's coming again will be the most glorious day. At that time, all the things of the world will be renewed. There will be a new heaven, new sea, and new sky. This is the day Christians earnestly expect to see. In the last days, all the elements of the world will dissolve, such as the sun, moon, and stars. When the sea, which is the center of earthly gravity, is greatly troubled, roaring and tossing on the earth, nations will be in anguish and perplexity. Men will faint from terror, apprehensive of what is coming (25-26). Peter also spoke about this in 2 Peter 3:10. "But the day of the Lord will come like a thief. The heavens will disappear with a roar; the elements will be destroyed by fire, and the earth and everything in it will be laid bare."

The day of the Lord will be really horrible for those who have lived for selfish purposes and rebelled against God as the haters of God. But for those who have lived for the sake of his name, it will be the day of glory and victory. The people of the world scoff (2Pe 3:4) and boldly commit sins. They reject Christians for no obvious reason and give them a hard time whatever they do. This is not the rejection of men; it is the rejection of the Son of Man. Godless men deliberately rejected the Son of Man. They crucified Jesus on a cross simply because he is the Son of God. They threw him outside the city wall of Jerusalem. They thought they would never see him again. But verse 27 says, "At that time they will see the Son of Man." They will see him with their own eyes, coming in a cloud with power and great glory. They must stand before him to be judged. This will be a bad day for those who rejected the Son of Man. On the other hand, this will be the day of salvation and honor and final victory for those who have sacrificed and cried many tears for the sake of his name. Read verse 27 again. "At that time they will see the Son of Man coming in a cloud with power and great glory."

How do we know this? Read verses 29-31. "He told them this parable: 'Look at the fig tree and all the trees. When they sprout leaves, you can see for yourselves and know that summer is near. Even so, when you see these things happening, you know that the kingdom of God is near.'" Generally, people see the world negatively and despair. But we must have prophetic insight to see the world from God's point of view and see that the future is glorious because the kingdom of God is near.

Still, there are many reasons for Christians to despair at the world's dark situation like the people of the world. So in verses 34 and 35, Jesus warns us to be careful. "Be careful, or your hearts will be weighed down with dissipation, drunkenness and the anxieties of life, and that day will close on you unexpectedly like a trap. For it will come upon all those who live on the face of the whole earth."

Read verse 36. "Be always on the watch, and pray that you may be able to escape all that is about to happen, and that you may be able to stand before the Son of Man." We must always be watchful so that we may be able to stand before the glorious King on that glorious day. Christians should not be negative about the world even though the world is filled with evil and darkness. We must rejoice in Jesus. We must love Jesus all the more. We must learn how to see the dark world from God's point of view. We must love one another and pray diligently. Also, we must have deep compassion on those who have no hope of the kingdom of God, and for those who do not have the joy of waiting for the second coming of Jesus. We must preach the good news of Jesus Christ to them without fail. We must be positive about the future world because the kingdom of God is near and Jesus is coming again with power and great glory.

Lesson 54

The Last Supper

Luke 22:1-38
Key Verse: 22:20b

I. JUDAS AGREES TO BETRAY JESUS (1-6)

1. As the Passover time approached, what were the religious leaders thinking about? At this time, what did Judas, one of the Twelve, do? What kind of attitude does one have who lets Satan enter his heart?

II. THE NEW COVENANT OF BLOOD (7-23)

2. What did Jesus tell Peter and John to do? Why might this have been hard to do? What did they learn from obeying his instructions?

3. Why did Jesus want so much to eat this Passover with his disciples? What is the historical background of the Passover? (Ex 12:7,12,29-32) In what ways does slavery in Egypt parallel slavery to sin?

4. In verses 16-18, what did Jesus teach about the kingdom of God, and how does Jesus himself fulfill the meaning of the Passover? (Jn 1:29; Rev 19:9)

5. What did Jesus teach about the meaning of the bread he broke and gave them? How can Jesus, the Bread of life, satisfy our spiritual hunger (Jn 6:35,56-57)

6. After supper, what did Jesus teach about the meaning of the cup? What does it mean that Jesus makes a blood covenant with us? (Ro 3:10, 5:8-9; 1Jn 1:7) Have you made a personal blood covenant with Jesus?

7. What did Jesus say about Judas? Though he ate at this love feast with Jesus, why could he not bear Jesus' love? What can we learn here about the tragedy of an uncommitted life?

III. THE TRULY GREAT MAN IN THE KINGDOM OF GOD (24-38)

8. What did the disciples argue about among themselves? What does this show about their spiritual condition? How should the disciples' way of serving be different from that of worldly people? What was the example of Jesus himself?

9. What is the glorious promise Jesus gave his disciples? What is the

prerequisite of ruling with Jesus in his kingdom?

10. What was Jesus' prayer topic for Simon Peter? Why was Simon especially vulnerable to Satan's attack?

11. What new instructions did Jesus give the apostles? Why did he give these instructions? What do they mean practically to disciples?

The Last Supper

Luke 22:1-38
Key Verse: 22:20b

> *"This cup is the new covenant in my blood, which is poured out for you."*

ESUS, BEFORE HIS CRUCIFIXION, ate the Passover in a large upper room. We call this event "The Last Supper," in which Jesus taught his disciples the meaning of the new covenant of blood. Let's participate in the Last Supper from our hearts so that we may somehow know better the meaning of the new covenant of blood.

I. Judas agrees to betray Jesus (1-6)

Read verses 1 and 2. The time of the Feast of Unleavened Bread, called the Passover, was approaching, and the chief priests and teachers of the law were looking for some way to get rid of Jesus, for they were afraid of the large crowd of people who came annually to the Feast. This crowd of people might turn to Jesus and follow him. So the chief priests and teachers of the law were so desperate that they were looking for someone who could be used to lay their hands on Jesus.

Read verse 3. "Then Satan entered Judas, called Iscariot, one of the Twelve." It is a big surprise that one of the Twelve betrayed Jesus. Judas Iscariot must have been able and trustworthy, for he was the treasurer of the apostolic band. In the past, as was customary, followers of a teacher loved their teacher more than themselves. It is hard to imagine why Judas Iscariot betrayed Jesus.

When we study the gospels, we learn that Judas had never displayed a high motive of service or commitment to Jesus. He did not follow Jesus to become one of his disciples; he followed him just because it seemed beneficial. He was happy to follow Jesus when Jesus was popular and his preaching ministry was successful. But when the world seemed to be standing against Jesus, Judas became uneasy. When Jesus came to Jerusalem to be slain as the Paschal Lamb, Judas could sense a kind of ominous presentiment. In the final analysis, Judas was wondering indecisively whether he should follow Jesus further or slip away. We don't know exactly why and how he could betray Jesus.

Both Luke and John say quite simply that Satan entered into Judas (3; Jn 13:27). It is amazing to see that Satan crept into Judas when Judas was wandering with an uncommitted heart. At that moment, Satan entered him. He became a servant of Satan and began to serve Satan.

Read verses 4-6. It is unbelievable that Judas went to the chief priests and officers of the temple guard and discussed with them how he might betray Jesus. They made a deal. Since then, Judas watched for an opportunity to hand Jesus over to them when no crowd was present. Those who have no commitment seem to be smart. But they must know that in the long run they only become like Judas Iscariot, one who should not exist in the world.

II. The new covenant of blood (7-23)

Now it was the first day of the Feast of Unleavened Bread on which the Passover lamb had to be sacrificed. Read verse 8. "Jesus sent Peter and John, saying, 'Go and make preparations for us to eat the Passover.'" It was customary for them to eat the Passover, but they could not afford a room in which to eat the Passover. So the disciples asked, "Where do you want us to prepare the Passover?"

Read verses 10-12. "He replied, 'As you enter the city, a man carrying a jar of water will meet you. Follow him to the house that he enters, and say to the owner of the house, "The Teacher asks: Where is the guest room, where I may eat the Passover with my disciples?" He will show you a large upper room, all furnished. Make preparations there.'" It was not unusual for Jesus to command his disciples like this. At the time when Jesus was preparing to make a triumphal entry into Jerusalem, Jesus said to his disciples, "Go to the village ahead of you, and as you enter it, you will find a colt tied there, which no one has ever ridden. Untie it and bring it here. If anyone asks you, 'Why are you untying it?' tell him, 'The Lord needs it'" (19:30-31).

But it is amazing that his disciples obeyed his impossible command. The city of Jerusalem, as well as its satellite towns, was packed with pilgrims. It was utterly impossible for them to find a room. Though they were fishermen, people in the labor class, they had awesome respect for Jesus' word, for they loved him. They were always ready to obey whatever he said. Peter had such an attitude from the beginning. One day, early in the morning, Peter was mending his nets after fishing all night on the sea. He was hungry and tired. He was at the point of blowing up. But when Jesus said to him, "Put out into deep water, and let down the nets for a catch," he said, "Master, we've worked hard all night and haven't caught anything. But because you say so, I will let down the nets" (5:4-5). It was his humbleness that made it possible for him to grow in Jesus as the greatest man who ever lived. Peter and John left and found things just as Jesus had told them. They say that this was Mark's house.

Read verses 14 and 15. "When the hour came, Jesus and his apostles reclined at the table. And he said to them, 'I have eagerly desired to eat this Passover with you before I suffer.'" Jesus was happy to eat the Passover at the table with them before he suffered. Jesus told them that there would be no more eating the Passover until the time of the heavenly banquet of those redeemed through the death and resurrection of Jesus Christ.

What was the significance of their eating the Passover? It had a historical meaning (Ex 12). It commemorated the deliverance of the Israelites from their bondage in Egypt. The life of the Israelites in Egypt was misery itself. Just to eat three meals a day, they had to undergo forced labor day after day. Their lives in Egypt were a life of sin because what they did was eat delicious food and sleep comfortably. They had no purpose or meaning in life. They had no mission of God. It was a cursed life. This describes human life under the power of sin.

God had mercy on his people and decided to deliver them. But Pharaoh, the symbol of the power of sin, did not let the Israelites go. God sent plagues on Egypt. As each plague came, Pharaoh promised to let the people go. But when each plague abated, he changed his mind. The plagues were repeated nine times. Finally, God gave Pharaoh a choice to make: either let the people go, or see God strike down all the firstborn of all kinds in Egypt (Ex 12:29). But Pharaoh did not listen to God's words through Moses. It was the plague of the angel of death. No firstborn was exempt, not even the firstborn of Pharaoh the king.

In the meantime, the Israelites were to slay a lamb. With a bunch of hyssop, they were to smear their doorposts with the blood of the lamb, and when the angel of death saw the doorposts so marked, he would pass over that house, leaving its residents safe.

Therefore, eating the Passover meant deliverance from the yoke of slavery in Egypt. It was the great commemoration of the great love of God who delivered them from the hand of Pharaoh. In order to eat the Passover, they had to slay a year-old male lamb without defect and sprinkle its blood on the doorposts for their deliverance. They also roasted the meat of the lamb and ate it. They dried the bones and used them as firewood. They dried the skin and used it as paper. The Paschal Lamb was completely sacrificed. This deliverance was made possible through the blood of the lamb. This is the so-called covenant of blood.

Read verse 16. "For I tell you, I will not eat it again until it finds fulfillment in the kingdom of God." Verse 16 implies that Jesus himself is the Paschal Lamb at this Passover. In John 1:29, John the Baptist said, "Look, the Lamb of God, who takes away the sin of the world!"

Now it was the last supper with his disciples before he would suffer. Jesus would eat no more Passover meals until the coming of the future kingdom. Finally, the fellowship would be consummated in the great messianic wedding supper to come. Revelations 19:9 says, "Then the angel said to me, 'Write: "Blessed are those who are invited to the wedding supper of the Lamb!"' And he added, 'These are the true words of God.'"

Read verse 19. "And he took bread, gave thanks and broke it, and gave it to them, saying, 'This is my body given for you; do this in remembrance of me.'" "This is my body given for you." The Israelites satisfied their stomachs by eating the meat of lambs. Likewise, men can really satisfy themselves when they take the body of Jesus. Jesus is the Bread of life. He who comes to Jesus will never go hungry, and he who believes in him will never be thirsty (Jn 6:35). These days many people are depressed or tired because they are not satisfied with what they have or with what they are doing. They must come to Jesus and take the body of Jesus. Then they can find real satisfaction from God. Jesus satisfies man's soul.

Read verse 20b. "This cup is the new covenant in my blood, which is poured out for you." Jesus came to the world to die on the cross so that he might pour out his blood for many. He had to sacrifice himself by shedding his blood because only his blood can be a ransom in delivering people from the bondage of sin.

Many young people want to live a noble and pure life. One young man I know wants to live a noble and pure life, quitting his immoral life. But he fails all the time because of the sin-sick blood circulating in his soul. As a result, the power of sin in him is in charge and in command.

Nobody can ransom such people. Only the blood of Jesus can deliver them from the slavery of sin. If one goes to the hospital for treatment, his doctor first checks his blood because sick blood makes a person sick. Likewise, only the blood of Jesus cleanses and purifies our sin-stained blood. The blood of Jesus cleanses us from all our sinful desires and from our sinful thoughts and habits. When we are healed from our sin-sickness by the blood of Jesus, we can see the love of God for us. It is the promise of God that he would send his Son to die on the cross to shed his blood for our sins. This is the new covenant in his blood.

Read verse 20b again, "This cup is the new covenant in my blood, which is poured out for you." We must have a personal blood covenant with Jesus. Otherwise, we are still sick with sins and not healed. Some people think they are not sinners. But Romans 3:10b says, "There is no one righteous, not even one." We are all sinners—morally, ethically, and spiritually. We need to come to Jesus for the new covenant of blood.

They were eating the Passover. But Jesus said in verse 21, "But the hand of him who is going to betray me is with mine on the table."

This man was Judas Iscariot. He was eating the meaningful Passover with Jesus. He had received all the love that Jesus could give, but he could not bear God's love through his Son Jesus because of his uncommitted life.

Jesus said in verse 22, "The Son of Man will go as it has been decreed, but woe to that man who betrays him." Judas Iscariot should not have been born into the world. How tragic it is to see that there are so many people who do not make any commitment like Judas Iscariot.

III. The truly great man in the kingdom of God (24-38)

Read verse 24. "Also a dispute arose among them as to which of them was considered to be greatest." In the very shadow of the cross, the disciples quarreled about who was considered to be greatest. They were still worldly.

Read verse 25. "Jesus said to them, 'The kings of the Gentiles lord it over them; and those who exercise authority over them call themselves Benefactors.'" According to the worldly pattern, a king who exercises power and authority over people is called "Lord" or "Benefactor" by the people. Rulers or men in power expect respect and honor from the people under them; otherwise, they get mad. In ordinary society, the youngest ones are supposed to serve the older ones. But in the kingdom of God, the greatest should serve the youngest, and the one who is in a ruling position must serve others. In ordinary society, greater people eat at the table and servants serve. If greater ones sit at the table, servants serve the food dish by dish. If the greater ones want something else, then they ring the table bell to call the servant to bring what he wants. But in the kingdom of God, things are quite contrary to this. Jesus always served his hungry disciples. Jesus' entire earthly ministry is a good example of this.

Read verse 28. "You are those who have stood by me in my trials." In this verse, "in my trials" refers to Jesus' entire earthly ministry during which he battled with Satan. His disciples had always been with him and had seen how he was with God. They had seen how he served people as his expression of his serving God.

Therefore, God was pleased with Jesus who served his flock, and

God entrusted to him the kingdom of God to rule. As God entrusted to Jesus his kingdom, so Jesus would entrust to his disciples the kingdom of God to rule. This is the promise that if his disciples learned how to serve God and how to serve his people as Jesus had done, they would attain power to rule in the kingdom of God together with Jesus, sitting on thrones judging the twelve tribes of Israel. Thank God for this promise. We, the children of God, must learn how to serve other sinners as ones who would rule in the kingdom of God together with Jesus.

At the critical moment, what was Peter's spiritual condition? He was in a great spiritual crisis. Satan was ready to devour him, for he was the top disciple of Jesus. So Jesus said in verse 31, "Simon, Simon, Satan has asked to sift you as wheat." Jesus knew that he would fail to keep his faith. But Jesus prayed for him so that when he had turned back, he might be able to strengthen his brothers. Read verse 32. "But I have prayed for you, Simon, that your faith may not fail. And when you have turned back, strengthen your brothers."

What was Peter's response? Read verses 33 and 34. "But he replied, 'Lord, I am ready to go with you to prison and to death.' Jesus answered, 'I tell you, Peter, before the rooster crows today, you will deny three times that you know me.'" Jesus knew that he would not keep his faith with human loyalty.

When Jesus saw his disciples, he could see that they were still vulnerable to Satan's attack, so he helped them prepare for the future without him. Jesus asked, "Did you lack anything when you were with me?" "Nothing," they answered. Then Jesus said to them in verse 36, "But now if you have a purse, take it, and also a bag; and if you don't have a sword, sell your cloak and buy one." This verse does not mean that they should buy swords and fight. It means that they must prepare spiritually to meet upcoming hardships and sufferings without Jesus. In this verse, Jesus urges them to arm themselves to stand in faith, absolutely depending on God.

Jesus illumines them about what is going to happen to him. Read verse 37. "It is written: 'And he was numbered with the transgressors'; and I tell you that this must be fulfilled in me. Yes, what is written about me is reaching its fulfillment." This is a quotation from Isaiah 53:12, which says, "Therefore I will give him a portion among the great, and he will divide the spoils with the strong, because he poured out his life unto death, and was numbered with the transgressors. For he bore the sin of many, and made intercession for the transgressors." This prophecy would be fulfilled in the body of Jesus. In this prophecy, Jesus suggests that he would be betrayed and handed over to the hands of men and would suffer many things. Finally, he would be considered as an evil man and criminal deserving capital punishment. But his disciples did not understand the spiritual meaning of his saying and said, "See, Lord, here are two swords" (38).

Lesson 55

Father, Take This Cup from Me, Yet ...

Luke 22:39-62
Key Verse: 22:42

I. JESUS PRAYS ON THE MOUNT OF OLIVES (39-46)

1. Why did Jesus go to the Mount of Olives? What do the words, "as usual," suggest about Jesus' prayer life?

2. What instructions did Jesus give his disciples before he withdrew to pray alone? What kind of temptation lay before them?

3. What was Jesus' first prayer request? What did he mean by the "cup"? What does this tell us about Jesus?

4. How did Jesus address God? What does this show about his relationship with God? What was God's will for him? (18:31-33) Did Jesus know that will? What was the nature of his spiritual struggle?

5. Describe Jesus' attitude of prayer. What can we learn from him about prayer?

6. What were the disciples doing while Jesus prayed? Why? Why was it so important for them to pray instead of sleep, even though they were exhausted? What can we learn here about the necessity of prayer?

II. JESUS ARRESTED (47-53)

7. What decision had Jesus made in prayer? How did Jesus' greeting to Judas make him aware of Jesus' identity and of the awfulness of what he was doing?

8. How did the disciples react when they saw what was happening? How does this show their spiritual unpreparedness?

9. In what respect were Jesus' attitude and actions a contrast to that of his disciples? Why did Jesus describe this hour as the hour "when darkness reigns"?

III. PETER DISOWNS JESUS (54-62)

10. What do the words "Peter followed at a distance" and "Peter sat down with them" suggest about Peter's attitude and spiritual condition?

11. Who recognized Peter first? What made him deny knowing Jesus? What were his other words of denial, and what motivated

him in each case?

12. When did Peter come to his senses and realize what he had done? What kind of look do you think the Lord gave Peter? What shows Peter's deep remorse and repentance? Did Peter ever meet Jesus again?

Father, Take This Cup from Me, Yet ...

Luke 22:39-62
Key Verse: 22:42

> *"Father, if you are willing, take this cup from me; yet not my will, but yours be done."*

IN VERSES 39-46, JESUS prays on the Mount of Olives. His prayer on the mountain was so important as a hinge of world salvation. After his prayer, Jesus was arrested (47-53). During the time of his trial, his beloved disciples scattered, and Peter, the top disciple, disowned him (54-62). Outwardly, Jesus looked utterly disowned by the people of the whole world and defeated by Satan. But it was not so. Jesus who prayed on the Mount of Olives was with God Almighty who rules the whole world on his throne. Virtually, he won the war against Satan before fighting. May God help us to learn Jesus' prayer on the Mount of Olives.

JESUS PRAYS ON THE MOUNT OF OLIVES (39-46)

I. Jesus went out to pray as usual (39-41)

Read verse 39. "Jesus went out as usual to the Mount of Olives, and his disciples followed him." The Mount of Olives is also called the Garden of Gethsemane in other gospels (Mt 26:36; Mk 14:32). As Jesus did not own such a garden flourishing with olive trees, obviously some wealthy friend had given him the privilege of using it, and it was there that Jesus went to pray as usual. "As usual" indicates Jesus' habit of prayer. The life of Jesus, from the beginning to the end, was a life of prayer. Mark 1:35 says, "Very early in the morning, while it was still dark, Jesus got up, left the house and went off to a solitary place, where he prayed." Mark was greatly moved by Jesus' early morning prayer life. Luke 21:37 says, "Each day Jesus was teaching at the temple, and each evening he went out to spend the night on the hill called the Mount of Olives." Luke the evangelist and historian saw that the life of Jesus was a life a prayer.

Jesus ministered to God's flock thronging to him by laying his hand of healing on the sick and by preaching the good news of the kingdom of God to those who were lost. Jesus also taught his disciples while eating or traveling on foot on the road. In terms of time, Jesus had no time to pray. But he prayed. He prayed very early in the morning. He prayed each evening, staying up late. Prayer is a personal conversation with God. Jesus, the Incarnate God, could have done everything with his own wisdom and power. But he did not. Early in the morning, Jesus talked with God in prayer. He renewed his mission and spiritual strength and worked all day long. When evening came, he went to solitary places and prayed.

Like Jesus, we must not do anything before praying to God. Even though we are able, we must listen to God first in prayer and do something with the wisdom from above. Then those who are around us can be blessed because of our prayers.

There are many kinds of people with many kinds of habits. Some people have a habit of worrying about everything for nothing. I know a man who formed a habit of self-pity when he was eight years old. He is now sixty-one years old with the same habit. It is easy to form a bad habit. But it is not easy at all to form a good habit. But we see that those who have good habits are prosperous and those who have bad habits are not happy, even though they have everything. When we deeply meditate on the concept of a habit, we learn that a habit is psychological dependence. Those who have a habit of drug abuse have a dependence on drugs. Jesus who had a habit of prayer had total dependence on God. In other words, Jesus had absolute faith in God. We must not habitually worry. We must not be slaves of bad habits. How wonderful it is to know that Jesus had a habit of prayer. We must do our best to imitate Jesus in forming the habit of prayer.

Jesus himself came to the Mount of Olives to pray, but he also urged his disciples to pray so that they would not fall into temptation, for the death of Jesus might be the best opportunity for the devil to tempt the disciples to stumble in their faith (40). Jesus also needed their prayer support. It was the only time for Jesus to battle to overcome himself in order to obey the will of God. So he withdrew about a stone's throw beyond them, knelt down and prayed (41). Read verse 42. "Father, if you are willing, take this cup from me; yet not my will, but yours be done."

II. Jesus prayed before the cup of suffering (42)

At that time, the "cup" did not refer to a championship cup of victory. The "cup" meant the cup of poison or death. The cup of suffering and death lay before Jesus, so he prayed, "Father, if you are willing, take this cup from me." He pleaded with God earnestly that he might not take the cup.

As we know well, human beings are clumps of desires—the desire for money, the desire for marriage, the desire for political power, the desire for world conquest, etc. Among the basic human desires, the desire for honor seems to be strong. A sense of honor is very important to each man. However, no one can deny that the desire for long life is the strongest. This may be the reason why people of the past blessed their king, saying, "Long live the king!" Everyone in their thirties struggles to improve their life conditions in this world, withstanding hardships and sufferings for a better future life security. In their thirties, no one wants to die.

Though Jesus is God, in his manhood, he must have hoped to live, as others do. Instinctively, he had never hoped to die. What's more, Jesus knew what crucifixion was like. It was known as capital punishment for criminals who were sentenced to death. The cross was known as a symbol of shame. Nobody wants to be shamed. Even drug dealers hide their faces before cameramen in order that their shame may not be revealed. Jesus had to bear the most shameful cross in order to bear all our shame.

The cross was the most painful punishment. It was the worst kind of punishment. But Jesus had to bear the cross in order to bear our burden of sin. Surely, the impending sufferings were pictured in his mind. The keen anticipation or apprehension of pain, which makes up so large a part of many human sorrows, overwhelmed him. He was afraid and did not want to drink the cup of death at all. If someone had asked you, "Do you want to drink the cup of death and die?" your answer would be, "No!" and a thousand times "No!" It must have been the same with Jesus.

Jesus knew very well what God's will for him was. But it was very difficult for Jesus to decide to take the cup. So he prayed, "Father, if you are willing, take this cup from me." Jesus' desire was to live in this world like other human beings and not die. God's will was that he die on the cross like a criminal for the sin of the world. But one thing is very clear. Jesus knew that he should overcome his own desire in order to accept God's will for him.

We see there are so many young people who long for the holiness of God. They are really yearning to be pure, noble, and different from others. But most of them do not know what to do with their overpowering desires. They just follow the ways their desires and thoughts direct them. Finally, they become slaves of their sinful desires. They become Satan's prey and the objects of God's sorrow and wrath (Eph 2:3).

Here we learn that we must go to the Garden of Gethsemane and kneel down on our knees and pray in order to overcome our own human desires and follow God's will for each of us. We must pray that our desires be changed into God's desires. May God sanctify and ennoble our desires into his own holy desires.

III. Jesus prayed to obey God's will (42)

Read verse 42 again. "Father, if you are willing, take this cup from me; yet not my will, but yours be done." These days, most people want to wear their own style of clothing. They have their own kind of lifestyle. They enjoy free will. They completely lost the spirit of true democracy and only make use of the benefits that democracy seems to offer. They don't want to obey anybody. The word "obedience" seems to offend all who have been educated in a democratic society. When such people have to do something which involves obedience to God, they immediately run away from the main issue and turn the subject into a theological argument and make the matter of obedience nonsense. When they discover that God's will for them demands sacrifice and obedience, many people habitually say, "I don't know if it is God's will."

When Jesus had to drink the cup of death all by himself after having served God so faithfully, Jesus did not doubt God's love. Jesus was willing to obey God's will, even if it meant death. But Jesus needed much prayer to do so.

Jesus knew that he was the Chosen One, the suffering servant as prophesied in Isaiah 53. Jesus knew that he had to be slaughtered like a lamb for the price of men's sins. Because he was sure of God's will for him to be the ransom sacrifice for the sin of the world, Jesus frequently told his disciples about the necessity of his rejection, suffering, and death. Luke 9:22 says, "And he said, 'The Son of Man must suffer many things and be rejected by the elders, chief priests and teachers of the law, and he must be killed and on the third day be raised to life.'" Jesus taught the principle of a kernel of wheat and about glory after death.

As we know, knowing is one thing and doing is quite another. To decide to do something is not easy. One man I know has been struggling for the last nine years to make a decision to get married, and as a result, lost all his hair. But he could not make a decision yet. It was not easy for Jesus to decide to obey the will of God. Through prayer, he overcame himself and decided to obey God's will to drink the cup of suffering and death.

IV. Jesus fought the spiritual battle in prayer (43-46)

Read verse 44. "And being in anguish, he prayed more earnestly, and his sweat was like drops of blood falling to the ground." Jesus was not overcome by human sorrow when he had to take the cup of suffering. He overcame his feelings. He was tired and helpless, but he overcame his tiredness and went up on the Mount of Olives to pray. When he began to pray, he knelt down.

Jesus struggled so hard that he was completely exhausted. Jesus had no more strength left to fight. When Jesus had done his best and had come to his limitation, God from above helped him through the angel (43). God helps those who cannot help themselves; God helps those who want to obey God's will.

Jesus' prayer was the greatest spiritual battle. Luke, who was a medical doctor, described in verse 44 how Jesus fought the battle in prayer to defeat the whisperings of Satan and to submit himself to the will of God. "And being in anguish, he prayed more earnestly, and his sweat was like drops of blood falling to the ground." Let's thank and praise Jesus who showed us how to fight spiritual battles in prayer.

What were the disciples doing while he was praying? When he rose from prayer and went back to the disciples, he found them asleep, exhausted from sorrow. They knew that they should have participated in Jesus' prayer labor, but they were so sorrowful about so many things that they became extremely tired. While enduring their human sorrows, they became exhausted. They grappled for a while and then fell asleep. They were still earthly men who had no spiritual qualities.

Peter had said, "I am ready to go with you to prison and to death" (22:33), but when he had to prepare himself in prayer to face the upcoming sufferings and death, he did not pray, but slept with a sorrowful mind. When Peter fell asleep, all the other disciples slept also.

Read verse 46. "'Why are you sleeping?' he asked them. 'Get up and pray so that you will not fall into temptation.'" Jesus said, "Get up and pray!" Jesus is also saying to us, "Get up and pray!" There are so many young people who cannot get up from their sorrows. There are so many young people who cannot get up and pray because of their human thinking.

We know what we have to improve the spiritual condition of the young people of this land. What is the secret to doing so? It is prayer. We must learn Jesus' life of prayer.

JESUS ARRESTED (47-53)

Jesus had already won the battle before fighting. After prayer, Jesus looked like a triumphant general. While he was still speaking, a crowd came up, and the man who was called Judas Iscariot, one of the Twelve, was leading them. Judas was a guide for the temple police in arresting Jesus. He approached Jesus to kiss him as a signal to those he brought.

What did Jesus say to him? Look at verse 48. "Judas, are you betraying the Son of Man with a kiss?" Jesus knew what Judas was doing, so he exposed Judas' secret attempt to kiss him as a signal to the enemies of God. It is unbelievable that one of the twelve disciples betrayed Jesus to get some money. There was a problem; Judas did not know who the Son of Man really was, so he was selling Jesus for a certain amount of money. In verse 69, Jesus explains who he really is: "But from now on, the Son of Man will be seated at the right hand of the mighty God." This verse implies that Judas will be held accountable for his evildoing at the time of judgment. Luke 9:26 says, "If anyone is ashamed of me and my words, the Son of Man will be ashamed of him when he comes in his glory and in the glory of the Father and of the holy angels." Jesus, the Son of Man, is the Son of God. Judas betrayed the Son of Man for 30 pieces of silver. But in fact, he betrayed himself.

Out of anger, one of the disciples struck the servant of the high priest, cutting off his right ear (49-50). According to John 18:10, it was Peter who cut off the ear of the high priest's servant whose name was Malchus. Jesus said, "No more of this!" (51). Jesus told Peter to resist no more. Jesus told Peter to persevere, even in this. And he touched the man's ear and healed him. Those who came to arrest Jesus were the chief priests, the officers of the temple guard, and the elders. They were supposed to be the face and conscience of the nation and the prayer servants and Bible teachers for God's flock, but they were not. Jesus rebuked their evildoing, saying, "Am I leading a rebellion, that you have come with swords and clubs? Every day I was with you in the temple courts, and you did not lay a hand on me. But this is your hour—when darkness reigns" (52b-53). Jesus taught the Bible to the people in the light, openly, before the eyes of all people (21:37-38). But the religious leaders did not lay their hands on Jesus then. When the time of darkness came, they came to arrest Jesus. Jesus was arrested by evil men. How stunning it is that the religious leaders came to arrest Jesus!

PETER DISOWNS JESUS (54-62)

Let's see how Peter denies Jesus three times. Judas' betrayal was a heart-breaking event. Another scratch on the broken heart of Jesus was Peter's triple denial. Peter was the top disciple and he was loyal to Jesus (22:33). He was overconfident and not prayerful. So in his human limitation, he denied his Master three times.

Read verse 54. "Then seizing him, they led him away and took him into the house of the high priest. Peter followed at a distance." Jesus was cross-examined while hangers-on huddled around the fire. While Jesus was on trial, the darkness of night hung over the dawn, and the morning air was sharp. Peter, exhausted, sat near the firelight in great fear. He crept near the blaze of the fire. A servant girl saw him seated in the firelight and said, "This man was with him" (56b). "But he denied it, 'Woman, I don't know him,' he said. A little later someone else saw him and said, 'You also are one of them.' 'Man, I am not!' Peter replied. About an hour later another asserted, 'Certainly this fellow was with him, for he is a Galilean'" (57-59). He must have been Malchus, whose right ear Peter had cut off with his sword. "Peter replied, 'Man, I don't know what you're talking about!' Just as he was speaking, the rooster crowed" (60). With his human loyalty, he could not follow Jesus to the end. He denied Jesus three times.

Nevertheless, Jesus deeply cared for Peter. Jesus was coming out of the courtroom and saw that Peter was there. Verse 61a says, "The Lord turned and looked straight at Peter." We owe the knowledge of this look of Christ to Luke only. Jesus was tired after enduring the all-night trial of the priests and false accusations. But when Jesus saw Peter, Jesus looked straight at him. Why did Jesus look straight at him? Jesus looked straight at him mainly to remind him of his promises to Peter. Luke 22:32 says, "But I have prayed for you, Simon, that your faith may not fail. And when you have turned back, strengthen your brothers." Matthew 16:18 says, "And I tell you that you are Peter, and on this rock I will build my church, and the gates of Hades will not overcome it." When he denied Jesus, Peter was like sand on the seashore. When Jesus looked at him, he looked at him with the hope of God that someday he would become Peter, a foundation stone of his church. As Jesus hoped, after his resurrection, Peter became the foundation of the Christian church.

At the moment Peter saw Jesus, he remembered the word the Lord had spoken to him: "Before the rooster crows today, you will disown me three times" (61b). Peter went outside and wept bitterly. This cry was the moment that Peter opened his spiritual eyes to see the love of God. This cry made it possible for him to meet the Risen Jesus at the seashore where he had first met him.

From this passage, we learn that Jesus prayed before the cup of suffering. We also learn that Jesus depended on God absolutely through prayer and decided to take the cup of suffering and death. May God help us not to be slaves of emotions, but warriors of prayer. May God use each of us as prayer servants in this generation.

Lesson 56

The Crucifixion of Jesus

Luke 22:63-23:56
Key Verse: 23:34a

I. JESUS BEFORE PILATE AND HEROD (22:63-23:25)

1. What was Jesus' testimony before the council? (22:67-69) With what did they charge him? (70-71) What charge did they bring against him to Pilate? (23:2) What did Jesus answer? What does this mean? (23:3; Mt 2:2; Mic 5:2)

2. How did Pilate try, but fail, to defend Jesus? (23:6-7) Describe Herod's base character. Why did Pilate compromise? What was the result? (23-25)

II. JESUS WAS CRUCIFIED AND DIED (26-56)

3. Describe Jesus' suffering on the way to the cross. What warning did he give? (26-31) Why did he suffer like this? (1Pe 2:24b; Isa 53:6b) Describe the crucifixion. Why was he crucified? (Isa 53:12; Jn 1:29) What did Jesus pray? (34) How did he help one man on the cross? (39-43)

4. What happened when Jesus died? (44-46) How did Jesus show his total dependence on God? (46) What confession did the centurion make? (47) How did Joseph show his faith? (50-53) What is the meaning of Jesus' burial? (44-56; Isa 53:9-10)

The Crucifixion of Jesus

Luke 22:63-23:56
Key Verse: 23:34a

> *"Jesus said, 'Father, forgive them, for they do not know what they are doing.'"*

THIS PASSAGE TELLS US of Jesus' trial, his crucifixion, and his death and burial. Though our Lord Jesus was treated like a criminal and crucified by men, he revealed that he is God and the Savior of the world during the time of his suffering and death. His suffering, crucifixion, and death remain forever in history as facts and truth for the salvation of mankind. Let's learn the meaning of his death on the cross.

I. Jesus before Pilate and Herod (22:63-23:25)

As we studied, during the night Jesus had been brought before the high priest. There, they unofficially cross-examined and arrogantly made accusations about Jesus, hoping to trap him. He was handed over to the temple police and they played cruel jests on him (22:63-65). When morning came, he was taken to the Sanhedrin to be tried.

To ordinary people, appearing before the Sanhedrin members for a hearing was like going into a den of lions. Nobody could stand upright before them. Nobody could keep their cool before them without breaking into a cold sweat. Read verse 67. "'If you are the Christ,' they said, 'tell us.'" There was a trap in this statement. The charge they were attempting to produce against Jesus was blasphemy. Jesus knew what the result would be if he answered incorrectly. But Jesus did not compromise. What did he say in response? Read verse 69. "But from now on, the Son of Man will be seated at the right hand of the mighty God." They treated Jesus like a criminal. But according to this verse, Jesus is the Sovereign Ruler and Judge over all mankind on the throne of God. "They all asked, 'Are you then the Son of God?' He replied, 'You are right in saying I am'" (70). In this way, their conspiracy was forged. However, the Jews in the time of Jesus had no power to execute the death penalty.

The whole assembly rose and led him off to the Roman governor Pilate to indict him (23:1-2). Look at 23:2. "And they began to accuse him, saying, 'We have found this man subverting our nation. He opposes payment of taxes to Caesar and claims to be Christ, a king.'" The charge they made against Jesus was based entirely on political crimes—sedition, refusing to pay taxes to Caesar, and assuming that he was the king of the Jews.

Pilate asked him, "Are you the king of the Jews?" What was Jesus' response? Read verse 3b. "'Yes, it is as you say,' Jesus replied." His "Yes" was undoubtedly going to cause him to receive the death sentence. But Jesus answered "Yes" in order to keep his identity as the Son of Man.

Pilate came to the realization that the charge was quite a religious matter and that it came from the religious leaders' jealousy. He announced to the chief priests and the crowd, "I find no basis for a charge against this man." But they insisted on their claims. Shrewd Pilate found an escape. He learned that Jesus was under Herod's jurisdiction, so he sent him to Herod. When Herod saw Jesus, he was glad, hoping that Jesus would perform some miracle and amuse him. He plied him with many questions, but Jesus gave him no answer. For the sake of his amusement and curiosity, he clothed Jesus in a king's robe and sent him back to Pilate.

Pilate did not want to condemn Jesus because it meant betraying impartial justice, which was the glory of Rome. More than that, he could not find any basis for their charge against him. His wife sent him a message, "Don't have anything to do with that innocent man, for I have suffered a great deal today in a dream because of him" (Mt 27:19). Pilate was a Roman governor, but before innocent Jesus he became helpless. Pilate was a judge, but in reality, it was a day for Pilate to determine his future destiny before Jesus. So Pilate called together the chief priests, the rulers, and the people, and said to them,

"You brought me this man as one who was inciting the people to rebellion. I have examined him in your presence and have found no basis for your charges against him. Neither has Herod, for he sent him back to us; as you can see, he has done nothing to deserve death (14-15)." Pilate asked for a compromise, saying, "Therefore, I will punish him and then release him." This proposition did not work. With one voice they cried out, "Away with this man." Wanting to release Jesus, Pilate appealed to them again. This time they shouted, "Crucify him! Crucify him!" (21) It is really a horrible thing to know that there was once a time this crowd of people had followed Jesus like sheep following a shepherd, like loyal people to their king. But now they became agents of the devil.

Read verse 22. "For the third time he spoke to them: 'Why? What crime has this man committed? I have found in him no grounds for the death penalty.'" He did his best to compromise with them. When the devil prevailed over him, he surrendered Jesus to their will. Because of this, he was branded as the one who condemned Jesus, the Son of Man, to death. Even the Roman governor Pilate found in Jesus no guilt for the death sentence. Jesus was innocent, sinless. But Jesus suffered and was tried. Why was he tried as the Son of God? It was for us. Because of our sins, we must appear before the judgment seat of God to be judged (2Co 5:10). But our Lord Jesus was judged in our places. People shouted all the more, "Crucify him!" We are the ones who should have been cursed and shouted at, "Crucify him!" But Jesus was cursed by men as the one who should be cursed.

II. Jesus was crucified and died (23:26-56)

Finally Jesus was taken from the judgment hall and set in the middle of a hallow square of four Roman soldiers. They laid upon his shoulders a heavy cross and led him to the place of crucifixion by the longest possible route while before him another soldier marched bearing a placard with his crime inscribed on it: "This is the King of the Jews." Jesus suffered so much and was so roughly treated that he was exhausted. The Roman soldiers whipped him. Blood dripped from his back and from his whole body. Carrying the cross on his shoulder, Jesus sank beneath the weight of the cross. Then they seized

Simon from Cyrene and put the cross on him. Let's hear what Jesus said on the road to Calvary.

First, Jesus carried the cross even though he is the Judge over all men. Read verse 27. "A large number of people followed him, including women who mourned and wailed for him." The women may have been a group of pious women who had been healed of their sins and sicknesses by the hand of Messiah. They had tasted the grace of the forgiveness of sin. They had tasted the love of God in Jesus. They believed that Jesus was indeed the Son of Man. When they saw this good Jesus falling down under the heavy cross that crushed his body, they mourned and wailed.

Read verse 28. "Jesus turned and said to them, 'Daughters of Jerusalem, do not weep for me; weep for yourselves and for your children.'" Jesus understood their feelings and appreciated their weeping, but he did not comfort them humanly. Rather, he comforted them by telling them who he really was. Read verse 29. "For the time will come when you will say, 'Blessed are the barren women, the wombs that never bore and the breasts that never nursed!'" They were now weeping for Jesus who was carrying the cross of salvation, but they did not have to weep for this. They should have wept because of God's impending judgment on the people who were crucifying the Son of God.

Nursing women are the symbol of human beauty, and pregnant women are the symbol of human blessing. But the judgment of God would be so severe on the people of Jerusalem that at that time, the situation of barren women would be better than those of nursing mothers, and unmarried old women would be better off than pregnant women. "They will say to the mountains, 'Fall on us!' and to the hills, 'Cover us!'" (30). Likewise, those wicked men who are crucifying Jesus in their evilness will ask a favor of the mountains and hills to help them die sooner in the anguish of God's severe judgment. Read verse 31. "For if men do these things when the tree is green, what will happen when it is dry?" The Son of Man was on his way to Calvary to be crucified. But he is God who came to this world in human form and lived for a while among us as a humble shepherd. He is the Son of Man who is seated at the right hand of the mighty God. People in their ignorance treated the Son of God like a criminal who deserved to be cursed and crucified. Many people say "Jesus Christ" when they are upset. Most people are hardly concerned with the Son of Man, appealing to him at random according to their feelings. But this is a great mistake. Those who treat Jesus like this will see that they should weep over their own sins against him.

Second, the cross of Jesus is the cross of the forgiveness of sins. Read verse 32. "Two other men, both criminals, were also led out with him to be executed." The authorities crucified Jesus between two criminals on purpose. It was staged so as to humiliate Jesus in front of the crowd, treating him equally with robbers. When they came to the place called the Skull, they laid his cross flat on the ground, laid him on it, and, stretching out his limbs on the cross, they began to drive the nails through his hands and feet. They hung him on a projected piece of saddlewood which bore his weight. Then they lifted up the cross and set it upright on its socket.

He was oppressed and afflicted. He was like a lamb being led to the slaughter. Why was he crucified on the cross in this way? It was not for himself. It was for the sin of the world. God sent his one and only Son as the Paschal Lamb to shed his blood for the sins of the world. John the Baptist knew this and cried out in John 1:29, "Look, the Lamb of God, who takes away the sin of the world!" Jesus carried the heavy cross so that he might unburden us from the burden of our sins. Jesus was hung on the tree so that he might bear all our sorrows and iniquities. He was crushed so that we might be healed. There are many people who look good. But each person who does not know Jesus has incurable pain and wounds. But Jesus was wounded on the cross so that whoever looks at him on the cross might be healed. Peter said in 1Peter 2:24b, "… by his wounds you have been healed." Jesus, as the Son of Man, took up all our infirmities and carried our sorrows. He took up all our iniquities and the burden of our sins in this way. He bore the burden of our sins so that whoever comes to him might find rest.

They executed Jesus in between two criminals—one on his right, the other on his left. According to Matthew 27:34, Jesus refused a drink of drugged wine, which would have eased the terrible pain. Jesus was determined to face death at its worst with a clear mind and unclouded senses.

On the cross, Jesus prayed, "Father, forgive them, for they do not know what they are doing." Jesus came to this world to give men the grace of forgiveness of sins. Jesus prayed, "Father, forgive them, for they do not know what they are doing." On the cross, his heart must have felt as if it were going to burst. But Jesus prayed for the grace of forgiveness for sinners who did not know what they were doing.

Many people think that sin is enjoyable and commit sin as easily as one drinks coffee. But sin makes man very sick within. As a result, people become angry and nervous, so nervous that they unintentionally damage the precious lives of others. They don't know that they are suffering from sin-sickness. But many people become so helpless because of their sin and guilty feelings that they have no rest. They all become like Cain, who was driven by fear and a sense of punishment and wandered aimlessly. So people want to escape from their restlessness of sin by taking drugs or seeking pleasures. We must hear Jesus' prayer on the cross, "Forgive them, for they do not know what they are doing." We must ask Jesus for the grace of forgiveness. 1 John 1:9 says, "If we confess our sins, he is faithful and just and will forgive us our sins and purify us from all unrighteousness."

In history, there have been many kings and heroes. But most of them died with their eyes unclosed because of their grudges against others. They did not know how to forgive others. So they lived and died as cursed men. Through Jesus' forgiveness on the cross, we must learn how to forgive others. There are many things to learn as we live our lives in this world. But to learn how to forgive others who wronged us is most important to all of us. This is the reason that Jesus taught his disciples in Matthew 6:12, "Forgive us our debts, as we also have forgiven our debtors."

Many people wonder why Jesus had to die on the cross like a criminal, thinking that there could have been a better way. But the death of Jesus on the cross is the only way to save men from their sins. "For God so loved the world that he gave his one and only Son, that whoever believes in him shall not perish but have eternal life" (Jn 3:16). God made his one and only Son the Paschal Lamb who shed his blood for men's sins. By shedding his blood, Jesus satisfied God's righteousness for those who believe in his blood. He shed his blood so that whoever believes in him may be healed of their sin-sicknesses. On the cross, he bore all our sorrows and infirmities. On the cross, he was stricken and smitten and afflicted in our places. He was cursed in our places.

Third, the cross of Jesus is the way to paradise. The people stood watching, and the rulers even sneered at him. They said, "He saved others; let him save himself if he is the Christ of God, the Chosen One" (35). The soldiers also came up and mocked him. They offered him wine vinegar and said, "If you are the king of the Jews, save yourself" (36-37) To Jesus, who was in terrible pain and at the point of death, "save yourself" may have been Satan's strongest temptation.

Satan's voice saying, "Save yourself," echoed in Jesus' ears. It annoyed Jesus continuously. One of the criminals who hung there hurled insults at him. "Aren't you the Christ? Save yourself and us!" They didn't know that Jesus was not saving himself in order to save men from their sins. They didn't know that God sent Jesus as the Lamb of God for the sin of the world. Jesus did not say anything to those who shouted, "Save yourself!"

The other criminal rebuked the first criminal. "'Don't you fear God?' ... 'We are punished justly, for we are getting what our deeds deserve. But this man has done nothing wrong'" (40-41). Then he said, "Jesus, remember me when you come into your kingdom." We have already thought about the former robber. He hurled insults and cursed Jesus by saying, "Save yourself." We don't know why he did such evil things to Jesus. But one thing is clear. He was stubborn and unrepentant to the end. He was a sick man, both psychologically and spiritually because of his hardened heart.

In contrast, the other criminal had the fear of God in his heart. For the last 20 years, I knew an old man who enjoyed all kinds of sports, especially football games, as well as eating at various restaurants. Even until last year, he had no idea about the kingdom of heaven. But now he is intensive care at the hospital. Now he has suddenly become interested in talking about the heavenly kingdom. Likewise, the second criminal probably was not interested in the kingdom of heaven during his lifetime. But on the cross, the kingdom of God became very real and the only place he could hope for. He admitted that he was a sinner who deserved the death penalty. He saw salvation in Jesus. So he said, "Jesus, remember me when you come into your kingdom." He was a shameless guy who lived a wretched life. But he wanted to go to paradise.

Read verse 43. "Jesus answered him, 'I tell you the truth, today you will be with me in paradise.'" On the cross, Jesus restored lost paradise and made it a new paradise. On the cross, Jesus also accepted this man's faith, and he became the first one who entered the kingdom of God. Jesus entered the kingdom of God with the man who was once a robber condemned on the cross. Jesus is the merciful God of salvation. Jesus cared for this one person who was cursed and condemned, even though it was the time when he could not care for others because of his own great pain on the cross.

Fourth, the cross of Jesus liberates men from the bondage of sin and Satan. Verses 44-56 tell us of Jesus' death and burial. Read verse 44. "It was now about the sixth hour, and darkness came over the whole land until the ninth hour." The representative of nature, the sun, stopped shining. So darkness came over the whole land until the ninth hour. The death of Jesus was so unreasonable that even nature mourned. Read verse 45. "… for the sun stopped shining. And the curtain of the temple was torn in two." The curtain of the temple which was opened once a year for the high priest to enter and offer sacrifices was torn in two. The door to God is now wide open through the death of Jesus on the cross. Up until our Lord Jesus' crucifixion, mankind was bound by the chains of Satan and groaned endlessly. But through his death on the cross, Jesus liberated all men who believe in him from bondage to sin and Satan.

Read verse 46. "Jesus called out with a loud voice, 'Father, into your hands I commit my spirit.'" Jesus did not die with a sad face. Jesus had no remorse or regret at all when he breathed his last. He called out with a loud voice, "Father, into your hands I commit my spirit." His crying out with a loud voice tells us that he had a life commitment to God. His loud crying out eloquently tells us that he won the victory over Satan and that God was pleased with him.

Fifth, the cross of Jesus gives light to men who are in darkness.

The Roman centurion, seeing what had happened, praised God and said, "Surely this was a righteous man" (47). There was a centurion who watched the execution of Jesus. But to this foreign soldier, Jesus was not a criminal. Jesus' death did not overshadow the centurion with the darkness of death. Rather, bright sunlight came into his heart. Jesus who died on the cross was not a criminal. He was a righteous man. The man exclaimed, "Surely this was a righteous man." Judah Ben Hur lived in the darkness of hatred toward his Roman friend who imprisoned his mother and sister and who sent him away as a slave on a warship. Even after his Roman friend was killed in a horse race, the hatred in Ben Hur's heart did not go away. But when he looked at Jesus on the cross, marvelous light came into his heart and the sword of hatred in his heart was pulled out. This is only a story. But historically, there are many who saw the marvelous light of life at the cross of Jesus.

The centurion was a witness to Jesus' death. There were more witnesses. The women who had followed him from Galilee stood at a distance, watching these things. They are also witnesses of Jesus' death forever until he comes again in glory and power.

Read verse 50. "Now there was a man named Joseph, a member of the Council, a good and upright man ..." Joseph, a member of the Council, a good and upright man, had not consented to their decision and action. He was waiting for the kingdom of God. He came to Pilate and asked for Jesus' body. He buried Jesus' body in a new tomb which he had originally prepared for himself (Mt 27:60). Jesus died on the cross for the sin of the world.

Lesson 57

The Resurrection

Luke 24:1-53
Key Verse: 24:6a

I.   HE IS NOT HERE, HE HAS RISEN (1-12)

1.   Who were the women? (10; 23:55) When and why did they go to the tomb? What might they have been thinking about on their way? What surprising things did they notice when they arrived?

2.   Who were the two men? What was the women's first reaction to them? What was their gentle rebuke to the women? What good news did they tell the women? Of what words of Jesus did they remind them?

3.   How were the women changed when they remembered Jesus' words? What did they do? To whom did they deliver the first resurrection message?

4.   How did the apostles respond to their message? Why were they unchanged? What did Peter do? What did he think? What was his problem?

II.   ON THE ROAD TO EMMAUS (13-35)

5.   Who were these two men? (13) What were they discussing? Why might they have not recognized the Risen Jesus when he joined them?

6.   Summarize the contents of their story to him. Why were their faces downcast, even though they had heard that Jesus was alive? What was their problem?

7.   How and why did Jesus rebuke them? What did he begin to do for them? (27) What happened when they urged Jesus to stay with them? How did these men finally rescue him?

8.   After recognizing him, what did they say? After being convinced of his resurrection, what did they do? What can we learn here?

III.   JESUS APPEARS TO THE DISCIPLES (36-49)

9.   What did the Risen Jesus say first to them? How did the disciples respond? How did Jesus prove to them that it was really him, the same Jesus? Why was it hard to believe, even after seeing? What did he prove to them by eating in their presence?

10.   How did he help them base their faith on the Scriptures? What

mission and promise did he give them?

IV. THE ASCENSION (50-53)

11. Describe Jesus' departure into heaven. What hope did this put in the hearts of his disciples? (Ac 1:9-11) What did they do after his ascension? Why? In what way were the disciples changed after believing in Jesus' resurrection?

The Resurrection

Luke 24:1-53
Key Verse: 24:6a

"He is not here; he has risen!"

I N THIS WORLD, MARRIAGE is considered very important and joyful. But in the eternal world, the resurrection is most important.
The Son of Man died on the cross so that he might be raised on
the third day.

Luke the evangelist and historian does not give us a theological
argument on the resurrection, but rather, the evidences of the resurrection of Jesus Christ from the dead. Most importantly, he tells us
what happened in the hearts of those who saw the resurrection of
Jesus. May the Holy Spirit help you to meet the Risen Jesus personally
so that great things and a great change may happen in your heart.

I. He is not here; he has risen (1-12)

It was on the first day of the week, at the first stroke of dawn. The
women who had followed Jesus from Galilee all the way to Golgotha
had wept, mourned, and wailed when they saw his crucifixion. These
women returned to their own places with a broken spirit. Probably
they felt ashamed that they had not died with Jesus. They must have
stayed up all night in consuming sorrow, thinking of good Jesus who
had been crucified by evil men. Very early in the morning, around
4 o'clock, they went to the tomb in order to express their love for the
dear Jesus who was dead by embalming his body with their spices.

As we studied, Jesus was buried in a new tomb of Joseph's, a member of the Council, the tomb which Joseph had prepared for himself.
The tomb was closed by a great circular stone. But when the women
came, they found the stone rolled away, and when they entered, they

did not find the body of the Lord Jesus.

Read verses 4 and 5. "While they were wondering about this, suddenly two men in clothes that gleamed like lightning stood beside them. In their fright the women bowed down with their faces to the ground, but the men said to them, 'Why do you look for the living among the dead?'" These women were looking for the dead body of Jesus in great sorrow to express their last respects and love. They were doing something beautiful, but in vain. They were looking for the living among the dead.

Read verses 6 and 7. "He is not here; he has risen! Remember how he told you, while he was still with you in Galilee: 'The Son of Man must be delivered into the hands of sinful men, be crucified and on the third day be raised again.'" During the time of his earthly ministry, Jesus had predicted his death and resurrection on a number of occasions (9:22,44; 18:31-33). At the time of his crucifixion and resurrection, the disciples failed to comprehend or accept what he had been saying. But look at verse 8. These women, who up until now had only listened over the shoulders of the disciples, immediately remembered when they heard the voice of the Risen Christ. When they heard the voice of the Risen Christ and remembered his words about his death and resurrection, they were no longer sorrowful women over the dead. They became the witnesses of his resurrection.

These witnesses were Mary Magdalene, Joanna, Mary the mother of James, and the others with them who told these things to the apostles. They were the women who had served Jesus and his company, not because they had money, but because they loved Jesus and his company. Mary Magdalene had been very sin-sick. But she was completely healed by Jesus. Since then, she had dedicated her life to Jesus' ministry. They were happy to follow and serve Jesus and his company. Jesus was the meaning and joy of their lives. But when they followed Jesus who was carrying the cross, they became helpless. When they saw Jesus crucified, they felt as if they were crucified. These three beautiful women became so wounded and endlessly sorrowful because of their Lord's death on the cross. But something great happened. When they heard the voice of the Risen Christ, sorrows melted away from their hearts and an inexpressible, eternal joy and life overflowed in their hearts. They had not eaten for several days because of their sorrow. But suddenly they felt great strength in their legs. Women of those times never ran, but they came running and told these things to the apostles.

How did the apostles respond to the women's saying? "They did not believe the women, because their words seemed to them like nonsense. Peter, however, got up and ran to the tomb. Bending over, he saw the strips of linen lying by themselves, and he went away, wondering to himself what had happened" (11-12). We can see here a sharp contrast between the women and Peter. The women went to the tomb with sorrowful minds, but when they heard the voice of the Risen Jesus and remembered his words concerning his death and resurrection, their sorrow turned into great joy. But Peter went to the tomb with his human loyalty, saw a few pieces of grave clothes lying by themselves, and went away, only bewildered. He needed to meet the Risen Jesus and remember his words concerning his death and resurrection.

Here we learn that Jesus is not someone we can only study. When we only study about Jesus, we become like the apostles who heard the women's words, but regarded it as nonsense. Studying is not enough. We must meet the Risen Jesus very personally. Then we can experience the power and glory of the resurrection like the women, whose sorrows turned into great joy and confidence.

II. On the road to Emmaus (13-35)

"Now that same day two of them were going to a village called Emmaus, about seven miles from Jerusalem. They were talking with each other about everything that had happened" (13-14).

Read verses 15-18. "As they talked and discussed these things with each other, Jesus himself came up and walked along with them; but they were kept from recognizing him. He asked them, 'What are you discussing together as you walk along?' They stood still, their faces downcast. One of them, named Cleopas, asked him, 'Are you only a visitor to Jerusalem and do not know the things that have happened there in these days?'"

Look at verses 19 and 20. "'What things?' he asked. 'About Jesus of Nazareth,' they replied. 'He was a prophet, powerful in word and deed before God and all the people. The chief priests and our rulers handed him over to be sentenced to death, and they crucified him.'" Verse 21 reveals what they had in their minds. They had hoped that he was the one who was going to redeem Israel. They saw that Jesus was a prophet, powerful in word and deed before God and all the people. They thought he was the one who was going to redeem Israel from bondage to the Roman Empire. But the chief priests and rulers handed him over to be sentenced to death, and they crucified him. They had had a hope of the redemption of Israel through Jesus. But contrary to expectation, he was crucified. All their wishful, bewildered regret is in their sorrowing words, "We had hoped that he was the one who was going to redeem Israel" (21a). These were the words of men whose hopes were dead and buried.

In addition, they were amazed by some of their women who went to the tomb early in the morning, but did not find his body (22-23a). Some of their companions went to the tomb and found it just as the women had said, but him they did not see (24). They despaired even more to think that his dead body was stolen. In their despair, they were running for their lives to Emmaus.

What did the Risen Christ do for these two men who had utterly despaired? Their disappointment and despair did not come from their situation which they were talking about. Their disappointment and despair came from their unbelief. Their disappointment and despair were right in their own hearts. During the time of his earthly ministry, Jesus taught his disciples about his suffering, death, and resurrection repeatedly, whenever it was necessary. But they were real men of the world, full of worldly and human desires. They did not accept his teachings concerning his suffering, death, and resurrection from their hearts. When the events of his death and resurrection actually happened, they were bewildered in fear and despair.

Jesus rebuked them for their unbelief. Read verses 25 and 26. "He said to them, 'How foolish you are, and how slow of heart to believe all that the prophets have spoken! Did not the Christ have to suffer these things and then enter his glory?' And beginning with Moses and all the Prophets, he explained to them what was said in all the

Scriptures concerning himself."

Read verses 28 and 29. "As they approached the village to which they were going, Jesus acted as if he were going farther. But they urged him strongly, 'Stay with us, for it is nearly evening; the day is almost over.' So he went in to stay with them." Here we learn that Jesus was waiting for them to invite him. When they invited him to come in, then he went in to stay with them. This scene reminds us of Revelation 3:20, "Here I am! I stand at the door and knock. If anyone hears my voice and opens the door, I will come in and eat with him, and he with me."

"When he was at the table with them, he took bread, gave thanks, broke it and began to give it to them" (30). Then, amazing things happened in the hearts of the two men. Their spiritual eyes were opened and they recognized him, and he disappeared from their sight. Read verse 31. "Then their eyes were opened and they recognized him, and he disappeared from their sight."

Read verse 32. "They asked each other, 'Were not our hearts burning within us while he talked with us on the road and opened the Scriptures to us?'" When they met the Risen Jesus and studied the Bible, a miracle happened. Their blind spiritual eyes began to open. Their dead hearts began to burn within them.

Before meeting the Risen Jesus, they were running away from Jerusalem. They were escaping from the realities of the world. They had contracted the disease of death, for at the end of escape is death. But after meeting the Risen Jesus, they got up and returned at once to Jerusalem where Jesus had been crucified and where secret policemen were scattered all around to arrest Jesus' people. Before meeting the Risen Jesus, they were full of human thinking which made them endlessly fearful. After meeting the Risen Jesus, they became so courageous that they were ready to fight against any kind of enemy. When they arrived in Jerusalem, "there they found the Eleven and those with them, assembled together and saying, "It is true! The Lord has risen and has appeared to Simon"" (33b-34) "Then the two told what had happened on the way, and how Jesus was recognized by them when he broke the bread" (35).

Let's pray that God may help us meet the Risen Jesus so that we may not escape from our own Jerusalem, but advance.

III. Jesus appears to the disciples (36-49)

Jesus came into the upper room where the Eleven were gathered. Jesus said to them, "Peace be with you" (36). "They were startled and frightened, thinking they saw a ghost" (37). They had been convinced of his resurrection through many witnesses. But still they were fearful. When they saw Jesus, they thought he was a ghost. Read verses 38 and 39. "He said to them, 'Why are you troubled, and why do doubts rise in your minds? Look at my hands and my feet. It is I myself! Touch me and see; a ghost does not have flesh and bones, as you see I have.'" The Risen Jesus was not a ghost. He was real. The Jesus who died was in truth the Christ who rose again.

Jesus took and ate in their presence the piece of fish they had given him. Read verse 44. "He said to them, 'This is what I told you while I was still with you: Everything must be fulfilled that is written about me in the Law of Moses, the Prophets and the Psalms.'" Jesus again taught them the Bible. Then their minds were opened so they could understand the Scriptures.

Read verses 46-49. "He told them, 'This is what is written: The Christ will suffer and rise from the dead on the third day, and repentance and forgiveness of sins will be preached in his name to all nations, beginning at Jerusalem. You are witnesses of these things. I am going to send you what my Father has promised; but stay in the city until you have been clothed with power from on high.'" These verses tell us several things:

First, the cross of Jesus was what all the Scriptures looked forward to as the bridge between death and resurrection. The cross of Jesus was part of the plan of God so that we can see his eternal love in a moment of time.

Second, the world mission task. We must deliver the message of repentance and forgiveness of sins to the peoples of all nations. Read verses 47 and 48. "… and repentance and forgiveness of sins will be preached in his name to all nations, beginning at Jerusalem. You are witnesses of these things."

Third, the coming of the Holy Spirit. Flesh is nothing; spirit is everything. Those who have no power from the Holy Spirit cannot do God's work. They must first wait for the coming of the Holy Spirit so that they may be clothed in the power of the Holy Spirit. Read verse 49. "I am going to send you what my Father has promised; but stay in the city until you have been clothed with power from on high."

IV. The Ascension (50-53)

Read verses 50 and 51. "When he had led them out to the vicinity of Bethany, he lifted up his hands and blessed them. While he was blessing them, he left them and was taken up into heaven." The ascension of Christ is the promise that he will come again, just as he had ascended. Acts 1:10-11 says, "They were looking intently up into the sky as he was going, when suddenly two men dressed in white stood beside them. 'Men of Galilee,' they said, 'why do you stand here looking into the sky? This same Jesus, who has been taken from you into heaven, will come back in the same way you have seen him go into heaven.'" The ascension of Jesus gives us the hope of the second coming of our Lord Jesus. When he came to this world first, he came as our Shepherd and Savior. But when Jesus comes again, he comes as our King and Judge. He judges all men according to the purpose of their lives. He gives the crown of life to those who were faithful to him, and he condemns those who did not accept the love of God through him.

The ascension of Jesus planted great joy and songs of praise in the hearts of his disciples. Read verses 52 and 53. "Then they worshiped him and returned to Jerusalem with great joy. And they stayed continually at the temple, praising God."